EUROPEAN HISTORICAL DICTIONARIES
Edited by Jon Woronoff

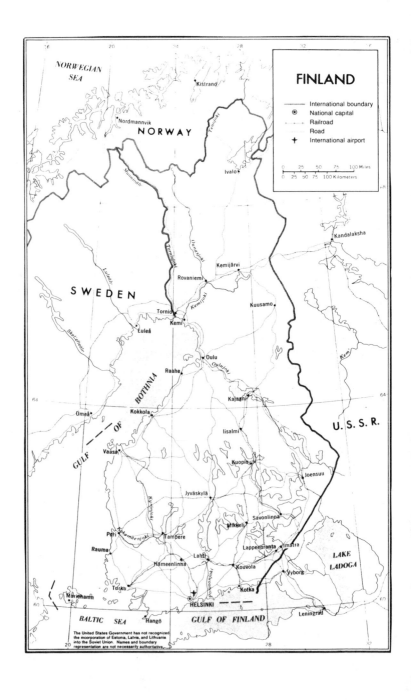

NORWEGIAN SEA

NORWAY

NORDMANNVIK

Kistrand

Ivalo

SWEDEN

Luleälv

Tornio
Kemi
Luleå

Rovaniemi
Kemijärvi

Kuusamo

Oulu
Oulujoki
Raahe

Kajaani

Umeå
Kokkola

Iisalmi

Vaasa

Kuopio

Joensuu

Jyväskylä

Savonlinna

Mikkeli

Pori
Tampere
Rauma

Lahti
Lappeenranta
Imatra

Kouvola
Hämeenlinna

Turku
Kotka
Vyborg

Mariehamn

HELSINKI

Hangö

BALTIC SEA

GULF OF FINLAND

Leningrad

LAKE LADOGA

U.S.S.R.

GULF OF BOTHNIA

FINLAND

International boundary
National capital
Railroad
Road
International airport

0   25   50   75   100 Miles
0 25 50 75 100 Kilometers

HISTORICAL DICTIONARY
OF
FINLAND

by
George Maude

European Historical Dictionaries No. 8

The Scarecrow Press, Inc.
Lanham, Md., & London

SCARECROW PRESS, INC.

Published in the United States of America
by Scarecrow Press, Inc.
4720 Boston Way, Lanham, Maryland 20706

4 Pleydell Gardens, Folkestone
Kent CT20 2DN, England

Copyright © 1995 by George Maude

British Cataloging in Publication Information Available

Library of Congress Cataloging-in-Publication Data

Maude, George.
Historical dictionary of Finland / by George Maude.
p.   cm. — (European historical dictionaries ; no. 8)
Includes bibliographical references.
1. Finland—History—Dictionaries.   I. Title.   II. Series.
DL1007.M38   1995   948.97'003—dc20   95–1497

ISBN 0–8108–2995–9 (cloth : alk. paper)

Printed in the United States of America

 The paper used in this publication meets the minimum requirements of
American National Standard for Information Sciences—Permanence
of Paper for Printed Library Materials, ANSI Z39.48–1984.

CONTENTS

EDITOR'S FOREWORD

Tucked away in the northeastern corner of Europe, tied into a special relationship with the erstwhile Soviet Union, Finland has long had a somewhat peripheral position of its own. It is now moving ever more rapidly and broadly into the mainstream of European affairs, raising an interesting identity question for the Finns. So this is a particularly good time to learn more about Finland. And this is an excellent place to start, with a historical dictionary that shows where Finland is coming from and where it is now while providing enough insight to suggest where it is heading.

Relatively large, and relatively underpopulated, by European standards at least, Finland is a very beautiful country. It has retained its forests, graced with countless lakes, and its people remain close to the land. The Finns have also developed an increasingly vigorous economy (although currently under many pressures) and fashioned a society and government that meets their needs. To find out more about the place, the people, the economy and polity, the society and its history, read on.

This story is told most ably and compellingly by Dr. George Maude, born in England but thoroughly assimilated to Finland, where he has lived and taught for three decades. Initially a lecturer in English, he is presently docent in international relations at the Law Department of the University of Turku. Over the years, he has written extensively on Finland and its external relations and become a member of the Turku Historical Society and the Porthan Society, Finland's oldest learned society. Recently, he was made a Knight of the Order of the Lion of Finland.

Jon Woronoff
Series Editor

v

PREFACE

In the writing of this text I have been influenced by many works and opinions, and my acknowledgements are printed on a separate page. I cannot, however, refrain from mentioning in this Preface two works of scholarship that have influenced me greatly. The first of these is Antero Jyränki's study of constitutionalism, *Lakien laki* ("The Law of the Laws," i.e., the Constitution), which was published by Lakimiesliitto in Helsinki in 1989. The second is the late Juhani Paasivirta's work, *Suomi ja Eurooppa 1939–1956* ("Finland and Europe, 1939–1956"), a book I have had the privilege of reading in manuscript form. The work was published in Helsinki in 1992 by Kirjayhtymä. Any gaucheries in this text derive from me, not from them.

As ever, the staff of the University of Turku library has responded magnificently to my needs. I have also had much help from the library staff of Åbo Akademi (the Swedish University in Turku/Åbo) and from the staff of the City Library of Turku.

Above all, I should like to express my appreciation for the cheerfulness shown by my wife, Helena, my daughter, Ulrika, and my son, Andrei, in the tense days of finishing a manuscript during a period of convalescence.

The approach in this work leans, in accordance with the publisher's wish and the author's own determination, toward the modern political history of Finland. Since Finland was a part of Sweden until 1809 (the term "Sweden-Finland" is a misnomer, for, on the whole, Finland had no separate status), readers interested in the earlier period must also be prepared to look elsewhere into the history of Sweden.

The approach in this work is strongly biographical, the personal vignettes being intended to serve as illustrations of more general moods and currents of opinion. The reader can make up his or her own mind about the role of the individual in history. For the record, I am sticking with Plekhanov. In so doing, what I have tried to relate is the story of a people struggling to proclaim a destiny.

ACKNOWLEDGMENTS

Apart from the acknowledgments made in the Preface, I should like to record my indebtedness, whether in the form of personal discussion or through acquaintanceship with their writings or television programs, to the following:

Risto Alapuro, Roy Allison, Christopher Andrew, Eugen Autere, Michael Berry, Göran von Bonsdorff, William Copeland, Bo Carpelan, William Copeland, Max Engman, the Finnish Meteorological Office, Oleg Gordievsky, Martti Häiklö, Tapani Harviainen, Ruth Hasan, Simo Heininen, Gordon Henderson, Riitta Hjerppe, John Hodgson, Aare Huhtala, Matti Huurre, Tarja Hyppönen, Juhani Ikonen, Mauno Jokipii, Kari Joutsamo, Osmo Jussila, Eino Jutikkala, Marja Keränen, David Kirby, George Kish, Urpo Kivikari, Matti Klemola, Matti Klinge, Keijo Korhonen, Auvo Kostiainen, Eerik Lagerspetz, Ahti Laitinen, Antti Lappalainen, Ritva Liikkanen, Leo Lindsten, Pekka Lounela, Michael Metcalf, Toivo Miljan, Juhani Mylly, Timo Myllyntaus, Jaakko Nousiainen, Felix Oinas, Jaakko Paavolainen, Esko Pajarinen, Eino Pietola, Tuomo Polvinen, Hannu Rautkallio, Marvin Rintala, Michael Roberts, Ari Rouhe, Hilkka and Keijo Salmi, Unto Salo, John Screen, Hannu Soikkanen, Timo Soikkanen, Markku Suksi, Elina Suominen, Aarre Tähti, Eero Taivalsaari, Jukka Tarkka, Päiviö Tommila, Martti Turtola, Kari Uusitalo, Pirkko Vallinoja, Vesa Vares, Olli Vehviläinen, Timo Vihavainen, Sakari Virkkunen, Pentti Virrankoski, Pentti Virtaranta, Eeva Vuorenpää, Esko Vuorisjärvi, Kalevi Wiik, Kauko Wikström, Heikki Ylikangas, and Seppo Zetterberg.

ALPHABETIZATION AND
LANGUAGE NOTE

The Finnish and Swedish letters *ä* and *ö* and the Swedish letter *å* have been treated for purposes of alphabetization as normal *a* and *o*, and the same applies to the German *ü*—it is to be treated as *u*.

The letters v and w, which are interchangeable in Finnish and Swedish, have been kept separate in the English alphabetical order.

The style of place-names normally used in this text is that of the Finnish-language version, with the exception of "Åland," since the area is officially Swedish in language. The hybrid form, from the Swedish "Österbotten," of "Ostrobothnia," is used for this important area of Finland, since it has become almost standardized.

For those readers more familiar with Swedish place names, a list of equivalents follows.

FINNISH AND SWEDISH PLACE-NAMES

Finnish	*Swedish*
Hamina	Fredrikshamn
Hanko	Hangö
Helsinki	Helsingfors
Käkisalmi	Kexholm
Kokkola	Gamlakarleby
Naantali	Nådendal
Oulu	Uleåborg
Pietarsaari	Jakobstad
Pori	Björneborg
Porvoo	Borgå
Raahe	Brahestad
Rauma	Raumo
Turku	Åbo
Uusikaarlepyy	Nykarleby
Uusikaupunki	Nystad
Vaasa	Vasa
Viipuri	Viborg

ACRONYMS AND ABBREVIATIONS

AKS	Academic Karelia Society
BALTAP	Baltic Approaches (a shortened form of COMBAL-TAP [Baltic Approaches Command] of NATO, covering the southern half of the Skagerrak, the Kattegat, the Danish Straits, the western Baltic, and Schleswig-Holstein)
CP	Center Party
CSCE	Conference on Security and Cooperation in Europe
EEA	European Economic Area
EEC	European Economic Community
EFTA	European Free Trade Area
EU	European Union (formerly European Economic Community, European Community)
FCMA	Treaty of Friendship, Cooperation, and Mutual Assistance
FINEFTA	Finland's agreement of association with EFTA
GATT	General Agreement on Tariffs and Trade
IBRD	International Bank for Reconstruction and Development (World Bank)
IKL	People's Patriotic Movement
IMF	International Monetary Fund
IWW	Industrial Workers of the World
KEVSOS	(agreements made between Finland and the Socialist countries of Easter Europe (from 1974 onward) for the gradual reduction of tariffs and other trade hindrances so as to parallel the conditions pertaining in trade between Finland and the Soviet Union, the EFTA countries, and the EEC)
MNC	Multinational corporation
MTB	Motor torpedo boat
MTK	Central Union of Agricultural Producers and Forest Owners

NAFTA	North American Free Trade Agreement
NATO	North Atlantic Treaty Organization
NCP	National Coalition Party
RBMK	(graphite-moderated nuclear reactors of the Chernobyl type)
SDP	Social Democratic Party
WEU	Western European Union

HEADS OF STATE

Tsar–Grand Dukes

Alexander I	1809–1825
Nicholas I	1825–1855
Alexander II	1855–1881
Alexander III	1881–1894
Nicholas II	1894–1917

Holder of Supreme Power

P. E. Svinhufvud	May–December 1918

Regent

C. G. Mannerheim	December 1918–July 1919

Presidents

K. J. Ståhlberg	1919–1925
L. K. Relander	1925–1931
P. E. Svinhufvud	1931–1937
K. Kallio	1937–1940
R. Ryti	1940–1944
C. G. Mannerheim	1944–1946
J. K. Paasikivi	1946–1956
U. K. Kekkonen	1956–1981
M. H. Koivisto	1982–1994
M. Ahtisaari	1994–

CHRONOLOGY

1809	Finland becomes a Grand Duchy of the Russian empire.
	March–September: Meeting of the Diet of Porvoo.
	September: Signing of the Treaty of Hamina between Sweden and Russia.
1854–1856	The Crimean War. The Finnish coast is bombarded, the fortress of Bomarsund on Åland destroyed, and in 1855 Sveaborg is shelled from the sea.
1863	The Diet is summoned once again.
1869	The Diet begins to meet regularly.
1890	The Postal Manifesto foreshadows further measures of unification with the rest of the empire. Senator Leo Mechelin resigns.
1899	February: The February Manifesto lays down the future lines for imperial legislation. The Finns draw up the Great Address to Tsar Nicholas II in defense of their autonomy. The International Cultural Address is also drafted with the same end in view.
1901	The separate Finnish army (with the exception of the Guards regiment) is abolished, and Finns are to be drafted into the Russian imperial forces. Resistance against the draft begins, led by the passive resistance movement.
1903	Leo Mechelin, leader of the passive resistance movement, is exiled to Sweden.
1904	June 16: Governor-General Bobrikov is shot by Finnish civil servant Eugen Schauman.
1905	October: The Great Strike in Finland, following upon the Russian Revolution. The Socialists, whose party was founded in 1899 and became

Marxist in 1903, show their strength. Danger of clashes between White and Red guards foreshadows the Civil War of 1918, but all forces become temporarily united to oppose Russian oppression.

November: Tsar Nicholas II rescinds many of the unification measures through his November Manifesto. The Finns begin to plan a reform of the Diet of Four Estates.

1907   The new unicameral legislature meets, elected by universal male and female franchise. Eighty Social Democrats are elected out of a membership of two hundred.

1908   Stolypin begins to reintroduce the concept of imperial legislation.

1909   The Old Finns leave the Senate and are replaced by Russians.

1910   June: The plans for imperial legislation go through the Duma.

1914   Shortly after the outbreak of World War I Finland is put under military rule.

1915   February: The first Finnish Jaegers begin their training at Lockstedt, near Hamburg.

1916   In a low turnout (55% of the voters) the Social Democrats win 103 seats in the legislature, but it is not allowed to meet.

1917   As a result of the March Revolution in Russia, the measures restricting Finnish autonomy are repealed.

Social Democrats join a coalition Senate.

July: The legislature, led by the Social Democrats, votes an enabling act, giving independence to Finland in all but external relations. In consequence, Carl Enckell, the last minister state-secretary of Finland in Saint Petersburg, gets Kerenski to dissolve Parliament.

October: In the new parliamentary elections the Social Democrats win only 92 seats.

December 4: A committee headed by K. J. Ståhlberg reports in favor in the establishment of a republic with a loose link to Russia.

	December 6: Finnish independence is declared. December 31: Lenin signs an act of recognition of Finnish independence.
1918	January–May: The Finnish Civil War ends in the defeat of the Reds. German troops are in Finland. October: Friedrich Karl of Hesse is elected king of Finland, but renounces the throne a few days later on Germany's defeat in World War I.
1919	July: Finland declared a republic. Mannerheim, the regent, resigns after the election of K. J. Ståhlberg as president.
1920	October 14: Signing of the Peace of Tartu, which regularizes the frontier with Soviet Russia. Many Finns remain dissatisfied with this treaty.
1922	February 22: The Academic Karelia Society is founded. October 14: The *Lex Kallio* renders a final improvement in the conditions of the crofters and the landless.
1929	The Lapua movement starts up.
1930	October 14: Members of the Lapua movement kidnap former President Ståhlberg and his wife.
1932	January 21: Finland and the Soviet Union sign a Nonaggression pact. February–March: The Mäntsälä Revolt occurs in a small village in southern Finland. The People's Patriotic Movement (the IKL) founded.
1935	December: Finland sets its course with Nordic neutrality.
1937	March: The "Red Earth" government of Social Democrats, Agrarians, and Progressives is formed.
1938–1939	Yartsev and Stein ask Finland for a military security arrangement or territorial concessions in light of the threat from Nazi Germany. The Finnish government refuses and maintains a strict neutrality, in spite of Mannerheim's wish to cede islands in the Gulf of Finland.
1939	August 23: The Nazi-Soviet Pact is signed, which,

by a secret protocol, puts Finland into the Soviet sphere of influence.

November 30: The Winter War begins after negotiations between Finland and the Soviet Union for territorial concessions lapse.

1940   March 13: The Peace of Moscow is signed, ending the Winter War. The Karelian Isthmus is lost. Hankois leased by the Soviet Union.

August–September: German troops on leave are allowed transit through Finland from Germany to Norway. The Finns orient themselves toward Germany.

1941   June 22: Germany invades the Soviet Union.

June 25: The Finnish prime minister states that Finland is at war with the Soviet Union after Finland is bombed by Soviet planes.

December 6: Great Britain declares war on Finland.

1944   September 19: The Soviet Union and Great Britain sign an Armistice Agreement with the Finns, though hostilities had already ceased on September 5. The Communists come out into the open.

1947   February 10: Peace treaty is signed in Paris, with no possibility of getting back any of the lands lost by the 1944 armistice.

1948   April 6: The Finnish-Soviet Treaty (the FCMA Treaty) is signed. Shortly afterward President Paasikivi makes moves to rid the government of Communists.

1952   January 23: The Agrarian party newspaper *Maakansa* publishes Kekkonen's Pajama-Pocket Speech.

1955   September: With the premature renewal of the FCMA Treaty, Finland secures the return of the peninsula of Porkkala, leased under the Armistice Agreement to the Russians for fifty years.

October: Finland enters the Nordic Council.

December: Finland enters the United Nations.

1958   Fall: The "Night Frost Crisis" with the Soviet Union extends over several months.

1959   January: The Night Frost Crisis is resolved.

1961   July 1: The FINEFTA agreement is put in force.
        October 30: A Soviet note to Finland begins the
        Note Crisis in connection with the presidential
        election.
        November 24: The rival candidate to Urho Kekko-
        nen, Olavi Honka, withdraws from the presidential
        race.
1963   May 28: Kekkonen suggests the creation of a
        Nordic Nuclear-Free Zone.
1966   The Communist are taken into the government
        once more.
1969   Finland begins to exert pressure on Western Eu-
        rope and the U.S. for the European Security Con-
        ference. Finland begins to host SALT I.
1971   Finland puts forward Max Jakobson as candidate
        for the post of U.N. secretary-general. He is beaten
        by Kurt Waldheim, an Austrian.
1973   July: The European Security Conference prelimi-
        naries begin in Helsinki.
        November: Parliament adopts the Free Trade
        Agreement with the EEC.
1974   President Kekkonen continues in office without an
        election.
1975   The European Security Conference meets in
        Helsinki.
1978   May: Kekkonen issues a revision of the Nordic
        Nuclear-Free Zone proposal.
1989   Finland joins the Council of Europe.
1990   September: Finland states that it is no longer
        bound by the military restrictions contained in the
        1947 peace treaty.
1992   January: Finland and Russia mutually renounce
        the 1948 Finnish-Soviet Treaty. New treaties, of a
        less military character, are made between Finland
        and Russia.
        March: Finland applies for EC membership on a
        proposal of President Koivisto adopted in Parlia-
        ment.
1994   October: by a 57% vote in the national referendum
        the Finns decide to join the European Union (for-
        merly European Community).

FINLAND: AN OVERVIEW

PHYSICAL GEOGRAPHY

Finland lies on the northeastern shore of the Baltic Sea, washed on the south by the Gulf of Finland and on the west by the Gulf of Bothnia. In terms of political geography, it is situated between Russia on the east and Sweden on the west. The Norwegian border runs along the northwest, while across the Gulf of Finland is the restored Republic of Estonia.

By European standards, Finland is a country of some 130,000 square miles, being thus larger than Great Britain, Ireland, and the Benelux lands combined and about half the size of the state of Texas. In historical times, and still today, Finland has been a forested land (the "green gold," which has been the source of the country's prosperity since the late nineteenth century). The forest is mainly spruce and covers roughly 65% of the land area. About 20% of the forest is owned by the State.

Finland has few long rivers. The longest is the Kymi River in eastern Finland, which is approximately 127 miles in length, and which empties into the port of Kotka. The Kymi River has been important for the floating of timber and for the power it provides for the sawmills and paper mills on its banks.

Finland has an extensive network of lakes, and the country has often been described—and often for tourist purposes—as the Land of Sixty Thousand Lakes. The transport route from the Gulf of Finland, through the Saimaa Canal into the Finnish eastern lake system, is of some navigational importance. It enables seagoing vessels to reach the inland port of Kuopio, deep in the east central interior of the country. This navigation was an interesting example of post–World War II Finnish-Soviet cooperation, for the Saimaa Canal was leased from the Soviet Union in 1963 (and deepened and widened by the Finns), but ran through territory taken by the Soviet Union from Finland in 1944. That area now belongs to the Russian Republic.

Finland is not a mountainous country, but in eastern Finland the hill of Koli, near Joensuu, rises to a height of well over 900 feet. In the north, in Lapland, there are fells that are three times higher than this. Both the Koli and the Lapland areas provide opportunities for winter skiing in the midst of beautiful scenery.

Due to the proximity of the sea (including the Gulf Stream in the north), the Finnish climate is a mixture of maritime and Continental influences. The average temperature in Helsinki is around 45°F, at Jyväskylä in south central Finland around 36°F, while at Sodankylä in Lapland the average is around 30°F. In summer, on the mainland, the temperature can reach to above 85°F, and can fall in winter to 5°F or below.

Rainfall varies from just over 24 inches per annum in Helsinki to just over 19 inches per annum at Sodankylä.

The extremes of temperature to be met with in Finland, and the possibility of summer frost the further north one goes, have helped to foster the image of a country in which agriculture survives with difficulty. Since much of the bedrock is granite (including the form known as *rapakivi,* which outcrops fairly regularly), and the soil is largely of morainic origin, the picture of a poor, infertile Finland has been imprinted on the minds of the Finns: the poets J. L. Runeberg and Z. Topelius have told them that this is the case. Historical events, like the famine of 1867–1868 (when the harvests failed in a broad swathe of territory from northern Sweden through Finland to northern Russia) reinforce the picture.

In fact, it is amazing how much of its population Finland has been able to support through agriculture. The traditional slash-and-burn techniques, fertilizing the soil with potash and phosphates, were still in use in the remoter parts of the country in the late nineteenth century. Over much of the land, however, the effects of the mid–eighteenth century Great Partition (permitting a uniting of strips of cultivation) added to the pioneering of new farms in the wilderness, producing an efficient mix of animal and arable husbandry.

So much was this the case that the population rose, and the slow rate of urbanization in early-twentieth-century Finland could not absorb the excess. Emigration has therefore been a characteristic of the Finnish population in this century.

In Finland farming has always gone hand in hand with forestry and fishing, whether in the lakes or on coastal waters, slowing the demise of agriculture. On independence in 1917 roughly 66% of the population was living by agriculture and forestry, and as late as 1970 the figure was still as high as 18%.

In 1944, at the end of the war with the Soviet Union, Finland had to cede one-twelfth of its territory. This meant, among other things, the resettlement of 10,000 farming families from the Karelian Isthmus refugee population, strengthening agriculture in Finland. Though today only a few percent of the population derive their living from the fields, agriculture has remained heavily subsidized at a level (as Finland now enters European Union membership) which even that pro-agricultural body will not tolerate.

Geographically, present-day Finland is a product of the retreat of the ice cap that began, in fits and starts, some ten thousand years ago. The distinctive seal population of Lake Saimaa, now threatened by navigation and pollution by factories and summer cottages, became closed into the eastern Finnish lake system approximately 8,000 years ago, as the land rose, cutting the region off from what is now the White Sea.

Deglaciation has not meant just land rise. The volume of meltwater released also meant eustasis, the rise of the sea level over land so that the archipelagoes off the Finnish coast were covered. For present-day Finland, and for the Finland of historical times, the significant fact has been isostasis—land uplift above the sea level—first explained by the Scottish geologist T. F. Jamieson in 1865 as being due to a compensatory movement of the earth's crust to cope with the pressures from the Quaternary ice sheets.

Isostasis has continued to occur in Finland, being of the order of close to three feet per hundred years in the Vaasa district and just over a foot in the Helsinki district. Historically, this has had a negative effect upon fishing in many areas and upon the ports of Vaasa and Uusikaarlepyy. It also means that Finland is gaining (whether for agriculture, recreation, or industry) approximately 600 square miles every hundred years. It has been estimated that Finland will be joined to Sweden across the Gulf of Bothnia in about 3,000 years, and in 5,000 years it will have gotten from the sea the equivalent amount of land to that lost to the Russians in 1944.

It is small wonder that a modern geographer, Michael Jones, insists on calling Finland "Daughter of the Sea," but this heritage of historical geography may not seem quite so meaningful to the modern Finnish citizen.

POPULATION AND HISTORICAL GEOGRAPHY

In 1991 the population of Finland, including foreigners, was 5,026,000. Among the Finns, women outnumber men in the population by 147,000.

Finland is officially a bilingual country, with 6.3% of the population registered as Swedish-speakers. The line between Finnish-speakers and Swedish-speakers should not be drawn ethnically, at least not very tightly.

The Finns, as a population, appear, according to fairly recent blood-group research, to have a three-quarters European ethnic inheritance with one-quarter from Asia. It is not known when the Finns moved from the East Baltic area, or from the East, into present-day Finland, or to what extent they mingled with preexisting Stone Age populations (the earliest known settlement in Finland was the Stone Age Askola culture from approximately 7000 B.C., from the period when much of the area of Finland was still under water due to the glacial meltwater of the great Yoldia Sea).

It was previously maintained that the entry of the Finns into what is known as Finland may have coincided with the Iron Age, though it was also known that movements from Scandinavia were then occurring and had occurred even in the Bronze Age. The view held today tends to place the period of entry of the Finns (or a Finno-Ugrian population) as early as the Neolithic period, perhaps 3000 B.C.

As Finnish settlement spread, the Finns came into contact with the Lapps, whose language is related to Finnish, and of whom just over 4,000 now live in Finnish Lapland. In the Middle Ages they lived much further south, even as far south as the upper area of Satakunta.

The historical-cultural inheritance of the Finns became more complicated in the course of the struggles between Christianity and older religions, between Catholic Christianity and Orthodox Christianity, the stamping of Lutheranism upon the country, the constant wars between Sweden and Russia, the switch in allegiance from Sweden to Russia, and the internal language conflict between Swedish-speakers and Finnish-speakers.

These stresses produced an identity crisis in large sections of the Finnish upper and educated classes in the nineteenth century, culminating in a search for the origins of the Finnish people (in Asia) and an identification with the common people who spoke Finnish.

An intense Finnish nationalism emerged, the negative aspect of which was stridently expressed by August Ahlqvist-Oksanen in his call for *yksi kieli, yksi mieli* or "one language, one outlook," a type of thinking that is the source of the authoritarianism behind much of the later drive for an internally imposed consensus.

Both language groups asserted themselves, and the wars of the twentieth century were seen as acts of survivalism: to be a Finnish Finn, to be a Swedish Finn, but not, of course, to be a Communist Finn (whose pretended internationalism would only, it was argued, have replaced the national state with that of an alien nation).

As the Finnish national state began to emerge in the twentieth century, and was realized in sovereign independence at the end of 1917, it failed to provide for large sections of the population in whose name it was supposedly also functioning. After the 1880s, 300,000 Finns emigrated permanently to the New World; in 1925 the population of Finland was only 3,322,000, so this emigration was a truly enormous proportion of the population. There was also an emigration of some volume eastward to the Petersburg region and, after 1917, clandestinely to Soviet Russia. After World War II approximately 200,000 Finns moved permanently to live in Sweden, and there was a smaller migration to Australia.

These figures speak of a country that industrialized only slowly and, when it did, developed an industry that was often, like the paper industry, capital intensive and technology intensive rather than labor intensive.

Yet, after World War II, the population that remained in Finland prospered (until the bewildering slump of the 1990s), and its prosperity was based on the ratio between a small population and a high productivity, with the possibility always of shedding excess members by emigration, or keeping others at home in heavily subsidized agriculture.

Correspondingly, the Finns have not seen any need to take in foreigners, not even as refugees. The Finns are heavy users of the resources of other countries, not only as emigrants but also as tourists, particularly in the Mediterranean. They do not, however, welcome any counterflow to their own high-priced country. It used to be said that of all the countries in Europe only Albania had fewer foreigners than Finland. Nowadays, it is simply said that of any country in Europe Finland has the fewest foreigners (approximately 30,000).

One aspect of the constitution of the Finnish population that has occasionally given grounds to a tentative debate about a need to take in more foreigners is the fact that a change in the balance of the population is occurring. In 1990 the proportion of the population sixty-five years old or over was 13.5%, but it is expected to rise to 23.9% in 2030. At the same time the number of those of working age is expected to fall from 65.9% of the population, which it was in 1990, to 59.4% in 2030. Young foreigners might support this aging population, it has been suggested.

Much of the debate in Finland about population questions revolves around utility rather than rights. In an integrating Europe, many Finns fear that their population will lose out, be relegated, be denied its share in what is felicitously termed in Finland "the international division of labor." This is the problem of a nation that feels itself to be peripheral, but brought up, nonetheless, upon a tantalizing combination of political self-sufficiency and international trading.

The problem is all the more acute since within Finland itself there exists a periphery/center (or rather southwest: the triangle of Helsinki, Tampere, and Turku) tension. Since World War II Finns have not merely migrated to Sweden, but internally down to the southwest, so that, for example, in the province of Uusimaa (in which the capital is situated) one-third of the present inhabitants have been born elsewhere. In this area, too, there is a concentration of the educated—in the local government district of Kauniainen, to take the most striking instance, university graduates constitute 25% of the population.

Successive governments, through regional aid programs which have included the establishment of provincial universities, have fought against this migration to the southwest. Some government offices have even been moved out to the provinces. The question remains of whether Finland, by a concentration of resources leading to the development of high-tech industry in only certain areas (the Oulu district has been suggested in addition to the southwest), can better withstand integration pressures.

In the slump of the early 1990s, integration or not, it looked as if Finland would initially at any rate, support itself up by a continued reliance on the paper industry and certain traditional engineering lines. The problem of where future areas of growth in Finland are going to be (possibly in the southeast with a revitalized trade with Russia) should be a matter of concern for infrastructure planning and population policies.

POLITICAL AND ECONOMIC HISTORY

Before there was a Finland there were Finns. Early historical knowledge about this people has been obscured by the fact that the term "Finn" has been used in the older Nordic world to refer to Lapps—the *Fenni* described by Tacitus (circa A.D. 100) may, in fact, have been Lapps.

The Finns may have come into Finland only temporarily at first from the Estonian shores, hunting for furs. The whole of the Baltic region was renowned in Roman times for the quality of its furs, and the Finns traded furs for metal goods and jewelry. The furs included not merely beaver, but also squirrel skins (the Finnish word for money, *raha,* originally referred to squirrel skin).

In these early historical times, the Finns, Scandinavians, and Slavs were penetrating the same areas, though living in Finland were also the descendants of earlier peoples, about whom only archaeology can tell. The invaders began to settle along the coastal regions and riverbanks, and a study of the development of their settlements over the centuries reveals much about a matter of considerable importance: the origin of states, or at least of political control.

The current identification of a state with a parcel of unified territory has been used, somewhat falsely, as a measuring rod for the remoter Finnish past. By this interpretation, Finland attained political reality only as a piece of territory added to the Swedish Crown in the struggles between Sweden and Novgorod.

Another conceptualization of political power, however, has now recognized that control over the southwestern shores of Finland became the goal of two sea empires, one centered on the Lake

Mälaren (near the present capital of Sweden), the other centered on the large islands off the coast of Estonia, especially Saaremaa. A boundary, including a sea boundary, between these empires has been located and the fact of their existence can be found in the Finnish national epic, the *Kalevala*. The goal of these empires was the profit wrung from taxation, perhaps a tribute to the importance of the fur trade then. The Finns (or the *Pirkkalaiset,* as the group was called) would much later tax the Lapps in the same way.

The two seagoing empires were identified with the spread of Christianity, and not only in the crusades against the old religions. Two competing forms of Roman Catholicism emerged: the cult of Saint Olaf (favored by the Mälaren empire) and the cult of Mary (favored by the Estonians and later by the Teutonic Knights, who took over Estonia). These two forms merged to struggle against the Orthodoxy of the Karelians and Slavs, though the Novgorod empire also had a strong Scandinavian component.

These factors of cultural diversity, combining strong maritime, trading, and tax-collecting elements of political enterprise, are repeated throughout early Baltic history in the *Drang nach Osten* of many western organizations—the Hanseatic League, the Teutonic Knights, and the Danish and Swedish kingdoms.

Ultimately, Finland became a Swedish possession, but it is incorrect to speak of Sweden-Finland (as many historians, alas, do) as if two states were joined in a kind of real union under the Swedish Crown. On the contrary, Finland became a part of Sweden, even though the Finnish language retained its vigor. Swedish laws were applied and, as the centuries wore on, the Finns were represented in the Swedish Diet.

The eastern boundaries of the Swedish state were given a general definition at the Peace of Pähkinäsaari in 1321. On the Karelian Isthmus the border was drawn at Rajajoki, which in fact remained the border between Finland and Russia until 1940. Novgorod retained Ladoga Lake, and the Karelians—their subjects—kept the northern Finnish lands with access to the sea on the northern Ostrobothnian shore. This was not lost to the Karelians until the Peace of Täyssinä of 1595; shortly afterward, at Stolbova in 1617, the Swedish state reached its furthest border eastward when the conquest of Ingria guaranteed it.

This eastward expansion of Sweden was motivated by economic considerations: the desire to control the trade of the Baltic littoral and Russian hinterland. Dynastic ambition and the sheer lure of territorial possession overtook it, however, most of all in the Great Northern War of 1700–1721, pursued ferociously by Charles XII. This led to the period known in Finnish history as the Great Wrath, when Finland was occupied and devastated by Russian invaders.

It could be argued that up to this point Finland had benefitted (as well as suffered) from the eastward expansion of the Swedish state. From the Great Wrath onward, while the country clung to the Swedish connection, the connection was a defensive one, symbolized most clearly by the decision in 1746 to build a great fortress at Sveaborg (later Suomenlinna) off Helsinki. Finland lost territory to Russia in 1721 and 1743, and nothing was regained in the Swedish-Russian War of 1788–1790.

By the second half of the eighteenth century leading Finns began to be haunted by a fear that Sweden might abandon Finland. This produced ambivalent reactions, as seen, for example, in the career of G. M. Sprengtporten, who first (through participation in the coup d'état of 1772) helped strengthen Swedish monarchical power, and later betrayed his monarch by going over to the Russian side.

When Russia finally took Finland in the war of 1808–1809, the outcome was positive for the Finnish ruling class for many decades. The treachery of Sprengtporten and the adventurism of G. M. Armfelt seemed justified, and it looked as if many Finns had too greatly feared a change of monarchical allegiance.

Finland became a state apart, an existence apparently acknowledged by the restoration of Old Finland (the lands lost in 1721 and 1743) in 1811. Since Swedish laws and institutions were maintained by Alexander I, the only de facto link with the Russian Empire was the fact that the monarchy was now Russian and not Swedish. De jure the monarchical link was confirmed (as against an administrative-institutional link) when it was laid down that Finnish matters be presented directly to the tsar by a minister state-secretary who did not consult any Russian ministerial colleagues.

As the Finns, later in the nineteenth century, thought about their political situation, they developed an almost contractual theory of their "State." They were loyal to the monarchical connection, because the monarch in turn was loyal to their institutional life, inherited from Swedish days. The shock of the bombardment of the Finnish coast during the Crimean War caused a certain interest once more in a restoration of the Swedish connection (among a minority of students), and a more considered debate on neutrality was spawned, which lasted for several decades. In fact, loyalty to the Russian connection was strengthened after Alexander II summoned the Diet of Four Estates to meet in 1863. It met regularly from 1869 onward.

By this time the antiquated Diet system had already been changed in Sweden. The truth was that, as far as political institutions were concerned, both Russia and Finland were not modern states. The problem became acute for Russia as the century wore on. A foreign-policy dimension entered into the issue with the development of a German Empire and the *Ausgleich* of 1867 that created Austria-Hungary. The Crimean War had already destroyed the role of Russia as the arbiter of absolutism in eastern Europe.

Attempts to modernize the Russian Empire became associated with a Russian nationalist populism. In Finland these Russian attempts to unify were therefore called "Russification," especially since in Finland the Russian language was hardly known—even many administrators had little knowledge of it. For the Russian unifiers, Finland became a symbol of what had to be ironed out to produce a Russian security state (abolition of the separate Finnish army, integration of its pilot and telegraph services into the imperial institutions, imposition of the Russian language as the means of communication among the higher administrative echelons).

All these changes were made possible after the promulgation of the 1899 February Manifesto. Among most of the Finnish leadership, this provoked the reaction that the tsar had broken his oath to uphold Finnish fundamental laws (which seemingly protected a wide range of distinct Finnish institutions).

A section of the Finnish leadership went further. Drawing the conclusion that the contract was being dissolved by the tsar's action, they felt justified in engaging in passive resistance, until such time as the status quo was restored. The group among the Finnish leadership known as the Compliants were no different in their goal: they wanted to come to terms with the tsar and his advisors in order to preserve as much of the status quo as possible. The difference between the Compliants and the supporters of passive resistance was only one of tactics.

In short, the Finnish elite had benefited greatly from the old Finnish autonomy that had endured from 1809 to 1899. In the second half of the nineteenth century restrictive economic laws had been done away with and trade liberalized so that a small but effective commercial and industrial bourgeoisie had built up a profitable export trade. Penetrating Russian as well as Western markets, these entrepreneurs were skillful to such a degree that Russian industry had to be protected against them. A tariff wall for many products was maintained between Finland and Russia at the request of Russian manufacturers (in the paper industry, for instance), and this constituted a stumbling block to greater unification measures from the Russian side.

In the meantime the Finnish elite had played language politics, debating among itself whether to be Finnish or Swedish. This toying with its own identity was part of a standoff to the Russian connection: it was confrontational but also mutually supportive, as Russian governors-general picked and shifted their allies.

What this politics ignored was the emergence of new classes and problems in Finland. This was not simply a question of the rise of an industrial proletariat, which remained pathetically small in relation to the rural proletariat—or near proletariat, in the shape of an insecure crofter and landless population. The new Social Democratic party, founded in 1899, tried to cover the problems of both industrial and rural proletariat. Characteristically, workers' leaders were ignored in the first instance when opposition to the February Manifesto was being organized by the traditional Finnish elite.

In a sense, this was important when the overwhelming majority of the population was unrepresented in the major representative organ, the Diet of Four Estates. The basic fact was that Finland, while it had been contrasted favorably with a reactionary Russia by Lenin in 1901, was in political terms run by an enlightened administrative elite of its own, which picked its own problems and issues to be solved, and which was not prepared to listen too closely to anything the common people might want to tell it.

Agreement about the evils of tsarism did exist between the older elite and the Social Democratic party, but for the latter it was part of a wider problem, the solution to which was international revolution and not a restoration of the status quo. For many of the Social Democrats the unicameral legislature of 1906 (meeting for the first time in 1907) came only because of the Russian Revolution of 1905 and the subsequent Finnish Great Strike at the end of the same year.

When tsarism went on to hamstring the work of the Finnish reformed legislature (the tsar refusing to sign many of the laws adopted), a truly working Parliament and the concomitant attainment of independence came to be only as a result of the second series of Russian revolutions, those of 1917. In other words, many of the Social Democrats thought, an independent state with a sovereign Parliament was the product of international revolution and not an alternative to it.

In July 1917 a Social Democratic–dominated legislature adopted an enabling act giving Finland independence, under Parliament, in all internal affairs. It was the bourgeois political forces (who had gotten Kerensky to dissolve this Parliament) who were, in the eyes of the Social Democrats, the true betrayers of constitutionalism. This later drove the Social Democrats (or a part of them) into another revolution, the Red rebellion of the Finnish Civil War.

In fact, constitutionalism was vitally important for the bourgeois political forces, and, indeed, a native constitutionalism of an independent state was what they, too, needed. For between 1908 and 1910 the Finns had been offered a chance to participate in Russian constitutionalism, with a share of seats in the Duma, where Finland and its interests would have been consistently outvoted.

It was the form of constitutionalism that the Social Democrats and the older elite disagreed about. The Social Democrats wanted a sovereign Parliament, the bourgeois forces a strong executive, to which they had always been accustomed. For the latter forces, the people could have their say through Parliament, but a constitutional balance, a *controlling* constitutionalism of an independent judiciary and executive, had to come into being.

After the White victory in the Civil War in 1918, many bourgeois politicians even dreamed of a Finnish monarchy. This arose not merely from their mistaken view of a German victory, but from the sense of a need to give legitimacy to the new state—at the top. In any case what was created was what Veli Merikoski has rightly called a presidential-parliamentary democracy.

The powers of the presidency revolved around the president's role as leader of the country's foreign policy, but his latent powers stretched everywhere—as, for example, when President Svinhufvud refused, in 1936, to accept the Social Democrats into his government.

The wars of the twentieth century (and Finland engaged in four of them) have ultimately tended to reinforce the power of the executive, though this, as was shown most clearly between 1940 and 1944, was sometimes a military as well as a presidential exercise of power.

Adjusting to the Soviet Union after World War II similarly helped fortify presidential power. The 1948 Finnish-Soviet Treaty was forced upon a reluctant legislature by the force of President Paasikivi's will.

Under his successor, President Kekkonen, foreign policy decision making in the strictest sense had to be combined with the making of delicate decisions in the field of economic policy: the FINEFTA agreement of 1961 and the Free Trade Agreement with the European Economic Community in 1973 were the most important of these. A country with a small population like Finland necessarily based its prosperity on a high level of exports, which had to be guaranteed on Western as well as Soviet markets.

Along with Finland's promotion of the CSCE process, Kekkonen used these concerns of foreign economic policy, as well as the difficulties of upholding good relations with the Soviet Union, as powerful pretexts to impose domestic unity upon the country. Presidential power reached out, in the late 1960s, not only to bind together parliamentary coalitions but also to foster the development of extraparliamentary means, such as wage policy that bound industrialists, trade unionists, and agricultural producers into an enforced harmony.

To borrow a term from Richard Rosecrance, Finland, in spite of its burden of a heavily subsidized agriculture, has become a trading state par excellence, its people little interested in such territorial questions as the return of the lands lost in 1944 to the Soviet Union.

A trading state is not, however, by definition inevitably any more democratic than a state motivated by the territorial imperative (which Finland was in the period of Swedish expansionism and in the period of cobelligerency with Nazi Germany in 1941–1944). Finland remains an administered country.

The revolutionary Finnish Social Democrats of the early twentieth century were able to appreciate that European peoples were living in an economic context that was breaking down the barriers between states. This process would, they thought, produce revolution and with it democracy.

The Finnish bourgeois forces, the dominant forces in Finland, had another vision. They strove avowedly to maintain and, they believed, develop an existing Finnish constitutionalism in a Europe of antagonistic and often warring states. Economically, they were promoters of an international trade that lacked a corresponding international political context, which was why the great Finnish constitutionalist Leo Mechelin died a sadly disappointed man. The irony was that the context of warring European states and the ensuing revolution was the context that brought Finland its independence, once the Russian Empire finally collapsed in 1917.

Now that the wars are over (or at least confined) and the states are beginning to break down barriers through an economically integrative process, the forces ruling Finland are edging into the process, proclaiming the maximum preservation of native independence compatible with the demands of the trading imperative. Since the latter imperative is increasingly the concern of a European Union that is not even a state, there is little reason to think that this context will be any more conducive to the promotion of democracy than the world revolution predicted by the early-twentieth-century Social Democrats (another economic imperative, in fact).

Finally, and with pardonable exaggeration, what might also perhaps be recalled is the early settlement of the Finns on the periphery of their land and their inclusion in trading empires operated from elsewhere.

THE DICTIONARY

-A-

ACADEMIC KARELIA SOCIETY (AKS: *Akateeminen Karjala-Seura*). This organization was one of the most important pressure groups in prewar and wartime Finland.

The Academic Karelia Society was founded in February 1922 by students. It arose as a reaction against the defeat by Soviet power of the uprising in East Karelia (q.v.) and the consequent retreat of Finnish irregular forces from that area. The society also reacted strongly against the Peace of Tartu (q.v.), believing that the Finnish government of the day had, in making peace with Soviet Russia, betrayed the interests of the East Karelians and Ingrians. Even more vehemently did the society, in its propaganda, attack the Soviet government for having disregarded the obligation to promote East Karelian autonomy laid down in Article 10 of the peace treaty and for having made statements at Tartu about the rights of East Karelians and Ingrians which that government had no intention of observing.

There was thus a frustrated kind of legalism in the AKS outlook. It represented an almost macabre version of the legalism which had been the main source of Finnish opposition to Russia in the pre–World War I Years of Oppression (q.v.). On the other hand, many of the AKS leaders had been Old Finns (q.v.) in their political inspiration. It was as if they, too, now found a moral and juridical justification for a contempt of all things Russian (the AKS always used the contemptuous Finnish term *ryssä* when speaking of a Russian).

The society was militant, and its goal was the creation of a Greater Finland (q.v.). In this connection the AKS found its own martyr figure in the person of Bobi Sivén, a young Finnish official, who, having lowered the Finnish flag in the

East Karelian parish of Repola after the "shameful" Peace of Tartu, shot himself. The bullet from his gun was sewn into the AKS flag. Mannerheim (q.v.) always lauded Sivén.

The Academic Karelia Society was dominant in student circles and has been studied as an example of the politics of a burgeoning academic elite. A few strong souls, like the future meteorologist Artturi Similä, who detested the authoritarianism of the society, kept clear of it. Urho Kekkonen (q.v.) also retreated from it.

The Academic Karelia Society rather swiftly became yet another embodiment of Finnish-language politics. Its links with the politics of the Activists (q.v.) restricted women from direct membership; a support organization was formed for them.

With regard to the influence of the society in terms of mainstream politics, it is evident that the role it played among the university-trained elite was a factor confirming the Finnish government's outlook in 1938 and 1939 on the unwisdom of making territorial concessions to the Soviet Union. As far as the Finnish occupation of East Karelia during the Continuation War (q.v.) was concerned, the policies then pursued by the Finnish military forces reflected much of the outlook of the AKS.

Along with such kindred organizations as the People's Patriotic Movement (q.v.), the AKS was automatically suppressed in accordance with Article 21 of the 1944 Armistice Agreement (q.v.), a prohibition repeated in Article 8 of the Peace Treaty of February 10, 1947 (q.v.).

ACT OF UNION AND SECURITY OF 1789. At the height of the Swedish-Russian War of 1788–1790 (q.v.), Gustavus III summoned the Diet of Four Estates (q.v.). His aims were to strengthen further the royal power and to secure from the Estates a grant of additional taxes for the prosecution of the war.

In securing these funds, Gustavus III was compelled to acknowledge the traditional role of the Diet in the granting of new taxes. He also confirmed the privileges of the Estates, which actually meant an improvement in the peasants' rights of landowning.

Through the Act of Union and Security, however, it was made clear that the monarch no longer needed the consent of the Estates for a declaration of war and that he could determine appointments to all official posts. The Council of the Realm was split up into a Supreme Court and a downgraded Administrative Office.

These royal powers especially affected the nobility, which refused to accept the act, the other Estates carrying it through only by the dubious method of acclamation, though many members of the Estate of Peasants and some of the Estate of Burghers were genuine in their support.

Along with the Form of Government of 1772 (q.v.), the Act of Union and Security was assumed in broad terms to be in force after 1809 in the Grand Duchy (q.v.) of Finland. Part of its significance here may have lain in the fact that it represented a warning against overmighty aristocratic pretensions. In actuality, in spite of the aristocratic rage that had led to the assassination of Gustavus III in 1792, the Estate of Nobility accepted the Act of Union and Security in 1800.

ACTIVISTS. The Activist group, a rather heterogeneous collection of patriots (often Swedish-speaking), emerged out of the frustrations of the passive resistance movement (q.v.), which had been founded to challenge the imperial policy of unification (q.v.), which had begun in earnest with the promulgation of the 1899 February Manifesto (q.v.).

The Activists were dissatisfied with the caution of the passive resistance leaders. In the opinion of the Activists, the populace had not been sufficiently drawn into the struggle, the number of young men refusing the imperial army draft having fallen substantially by the spring of 1903.

Thus the Activists, who came out vociferously against the passive resistance leaders at the Stockholm conference in September 1903, were not merely inclined to violence but identified violent resistance with popular resistance. The poet Arvid Mörne, for instance, sought the involvement of the working class, and many Activists advocated sweeping away the old Diet of Four Estates (q.v.) and the setting up of a democratic, unicameral legislature (q.v.).

Among the Activists, therefore, there was a feeling that the struggle against the Russian imperial power must be accompanied by internal change in Finland.

Like the Russian revolutionaries (particularly the Social Revolutionaries), with whom they were prepared to cooperate, the Activists also believed in individual acts of terror. They planned the assassination both of Russian officials in Finland and of Finnish officials whom they believed to be working with the imperial power. Thus they tried to assassinate the Russian governor-general of Finland, Nikolai Ivanovich Bobrikov (q.v.), an act finally accomplished on June 16, 1904, by a young official of the Central School Board, Eugen Schauman, who promptly committed suicide. As well as having political motives, Schauman was in a state of personal distress, having been crossed in love.

A very different type of Activist, the arrogant Lennart Hohenthal, shot the procurator of Finland, J. M. E. Soisalon-Soininen, early in 1905. The procurator was an Old Finn (q.v.), whose patriotism comprehended neither passive nor active resistance.

In the meantime another Activist, Konni Zilliacus (q.v.), planned the smuggling of quantities of arms into Finland, a prelude to more large-scale operations than anything the spectacular acts of assassination could achieve.

By the turn of 1904–1905 the Activists had organized themselves into a party, but it remained very much of a secret society. What was even more ominous was that when the Russian Revolution of 1905 led to the Great Strike (q.v.) in Finland of November 1905, both White Guards and Red Guards were formed and nearly came into prolonged conflict. So the pretended interest of the Activists in joint action with the common folk of Finland failed to come to fruition.

Nevertheless Activism was revived in the early months of World War I through the institution of recruitment for a Finnish Jaeger (q.v.) battalion in Germany. Many young Social Democrats (q.v.) were recruited, including the son of the Social Democratic leader, Yrjö Mäkelin.

In independent Finland a few of the Activists who worked for the independence movement in World War I gained leading positions. Dr. Rafael Erich, who worked for Finnish independence in Sweden and Germany, became prime minister in 1920. It was perhaps typical of the old relations between the Activists and the Left that O. W. Kuusinen (q.v.), the Finnish Communist leader in exile, then thought that he could write to Prime Minister Erich, privately, about the making of peace between Finland and Soviet Russia — with the offer of Petsamo (q.v.) for Finland. Erich and Kuusinen had also been schoolfellows; it was a small world for the elite in pre–World War I Finland.

The last fling of the Activists, in which Erich actually played a role, was the proposal in 1940 for a political union with Sweden. By this time, of course, whatever individual schemes might be dreamed up, a large part of the Finnish population had embraced many of the basic tenets of the original Activism: forceful resistance to Russia and aid, if not from Sweden, then from Germany.

AGE OF LIBERTY. The Age of Liberty in Sweden, which lasted from 1719 to the royal coup d'état of Gustavus III in 1772, began as a reaction against the disastrous wars of Charles XII. In succeeding her brother in 1719, Ulrika Eleonora had to agree that she ruled not by hereditary right but by the election of the Estates. With even greater justification the same doctrine was applied when her husband, the landgrave of Hesse-Cassel, took over the Swedish throne from her, as Frederick I, in 1720.

These monarchs were bound by strict constitutional provisions, but the essence of the Age of Liberty was not merely the power of the Estates as a legislature, but also the fact that in many respects the Estates served as the executive. They were able to act in this way by using or threatening to use a power of impeachment (*licentiering*) against recalcitrant members of the Council of the Realm (the monarch's advisors). But the Estates also set up their own Secret Committee, a de facto executive.

The Secret Committee was dominated by members of the Estate of Nobles. Indeed, the peasants, the fourth Estate of the Diet, were not represented on the committee at all. This fact indicates a great deal about the Age of Liberty. It was partly a protest of the nobility, which had increasingly become a nobility of service, against monarchical power.

On the other hand, in the functioning of the Diet all the Estates played important roles. From Finland the Estate of Clergy produced the great parliamentarian Anders Chydenius (q.v.). For the peasants (especially in Finland) the changes in landholding, inter alia, the Enclosure Act of 1747 and the permission for peasants to take crofters (q.v.) on their lands, strengthened peasant agriculture. In fact, the royal coup d'état of 1772 may well have frustrated a more powerful expression of peasant demands.

For Finnish conservatives the Age of Liberty seems to have left an unpleasant image. Thus, when the Finnish unicameral legislature (q.v.), in July 1917, passed an enabling act which granted it vast executive powers, the minister state-secretary for Finland in Saint Petersburg, Carl Enckell (q.v.), ran to Kerenski to get the legislature dissolved. His explanation after the event was that he had not wished to see a return to the Age of Liberty.

AGRARIAN UNION–CENTER PARTY. The Agrarian Union was founded in the Oulu area and in southern Ostrobothnia in 1906, and in the first elections for the unicameral legislature (q.v.) in 1907 it won only a handful of seats. The Finnish peasantry had been represented in the old Diet of Four Estates (q.v.) and had, therefore, both a political and constitutionalist tradition. Besides, the Finnish-speaking peasantry had been the darling of the Fennoman movement (q.v.) and had developed a certain self-confidence.

This enabled its leaders to form counterpolicies to what they perceived to be the encroaching danger of the values of urbanized and industrializing society. Not merely did the Agrarian Union prosper as a political party, but it was part of a general defense of the rural way of life that included, for example, the creation of farmers' cooperatives and, above all, in 1917 of the powerful MTK, the agricultural producers' association. This special interest group worked closely with the Agrarian Union, though officially distinct, with it developing, especially after World War II, a heavily subsidized agriculture.

In the Finnish Civil War (q.v.) the Agrarians were White, and the peasant army of Ostrobothnia formed a key element in the White victory. Yet both before the Civil War and gradually after it, the Agrarians showed that they were able to cooperate with the Social Democrats.

The Agrarian Union was flexible. Many of its members were later drawn to the Lapua movement (q.v.). Only at the end of the 1930s, under the presidency of Kyösti Kallio (q.v.), was a modus vivendi restored with the Social Democrats.

The Agrarian Union was the quintessential Finnish party, in spite of a formal prewar linkage with a "Green International" of other European peasant parties. At its conferences people sat in national dress, and folk dancing was an important part of the program. The party was national, not ideological, and the basic interest it represented was quite clear.

After World War II, the Agrarian Union, despite an industrializing Finland, secured its future by maintaining a strong agriculture and promoting its supporters to key offices by an effective use of the spoils system. And since the Communists were not, it appeared, destined to possess Finland, the Agrarians succeeded in monopolizing the handling of relations with the Soviet Union so that the legitimacy of the whole state often seemed to be in their hands.

Finnish farmers grew much timber, a fact which bound the agrarian interest, whatever its proclaimed ideals, to the most important export sector of Finnish industry: paper, pulp, and sawmill production. Since urbanization went on apace, however, the Agrarian Union decided to do what its Swedish counterpart had done. In 1965 it changed its name to the Center party and tried to broaden its image.

The first results were disastrous in terms of election losses from dissatisfied voters in the countryside who initially turned to the populism of Veikko Vennamo. To some extent, the Center party has obviously succeeded in becoming an alternative bourgeois party for those angered with the National Coalition party (q.v.), a fact seen in the 1991 election, when the Center Party captured some of the anti-Helsinki vote.

The result? A truly Finnish one: a coalition government based on the axis of Center party–National Coalition party cooperation. And the goal of the government? An application for membership in the European Union (accepted in 1994), a move deeply feared at first by the majority of Center party supporters in the Finnish countryside.

AGRICOLA, MIKAEL (ca. 1510–1557). Church reformer and father of written Finnish. He was born in the parish of Pernaja, near Turku (q.v.), the son of a prosperous peasant. It remains unclear whether Agricola's home language was Finnish or Swedish, but he was educated at the Viipuri Latin school. Thereafter he became a clerk to Bishop Martinus Skytte in Turku and subsequently studied at Wittenberg when Luther and Melanchthon were in their prime.

Even before his attendance at Wittenberg, Agricola seems to have accepted the teachings of the Reformation and had already begun to translate the New Testament into Finnish. His productions in the Finnish language—a primer, catechism, prayerbook, psalms, work on the liturgy, and translations of parts of the Old Testament, as well as the whole of the New Testament—were undertaken in the light of the Reformation view that the laity should have direct access to the word of God in their own tongue. Research has shown that Agricola regarded this literary work as a necessary chore, and he bemoaned the lack of support from the civil authorities.

Agricola rendered great service to later Finnish folklore studies by listing the pagan gods of the Finns of Häme and of Karelia. In his time paganism, as well as Catholicism, still competed with the teachings of the Reformation.

Agricola ended his days as bishop of Turku, but he was compelled by Gustavus Vasa to join the delegation negotiating with Ivan the Terrible for peace on the Karelian frontier. On returning from Russia, after the Peace of Novgorod, Agricola died on the Karelian Isthmus (q.v.) at Kuolemajärvi, "Death Lake."

A statue of Agricola may be seen outside the cathedral of Turku.

ÅLAND ISLANDS. A group of islands between Finland and Sweden in the southernmost extremity of the Gulf of Bothnia. There are over six thousand islands in all, of which only seventy are permanently inhabited. Geographically, the Åland Islands comprise the western part of the extensive archipelago running from Turku (q.v.) to the open sea. So distinct in character, however, are the Åland Islands that their inhabitants even claim to have an archipelago of their own, made up of the five local government districts of Brändö, Föglö, Kumlinge, Kökar, and Sottunga.

Historically, culturally, administratively, linguistically, and to a great degree ethnically, the Åland Islands are a separate society. The 25,000 Ålanders do not even like to be called Finns. They are descended from Swedish settlers, who first came to Åland as early as the sixth century. The distinguishing mark of the Ålanders has continued to be the Swedish language (q.v.), which has an unchallenged position on the islands, the Finnish language (q.v.) not being an official language there.

By the 1809 Peace of Hamina (q.v.), the Åland Islands were taken with Finland into the Russian Empire, though there was some wrangling about them in the treaty negotiations. The islands were occupied by the British and French in the Crimean War (q.v.), and the Russian fortress of Bomarsund was destroyed. By the Åland Convention of 1856, an annex to the Treaty of Paris, the islands were neutralized. The Swedes undoubtedly wanted to repossess them, but as they "had not taken the fortunes of war" before this, they had to content themselves with neutralization. All these decisions were nevertheless a reflection of Western fears lest the islands became a base for Russian expansion.

In March 1918, in the Brest-Litovsk period, the islands were occupied by German troops before German contingents arrived on the Finnish mainland, in April 1918, to fight on the White side in the Finnish Civil War (q.v.). The inhabitants of Åland, in this period of confusion around the birth of the independent Finnish state, expressed their preference for Swedish rule, and Swedish troops were sent. Great Britain raised the issue in the League of Nations, though Finland was not yet a member. The League decided for Finland—against the wishes of the Ålanders.

The League's decision was based upon recognition of the strategic link between Åland and Finland and also upon the view, vociferously argued by Swedish-Finnish emissaries, that possession of Åland would strengthen the position of the Swedish-speaking minority in Finland. In the latter matter, as things have turned out, it does not seem to have made much difference.

The League's decision, in June 1921, also involved the grant of autonomy to the Ålanders, but the Finnish government had already recognized this the previous year. Thus the islands have a parliament of their own, the Landsting.

The islands were again declared neutralized by the Åland Convention of October 1921, but in January 1939 the Finnish and Swedish governments began to plan for the fortification of the islands. Many Åland leaders felt that this would lead to Finnicization. They need not have feared. In June 1939, as a result of Soviet antagonism, the Swedes withdrew from the scheme. Wrangling over the fate of the Åland Islands also played a significant part in the failure of the 1939 negotiations among Great Britain, France, and the Soviet Union, and thus helped precipitate the Nazi-Soviet Pact (q.v.).

The islanders are exempt from military service, but in World War II they did valiant work in the merchant marine. At the end of hostilities rumors abounded that Åland, not Porkkala, was to be taken as the Soviet base area.

Since World War II the autonomy of the Åland Islands has been enhanced. In 1954 they got their own flag. They have their own stamps, and now they want their own money, which, in specimen form, has already been minted. By using the right of domicile in the strictest manner (with regard to the language requirement), they keep out Finnish-speaking settlers. Some Ålanders are certainly attracted by "off-shore island" possibilities.

The Ålanders claim that they contribute more to the Finnish state budget than they get out of it. Though represented by one member in the Finnish Parliament, they have two out of the eighty-nine members in the Nordic Council (q.v.).

ALLIED CONTROL COMMISSION. The Allied Control Commission was in Finland from the Armistice Agreement (q.v.)

ending the Continuation War (q.v.) until the signing of the Peace Treaty of February 10, 1947 (q.v.).

The task of the commission was to ensure the enforcement of the conditions of the Armistice Agreement. To this end, Andrei Zhdanov, the chairman of the commission, felt obliged to interfere in the sentences passed in the war trials (q.v.) when he regarded them as too mild.

Zhdanov was often away from Finland, however, because of his concerns for Leningrad. Thus his deputy, Major General G. Savonenko, took over. Of distant Finnish origin, he nonetheless seems to have been even more difficult to get on with than Zhdanov.

In spite of these personality conflicts, on the whole the Allied Control Commission behaved punctiliously with respect to its tasks. Paasikivi (q.v.) feared that it might turn into an alternative government, but this was not the case. Paasikivi took care, however, always to have relations with the commission directly under his own thumb—another example of the utility of strong presidential power in Finland. He was sometimes seen laughing with Zhdanov.

Since Great Britain had declared war on Finland, there were also British officers on the commission, one of whom, J. H. Magill, was known to many Finns from his earlier connections with their country. His instructions were to do nothing to upset the Russians. The U.K. political representative to the commission was F. M. Shepherd, formerly His Majesty's Consul General at Leopoldville in the Congo.

Considering Soviet behavior in Eastern Europe, the correctness of behavior of the Allied Control Commission in Finland, dominated as it was by the Russians, testifies once again to the fact that the Soviet government did not intend to take Finland over.

ANJALA COVENANT. This document was signed by a group of officers, meeting at Anjala, an estate in southern Finland, in the early weeks of the Swedish-Russian War (q.v.) in 1788. It was drafted shortly after the Liikkala Note (q.v.), but while there were only seven signatories to the note, the covenant was signed by 113 officers.

The men of Anjala declared their loyalty to the Swedish king, Gustavus III, an act he had demanded on hearing of the Liikkala Note. They also stated, however, that insofar as the empress Catherine was prepared for peace, they were ready to lay down their arms. They called for the summoning of the Diet and for the safeguarding of the privileges of the nation and the Estates.

It may well have been that the intriguers of Liikkala had given too rosy a picture of Catherine's intentions. In any case, Gustavus III, hardly surprisingly, regarded the Anjala men as conspirators, even if he took his time in dealing with them.

In the background lurked his jealous brother, Duke Charles of Södermanland (later king himself as Charles XIII, reigning from 1809 to 1818), who had contacts with the men of Anjala. On hearing, however, that a dissident Finnish aristocrat in Russian service, G. M. Sprengtporten (q.v.), was planning the separation of Finland from Sweden, Duke Charles denounced the Anjala conspiracy.

Major J. A. Jägerhorn, the bearer of the Liikkala Note, and Lieutenant K. H. Klick, the drafter of the Anjala Covenant, managed in any case to flee to Russia. Only one of the conspirators, Colonel J. H. Hästesko, who had been involved both at Liikkala and Anjala, was executed. His beheading was deeply resented by his fellow officers and aristocrats and was a factor in the intrigues leading to the assassination of Gustavus III in 1792 (an event around which Verdi wrote his opera *Un Ballo in Maschera*).

Notwithstanding the hesitant nature of the Anjala enterprise, it has been seen by the late President Kekkonen (q.v.), among others, as a distinct Finnish attempt to come to terms peaceably with Russia by rejecting the role for Finland of "outpost of the west" (q.v.), or vanguard.

In its time the Anjala conspiracy had no popular support and was an aspect of the conflict between the monarch and certain aristocratic circles.

ARMED FORCES. In the old Kingdom of Sweden, until the late seventeenth century, infantrymen were conscripted and cavalrymen volunteered in return for a certain remission of their farm rents insofar as they farmed Crown lands. It is probably the case that Finns served the Swedish kings in numbers that were quite disproportionate to the paucity of population in Finland, a point underlined later by Snellman (q.v.) in his rejection of the Swedish connection.

Still, Finns seem to be proud of the ferocious reputation their troops had in the Thirty Years' War. The Finnish cavalryman, who in that war was known as *hakkapeliitta* (a corruption of the cry *Hakkaa päälle* "Down with the enemy"), has this century had a reinforced snow tire named for him.

In 1682 an attempt was made at a comprehensive reconstruction of the armed forces of the Swedish kingdom on an *indelta* system: a group of farms had to support an infantryman and larger farms had each to support a cavalryman, while noncommissioned officers and officers were given farms from Crown lands for their support. This system actually endured till 1810 and even had a brief revival in the mid–nineteenth century as a result of the Crimean War (q.v.).

Nevertheless one of the greatest achievements of the Diet of Porvoo (q.v.) in 1809 was to beg successfully from the new ruler, Tsar Alexander I, a fifty-year period of exemption from general military service for the inhabitants of the Grand Duchy (q.v.). Some volunteer troops were indeed assembled in the crisis year of 1812, and they helped to guard Saint Petersburg. From these forces later derived the sharpshooters' battalion and the Finnish Guards.

Throughout the nineteenth century officers continued to be trained in Finland, first at the Topographical School at Haapaniemi and then at the Hamina Cadet School. These officers could then serve either in the small Finnish army or in the imperial forces, where there existed a merit system for Finns. After the great reform in military service in Russia in 1874, military service was introduced into Finland in 1878, though it was service by lots and was only half the length of service in the Russian army.

The abolition of the separate Finnish army in 1901, of the Hamina Cadet School in 1903, and of the Finnish Guards in 1905 were aspects of the process of unification (q.v.) in the Russian Empire. These steps were deeply resented by the Finns, with many young men refusing to be drafted into the

Russian army. In the end the matter was settled when the Finns agreed to pay a financial contribution in lieu of recruits, a system that saved most Finns from the battlefields of World War I.

In the Civil War (q.v.) of 1918 both sides imposed a draft. The present-day Finnish armed forces, also based on the draft, are the heirs of the victorious White Army of the Civil War.

In the first few years of its existence, however, the army of independent Finland was riven by feuding in the officer corps between those who had formerly served in Russia and the officers trained through the Jaeger movement (q.v.) by the Germans. In 1926 General Karl Fredrik Wilkama was forced out of command by the Jaegers.

In spite of this disgraceful beginning, the armed forces of independent Finland have on the whole been a unifying force in the country. This was seen at its clearest in the Winter War (q.v.), where the army's heroic stand of three and a half months was an expression of the national will. Indeed the Finnish defense forces, as they are officially styled, even in the mutuality of their post–World War II relationship with the Soviet Union, laid down in the 1948 Finnish-Soviet Treaty (q.v.), were still a traditional manifestation of the Finnish determination not to be Russian.

At the present time military service is for a minimum period of eight and a half months, with three further months for those who are being trained as reserve officers at Hamina. Trainee professional officers, having completed their military service, then go on to the Cadet School in Helsinki.

In spite of the limitations on certain types of weaponry, and on the number of personnel at least in peacetime, originally decreed (until the Finns in 1990 unilaterally declared otherwise) by the 1947 Peace Treaty, it has been estimated that the Finns would have been able in the post–World War II period to field hundreds of thousands of men in a war or crisis.

They justify a mass army, inter alia, by the vast extent of Finland and its difficult terrain. It is not easy to see how they could cope with the accurate aerial bombardment by night of key civil and military targets characteristic of one side's activity in the Gulf War or with the admitted problem of seaborne and airborne cruise missiles.

Notwithstanding disarmament plans elsewhere in Europe, the Finnish defense forces are making no gesture in this direction. Backup opinion will point out that disarmament is relative or that internal circumstances in the former Soviet Union or Eastern Europe may worsen—a point seemingly confirmed by the allegation that in the Russian parliamentary elections of 1993 a strong section of the Russian army voted for the fire-eater Vladimir Zhirinovsky, who once declared that Finland should be taken back into the Russian Empire.

Few refuse military service in Finland (alternative non-military service is thirteen months at the moment), and now, thanks to the female defense minister, Elisabeth Rehn, the voluntary enlistment of women in the armed forces will soon be possible. This will hardly improve the situation for the conscripted men.

The Finnish defense forces continue to stand for a defensive machismo, an uncritical backs-to-the wall mentality, which does not welcome controversial discussion of security policy questions and the role of the army vis-à-vis civil society.

ARMFELT, GUSTAF MAURITZ (1757–1814). Soldier and courtier, statesman and intriguer, Armfelt was born on his father's estate at Marttila in southwestern Finland. After a brief period of study at the University of Turku, he became an ensign in the Life Guards.

Notwithstanding the brilliance of his subsequent court and military career, Armfelt, while commanding troops against Russia in the Swedish-Russian War of 1788–1790 (q.v.), entered into secret relations with the Russian side. After the assassination of Gustavus III in 1792, Armfelt, then envoy of Sweden at Naples, intrigued against G. A. Reuterholm, the favorite of Duke Charles, the regent, and even envisaged calling up the aid of Catherine II. For this Armfelt was condemned to death in absentia.

He fled to Russia and, after a period in internal exile there, he ended up in dalliance at the court of the widowed duchess of Courland. With the accession of Gustavus IV Adolphus,

Armfelt was pardoned and returned to Sweden to a succession of military and diplomatic posts.

In 1807 he commanded the Swedish troops that threw the French out of Swedish Pomerania. Though his relations with Gustavus IV Adolphus worsened, when the latter was driven into exile in 1809, Armfelt—as a true Gustavian (q.v.)—could not stomach the thought of the Bernadotte succession. By 1811 Armfelt decided that he could manage the oath of allegiance to Tsar Alexander I, and so he was able to return to his Finnish estates.

In Finland Armfelt rapidly rose to prominence. He helped ensure that the Committee of Finnish Affairs would be composed only of Finns—this against the wishes of Mikhail Speransky (q.v.), who wanted Russians also on it. Armfelt was instrumental in securing, at the end of 1811, the incorporation of Old Finland (q.v.) into the rest of Finland. He succeeded Speransky as chancellor of the University of Turku, a post he had previously held in 1791.

This final fling of Finnish patriotism, quite important for the future of the Grand Duchy (q.v.), testified to the root problems of the Finnish Gustavian aristocracy, torn between Sweden and Russia, and threatened by new social forces. Armfelt's notorious love affairs, so clearly mixed up with ambition and politics (his former mistress, Magdalena Rudenschöld, was humiliated at the pillory in Stockholm in 1794 for her part in Armfelt's attempt to oust Reuterholm), were a more personal expression of his constant uncertainty.

ARMISTICE AGREEMENT. The hostilities of the Continuation War (q.v.) ended on the Finnish side on September 4, 1944, and on the Russian side on September 5, but the Armistice Agreement was not signed in Moscow until September 19.

The period in between was far from pleasant for the Finnish delegation. They were made to wait because of the Romanian negotiations, and they were accused by Molotov of already having made a gentlemen's agreement with the Germans, who were drawing back from Finland in peace and at a stated pace. As if to add weight to Molotov's complaint, Soviet troops crossed the northern Finnish border at two places on September 18.

The British, who had declared war on Finland on December 6, 1942, were also making a fuss, claiming that the Russians were keeping them in the dark about the Finnish armistice. In fact, the Russians would have liked to settle the whole thing by making a peace treaty then and there with the Finns, but the British wanted to hold off until peace treaties were made with all the former enemy states.

What difference this would have made to the Finnish position had the country been able to make a peace treaty in 1944 is difficult to say. The Finnish armed forces would have had fewer restrictions imposed on them. Finland might have entered much earlier into the United Nations (as it was, Finland's membership was delayed until the end of 1955 because of Cold War wrangling), but how far U.N. membership immediately after World War II would have eased Finland's position is uncertain.

The United States, which never declared war on Finland but had broken off diplomatic relations at the end of June 1944, would have liked to help Finland but dared not upset the Soviet Union at this juncture by direct intervention in negotiations in which the U.S. had no *locus standi.*

The negotiations were really more like dictation. Article 6 confirmed the territorial concessions made by Finland to the Soviet Union by the Peace of Moscow (q.v.), which had ended the Winter War (q.v.). Thus the lost lands were lost again, only this time the vast area of Petsamo (q.v.), bordering on the Arctic Ocean, was also, by Article 7, to be lost to Finland. Molotov averred that it had been an area used as an aggressive springboard in the Continuation War, but there were nickel deposits (q.v.) in Petsamo, which may have been a more important reason. The strategic value of Petsamo in the Continuation War had not proved to be of overriding importance.

Article 8 of the Armistice Agreement saw the Soviet Union renouncing its lease of the Hanko Peninsula: instead the Soviet Union leased the Porkkala Peninsula, which was even nearer Helsinki (q.v.), a matter that drove President Mannerheim (q.v.) to think of moving the Finnish capital to Turku (q.v.). Mannerheim's idea that the Russians should be offered a base on Åland (q.v.) in place of Porkkala was not even brought up by the Finnish delegation. They were faced with a fait accompli, and the Swedish government—which had gotten wind of the Åland suggestion—were in any case furious with the Finns.

The lands lost to the Soviet Union covered more than one-tenth of Finland's area, and more than 400,000 people had to move (nearly all the Finnish population left these areas).

In addition, by Article 11 of the agreement, Finland had to pay a war indemnity to the Soviet Union of $300 million, assessed at 1938 world prices. Thus, though Finland later received a reduction of $73.5 million from this sum, the total amount of war reparations (q.v.) actually paid was equivalent to $444 million.

Many of the stipulations of the Armistice Agreement required a change in Finnish society. This was particularly the case with Article 13, which required war trials (q.v.), and Articles 20 and 21, which removed "discriminatory legislation" against those who had worked for the United Nations (thus legitimizing the Communists) and imposing discriminatory legislation against fascist organizations or those which had worked against the United Nations. This matter was interpreted widely, so that the Lotta Svärd women's voluntary organization for the defense of Finland became forbidden.

As the Armistice Agreement closed one war, so it opened another, for by the second article of the agreement the Finns were compelled to disarm and hand over their former German *Waffenbrüder*. This meant the outbreak of real hostilities between the Finns and the German troops on Finnish soil; the ensuing war is generally known in Finland as the Lapland War (q.v.).

Finally, by Article 22, the Armistice Agreement imposed on Finland an Allied Control Commission (q.v.). Whether this institution would have been avoided had a peace treaty been made is somewhat doubtful, but the thought is there.

The best thing about the Armistice Agreement is that it solved Finland's fate before the partition of Europe at Yalta in February 1945. In general the Allies seemed to want to keep an independent Finland if only the Finns would lay down their arms against them in time. It is worth remembering nonetheless that in the early fall of 1943 (several weeks before the Teheran Conference, where he changed his mind again), Roosevelt is said to have envisaged a postwar "restoration" of Finland to Russia.

ARMS CACHING. Sometime between the spring and early fall of 1944 the Finnish General Headquarters decided to build up secret stores of arms all over Finland. Discussions were certainly held in the fall between Colonel V. K. Nihtilä, the head of the operations section, and his assistant, Lieutenant Colonel U. S. Haahti, on this project. These officers later bore the main share of the guilt, but it is improbable that they planned all this without the cognizance of their superiors.

The plan, intimately connected with the Stella Polaris (q.v.) operation, was a typical piece of military politics. The eventuality that inspired these people was the imminent breakdown of relations between the West and the Soviet Union, which they envisaged as a "hot" war in which Finland might be occupied by Soviet armed forces, and a native resistance movement arose.

While Finland was entering into hostilities with Germany in the Lapland War (q.v.), German intelligence was aware of these plans to build up a secret arms network in Finland for use against the Soviet Union. The Germans harbored similar thoughts about a West-Soviet conflict.

The activities were revealed in the spring of 1945, but the Allied Control Commission (q.v.), after an initial flurry of concern, left the whole matter in the hands of the Finnish authorities. Prime Minister, later President, Paasikivi (q.v.) and then Minister of Justice Urho Kekkonen (q.v.) showed intense anger at the conspiracy. Indeed, it is a wonder that the revelation of the conspiracy did not seriously undermine the politics they were trying to pursue. But—let the fact be known—the Soviet Union in the immediate post–World War II period showed a tolerance toward Finland it did not show to other small states.

The trials dragged on for several years and are said to have been the longest in Nordic history. Over four hundred officers were given prison sentences, but the generals (and marshals) were either acquitted (like General A. F. Airo—who spent three years in prison while awaiting his trial and during it) or were never considered for trial.

A recent minister of defense, Elisabeth Rehn, said she regarded the officers involved in the arms caching as patriots.

AUTONOMY. From 1809 to 1917 Finland was an autonomous Grand Duchy (q.v.) of the Russian Empire. In 1809 Finland's position was not explicitly defined in this way; rather, what was stressed was a certain special relationship with the tsar.

The constitutionalist argument from the Finnish side, as it developed gradually in the nineteenth century, tried to make concrete something that had not been very clearly articulated in terms of political theory. For the horrified Russians, talk of autonomy (and Mechelin [q.v.] went further even into the doctrine of real union, as if Finland and Russia were two distinct states joined only by a common monarchy) was uncomfortably close to separatism.

From another angle, the obsession of Finnish leaders with defining and defending autonomy took their concern away from many important social questions at home; the emergence of Socialism, for example, crept up on them unawares.

- B -

BANK OF FINLAND. Outside the Bank of Finland there is a statue of J. W. Snellman (q.v.) and even the street on which the bank is situated is named for him, yet Snellman was not the inaugurator of the bank. It had been founded in 1811, largely to provide credits and other assistance for landowners who had outstanding mortgages with Swedish financial institutions. Not until 1840 did the Bank of Finland begin to discount bills, and by the middle of the century it was still granting few loans to industry.

In 1863 Snellman became head of the Senate (q.v.) Finance committee. He realized that the chief benefit the Bank of Finland could bring to Finnish industry and commerce would be the establishment of a sound currency. Hence he continued the work started by his predecessor, Fabian Langenskiöld, for the institution by the Bank of Finland of a separate Finnish silver mark. This would be distinct from the notoriously fluctuating currency of the Russian Empire.

Snellman did not succeed in eradicating the Russian silver ruble (though ruble notes were no longer to be legal tender in Finland), but he secured parity for the silver mark with the silver ruble.

As silver weakened internationally in the 1870s, Finland went on the gold standard in 1878—almost twenty years before the same change occurred in Russia.

This striking testimony to the strength of Finnish autonomy (q.v.) has not been without its problems as far as the role of the bank in independent Finland is concerned. The bank was created well before Finnish representative organs began to meet regularly, and it has retained its distance from them.

It is true that the Diet of Four Estates (q.v.), as early as 1868, elected representatives of its own to the bank, a practice continued by the Finnish Parliament. This form of control, however, originally instituted to safeguard the bank from Russian imperial interests, has proved weak in independent Finland.

The board of the bank is a separate organ, and its members are appointed by the president—yet another example of the strength of presidential power in Finland. It is often asserted that the Bank of Finland is more independent than comparable institutions in other lands. In terms of democratic supervision, this assertion is correct, but otherwise the bank often seems to be prey to presidential diktat (as with the attempt to maintain a high mark in 1991), or to pressures from the Finnish wood and paper industry (as with the reluctant devaluation in the fall of 1991), or to the wishes of the commercial banks (as with the appointment to the post of head of the Bank of Finland).

BECKER BEY (Becker, Ewert Gustaf Waldemar) (1840–1907). This colorful figure came of military stock in the Helsinki district. He himself trained as an officer at the Hamina Cadet School, seeing service in the Finnish Guards before going off to fight for the Spaniards against the Moroccans. Returning to the Russian Empire, Becker served in the Grodno Hussars, but then fled with a married woman to the United States. The love affair was soon over—as was Becker's career in the Russian imperial service.

Becker, who lived the rest of his life abroad, fought for Maximilian in Mexico, served briefly in the Papal Zouaves in Rome, was in the army of the khedive of Egypt (hence the title "Bey"), and fought for the Serbs against the Turks. His early Catholic passion to see the destruction of the Turkish Empire was later overtaken by a zealous concern, expressed in many writings, about the need to bridle Russian expansionism ("Pan-Slavism," he dubbed it).

In thinking originally about the liberation of subject peoples (Greeks, Serbs, Albanians, Kurds), Becker thought in terms of joint risings of oppressed nations. Later, however, in dwelling on the problem of Finland, he came to believe that change would come only through an international breakdown in the relations between the powers. He thus argued that it would be in the interests of Austria-Hungary, a united Germany, and Great Britain to thwart Russian expansion whether in the Balkans or Scandinavia. In the outcome of a politics of this kind, Finland could arise as an "independent and neutral state" to be guaranteed by the three powers.

Becker had links with the liberalism of the *Helsingfors Dagblad* newspaper, which opened its columns to him. Where he differed from the earlier "Scandinavians" was in no longer placing reliance on Sweden.

For Snellman (q.v.), who attacked the "adventurer" Becker as a man of illusions, there could be no reliance on any of the powers Becker had cited. Even up to the Russo-Japanese War, however, Becker Bey continued to work on his scenarios.

BOBRIKOV, NIKOLAI IVANOVICH (1839–1904). Governor-general of Finland from 1898 to 1904. In Finnish eyes Bobrikov became the embodiment of Russian arbitrary rule, and he was assassinated by a young Finnish civil servant of Activist (q.v.) sympathies.

In spite of some scurrilous attempts in Finland to cast aspersions on Bobrikov's parentage, he was, in fact, the son of a privy councillor. As a soldier with a meritorious record, Nikolai Bobrikov had the right background for the post of governor-general, who was inevitably a soldier for, among other things, he commanded the military establishment in the Grand Duchy (q.v.).

For the Finns, nothing was right about Bobrikov. Before taking up his post, he had submitted a policy statement to Tsar Nicholas II, according to which his goals were political, based on a principle put forward a decade earlier by K. F. Ordin. This was that in the War of 1808–1809 for the Possession of Finland (q.v.) the Finns were well and truly conquered and could, therefore, in the last resort be subjected to the imperial will.

He pleaded for the abolition of the separate Finnish army and the recruitment of young Finns into the Russian forces (goals attained after 1901). He also suggested to the tsar the suppression of the Finnish customs authority and separate monetary system (advocated earlier and never attained even by Bobrikov), thus also expressing his concern for the military weakness and unreliability of Finland. Before coming to Finland, Bobrikov had been chief of staff of the Saint Petersburg military district. From Ordin he had learned, erroneously, that Russian policy toward Finland had always been motivated by fears for the security of the Russian capital.

By the turn of the century it was not Sweden as such that was feared, but the possibility of Sweden's attacking as part of a wider European grand alliance, led presumably by Germany.

In office, and once the February Manifesto (q.v.) was promulgated, Bobrikov's first important measure was to secure a decree imposing the Russian language as the language of the higher administrative bodies. Because of this, his line of policy (as indeed that of other Russian administrators and publicists) was always dubbed "Russification" by the Finns.

Such a designation may be misleading, for it might be thought to signify a policy based essentially on the emotional content of a Pan-Russianism. There was a deeper rationale in Bobrikov's policy, even if it was given a ruthless expression. The Russian Empire, in the face of the increasing effectiveness of the German Empire and Austria-Hungary, was desperately trying to modernize its institutions, one aspect of which was their unifying. For the Finns such a unifying could not possibly mean modernization, but a downgrading of what they had. Yet Bobrikov was impressed neither by the modernity of the Finnish armed forces (q.v.) nor, for example, by the coastal pilot service.

Receiving dictatorial powers in 1903, Bobrikov exiled Leo Mechelin (q.v.) and other leading members of the constitutionalist passive resistance movement (q.v.). The Activists then came to the fore, and one of them killed him.

BRAHE, PER (1602–1680). Governor-general of Finland from 1637 to 1640 and from 1648 to 1654. Brahe, the son of an aristocrat, was born at Rydboholm in Sweden. He studied at the universities of Giessen and Strasbourg and traveled in Italy. A man of cultivation, he also served with distinction as a soldier in the Thirty Years' War.

Finland did not usually have any separate status in the Swedish kingdom (unlike the Baltic lands). In reviving the Finnish governor-generalship for Brahe, Chancellor Axel Oxenstierna and later Queen Christina were getting rid of a potentially dangerous rival, one who believed strongly in aristocratic power and rights.

On the other hand, there had been governors-general of Finland shortly before Brahe, including a relative of Oxenstierna. The Swedish state was tightening up its administration (the same trend was occurring in the provinces recovered from Denmark). The Thirty Years' War was an obvious factor here, but in the case of Finland there was a residue of uncertainty deriving from the events of the last decade of the sixteenth century, particularly the attraction exerted then by Sigismund (q.v.) and the Polish connection.

Brahe thus came to Finland as a unifier, but in seeking to raise standards (he regarded the Finns as lazy and superstitious) he inevitably helped foster to some extent a Finnish identity. Brahe did much for Finland. He decreed the establishment of several towns, including the port of Raahe (a corruption of his name) in northern Finland, as well as Hämeenlinna and Savonlinna; he also ordered moving Helsinki (q.v.) from the mouth of the Vantaa river to its present location. Brahe founded the first Finnish university at Turku (q.v.) in 1640; his aim was to create a training school for administrators and not, as happened, for the clergy.

In spite of his dislike for the relics of the old Finnish religions, Brahe grasped the significance of the Finnish language (q.v.), even as a political factor linking Finland with the peoples outside its eastern borders. He successfully secured the translation of the whole Bible into Finnish, thus completing the work begun the previous century by Mikael Agricola (q.v.). According to Brahe, even a Swedish king should learn Finnish.

No wonder the Finns have an expression, *juuri kreivin aikaan* ("just in the time of the count," that is, just at the right time). The count was the efficient Per Brahe. He knew his worth, however. On Walter Runeberg's statue of him, outside Turku cathedral, are inscribed his own words: "I was quite satisfied with the country and the country with me."

- C -

CAPS. *See* HATS AND CAPS

CASTREN, MATTHIAS ALEXANDER (1813–1852). Linguistic scholar and ethnographer, he was born in the parish of Tervola, the son of a clergyman. He graduated in 1836 and under the influence of the *Kalevala* (q.v.), then just appearing in print, abandoned his original intention of specializing in Oriental languages and turned to the study of the Finno-Ugrian language group (q.v.). This led him to undertake vast journeys into inaccessible regions in the Russian Empire. It was Castren who found the connection between the Finno-Ugrian and Samoyed languages.

In 1851 he became the first professor of Finnish at the University of Helsinki, beating Lönnrot (q.v.) to the post, but Castren had to deliver his lectures in Swedish—his spoken Finnish not being good enough for the purpose of academic delivery. Shortly after his appointment Castren died as a result of the privations suffered on his exploratory journeys. Lönnrot succeeded him in the post.

Since in Castren's day the distinction between language and race was not clear, Castren had mixed feelings about what he felt to be the conclusion of his work: that the Finns had relatives of Asian stock (blood-group research has confirmed the partial truth of this). He did feel pride in the knowledge that he had proved that the Finns were no longer "an isolated swamp people" (the customary interpretation of the word *Suomi*—which is the Finnish word for Finland—was that it came from the word *suo* meaning "swamp"; it probably means "people"). Castren went on to show that the Finns were related to one-seventh of mankind, as he put it, referring to the vast Asian connections of his race.

As he feared, after his death, the alleged Mongol connections of the Finns were held against them, particularly by Swedish nationalists. What is interesting about Castren is that, these fears notwithstanding, he harbored dreams that someday all these peoples would rise against the Russian yoke—and Finland would be freed.

CATHOLICISM. There are today only a handful of Catholic churches in Finland and many of the parishioners are of foreign origin. Yet Finnish culture owes much to Roman Catholicism (q.v.), for in the Middle Ages both Turku (q.v.) and the neighboring town of Naantali were centers of learning fostered by religious orders. Finland originally took its "Western" culture from the Roman Catholic church, since part of the force of the Crusades in the early Middle Ages was directed against the Orthodox church (q.v.) to which many of the Karelians, in fact, submitted.

These Crusades, with their saintly bishops Henry (q.v.) and Thomas, have gone into Finnish history with an almost legendary significance, but the Crusades were complex phenomena in which it is far from easy to disentangle and then weave together again the diverse motivations behind them. Apart from the obvious connection of a Swedish imperialism, there is also the question of how far Finland *was* pagan—and of how far lapses into paganism kept occurring. In addition many historians have pointed to a conflict within the Catholic church between the two cults of Olaf and Mary, with different geographical bases—a conflict, alas, not unconnected with tax-collecting interests.

Be that as it may, in most of Swedish Finland by the sixteenth century the population adhered to the Roman Catholic church; its conversion to the Lutheran church (q.v.) was imposed, as in so many countries, from above, helped nonetheless by priests who did not always abandon the ceremonies of the old church.

CHYDENIUS, ANDERS (1729–1803). Clergyman and political reformer. The son of a clergyman, Chydenius was born in the impoverished district of Sotkamo. He studied at Turku (q.v.) and Uppsala, graduating from the former university in 1753, thereafter serving as a clergyman in northern Ostrobothnia.

Chydenius was a representative of the Estate of Clergy in three Diets. He was first an ardent Cap (s.v. Hats and Caps) and then, after the Gustavian coup d'état of 1772, a supporter, at least professedly, of the monarchy.

Ever bristling with reform projects of a liberalizing nature, Chydenius's chief claim to fame is that in his text *Den nationnale vinsten* ("The National Gain"), published in 1765, he championed, eleven years before the appearance of Adam Smith's *Wealth of Nations,* the doctrines of free trade. His case is often cited in Finland as an example of the absence of global recognition for the original thinkers of the less well known cultural areas.

Chydenius was a man of practical vision, who did much, both inside and outside the Diet, to advocate (and in the end successfully) the right of the northern Ostrobothnian coastal towns to trade directly overseas and not to have to leave their wares (principally tar) with the monopolistic ring of Stockholm merchants.

Being more influenced than Adam Smith by the early Physiocrats, and as a Cap representing an area of flourishing agriculture, Chydenius devoted much thought to the problems of agriculture, especially in relation to the poorer classes. An exaltation of the division of labor, in terms of a specialization of function in production, was hardly characteristic of his thinking. On the contrary, in demanding the end of restrictions on earning a livelihood, he seemed to argue the merits of an interchange of function.

For Chydenius, the land was rich in resources. The Swedish realm needed no more conquests, but rather the development of what it already had—as, for example, through the colonization of Lapland. This meant the utilization of human resources, especially by freeing the common people to take charge of their own lives and livelihoods.

Chydenius had a distaste for the aristocracy, which in part explains the hopes for Gustavus III to bridle aristocratic power. In the aristocracy Chydenius saw a privileged landed class, one which compelled a landless peasantry into servitude. Chydenius spoke for the intensive cultivation of the small homestead, where the family income was supplemented (as in aristocracy-free Ostrobothnia) by the production of handicrafts or the burning of potash.

Chydenius was a clergyman from conviction in Christ. Though a Pietist, he did not attribute the misery in which many of the common folk lived simply to lack of moral striving. His Christianity was combined with a social thinking that made him see how many potentially worthy members of society were stifled in their lives by the privileges of others.

These social concerns, reflected in his Christianity and in what he saw of the environment in the Swedish realm (and he seems, by the way, to have spoken Finnish as fluently as he did Swedish), set him apart, if not entirely from Adam Smith, at least from the latter-day Adam Smith Institute.

CIVIL GUARDS. This term is often used in English as a translation of the Finnish institution known as the *suojeluskunta,* which arose out of the White Guard organization in the Civil War (q.v.). The Civil Guards were thereafter a kind of volunteer, part-time military force, a bit like the National Guard in the United States or the Territorials in Great Britain.

Ideologically they were anti-Red, and thus the Civil Guards between World War I and World War II were a force of indoctrination. In many areas being a member helped one get a factory job.

They were commanded in this period by a general of their own, Lauri Malmberg, who was implicated—and heavily—in the Mäntsälä Revolt (q.v.) of 1932. Many of the Civil Guards, however, refused to join this coup and remained loyal to the government. After all, their own greatest sympathizer, P. E. Svinhufvud (q.v.), was now president.

In World War II, the Civil Guards performed many functions—among others, that of guarding Soviet prisoners of war (q.v.). On the signing of the Armistice Agreement (q.v.), they were disbanded as an organization working contrary to the principles of the United Nations.

CIVIL WAR. On the evening of January 26, 1918, a red lantern was lit on the tower of the Workers' Building in Helsinki (q.v.). This was the official signal for the attempt to seize power by the revolutionary Social Democrats (q.v.). Violence had broken out a few days earlier in Viipuri on the Karelian Isthmus (q.v.), while in November 1917 a general strike had taken place and incidents had occurred in the countryside—at Mommila, for example, one of Finland's leading entrepreneurs, Alfred Kordelin, had been killed, and a future president of Finland, Risto Ryti (q.v.) and his wife, Gerda, had narrowly escaped the same fate.

It could persuasively be argued, therefore, that many of the Social Democratic leaders committed themselves reluctantly to revolution in order to exert control over an already deteriorating situation. They were confused men who had come to believe in the theory of the popular will, but had really wanted to see it expressed through a Parliament controlled by a working-class majority—and the Social Democrats had had a majority of 3 (103 out of 200) in the Parliament dissolved by the machinations of Enckell (q.v.) and Kerensky in July 1917. In the subsequent election the Social Democrat representation had fallen to 94. Since the Social Democrats had also taken part in the Senate (q.v.), they felt doubly frustrated with a political system that ought to have given them power but actually denied them it.

They were also Marxists, for whom resort to revolution was natural since the bourgeoisie would always manipulate the political system against them. Enckell's behavior seemed to prove that Marx was right. In any case in Russia the Bolsheviks were pulling off a revolution, and in November 1917 Stalin came to Finland to urge revolution and promise arms from the Bolsheviks.

The seizure of Helsinki by the Social Democratic revolutionaries was a form of the revolution the young Marx himself had delighted in—from his studies of France—and rested upon the idea of a political coup from the center, with the rest of the country to follow. And certainly throughout the south of Finland there were plenty of spontaneous revolutionary forces to link up with.

On the other hand, Marxism also sowed the seeds of doubt. Finland was not the most industrialized country in Europe—far from it—and the revolution should have erupted first in a country like Germany.

If anything, therefore, chances for the development of a powerful industrial proletariat in Finland were inadequate. In spite of emigration, there was a rural proletariat, landless and unable to find employment in the urban areas or in the rural factory communities of the paper, pulp, and sawmill industry. The breakdown of trade with Russia in 1917, after almost three years of booming war conditions, worsened once more the chances of this rootless population's gaining employment.

In the meantime, the small, trained industrial proletariat, conscious of the value of its role in the revolutionary process and aware of the virtues of "the people" through years of Fennoman movement (q.v.) indoctrination, felt itself to be, notwithstanding its smallness, the leader of the future.

The White forces, however, under an unemployed tsarist officer named Carl Gustaf Mannerheim (q.v.), grouped themselves in Ostrobothnia, an area of independent peasant holdings. A peasant army, combined with the newly returned Jaeger (q.v.) forces from Germany, swept the Finnish Reds into defeat. The civilian White leader P. E. Svinhufvud (q.v.) called in German troops (against the wishes of the pro-Entente Mannerheim), but this aid was not decisive.

What was decisive, as the historian Jussi Lappalainen has pointed out, was Brest-Litovsk. At this peace between Germany and Bolshevik Russia, the Bolsheviks agreed to desist from any intervention in Finland. It was here, in March 1918, that imperial Germany and the Finnish White cause truly coalesced.

Kuusinen (q.v.), the Finnish Red leader, then tried to get the Germans, who were already on Åland (q.v.), to mediate a peace between Finnish Reds and Whites. His proposals were reasonable, but the Whites rejected them. They intended to win, and by May they had.

During the Civil War, the Reds killed 1,649 Whites outside the field of battle; the victorious Whites killed 8,380 Reds. After the war, 12,500 Red prisoners in White concentration camps and prisons died of starvation or disease.

The Civil War *was* a revolution, for it was an expression of a need for direct rule by the people. A section of the Social Democratic party had not been involved in the revolution and, after a brief lapse of time, fit rather well into the constitutionalist state, which on a somewhat narrow base gradually emerged in the 1920s.

CLUB WAR. The social outburst known as the Club War was a peasant rebellion—one that, according to some historians, took on the dimensions of a civil war, for some of the leaders were comparatively well-to-do.

The Club War took place between November 1596 and February 1597. It was so called because the peasants used clubs tipped with metal, a useful weapon against armor-clad foes.

The Club War started in Ostrobothnia, but spread throughout large parts of Finland (Sweden was untouched). The rebellion was badly coordinated, and the Ostrobothnian leader, Jaakko Ilkka, was taken prisoner and executed even before the rebellion had got going in other regions.

The peasantry had many complaints. Having borne much of the fighting and the expenses (including the compulsory transporting of military supplies) of the Long Wrath (q.v.), they found that after the Peace of Täyssinä (q.v.), the exactions of the *linnaleiri,* or the billeting of and taxing for troops recruited by the nobility, continued. This was justified—when he needed a justification—by the governor of Finland, Klaus Fleming (q.v.), as being due to the uncertainty of the Täyssinä peace.

Fleming, however, was head of a massive system of exploitation, of which the *linnaleiri* exactions were but the most outrageous feature. The militarization of the country had become part of an increasing centralization, in which an upper class and its aspirants collected lands, judicial offices, and taxes.

More than 3,000 peasants died in the Club War. Some of them had surrendered on the strength of a false promise by a priest, Henricus Plåck, that their lives would be spared. They were then massacred to a man by the military commander, Iivari Tawast, a noble. Both Plåck and Tawast were later executed by order of the regent, Duke Charles.

Thus the Club War, a desperate expression of popular political will, occurred against a background of high politics: the struggle between the two factions of the Vasa dynasty, the one led by Sigismund (q.v.), king of Poland and nominal king of Sweden, the other led by his uncle, the regent in Sweden, Duke Charles. The latter aimed for the Swedish throne, which he attained in 1604.

Fleming was a supporter of Sigismund, an absent king, a fact that enabled Fleming and his followers to consolidate their power in Finland. In suppressing the peasant rebellion, therefore, Fleming accused them of disloyalty to their monarch. The peasants had certainly tried to send complaints about their plight to the regent in Stockholm, but the regent did not support the rebellion (though there is some evidence that he encouraged the northern Ostrobothnians to take the law into their own hands). For one thing, the Council of State in Stockholm, a body composed largely of nobles, was unwilling to see the regent countenance a peasant rebellion.

But the regent Charles nonetheless profited from it. Once the rebellion was suppressed by the Finnish nobility, Charles, after Fleming's death, began to reduce Finland—and its nobility—to order. This was done on the justification of righting the wrongs that had occurred in the suppression of the rebellion.

It has been argued that Charles's policy of reduction in Finland (meaning particularly thereby the replacement of the native Finnish nobility by Swedes and even Baltic Germans) sounded the death knell to a burgeoning Finnish autonomy. As has been pointed out by more recent historical research in Finland, however, this argument, which is based upon the folly of the Club War, rests upon an imputation of peasant ignorance and barbarity. The truly ignorant and barbaric were Fleming and his followers, who undermined by their rapaciousness the loyalty of the people.

COBELLIGERENCY. By the use of this term, the Finnish government explained its relationship to Nazi Germany in the

Continuation War (q.v.). Though the term was clearly concocted by the propagandists, it did explain a part of the Finnish outlook.

The Finns claimed to be engaged in a limited war (though their war aims were never specified). This was certainly belied by Mannerheim's (q.v.) order of the day of July 10, 1941, in which he proclaimed a crusade into East Karelia (q.v.). Yet a degree of hesitancy in the Finnish position is reflected in the term "cobelligerent." The Finns, willing to accommodate themselves to the New Order of Nazi-dominated Europe, were not Nazis. They were constitutionalists and wanted to put distance between their stand and the aspirations of the Nazis. There was also the United States to think about, where Finland had many friends.

When the United States entered the hostilities, it never declared war on the Finns. Perhaps the designation of "cobelligerency" helped in this case.

COMPLIANTS. The line of compliance to Russian policy became a component of Fennoman party politics, as the Fennoman movement (q.v.) strove to represent itself to the Russians as a form of Finnish identity not offensive to Russia.

Compliance was particularly associated with the period of the Bobrikov (q.v.) governor-generalship, and the Old Finns (q.v.) did not oppose the promulgation of the February Manifesto (q.v.) in 1899 (though not all the senators voting for its promulgation were Old Finns). Old Finn senators stayed in office till the Great Strike (q.v.) of 1905.

The key to understanding their position as compliants was the fact that they cherished a belief that Russia was not pursuing maximalist goals in Finland. The Old Finn politicians tried to come to terms with V. K. Pleve, the Russian minister of the interior and minister state-secretary for Finland in Saint Petersburg. This very combination of offices was abhorrent to the constitutionalists, but the Old Finns struggled nonetheless to effect a compromise with Pleve. In this respect they were working at a level of practical politics that had something to recommend it.

In compliance lies the great paradox of the traditionalist

Fennoman forces. They were authoritarian in their remorseless pursuit of national identity, but they were prepared to tack to and fro—to play, in short, a very sophisticated game of politics, with the external imperial power. This was a form of foreign policy.

Unfortunately for them, the external power and its representatives were not always so sophisticated. Pleve seems to have been willing to compromise. Bobrikov, a soldier, with the military demands of the Russian Empire uppermost in his mind, was not.

Notwithstanding the failure of the compliants in the years before World War I, their viewpoints remained an important element latent in the Finnish position. After World War II, under the presidency of J. K. Paasikivi (q.v.), who had been nurtured on their ideas, a foreign policy of good relations with Russia was established for Finland based on the hope, if not exactly the conviction, that Russia had only minimalist aims as far as Finland was concerned.

CONFERENCE ON SECURITY AND COOPERATION IN EUROPE (CSCE). Finnish advocacy of this conference in the late 1960s and after has been described by Martti Häikiö as "the most successful initiative in the history of Finnish foreign policy." From the conference, two sessions of which were held in Helsinki (q.v.)—in 1973 and 1975—has sprung a whole process and system covering European security, one which also includes the two North American states.

The Finns have always stressed the importance of having the latter states in the process. The Finnish note of May 5, 1969, unlike the Warsaw Pact note of March 18 proposing a security conference, was thus sent to the United States and Canada, the Finns taking a hint here from a NATO communiqué of April 11.

This was the high point of the Kekkonen (q.v.) era, when the Finns were prepared to take initiatives they had not dared to take, for example, in 1954 when faced with a Soviet proposal then for a conference of this kind. Under Kekkonen, in contrast to his predecessor Paasikivi (q.v.), the Finns had developed a certain confidence in their ability to mediate between the West and the Soviet bloc states. It even became an aspect of their neutrality (q.v.) to do so. No one who looks back on the antagonism of the Cold War can fail to appreciate the significance of Finnish activity, under Kekkonen, in this period, when Finland became a center of reason in a Europe short on that commodity.

The European Security Conference process embraced not merely both blocs but also the states outside the blocs, the neutrals and the nonaligned, states like Finland and Yugoslavia, states that began to cooperate in an "N & N" group within the CSCE. Such a system could work only by consensus, and its high politics, as far as Kekkonen was concerned, was a reflection of a domestic political consensus he was maintaining. He was even encouraging domestic consensus (and his own continuation in presidential office without an election) in the name of European Security Conference needs.

For the Finns, the conference process is an important aspect of their security policy. The sanctity of frontiers, written into the Helsinki Accord of 1975, seemed to guarantee Finland its existence between the blocs. Meanwhile the measures drafted at the 1986 Stockholm Conference, in respect of the notification of military maneuvers, reduced the threat of covert military action.

With the emergence of new states in Eastern Europe and the Soviet area, the CSCE confirmation-of-frontiers principle has been regarded as an obstacle. It is noteworthy that the Finns have not been among the first to welcome these new states.

On the other hand, the stress on human rights in the Helsinki Accord (which gave rise to the Helsinki groups of human rights advocates in the Soviet bloc countries) has helped in the transformation of these lands, as has the CSCE principle of freedom in the exchange of information among countries.

The utilization of these aspects of the CSCE process took the Finns somewhat by surprise, and there was a distinct fear among leading Finns that the United States would exploit these issues for another bout of Cold War politics. The impact of the low, grass-roots politics of certain Eastern European countries and the Baltic lands produced a process of its own that ultimately obviated the politics of global confrontation. In all this, the CSCE ethos played its part. Significantly, the current extension of CSCE membership to certain Central Asian states requires as a sine qua non the adherence of these states to the CSCE rights package: a fusion of high and low politics, undoubtedly a valuable combination in juxtaposition with Pan-Islamism.

So, way back in 1969, in the depressed period after the Soviet occupation of Czechoslovakia, the Finns helped start a dynamic, the further reaches of which have been rather surprising.

CONSENSUS. The hallmark of the Finnish political system, whose foremost domestic critics will immediately focus on consensus.

Consensus springs in part from certain structural features of the constitution (q.v.). A two-thirds majority is needed for permanent legislation and five-sixths for constitutional change itself. Alongside these conservative features must be placed the authoritarian role of the president as the symbol and enforcer, where need be, of the unity of the nation.

A system of voting based on proportional representation also plays a part, requiring the compromises (or horse-trading) without which coalition governments cannot be formed. It should be remembered, however, that Sweden, with an electoral system also based on proportional representation, manages to produce a somewhat more adversarial style of politics than Finland.

In short, proportional representation in Finland readily reflects a degree of socioeconomic and cultural diversity; for example, a Left/Right polarization is offset by the existence of a powerful agrarian interest expressed in the Center Party (s.v. Agrarian Union), the major party in the present government. The Swedish People's party (q.v.), also in the present government, seems willing to join any coalition as long as its demands for upholding the Swedish language are granted. Thus political bargaining, and not political alternative, is born.

Consensus in Finland is a deeper phenomenon than is contained in the politics of bargaining, however. Beneath the fragmentation is a bedrock of cultural uniformity, most obviously seen in the fact that nine-tenths of the population is officially Lutheran (q.v.). Conversely, when things have fallen apart in recent historical memory—in the Civil War (q.v.) of 1918—this produced a set of events from which nearly all Finns today recoil in horror. In addition, the problems caused by the Soviet Union have had an overwhelming role in helping foster a Finnish national stereotype. Cynics have pointed out that the unity of the Winter War (q.v.) of 1939–1940 redeemed the shame of the divisions of the Civil War.

Many critics of consensus would rather regard the phenomenon nevertheless as a product of the political manipulation of the post–World War II era, and especially of Kekkonen's (q.v.) twenty-five-year-long tenure as president. His insistence was on the minutiae of the ostentatious upkeep of good relations with the Soviet Union and on the paramount interests wherever of the export industries. This compelled a conformity of institutional behavior and an interlocking of institutional life reminiscent of Joachim Hirsch's model of the *Sicherheitsstaat*. A quasi-governmental system emerged, subordinating the labor-market organizations, the press, and the elites.

This has been regarded as a source of corruption. As parties become institutionalized, even receiving state subsidies, they become ever more greedy for funding, covert power, and jobs for their members. In the Noppa case, to take but one example, the Center party, the Social Democratic party (q.v.), and the National Coalition party (q.v.) (the Conservatives) were all in varying degrees involved in taking handouts from building contractors.

The next stage is the appearance of political alienation on the part of the voters, as the parties become ends in themselves. They cease to commit themselves in their election campaigns to clear and definite stands, for they may have to compromise later and would not wish to comprise themselves in advance.

On the other hand, consensus has had its good side, producing after World War II one of the most effective welfare states (q.v.) in the world, the current partial dismantling of which is much resented by many responsible Finns.

CONSTITUTION. The Finnish constitution has often been described as being presidential-parliamentary. At first glance it appears to fulfill the requirements of the Montesquieu tripartite division. The court system is distinct, but there is no supreme court in the U.S. sense, with a developed power of judicial review or a capacity to investigate cases of infractions of constitutional rights.

Parliament is a unicameral legislature (q.v.), following upon the model laid down by the great reform of 1906. The absence of a second chamber makes many Finns think that their legislature is more democratic than the legislatures of most nations, a fact that seems further confirmed by a electoral process deriving from proportional representation. Pundits have found yet another democratic peculiarity in the Finnish legislature: it controls the legality of its own operations through committees of Parliament.

On simple majoritarian grounds, however, the Finnish Parliament is an ineffective organ. Only temporary laws, having a duration of one year, can be adopted by a simple majority. Permanent legislation requires a two-thirds majority, while a change in the constitutional law requires a five-sixths majority. In practice, therefore, a minority may determine what goes on. This may be called consensus (q.v.) politics perforce, so that prominent political alternatives are not a feature of the Finnish system.

These built-in restraints on the operation of the parliamentary process go hand in hand with a strong executive power—a presidency—should the occupant of the presidential office care to use this power. Most of them have—particularly Urho Kekkonen (q.v.), who even wiped out the original Finnish Academy, so widely did he view his jurisdiction.

A strong presidency, whose occupant was indirectly elected through an electoral college (though this is now being changed), was part of the antimajoritarian solution to the Civil War (q.v.). K. J. Ståhlberg (q.v.), who devised a presidency of this kind, and who then went on to be the first president of Finland, actually put the scheme on paper before the Civil War broke out.

Breaking away from Russia, the framers of the Finnish constitution between 1917 and 1919 were obsessed by the need to settle the executive power. It became for them the mark of statehood, and indeed produced a conflict between Monarchists (q.v.) and Republicans, resolved to the latter group's advantage but with a strong presidential office acceptable to the antidemocratic Monarchists.

In the exercise of post–World War II foreign policy, a strong presidency (and the direction of foreign policy is a prerogative of the presidential office) was crucial to the creation and, some would say, maintenance of good relations with the Soviet Union. On the other side, it could be argued that in 1940 and 1941 presidential government capitulated to the military and that a more alert Parliament would have given greater consideration to other options.

The Finnish constitution bears with it a rights package, and the protection of private property, enshrined in Article 6, is reflected throughout all subordinate legislation, such as the Building Law, rendering public land policy for housing difficult and even hindering the protection of historic buildings.

In the same article of the constitution, there was inserted in 1972, thanks to the initiative of the Finnish People's Democratic League (s.v. Finnish Communist Party) a requirement enjoining the state to provide work for its citizens. Alas, in contrast to the protection of private property, the employment provision is not a civil right. In the early 1990s the unemployment rate in Finland was 18%.

In 1989 Finland joined the Council of Europe, and the rights of its citizens, and even of foreign residents, have fallen under the scrutiny of the Council of Europe rights regime. This has provoked the official establishment in Finland of a committee to draft a new set of basic rights to be added to the constitution. Some of these, particularly the rights of foreigners and the cultural and linguistic rights of small minorities like the Lapps and Gypsies, owe at least part of their inspiration to Western Europe. Other rights, such as the citizen's right to security of income, are reflections of a need to defend the Scandinavian welfare-state-rights concept against possible pressures from an integrating Europe.

As with all written constitutions, much escapes the Finnish constitution. Special mention should be made of the development of a powerful wage policy, based on the deal between such interest groups as labor unions, employers, and agricultural producers on the one hand and the government on the other. This phenomenon has been in part spin-off of Kekkonen's strong presidential government. The results of this policy have been more or less rubber-stamped by Parliament, an aspect of a wider budget politics—a consensus—which Parliament itself has never seriously wanted to challenge.

By the fall of 1993, however, wage-policy politics had been shattered, a casualty not of a revived constitutionalism but of a center-conservative government unable or unwilling to resist the liberalist economics of the Employers' Federation.

CONSTITUTIONALISM AND CONSTITUTIONALISTS. The core of the difference, for leading Finns, between the situation in the Grand Duchy (q.v.) of Finland and that in the rest of the Russian Empire was that Finland was a constitutionalist state, and, in consequence, also a *Rechtsstaat*. In contrast, these Finns thought, Russian rule was arbitrary.

The development, after the 1905 Revolution in Russia, of a species of constitutionalism through a Duma presented therefore a problem, which could be countered only by insisting that beyond all the diverse political forms was one great Russian chauvinism.

The term "constitutionalist" often meant the passive-resistance (q.v.) supporters in Finland from 1899 onwards—a line being drawn between themselves and the Compliants (q.v.), who were willing to try to come to some arrangement with Russia. In fact, at heart the Compliants were constitutionalist, too, as their behavior in leaving the Senate (q.v.) in 1909 showed.

For many Finns, the difference between tsarism and Bolshevism was somewhat trivial. Both were anticonstitutionalist forms of Russian chauvinism that would, so the argumentruns, have flattened Finland given half a chance. Thus the

Russian Whites in Paris after World War I were not willing to agree to Finnish independence (q.v.). Actually, independence was granted by Lenin (q.v.) and the Bolsheviks, who rarely get credit for this though it was quite in accordance with early Bolshevik principles. Circumstances alone, it would seem, freed the Finns.

CONTINUATION WAR. On June 22, 1941, in accordance with the Barbarossa Plan, German forces invaded the Soviet Union. On June 26 President Risto Ryti (q.v.) made a public declaration that Finland now considered itself to be at war with the Soviet Union. Hostilities endured until September 4, 1944, on the Finnish side, while the Russians continued to pound the Finnish lines until September 5. The Armistice Agreement (q.v.) came into full force on September 19.

The name of this war is an indication of how the Finns viewed it: as a continuation of the Winter War (q.v.) of 1939–1940. In the Continuation War the Finns endeavored (and in 1941 succeeded) in getting back nearly all the lands ceded or leased to the Soviet Union by the Peace of Moscow (q.v.) of March 13, 1940.

The war was, from the official Finnish standpoint, a Continuation War in the sense that once again, it was maintained, the Soviet Union was the aggressor. When the Germans had invaded the Soviet Union, Finland had first said that it was neutral, but Soviet planes had, from June 22 onward, bombed ports in southern Finland. This action on the part of the Soviet air force was due to the misconception that the German bombing of Leningrad had taken place from Finland. On the other hand, German naval vessels were certainly in Finnish waters.

The Soviet bombing nonetheless accorded ill with Molotov's request to the Finns that they should remain neutral in the hostilities between Germany and the Soviet Union.

In truth the Soviet bombing was a gift to the supreme Finnish leadership, which intended anyway to take Finland into the war. Ever since August 1940 relations between the Finnish High Command and Nazi Germany had been strengthening. In that month Herman Göring's righthand man, Lieutenant Colonel Joseph Veltjens, unexpectedly arrived in Finland, offering German arms to the Finnish armed forces (q.v.). What Veltjens also wanted—and got—was the right for the German forces in occupied Norway to send their troops on leave back and forth through Finland.

Who exactly made this deal from the Finnish side is still a mystery, but it is also a somewhat technical question since the Finnish High Command was overjoyed at the prospect. Equally important is the fact that the civil administration was kept in the dark about it. Thus when, at the end of September, the first German transit troops arrived at Vaasa, the local authorities were in complete bewilderment about what to do. Since a transit agreement with the Soviet Union had already been made by the Finns to permit the passage of Soviet troops by rail through Finland to the Hanko base (leased from Finland at the Peace of Moscow), the idea of balancing this by a transit agreement with the Germans was a reasonable price of realpolitik.

Unfortunately military discussions between the Finns and the Germans continued, culminating in the Salzburg talks of May 1941. No agreement was formally made even then, but by the second week of June German attack forces were in Lapland and on June 15 (eleven days before President Ryti declared that Finland was in a state of war with the Soviet Union) Finnish troops in Lapland were placed under the German military command.

All these arrangements were kept from Parliament and its Foreign Affairs Committee, who were told about them when they were already in force. This was a serious infringement of democratic practice and prevented the effective discussion of alternative courses of action.

Much of the subsequent analysis about Finland's entry into the war in June 1941 has drawn the conclusion of necessity, and reputable foreign historians have written books about Finland's choice only to show that Finland had no choice.

In maintaining a contrary position on this complicated question, a great deal revolves around the interpretation of how important Finland was to the German cause. Here it may be argued that since a large part of the Continuation War consisted of rather stationary warfare—basically pinning Soviet troops down—then this same goal could have been attained, at least for some time, by an ostentatious mobilization of Finnish troops without direct engagements in hostilities. A further justification for such a policy lies in the fact that the German invasion of Russia was meant to be a blitzkrieg anyway.

Bearing in mind how the war actually developed, it should be recalled, in light of the above argument, that the Finns never took part in major operations against Leningrad and that, in the very beginning of hostilities, they were unable to cut the Murmansk railroad; shortly thereafter, to curry favor with the Allies, they stopped trying.

The German-led operation from northern Finland, *Silberfuchs* (Silver Fox), as it was called, the goal of which had originally been the capture of the port of Murmansk, was pared down to something much less ambitious even before hostilities began.

In the end, when Finland succeeded in making a separate armistice with the Russians in September 1944, the Germans began to make a careful retreat on the basis of an understanding with the Finnish army, a reaction that would hardly have arisen had Finland been of first-class strategic importance to the defense of Germany. Only Soviet pressure on the Finns upset this modus vivendi and resulted in the hostilities between Finns and Germans known as the Lapland War (q.v.).

To the average Finnish citizen, the Continuation War meant the rightful return of the lost lands, though here again it could be argued that the Soviet Union might have evacuated parts of these lands, simply letting Finnish troops occupy them. On July 10, 1941, only two weeks after the outbreak of the Continuation War, Marshal Mannerheim (q.v.), the Finnish commander in chief, issued an order of the day proclaiming the intent of the army to liberate East Karelia (q.v.), a part of the Soviet Union that had never belonged to Finland. The order was issued without consulting either the civilian government or President Ryti, though a few months earlier Ryti had indeed discussed such a possibility. Many ordinary Finnish soldiers were deeply resentful of this extension of the hostilities into East Karelia, and the occupation of most of the region by the Finns exacted a high toll in casualties.

East Karelia was put under military rule—one example of the enormous power wielded by the Finnish military command as a result of the Continuation War and the preparations for it. Marshal Mannerheim himself, whom many Finns believed was respected both in the West and in the Soviet Union, remained a possible rallying point for those who wanted to get out of the war. In February 1943 there was even an abortive move, supported by the Peace Opposition (q.v.), to get Mannerheim elected president in place of Ryti. In August 1944, in order to get Finland out of the War, Mannerheim did replace Ryti as president.

The Finns had never defined their war aims, but the propaganda concept of claiming to be a "cobelligerent" (q.v.) rather than an "ally" of Nazi Germany did contain some truth. Most Finns did not like the Nazi ideology, and throughout the Continuation War the formalistic constitutionalist system functioned in Finland, even though the military command often ignored it.

It still needs saying that the limiting of Finnish aims in the war was proportionate to its length. From 1943 onward the Finns were looking for ways of extricating themselves from the war. They were helped by the Swedes, by the United States (which, unlike Great Britain, never declared war on Finland), and by the superb Soviet minister to Stockholm, Alexandra Kollontay.

But in 1941 the Finnish leadership (the consent of the people was simply assumed) wanted a place for Finland in the New Order guaranteed by Nazi Germany. All this encompassed the destruction of the Soviet state and the emergence of a truncated Russia miles away from the Finnish border.

The Finnish leadership made a mistake. It cost the nation 86,000 dead and 57,000 invalids—and the lost lands were lost again.

CRIMEAN WAR. When the Concert of Europe broke down in 1854, as a result of the Western powers' attempt to prop up the Turkish Empire against the alleged encroachments of the Russian Empire, Finland found itself at war against Great

Britain and France. Though the major part of the operations took place near the Black Sea, there were hostilities also on the Finnish littoral. This was greatly to the astonishment of many Finns, who had thought of the conflict as having something to do with the East (hence the term for this war in Swedish and Finnish, the "Oriental War") and even as having something to do with a fight between Christian (Russia) and heathen (Turkey).

In May and June 1854 the British fleet appeared off the Finnish coast and bombarded it from Hanko to Oulu, setting fire to naval stores of timber and tar, some of which were destined for export to England. The British officer in charge of these operations, Vice Admiral Plumridge, became known to the Finns as "Admiral Plundridge."

The British and French also landed on Åland (q.v.), from which the Finns have derived another name for the war—*Oolannin sota*—the "war of Åland." On Åland the allies destroyed the fortress of Bomarsund and then retreated for the winter. In 1855 the allies were back in Finnish waters, bombarding the naval fortress of Sveaborg (later Suomenlinna, q.v.) off the Helsinki (q.v.) shore.

The main purpose of these operations was to confine the Russian fleet into the eastern half of the Gulf of Finland and to destroy permanently the chances of an expansionist Russian naval power in the Baltic. Thus, in 1856, at the Peace of Paris, Åland was demilitarized.

Though tempted, Sweden had not entered the war. Had hostilities continued deep in 1856, Sweden would probably have joined in. Having in the end failed to take "the fortunes of war," however, the Swedish king was unable to get back Åland for Sweden—a goal he aspired to.

Had the Swedes invaded Finland, it is difficult to say what would have been the general Finnish reaction, though the Swedish crown prince (who was more bellicose than his father) assured the British that with such an invasion "the Finns would rise to a man."

In 1855, at the height of hostilities, the Finnish poet and publicist Emil von Qvanten, then resident in Sweden, projected the idea of a Scandinavian Union, to include Finland, under the Swedish Crown. It is certain that, in spite of the

Swedish failure to act during the conflict, Pan-Scandinavianism (q.v.) grew among some circles in Finland—a mood to which the young scholar and scientist Nordenskiöld (q.v.) surrendered.

As against the Western allies, however, the Finns remained loyal to the Russian connection, even fighting back against the British on some parts of the coast, as at Kokkola. This loyalty undoubtedly helped the new monarch, Alexander II, to view Finnish constitutionalism (q.v.) favorably.

At the same time the lure of neutrality (q.v.) began to exercise its charm upon a certain number of influential Finns. Over the next few decades a fitful debate surfaced on whether Finland's future would owe more to loyalty to the Russian tsar or to seizing the opportunities sometimes provided by international events.

CROFTERS. This is the term generally used in English as an equivalent to the Swedish *torpare* or the Finnish *torppari*. It is adequate if one bears in mind that the term "crofter" in English originally meant one who owed a number of days of unpaid labor and other obligations in return for tenancy of land.

Practically speaking, Finland, like Sweden, did not experience serfdom, but in historical tradition a certain negative connotation has grown up around the term "crofter." In the eighteenth century one of the reforms brought about by the Age of Liberty (q.v.) was the extension of the right to establish crofts to the ordinary peasantry. Crofting became a key element in the pioneering agriculture that broke new ground in the forests of central and northern Finland, for example. In an age in which money was scarce, the exaction of so many days of unpaid labor in return for the farming of land was understandable enough.

By the twentieth century, however, the system had become irksome, in part perhaps because of the spread of a money economy and the sense of opportunities elsewhere—in cities or overseas. In 1900 one-sixth of the agrarian population lived as crofters. In 1909 a leaseholding act went through the unicameral legislature (q.v.) and even received the assent of the tsar so that henceforth crofter contracts were to be under the scrutiny (and thus protection) of public land-lease boards. What the crofters really wanted was to own, not lease, the land.

The role of the crofters in the Civil War (q.v.) has been exaggerated, an exaggeration that Linna's moving novel *Here Under the North Star* has helped perpetuate. Only about 8% of the Red Guards were of crofter origin; the role of the landless was much more important.

In any case legislation swiftly changed the crofters' conditions: the Lex Kallio, as it was called, brought in by Kyösti Kallio (q.v.) finally removed, after the Civil War, the injustices of the system. The crofters became owners of their plots, and Social Democracy withdrew from rural life to the benefit of the Agrarian Union (q.v.).

-D-

DIET OF FOUR ESTATES. The constitutional organ of autonomous Finland (until 1907), inherited from Swedish times. In the old Kingdom of Sweden, Finland had no separate representative body, but sent its representatives to the Swedish Diet. This was composed of four Estates: nobles, burghers, clergy, and peasants. The representation of the last (Crown peasants only) was one of the most remarkable features of the Swedish constitution. Broadly speaking, serfdom in Sweden was unknown.

As far as Finnish representation was concerned, it has been estimated that in 1751, during the Age of Liberty (q.v.), out of a population of 430,000 approximately 198,000 (including some women) had the vote. Numerically speaking, the situation worsened, due to taxation and population changes, in the period of autonomy (q.v.). In 1906, the year of the final session of the old Diet, out of a Finnish population of 2,929,431 only about 126,000 were entitled to vote. Particularly galling, due to the property qualification, was the absence of the franchise for the urban proletariat, the rural proletariat, and women.

Yet the Diet of Four Estates, whose antiquated form charmed English historian E. A. Freeman when he was told about it by Edvard Westermarck in the early 1890s, represented a constitutionalism (q.v.) that the Grand Duchy (q.v.) of Finland possessed and the Russian Empire did not (not even with the establishment of the zemstvos in 1864).

The adherence to this constitutionalist tradition in the Grand Duchy was all the more remarkable since after the Diet of Porvoo (q.v.) in 1809 Finland had been administratively run. The diet did meet again till 1863 (the Polish rebellion indirectly helped Finnish constitutionalism) and only began to meet regularly after 1869.

In 1899 the Diet, unlike the Finnish Senate (q.v.), was courageous enough to reject the tsarist proclamation of imperial unification (q.v.) known as the February Manifesto (q.v.).

The House of Nobles and the separate building in which the three other estates met (*säätytalo*) can still be seen in Helsinki.

DIETS. *See* DIET OF FOUR ESTATES; PAASO, Diet of; PORVOO, Diet of

-E-

EAST KARELIA. Except by conquest in the Continuation War (q.v.) of 1941–1944, Finland has never possessed East Karelia, which consists, basically, of the two regions of Viena and Aunus (Olonetz).

The original inhabitants of East Karelia (in historical times) were Karelians, who spoke the Karelian language, which is distinct from Finnish, though they are more or less mutually intelligible. The Karelians were Orthodox and therefore under Russian rather than Western influence, their sense of difference from the Finns who were under Swedish influence being confirmed by the 1323 Peace of Pähkinäsaari (q.v.).

Nonetheless, Finnish and Karelian cultures were historically bound together by linguistic, ethnic, and certain cultural similarities. Thus, when the Finn Elias Lönnrot (q.v.) collected the oral poetry he put together in the Finnish epic, the *Kalevala* (q.v.), he drew much of his material from East Karelian peasants.

East Karelia became a culturally alluring spot for Finnish nationalists. Since this area was one of the most backward regions in the old Russian Empire, a sense of mission permeated many of the Finns when they thought about the fate of East Karelia and its *Karelian* population—for by the turn of the century the Russian population already outnumbered the Karelians. It was also noted in Finland that the region was rich in timber, but that neither the Russians nor the Karelians seemed capable of exploiting it.

So, all in all, East Karelia became the core area for those who dreamed about a Greater Finland (q.v.).

In 1918, during the Finnish Civil War (q.v.), the commander of the White forces, C. G. Mannerheim (q.v.), wanted to invade East Karelia, but was restrained by the Germans. In 1919, as regent, part of his interventionism concerned this area, but this time the Allies would not support him, as his policy conflicted with what they interpreted intervention to mean.

Finnish troops nevertheless occupied the parishes of Repola and Porajärvi, but had to get out on the signing of the Peace of Tartu (q.v.) in 1920. A rebellion in East Karelia was subsequently crushed by the Bolsheviks.

The Finnish Reds had been thinking about East Karelia, too. In June 1918 one of the defeated Finnish Reds in exile, Edvard Valpas-Hänninen, proposed that the Bolshevik government in Russia should grant East Karelia to Finland in return for the establishment of a coalition government in Finland in which the defeated Reds could take part.

No deals were to be made, however, and in this way East Karelia was not to enter internal Finnish politics. With the foundation of the Academic Karelia Society (q.v.) in 1922, though, the East Karelian issue came in from the other end of the spectrum, from the disgruntled Activist (q.v.) Right.

The AKS charged the Soviet government with neglecting the provisions of Article 10 of the Peace of Tartu, which laid down "self-determination" for East Karelia. At the same time, the Finnish Reds were rapidly building up East Karelia as a kind of "second Finland."

In 1920 Edvard Gylling, a Finnish Red leader who had been in favor of resettling the Finnish exile population in East Karelia after the Civil War—as had Oskari Tokoi, the

founder of the Murmansk Legion (q.v.)—was called by
Lenin (q.v.) to build up the area. A Karelian Workers' Com-
mune was established, which in 1923 became the Karelian
Autonomous Socialist Republic with an extended territory.

And so, while the AKS in Finland sought to agitate politics by pronouncements about the Bolshevization of East
Karelia, the Finnish Reds, in power over there, produced a
school system in which the major language of instruction
was Finnish, not Russian, and certainly not Karelian. The
Finns made up only one percent of the population, but
Gylling summoned Finnish-American Communists from the
United States, who came over with their families, with capital, with equipment, and with expertise, forming a kind of superior class of technicians and technocrats.

It did not last. The Karelian Republic was jealously watched
by the Leningrad party, even before the assassination, in December 1934, of S. M. Kirov, the Leningrad party boss (an act
with which the Finns had nothing to do). It did not take long
before the Finnish Red leaders in East Karelia were accused
by the party of "bourgeois nationalism." They were liqui-
dated, and Karelian replaced Finnish in the schools.

But the apparent usefulness of the Finnish connection was
not yet at an end. In the negotiations with the Finnish government in the fall of 1939, the Soviet Union offered East
Karelia to Finland in exchange for territorial concessions on
the Karelian Isthmus (q.v.). When the puppet Terijoki government (q.v.) was set up on December 1, 1939, it made this
trade in the name of "Finland."

In the Continuation War most of East Karelia was occupied by the Finns and put under Finnish military administration. Mannerheim made the decision to go into the region in
his famous (or infamous) order of the day of July 10, 1941,
in which he recalled that in 1918 he had pledged not to
sheathe his sword till East Karelia was freed. President Ryti
(q.v.) did not disagree, but many ordinary Finns were disturbed.

Once again, East Karelia had entered Finnish politics—to
the delight, at last, of the AKS, whose members were soon in
the military administration in the region. Finnicization began
there. For a second time, Finnish became the language of the

schools. Mannerheim, not generally considered a racist, had already drawn up plans for the "concentration" (in camps) of the bulk of the Russian population in East Karelia. Until the fall of 1943, Karelians, as a kindred nation to the Finns, received higher rations than Russians.

With few exceptions, the population—whether Russians, Karelians, or Finns—seems to have been hostile to the Finnish army of occupation and loyal to the Soviet system.

Since World War II, there has been a decline of Finnish in East Karelia, but a theater (now in difficulties as actors leave for Finland), a newspaper, and educational institutes were kept going. Boris Yeltsin has argued for a set of reciprocal arrangements between the region and Finland, which the new treaty covering border cooperation will certainly promote.

EDUCATION. Traditionally in Finland education was closely associated with the Church. In the Middle Ages the monastery and cathedral schools of Rauma, Viipuri, and Turku taught the trivium of Latin grammar, rhetoric, and dialectics, but not the more advanced quadrivium of music, astronomy, and the two branches of mathematics. Students went on to the Continental universities, including Paris (where an occasional Finn even became rector). There were then no universities in Finland.

The Reformation ultimately gave a boost to the development of popular education—in the vernacular languages— because of the Lutheran belief that all Christians should be able to read the word of God themselves. In 1686 Bishop Johannes Gezelius the Elder made it explicit that the illiterate could partake neither of the sacrament of Holy Communion nor that of marriage.

The teaching of reading was considered in the first place the duty of the home and only in the second place that of the school. If the child had learned neither at home nor school, he or she was to be taught to read by the local cantor at the compulsory confirmation classes.

In 1762 it was decreed that there was to be a schoolmaster in each parish, but because of the effect of the midcentury enclosure movement with the concomitant breakup of the old villages, many of these teachers were perforce itinerant schoolmasters. They instructed girls as well as boys.

With the approval of Tsar Alexander II, an elementary school system for the whole country was established in 1866. In 1869 it was freed from Church control. It was not, however, until 1921 and the attainment of Finnish independence that compulsory schooling (a six-year elementary school) was inaugurated.

The growth of a popular education system, and its separation from the Church (even though the Lutheran religion continued to be taught in the schools) was an aspect of modernization as well as patriotic endeavor. Further, in the nineteenth century, the Fennoman (q.v.) and Svecoman (q.v.) movements competed to promote the establishment of secondary schools, including schools for girls. From the second half of the century, girls began to constitute a source of trained but cheaper labor as Finland gradually built up a network of post offices, banks, schools, and hospitals.

In spite of the founding of a mass of agricultural schools and folk high schools, the latter on the Danish model pioneered by Bishop Nikolai Grundtvig, the total impact of the spread of education in Finland has been to serve urbanization.

Since World War II educational reform has also been intended to serve democratization—though the reforms have generally been concocted by a handful of officials. The key reform, trumpeted by President Kekkonen (q.v.) in his 1965 New Year's speech, was the creation of a uniform comprehensive system of education for all children from the ages of seven to sixteen. There has also been a vast increase in the number staying on in the senior high school (ages sixteen to nineteen), who thus go on to gain the coveted white student cap (a bit like a yachting cap) on school graduation.

Nonetheless, while 55% of sixteen-year-olds entered senior high school in 1990, only about 15% could expect to find a place later in the Finnish universities, though other forms of technical and professional training were open to them.

Finland now has twenty universities, a far cry from the past when the university founded by Governor Per Brahe (q.v.) at Turku (q.v.) in 1640, and later transferred to Helsinki (q.v.), served the country as the sole university for more than two and a half centuries.

An interesting feature of the current Finnish educational system is its feminization—in regard to senior high school pupils, the teaching profession (though not the professoriate), and university students. In 1990 in the Department of Humanities of the University of Turku there were 2,693 women students out of a total student number of 3,468, and even the staid Department of Law had 467 women students out of a total of 985.

The history of Finland could be written in terms of the changing ethos of its educational system. With the contemporary "European integration fever" the system is looking fitfully, and sometimes desperately, for ways to internationalize itself.

ENCKELL, CARL J. A. (1876–1959). Enckell was the last Finnish minister state-secretary in Saint Petersburg and the first Finnish minister to Russia. He was the son of a Finnish general in the service of the tsars, while his mother was of Polish origin. Carl Enckell was trained as a soldier himself in the Hamina Cadet School, after which he served for three years in the Ismailov Guards Regiment. He then left the Russian army to train as an engineer at the Dresden Technical University, and became a businessman in Finland.

Promoted after the first Russian Revolution of 1917 to be Finnish minister state-secretary, Enckell played a decisive role in the fortunes of his country. His is the classic case of how far the individual can determine the course of history, or alternatively, of how far the individual is acting as an embodiment of social forces.

In July 1917 the Finnish unicameral legislature (q.v.), in which the Social Democrats (q.v.) had a slight majority, adopted an enabling act, declaring their country independent in all matters except foreign affairs, defense questions, and issues relating to Russians in Finland. Enckell thereupon put pressure on Kerensky, the head of the Russian Provisional Government, to dissolve the Finnish legislature.

In the ensuing autumn elections the Social Democrats lost

their majority, a fact which undeniably encouraged that section of the party most interested in direct action to take up arms. Yet before Enckell made his move, the Social Democratic party in Finland had been deeply committed to parliamentary action, and the adoption of the enabling act had occurred with the support of Agrarians and some Young Finns (q.v.).

It was Enckell who did not like Parliament, preferring even to delay independence (q.v.) rather than see his country ruled by a legislature dominated by popular forces he distrusted. He feared, he said, a return to the times of the Age of Liberty (q.v.) of the Swedish period, when Parliament had ruled. He also found a justification for his caution in the fact that there were still large bodies of Russian troops in the country, but the truth was that the Social Democrats got on reasonably well with these troops, so that Enckell's ultimate fear was of profound social change.

To himself and to his colleagues, he spoke for the necessity of regulating de jure and de facto the executive power. In the meantime he preferred a Russian executive to a Finnish democracy. This all became tied up with the need to transfer "sovereignty" in the proper way — to an embodiment of those forces closest to Enckell's own heart and interests. The strong executive of the future Finnish constitution was implicit in his outlook.

Like Mannerheim (q.v.), Enckell, a Monarchist (q.v.) by conviction, was an aristocrat who went on to serve the bourgeois Republic of Finland. He was to perform many tasks for his country, helping negotiate the Armistice Agreement (q.v.) of 1944, the Peace Treaty of February 10, 1947 (q.v.), and the Finnish-Soviet Treaty (q.v.) of 1948. It is questionable, however, whether his part in any of these negotiations was as fateful as the part he played in July 1917.

ERKKO, ELJAS (1895–1965). Foreign minister of Finland from December 1938 to the end of November 1939, the crucial period leading up to the outbreak of the Winter War (q.v.) with the Soviet Union. In light of the condemnation passed upon him by J. K. Paasikivi (q.v.), the chief Finnish negotiator in Moscow in October and November 1939, Erkko's handling of relations with the Soviet Union has generally been regarded as inept.

Erkko, a graduate in law of the University of Helsinki, was the son of a newspaper editor and proprietor. Eljas Erkko himself served as editor of the same newspaper, the *Helsingin Sanomat,* for ten years before becoming foreign minister. Like his father, he was a prominent member of the liberal progressive party (q.v.) and took seriously its traditions of standing up to Russia.

As foreign minister, Erkko first won respect, both in Finnish political circles and in Nazi Germany, as a contrast to his temperamental and indiscreet predecessor, Rudolf Holsti. In substance, Erkko's line of policy was not very different from Holsti's, resting primarily upon the observance and preservation of a strict Nordic neutrality (q.v.).

Like Holsti, Erkko was an Anglophile (he even had a wife of English origin), but in foreign affairs Great Britain could not help him. As Holsti had done, Erkko fended off Soviet proposals for improving the security of Leningrad by leasing from Finland islands in the Gulf of Finland on which to establish Soviet naval bases. In this intransigence Erkko was backed up by the Swedish defense minister, Rickard Sandler, whose own plans for a joint Swedish-Finnish defense of Åland (q.v.) came to naught in June 1939.

As Soviet demands on Finland edged upward in the fall of 1939, Erkko could not bring himself to yield in respect of the island of Jussarö and other smaller islands near the mouth of the Gulf of Finland and close to the Finnish mainland. In October and November 1939 he sometimes appeared even optimistic, being buoyed up by President Roosevelt's appeal to Soviet president Kalinin of October 12 or by the thought that the World War might soon be brought to an end by mediation—and therewith Finland's own position automatically improved.

Instead hostilities between the Soviet Union and Finland broke out. Paasikivi called it "Erkko's War." In defense of Erkko, it has more recently been suggested that he really expected to receive a Soviet ultimatum, after which he could yield in the face of this force majeure. Such a response is well known in Finnish politics and enables politicians to tell the public that there is no alternative. If this is the explanation for Erkko's attitude he miscalculated again, for the Russians used a greater force upon Finland than that of an ultimatum.

-F-

FEBRUARY MANIFESTO. The issuing, on February 15, 1899, of this ukase of Tsar Nicholas II proved to be the watershed in relations between autonomous Finland and the imperial administration.

The manifesto itself was brief. It laid down that in areas of joint concern to the empire common legislation, applying both in Finland and the rest of the empire, should be enacted. Since these matters of joint concern were not listed, the Finns believed that the manifesto was the start of a serious, far-ranging policy of unification (q.v.). Earlier unification measures, like the 1890 Postal Manifesto (q.v.), had been specific and comparatively mild.

The February Manifesto was a product of imperial concern for the security of Saint Petersburg in a period in which the Great Powers were enhancing their military efficiency. A concrete result of the manifesto was therefore the abolition of the separate Finnish armed forces (q.v.) and the attempt to call up young Finnish males into the imperial forces.

The additional instructions attached to the manifesto laid down for the future a system of imperial legislation in respect of which the Finnish Senate (q.v.) and the Diet of Four Estates (q.v.) were to be allowed simply to give their opinions — without the right of rejection.

In actual fact the Finnish Senate promulgated the manifesto by a tied vote of ten to ten. The Diet refused its consent. The manifesto provoked the counterreaction of a national Great Address (q.v.) and, in Europe, of a distinguished set of signatures to the International Cultural Address to the Tsar (q.v.).

The February Manifesto was a watershed in the widest of senses. In Finnish politics it provoked the emergence of a clearer than ever division between Compliants (q.v.) and Constitutionalists. And it made most politically conscious

Finns aware that reliance on the coronation oath of the Russian tsar to respect Finnish liberties was reliance on an outdated instrument. Modern politics, with all its attendant strife, was being born.

FENNOMAN MOVEMENT. The philosopher of Finnish nationalism, J. W. Snellman (q.v.), made the point that the inhabitants of the Grand Duchy (q.v.) of Finland had no alternative but to be Finns. This truism was based upon the conviction that they had been rejected by the Swedes in the War of 1808–1809 for the Possession of Finland (q.v.), and, however, could never become Russians.

Being a Finn meant adopting the Finnish language (q.v.) in place of the Swedish language (q.v.) as the language of culture. This was a political choice. As such, it brought the upper class into a relationship with the common people, the majority of whom, except in certain coastal regions, spoke Finnish.

For Snellman, this was the only possibility for developing Finland into a Hegelian national state. The Hegelian logic— thesis (the Swedes), antithesis (the Russians), synthesis (the Finns)—can easily enough be discerned in all this, but it could, more coldly, be argued that this type of state gave the upper class a bulwark in the common people.Of course, it could be looked at, and was looked at, the other way round: that the upper class reached down to the common people and championed them, while replenishing itself with fresh blood from them. How far the Fennoman movement promoted the last-mentioned upward mobility and how far an upper and educated class simply Finnicized itself is yet another of the unresearched and unspoken themes of Finnish history.

As far as reaching down to the common people was con- concerned, the record of the Fennoman movement is a devious one. Elias Lönnrot (q.v.), a non-Hegelian, a true democrat both in manner of life and conviction, quite early advocated the emergence of a "low politics" by granting ordinary people the right to elect their own representatives ("men of trust") in local government. But many of the more politically minded Fennoman leaders, once the Fennoman movement had captured the Estates of Clergy and Peasants, set themselves the goal of capturing the Estate of Burghers (and hence gaining a majority in the Diet of Four Estates [q.v.]). Political manipulation as a means of blocking off the Svecoman movement (q.v.) and of claiming the right to represent Finland in dealing with the Russians became the twin goals of the Fennoman movement.

Thus the older Fennoman leaders were obsessed by using the Finnish language as an instrument of "high politics." By the end of the nineteenth century they were well known for treading the "road to Saint Petersburg" (q.v.).

In 1881 a Fennoman group formed around the periodical *Valvoja* to try to widen the issues of concern to the movement, but in 1894 an even more radical group of Young Finns (q.v.), including K. J. Ståhlberg (q.v.), began to meet and draw up alternative programs. The Fennoman movement started to split into two parties.

FINEFTA AGREEMENT. The creation of a European Common Market by the "Six" in 1957 was not in itself considered a threat by Finnish exporters, since all the forest-industry producing countries of Europe were together outside the market. In particular, Great Britain, a country vital for Finnish exports, was also outside the market. When Great Britain made its countermoves to establish a European Free Trade Area (EFTA), however, the matter became more serious for Finland, especially as Norway and Sweden clearly intended to join this body. Finland's concern was also motivated by the collapse of the Nordic Customs Union (q.v.) project.

So Finland joined EFTA by an agreement of association (the FINEFTA Agreement) signed on March 27, 1961, and coming into force on July 1 of that year. Finland did not become a full member because of its relationship with the Soviet Union; it became a full member only in 1986.

The Soviet Union had been given most-favored-nation status in the 1947 Finnish-Soviet Trade Agreement. This was retained by the FINEFTA Agreement—exceptionally, since no other EFTA country was allowed this privilege. Nevertheless, the EFTA negotiators understood the importance of trade with the Soviet Union for Finland, then running at one-fifth of Finland's foreign trade.

The Finnish negotiators also secured the maintenance of import restrictions on fuels and certain fertilizers. This safeguarded these imports from the Soviet Union, as they were an essential part of the barter upon which Finnish-Soviet trade was based. Since the EFTA Agreement did not concern agricultural products, then wheat, fodder, cotton, and sugar—all possible imports from the Soviet Union—were also on the protected list.

There was no heartache in Finland about this, since, correspondingly, the Soviet Union offered a protected market for many Finnish exports. And apart from the export-import pattern, Finnish agriculture continued to enjoy its monopolistic position on the home market.

In a wider sense, however, the FINEFTA Agreement, limited as it was, has been regarded as the true breach of Finnish protectionism—much more so than Finland's entry into GATT in 1950. A large part of Finnish industry was placed in a competitive position, but EFTA gave time for the sensitive fields of textiles and footwear to respond. One of the most remarkable consequences of the FINEFTA Agreement was the enormous growth of trade with Sweden, a country with a similar economy—a result that had not been foreseen, though the abortive Nordic Customs Union negotiations had certainly been moving in the same direction of stimulating intra-Nordic trade.

Finland entered the FINEFTA Agreement with the plea of necessity, while at the same time proclaiming a neutrality (q.v.) that was even interpreted economically (Finland traded with both West and East) and a neutrality that refused membership in a supranational organ and accepted only an associate membership in an allegedly purely functionalist arrangement. This had something to do with Finnish-Soviet relations, but, as noted, there were benefits for Finland, too, arising from that connection. It is further worth dwelling on the fact that the prime mover for Finland here was not the Soviet Union but Great Britain, whose own foreign trade requirements dictated Finland's EFTA relationship.

FINLANDIZATION. This theory reflected the fears of certain Western publicists about the dangers hidden in the détente process with the then Soviet Union. The theory was based upon an analysis of Finnish-Soviet relations, and it rested on the conviction that the Finns, after World War II, trimmed their system and policy to suit Soviet needs, even by anticipation. The picture was one of creeping Sovietization: Finland today, the rest of Europe tomorrow.

As a concept, Finlandization finds its origin in the alarm about a *finnische Politik* put out in 1953 by Austrian politician Karl Gruber. He feared that Austria, to regain its unity and formal sovereignty, would truckle to the Soviet Union, as Finland had allegedly done, thereafter losing its real freedom of action.

In the late 1960s and for most of the 1970s the idea of *Finnlandisierung* came to be current as a result of the writings of Richard Lowenthal (who later came to regret it somewhat), Walter Laqueur, and others, many of whom felt that détente was a trick. In 1974, in defense of détente, however, George Kennan gave a historical defense of postwar Finland, pointing out that the Allies after World War II had urged Finland to come to terms with the Soviet Union.

Still, while tangling with the conclusions, it would be foolish to deny the facts upon which the theory of Finlandization has been built up. Apart from censorship, especially in the form of self-censorship (Solzhenitsyn's *Gulag Archipelago* was first published in Finnish in Sweden), the theory does tell something about the emergence of a certain symbiotic relationship between aspects of Finnish institutional life and the Soviet system. The strong presidency of Urho Kekkonen (q.v.) is the clearest example.

The question might also be put, even though the proponents of the Finlandization theory never went so far, as to how many other authoritarian aspects of Finnish life owed their continuance to the proximity of the Russian state, without which it is difficult to see any need for the Finnish armed forces (q.v.).

On the other hand, there is reason to argue that the doctrine and practice of peaceful coexistence gave a boost to Finnish institutional life (by putting, for example, the Communists into Parliament and other organs, until, that is, their impact was ultimately wiped away by consensus [q.v.]).

Finlandization was a crude theory which needed development. Its exponents ignored the tradition of authoritarian
constitutionalism in Finland. They have hence been unable
to see, in the period of integration (q.v.) in Europe, that the
Finns were trimming their legislation to the norms of Brussels (even before entry to the European Union in 1994), a policy that may have infringed political choice far more than the
previous relations with Moscow (where two *different* systems were relating).

A further line of development would be to utilize the basic elements of the Finlandization theory as a tool of analysis in respect of the interaction between the foreign and domestic policy of other countries. For instance, some years
ago a British foreign secretary, David Owen, intervened
against the showing of the TV program "Death of a Princess"
for fear of offending the oil-kingdom of Saudi Arabia.

FINNISH COMMUNIST PARTY and FINNISH PEOPLE'S
DEMOCRATIC LEAGUE. The Finnish Communist party
was founded in Moscow in August 1918 by revolutionary
Social Democrats (q.v.) who had fled from Finland after the
failure of the Red cause in the Civil War (q.v.). This alien origin and upbringing was to tarnish the Finnish Communist
party throughout its existence.

Not all the exiles in Russia were satisfied with the establishment of a Communist party there. Some harbored hopes
of a reconciliation that would get them back to Finland—and
into the Finnish parliamentary system once more. The very
process of birth of the Finnish Communist party was something of a ruthless operation with dissenting voices soon shut
out. The subsequent proclamation of the necessity of a dictatorship of the proletariat, and with it a wringing of hands of
exiled Finnish leaders about the mistakes they had made in
the Civil War, was far from being acceptable to all members
of a grass-roots movement that had had in Finland a strong
parliamentary contact.

With the creation of a Finnish Communist party in Russia
the cause became conspiratorial. In Finland, however, a
group of left-wing socialists broke away from the still-exist-
ing "legal" Social Democratic party and established a more

radical Socialist Labor party (sometimes translated as "Socialist Workers' party") in 1920. The party, unlike the Finnish Communist party, which urged the boycotting of elections, was parliamentary and in favor of trade union activity.

Even here the conspiratorial element was not entirely absent, for behind the scenes was Otto Wille Kuusinen (q.v.), a master tactician and a founding member of the Finnish Communist party in Moscow. He was prepared to use the Socialist Labor party against the Finnish Communist party until such time as his own triumph in that latter party was assured.

In the end, Moscow was not needed to kill off the chances of the Socialist Labor party. In 1923 all its parliamentary members were arrested by the Finnish police, and the Socialist Labor party was suppressed. Thus, the extreme Left was denied a breathing space within the Finnish constitutionalist system, whose framework and basic norms it had — through the Socialist Labor party — been prepared to accept.

The extreme Left (not necessarily Communist in the sense of how the Finnish Communist party spoke) was driven back. It entered into conspiracy, trade union strike action, and the kind of outraged protesting that provoked, later in the decade, the Lapua movement (q.v.) and a crackdown on any form of activity that could be called "Communist."

It was the approaching victory of the Allies in World War II, and Finland's Armistice Agreement (q.v.) in September 1944, that finally freed the extreme Left in Finland, an interesting example of the impact of foreign relations upon internal politics. Being brought into the open once more in Finland, the Finnish Communist party went in, almost immediately, for popular-front tactics, primarily the establishment of what was meant to be an umbrella organization for all progressive forces: the Finnish People's Democratic League. These tactics were certainly endorsed in Moscow, but they suited well the desperate need of the extreme Left in Finland to come into the constitutionalist fold.

As it turned out, the Finnish People's Democratic League attracted only a group of radical figures from the Social Democratic party, the bulk of the SDP continuing to distrust any closer arrangement with the Communists. This also applied to the Agrarian attitude toward the Democratic League.

Still, the Communist party felt that time was on its side. The statement made in 1948 by Hertta Kuusinen (the daughter of Otto Wille Kuusinen)—"Czechoslovakia's way is our way"—should probably be seen as an expression of the belief that destiny had arrived rather than as an incitement to a coup d'état.

With the conclusion of the Finnish-Soviet Treaty (q.v.) in April 1948, President Paasikivi (q.v.) thought he could cheerfully drop the Communists and the Democratic League from the government, which he did in July 1948. The coalition government in which they had served was replaced by a minority Social Democratic government, an interesting case of how Finnish constitutionalism (q.v.) has bent the Left to its will.

The Communists and the Democratic League were not in the government again till Urho Kekkonen (q.v.) brought them back in 1966. This participation in consensus (q.v.) politics ultimately produced a split in the Communist party itself. A radical but rigid group of Stalinists, as they were unfortunately often called, objected to the acceptance of a wage policy and to the fact that Communist participation in the government produced no fundamental restructuring of Finnish society.

In fact, a restructuring had taken place, but in global terms. Finland, due to its export successes (including trade with the Soviet Union), had entered the ranks of the top nations, economically speaking. Its own class struggle was dwarfed by its international economic role, which placed it among the "have" nations.

The collapse of the Soviet Union completed the collapse of the Finnish Communist party and the Democratic League. There now exists only a very small reconstituted Communist party. But there is a new left-wing alliance with several M.P.s, and, in the economic recession of the 1990s in Finland, faint signs of a rapprochement with the Social Democratic party appeared to be in the air. It will be interesting to see how "Left" all this might turn out to be.

FINNISH LANGUAGE. Finnish is a non-Indo-European language; it is one of the principal languages of the Finno-Ugrian language group (q.v.).

By the early nineteenth century the importance of the Finnish language for the study both of language structure and of folklore was being recognized, and not merely in Northern Europe. By the bureaucracy of Finland, however, the language was considered to be a peasant tongue: fit for prayers in church but not for the deliberations of a court of law, as the great Finnish nationalist A. I. Arwidsson pointed out.

Arwidsson, somewhat ironically, had to clear out to Sweden, but his work was taken up a few years later by the student leader J. W. Snellman (q.v.), who, as early as 1833, was bold enough to harangue Nicholas I on the need to establish Finnish as the language of education and official communication. Snellman also pointed out to His Imperial Majesty a certain advantage that would accrue politically for Russia by alienating Finland from the Swedish connection—a point that Arwidsson had been unable to make.

In Snellman's 1833 speech can be found all the elements of Finnish linguistic nationalism that formed the core of the political Fennoman movement (q.v.). These can be seen in the mental attitudes of many Finnish-speakers today: a cultivated sense of isolated identity, a proclaimed belief in democracy along with a determined application to authority to get one's way. It is not the structure of the language that is important, but the politics that molds its milieu.

The gradual acceptance of the language of the majority had strange consequences. As Snellman went on to tread the "road to Saint Petersburg" (q.v.) to get equal status in courts and offices for Finnish with Swedish, a literary genius of the first order, Aleksis Kivi, was producing bold portrayals of Finnish peasant life. These were so bold that the arbiters of taste in the Finnish language condemned Kivi for depicting the Finnish people as barbarians. The furor over Jouko Turkka's recent TV version of Kivi's novel Seitsemān veljestā or Seitsemän veljestä ("The Seven Brothers") shows that this issue is not dead.

The exaltation of the Finnish language has, in spite of the prim and proper mandarins of taste, succeeded in engendering a many-sided literature, some of the precepts of which have been beyond the ability of the nation to absorb. Thus Kivi's view of war, as seen through his play *Olviretki Schleusingenissa* is very different from that of Runeberg's (q.v.). Circumstance has compelled the Finns to lean, however, more toward the Runeberg standpoint.

FINNISH-SOVIET TREATY. This treaty, first signed on April 6, 1948, was entitled the Treaty of Friendship, Cooperation, and Mutual Assistance (hence in English it is often referred to as the FCMA Treaty).

The treaty was to run initially for a period of ten years, but was renewed prematurely in 1955 (for a period of twenty years) as a condition for the premature return of the Porkkala base area to Finland. The treaty was renewed in 1970, prematurely and again for a period of twenty years, presumably because the Soviet Union needed reassurance against threatening extensions of the EEC. In 1983, in the uncertain first months of the post-Brezhnev era, the treaty was again prematurely renewed for twenty years as Yuri Andropov took power.

In spite of these renewals, the text of the treaty remained unaltered, though it is known that in 1970 Urho Kekkonen (q.v.) desperately wanted a recognition of Finnish neutrality (q.v.) written into the text.

The original treaty was not desired by the Finns. A certain ex post facto justification for the treaty nevertheless grew up from the Finnish side along the lines that it regularized a Finnish input into the Finnish-Soviet relationship, particularly in a crisis period. Arguments reaching back to Marshal Mannerheim's (q.v.) draft for such a treaty in the spring of 1945 were false; the aged marshal was tricked by Andrei Zhdanov into this effort. All the marshal had wanted had been heavier artillery for the Finnish armed forces (q.v.), who were then trying to prove their worth to the Allied cause.

The Finnish fear of such a treaty was seen not merely in the consternation of President J. K. Paasikivi (q.v.) when the Soviet request for a security treaty was transmitted, but in the fact that the Finnish negotiators did not want to accept the models of the Hungarian-Soviet Treaty or the Romanian-Soviet Treaty proffered by Stalin.

The Finnish negotiators, especially Urho Kekkonen and J. O. Söderhjelm, were skillful. They ensured that the treaty, in respect of the military obligations laid down in Article 1, would be limited to repelling "an armed attack by Germany or any state allied with the latter" against Finland "or the Soviet Union through Finland." This meant that the territorial application of the military obligations of the treaty was restricted to Finnish soil and that Finnish troops would not serve outside Finland. Thus there were no grounds for participation in any future, wider pact. Further, even Soviet help for the defense of Finland was to be "subject to mutual agreement."

Still, the establishment of NATO in 1949 did not improve the context for the treaty, since the NATO states could easily be included under the category of "states allied with Germany."

Article 2 of the treaty was a consultations clause should "the threat of an armed attack as described in Article 1" be in existence. This meant that the application of the treaty was by no means automatic, but the fact that these consultations would have taken place in peacetime (a crisis period, admittedly) cast a shadow over the Finnish claim to neutrality. (In the preamble to the treaty the Finns had managed to get inserted a statement to the effect that they wished "to remain outside the conflicting interests of the Great Powers"—the nearest they got to an endorsement of neutrality.)

Article 5 of the treaty was useful, for it gave cover to the development of economic relations with the Soviet Union. The collapse of Finnish-Soviet trade has been a severe blow to the Finnish economy.

The making of this treaty was originally, from the Soviet perspective, part of a "barrier politics" against a revived, aggressive Germany. By the turn of the 1990s much of the nature and style of the treaty had become anachronistic. Germany was now reunited, and the Soviet Union wanted to have the best of relations (including economic relations) with it. The Finns were fumbling toward a form of economic integration (q.v.) with Western Europe, in which the kingpin was Germany, even if, politically, the Finns have tended to prefer the British model of integration.

In 1991 the Finns and the Soviet authorities began, therefore, to plan a new "Treaty of Good Neighborliness and Cooperation" to replace the 1948 treaty. The treaty was to run for ten years, and jokers were soon querying whether the Soviet Union would last that long.

They were more than right, and the new treaty had to be abandoned at the very point of its signing, remaining in one sense a memorial to the pathetic inability of the Finnish foreign policy leadership (including the president) to visualize a world without the Soviet Union.

Alternatively, it may be argued that the treaty was not negotiated in vain. It was simply taken over to form the core of a treaty with Russia. Hence, on January 20, 1992, the old 1948 treaty was renounced by both parties, who then signed a treaty between Finland and Russia, which contained several key points from the aborted draft Treaty of Good Neighborliness and Cooperation. The military clauses of the 1948 treaty were whittled away, leaving only a statement that neither country would allow its territory to be used for an attack on the other treaty party and would deny military aid to any attacker. At the request of the Russian side, recognition was given to the common frontier between the states, thereby leaving the question of the lands ceded by Finland to the Soviet Union in 1944 unconsidered.

On the other hand, there is an extremely interesting point about the support both parties will give to protecting Finnish peoples and Finnic nationalities in Russia that recalls traditional demands expressed by Finland, for example, at the negotiations for the Peace of Tartu (q.v.). A corresponding obligation is imposed on Finland in the new Finnish-Russian Treaty with respect to recognition of the cultures of Russia in Finland.

According to the treaty, the leadership of the countries will continue to consult each other. In connection with the signing of the treaty, the Russian deputy-prime minister, Gennadi Burbulis, said that Russia would support any application Finland might make for membership in the European Community.

Two other treaties between Finland and Russia were also signed on January 20, 1992. The first concerned economic affairs and replaces the 1947 Finnish-Soviet Trade Treaty. The second concerned cooperation—economic and environmental, for example—between Finland and certain border areas, the Murmansk, Karelian, and Petersburg regions. This latter treaty may have great political significance in helping circumvent the emergence in Finland of stronger irredentist and quasi-irredentist demands vis-à-vis the Karelian areas.

FINNO-UGRIAN LANGUAGE GROUP. It is worth pointing out that this vast group of languages, spoken by peoples of many different life-styles, does not necessarily imply an ethnic identity among the speakers of these related languages, as, indeed, was assumed to be the case by the nineteenth-century savants. Nowadays, if the term "Finno-Ugrian peoples" is used, it simply means peoples who speak the Finno-Ugrian languages.

Naturally, some of these peoples are ethnically related. This goes for the Baltic Finns (composed of the Finns of Finland), the Karelians and Vepsians of East Karelia, the Estonians, and the few remaining Livs of what was once Livland. Recent blood-group research has also revealed that these peoples derive at least one-quarter of their ethnic inheritance from Asia. Still, the ethnic differences between the Finns and the Ugrians are quite pronounced.

That a relationship existed between the Finnish and Hungarian *languages* was already known in the sixteenth century. The languages are not mutually intelligible at all, but etymological connections can be traced (the Finnish word for "fish" is *kala;* in Hungarian it is *hal*). Hungarian and the Ob-Ugrian languages of western Siberia—Vogul and Ostyak—constitute the Ugrian component, the term coming from an old Russian word for "Hungarian."

Among the characteristics of the Finno-Ugrian languages are vowel harmony, a dislike of initial consonant groups, consonant gradation, compounding, and a well-developed case system (fifteen in Finnish).

Through the Samoyed language the Finno-Ugrian language group belongs to a larger group, the Uralic, and there is the assumption of a proto-Uralic language. A study of linguistic palaeontology shows, for example, that the common words for "bee" and "honey" reveal that the original homeland was actually west not east of the Urals, for the bee was then unknown in Siberia.

The nineteenth-century conviction that would connect a Uralic with an Altaic culture (and even a Turkic one) finds few supporters today.

The inspiration of a Finno-Ugrian cultural complex has had some significance in the building of a sense of political nationality in Finland. It has been the component behind the Greater Finland (q.v.) dreams. Abroad, however, it has had a certain negative impact upon the image of the Finns, putting them into the category of a tribal people, whose institutional life, as Max Müller liked to argue, owed everything to late Germanic influence.

FLEMING, KLAUS (ca. 1535–1597). Governor of Finland and Estonia from 1591 to 1597. The most famous anecdote about Fleming relates to both his death and his life. After his death, his great enemy, the regent of Sweden, Duke Charles, came to the castle of Turku (q.v.) and demanded that Fleming's coffin be opened. When it was opened, Duke Charles pulled Fleming's beard, saying, "If you were alive now, your head would not be very secure." Widow Fleming is then said to have retorted, "If my master and late husband were alive, your princely grace would never have entered this chamber." This macabre scene was the subject of an 1878 painting by Albert Edelfelt. From the painting it would seem clear that Edelfelt's sympathies were with the widow and the deceased.

Such an essentially patriotic interpretation of Fleming's career—seeing him as a tough Finn who resisted the personification of Swedish (read "alien") power—is hardly a valid one. Fleming, who was the son of a member of the Council of State, was born in southwestern Finland and belonged to the rich landholding class of that area. He gained fame as a young man because of his prowess in battle against the Russians and against John (later John III [q.v.]), challenger to the throne of Eric XIV.

Fleming accumulated important offices and estates, but then changed sides, in favor of John. In fact, Fleming went on to support John—and the Polish connection brought through John's marriage to Catherina Jagellonica—for the whole of John's reign. This did not, however, stop John from fining Fleming in 1575 the enormous sum of 4,624 dollars in respect of the latter's illegal appropriations.

Fleming, with John's approval, became an open supporter of the Sigismundian succession and, after John's death, of Sigismund (q.v.) himself. This he justified by the need of Finland to have a Polish ally against Russia. In practice the Sigismundian succession meant that there would be an absent king in Poland, while in Finland Fleming, in that king's name, could rule as he liked.

The illegalities of Fleming, and his upper-class and upstart followers, continued. Fleming's misgovernment helped produce the peasant rebellion known as the Club War (q.v.). He was personally cruel. It is said that when he caught a petitioner, who had been to Sweden to complain to the regent, Duke Charles, about Fleming's exactions, the man had his tongue torn out on Fleming's orders, Fleming saying to him, "Now go and cluck." Fleming suppressed the peasant rebellion, but died shortly afterward.

He was a freebooter, but the politics of plunder he and his followers pursued, bringing destruction both to Finnish society and to Fleming's own family, were rendered possible only because of the even larger politics of violent appropriation inherent in the eastward expansion of the Swedish state.

FORM OF GOVERNMENT OF 1772. This was the constitution that came out of the royal coup d'état of that year. Gustavus III forced this constitution on the assembled Estates by training guns on them (a *ius canonicum,* as one cynical bishop observed).

The Form of Government was a defeat for the Caps (s.v. Hats and Caps) and especially for their idea of "principalship," according to which the elected Estates directly reflected the wishes of the nation. Henceforth, the enlightened monarch, "first citizen among a free people furnished with rights," was to perform this task.

The Form of Government was thus intended to restore royal power. The Diet of Four Estates (q.v.) was no longer to meet regularly, but only when called by the monarch. The

Diet was to continue to take part in law-making, but only when general and not administrative law was in question. Gustavus III also bridled the authority of the Council of the Realm (in short, of aristocratic rule): the monarch had to listen to the advice of the council, but the decisive vote was his.

This highly monarchical constitution was still a piece of constitutionalism (the consent of the Diet for the granting of new taxes remained in force, for example). The restrained constitutionalism of the Form of Government, together with that of the Act of Union and Security of 1789 (q.v.), smoothed Finland's transition into the Russian Empire as a constitutionalist entity.

FREE TRADE AGREEMENT WITH THE EEC. On October 5, 1973, a Free Trade Agreement was negotiated with the European Economic Community, which came into force on January 1, 1974. The agreement is one of the most important treaties signed by Finland.

The starting point of the politics that led to it was the abandonment of EFTA (the European Free Trade Area) by Great Britain when that country successfully applied for membership in the EEC. Since Finland had its own special arrangement with EFTA in the FINEFTA Agreement (q.v.) of 1961, the core of which was the maintenance of Finnish exports to Great Britain, it looked as if British membership in the EEC would jeopardize Finnish exports to Britain. But the successful conclusion of the 1973 Free Trade Agreement ensured not only the continuance of exports to Great Britain, but an opening of the whole EEC area to Finnish exports. Thus the Finns turned necessity to greater use. They were not alone; similar agreements were made by other EFTA countries.

It was, however, harder for the Finns to reach their agreement. There were strong internal forces on the extreme Left which opposed it, and the Soviet Union had to be reassured, a complex politics involving the so-called Zavidovo (q.v.) negotiations and revelations. The making of the KEVSOS agreements with the Eastern European socialist states went some way (in principle) toward balancing what might otherwise have appeared as a sudden lurch into the Western politicoeconomic orbit, since the Soviet Union suspected the politics of anything having to do with the EEC. The Finns also trumpeted, as a matter of course, their strict political neutrality.

The Free Trade Agreement worked in light of Article 24 of GATT. In the initial transition period of three and a half years, EEC tariffs were reduced on goods from many Finnish labor-intensive industries (such as textiles and pharmaceuticals) and from capital-intensive fields like chemicals and lumber. In return Finland withdrew its tariffs on many EEC consumer goods, semifinished products, and investment goods. Over a longer transition period, ending on January 1, 1984, the EEC agreed to dismantle tariffs on more capital-intensive paper industry products (a weak sector for the EEC's own industries). In turn, over this longer period, Finland agreed to dismantle its own tariffs in certain sensitive labor-intensive fields, which needed a transition period of a longer duration to adapt to the EEC competition.

This agreement of Kekkonen's (q.v.) (the making of which constituted a pretext to keep him on as president—even without a presidential election) has worked. Since it has worked and endures, it is sometimes pointedly asked why Finland should now take the further step of applying for European Union membership. It is true that the Free Trade Agreement allowed Finland to keep quantitative restrictions on the import of fuel and certain fertilizers, thus protecting these items of Soviet trade. With the near-collapse of this trade, however, these restrictions lose their validity. It is interesting to note that agriculture was kept out of the Free Trade Agreement; it cannot be kept free from full membership.

FRIENDSHIP, COOPERATION, AND MUTUAL ASSISTANCE TREATY. *See* FINNISH-SOVIET TREATY

-G-

GRAND DUCHY. In 1809 Finland became a Grand Duchy of the Russian Empire, and the term should be seen in this connection and not as the continuation of a status previously granted in the period of Swedish rule.

It is true nevertheless that in the Middle Ages in the Swedish struggles with Novgorod the Swedish monarchs had occasionally referred to a Grand Duchy as if to make a claim for the area they were bent on conquering and holding. It should be remembered, however, that the term "Finland" referred then only to the southwest of the present country, the province then known as Finland proper.

In the sixteenth century Duke John had a duchy in Finland, though its boundaries fluctuated. Well into the eighteenth century the concept of "Finland" remained vague—Chydenius (q.v.) seems to have meant by it the region south of Ostrobothnia. Snellman (q.v.) was right: it was the Russians who brought statehood and the opportunity for national identity. The Grand Duchy was a firm vehicle for both.

GREAT ADDRESS. The collection of almost 523,000 signatures on a national address to the tsar, protesting against the provisions of the February Manifesto (q.v.) of 1899, was one of the first countermeasures from the Finnish side taken against imperial Russian unification (q.v.) schemes. While it foreshadowed future Finnish passive resistance (q.v.) policy, it was not in itself exactly an act of resistance. Rather it was an appeal, albeit intended as a measure of pressure, couched in terms of whether the tsar really understood what he had been doing in signing the manifesto.

Tsar Nicholas II replied in kind. He refused to see the five-hundred-man delegation that brought the Great Address to Saint Petersburg, but said that he was not angry with the members of the delegation either. He recommended they use official channels of the bureaucracy, the very system that the Finnish ruling elite had always employed to mediate their cause with Saint Petersburg but which was now being used to crush their protests.

In regard to the development of Finnish internal politics, therefore, the Great Address had a double character. It represented a mobilization of the latent strength of the people; nearly half the adult population of the Grand Duchy (q.v.) signed it, and many peasants were among the delegation that took the address to Saint Petersburg.

Conversely, the organizing of the Great Address can also be seen as a reflection of the hierarchical nature of Finnish society. The Great Address was planned by a committee of leading Finns in Helsinki (q.v.) and taken out to the people for signature by roving groups of students.

The ordinary people were certainly destined to be affected by future imperial unification measures—for one thing, after 1901, their sons were going to be called up into the Russian army, though this was not exactly known at the time of the Great Address. On the other hand, most of the Finnish people were, in 1899, without political rights in their own country, and in signing the Address they were only doing what their immediate Finnish superiors wanted them to do. Particularly vulnerable to pressure were the crofters (q.v.).

Of deep significance was the fact that the budding socialist movement had no representatives on the committee that planned the address. Due to Matti Kurikka's clearly made protests, the movement was later taken note of by the constitutionalist leaders. Within the next few years the socialist movement was to make itself even more forcefully felt. *See also* INTERNATIONAL CULTURAL ADDRESS TO THE TSAR

GREAT NORTHERN WAR (1700–1721). Ferocious though he was, the young king of Sweden, Charles XII, did not start the Great Northern War. It was started by Augustus II (Augustus the Strong) of Saxony, king of Poland, who invaded the Swedish possession of Livonia in February 1700. He was allied with Denmark and Russia, so a struggle for supremacy in the Baltic regions now began.

In the early years Charles XII triumphed. A largely Finnish army expelled the troops of Augustus from Livonia, and the Russians were defeated at Narva. Charles succeeded in putting Stanislaw Leszcyński on the Polish throne, but this intervention in Poland and Charles's determination to march on Moscow were aspects of a fatal adventurism that had eaten into his soul.

Sweden was overextended after the Peace of Stolbova (q.v.) of 1617. In terms of politicomilitary action Charles XII sought to solve this problem by swift acts of aggression that would reconstitute the whole Baltic-Russian environment. He failed. Finland was a principal sufferer from his failure.

After 1714, Finland was left to shift for itself as Charles turned his interest westward. The period known in Finnish history as the Great Wrath (q.v.) began. Though Charles was killed in Norway in 1718, the Great Northern War continued until 1721, when, at the Peace of Uusikaupunki (q.v.), Finland lost much territory.

Instead of being a gainer (just), Finland was now a loser from dynastic territorialism.

GREAT STRIKE. The breakup of the Russian Empire, due to the strains imposed by the Russo-Japanese War in 1904 and 1905, was characterized from October 25, 1905, onward by a new series of strikes that became the culminating point of what is often called the First Russian Revolution.

On October 30 strikes began in Finland, and the whole phenomenon is known as the Great Strike. No additional troops to suppress the strikers could be sent down the railroad from Saint Petersburg since the Finnish railroad workers who operated the Russian section of the Saint Petersburg–Helsinki railroad had already gone out on strike the day before.

In the Finnish Great Strike three political groups can be distinguished. The first of these was the workers' movement; the second was composed of the mainly nonsocialist bourgeois group known as the Activists (q.v.); and the third was the leaders and followers of the traditional constitutionalist forces, at the head of whom was Leo Mechelin (q.v.). All three groups were opposed to Russian imperial policy in regard to Finland, but the three groups had some difficulties in working together and in hammering out a common policy of their own.

There was much that was spontaneous about the workers' involvement, but their interests, unlike those of the old-style constitutionalists, were by no means confined to getting rid of the illegalities allegedly perpetrated since 1899. The preceding April in Helsinki (q.v.) a meeting of 35,000 workers had demanded universal suffrage. Now the Helsinki workers, urged on by Matti Kurikka, were calling for a national assembly, a demand that the Activists, too, had some sympathy with.

Workers from the industrial city of Tampere, led by Yrjö Mäkelin and Eetu Salin, clamored for the establishment of a provisional government, even one in which the workers' representatives were in a minority, as long as it represented a reconstituted society in Finland.

Here was the rub. The workers and many Activists were antitsarist as a prelude to the reforming of Finnish society, whose antiquated Diet of Four Estates (q.v.) represented only a fraction of the Finnish population. Mechelin and his followers were mainly concerned with getting control of the Senate (q.v.) and expelling the Compliants (q.v.). Then the enlightened rule of wise administrators, knowledgeable in the Finnish legal and constitutional tradition, could continue. The discredited Old Finns (q.v.), most of whom were Compliants, tried in vain to mediate between the factions.

Tsar Nicholas II issued the so-called November Manifesto (q.v.) on November 4. It was largely based on a draft of Mechelin's that did recommend the establishment of a legislature based on universal suffrage—thus the wind was taken out of the strikers' sails.

The 1905 Great Strike, which was mostly peaceful, has been regarded as a triumph for the principles of passive resistance beyond the somewhat restricted circles of Mechelin's own constitutionalists. On the other hand, the common people, both in towns and rural areas, were expressing clear grievances against the traditional Finnish system, and it remained unclear how far the constitutionalists really understood politics of this kind.

In the latter connection an ominous feature of the final days of the strike was the growing tension in relations between the Red Guard and the White Guard, two forces that had been set up to do policing work while the regular police were on strike. This upset the understanding that had hitherto existed between the workers' movement and the Activists. It prefigured a reforming of political alignments along class lines, a uniting of the three sections of the bourgeoisie (Constitutionalists, Compliants, and Activists) against the workers. This was to occur, a little over twelve years later, in the Finnish Civil War (q.v.).

GREATER FINLAND (*Suur-Suomi*). The linguistic scholar and ethnographer M. A. Castren (q.v.) found, in the first half of the nineteenth century, a certain political delight in contemplating the connections between his fellow countrymen and the Finnic peoples of the Russian imperial hinterland. It was not until the twentieth century, however, that political propaganda began to emerge in Finland on this theme.

There were several versions, of which the most famous was the ballad that came out during the Continuation War (q.v.) about "the march to the Urals." This was probably the least representative version; as far as the treatment of Soviet prisoners of war (q.v.) was concerned, those who came from the Finnic "tribes" got shorter shrift the nearer their homeland was to the Urals.

The idea of Greater Finland included, more particularly, the close neighbors of the Finns, related clearly both in language and blood (less Mongolic, as it were, than the Finnic tribes further east). After World War I, the darling recipient of the Greater Finland message was the East Karelian (q.v.). He was held to be the repository of a valuable historical culture, for much of the Finnish national epic, the *Kalevala* (q.v.), had been compiled from his lips; but he was also primitive and in need of the sort of modern education the Finns could offer. His lands were rich in timber, which the Russians had failed to exploit. Then there was the question of getting a natural frontier for Finland, and it appeared the river Svir would serve this purpose well.

Around this core, plenty could be built. In 1919 the Karelian Citizens' League, a kind of precursor of the Academic Karelia Society (q.v.), envisaged a defensive alliance between Finland and an independent Estonia and Ingria (q.v.), the latter probably controlling Petersburg. In this scenario Finland would take in the Kola Peninsula, though the ethnic ground for this was a bit shaky.

There was thus a mixture of considerations in the Greater Finland idea complex, but its protagonists rebutted the charge that they might be imperialists and founded their case on ethnic self-determination and the principles of the League of Nations. Their ideas were redolent of contempt for Russians, however, and during World War II books were published about *Finnlands Lebensraum* and concentration camps for Russians set up in East Karelia. The end product of this ideology was racism—even on occasion toward the East Karelians.

Thankfully, post–World War II Finnish foreign policy, as well as Finnish scholarship, has rejected these ideas. Present, tentative moves by Finland toward cooperation across the border are, on the one hand, more functional, and on the other, more humanitarian.

GUSTAVIANS. This term describes a group of Finnish noblemen, including J. F. Aminoff, G. M. Armfelt (q.v.), and C. E. Mannerheim (the great-grandfather of Marshal Mannerheim, q.v.), who had served the Swedish monarchy (q.v.), but after 1809 (in Armfelt's case, 1811) served the Russian monarchy in Finland. Some of them, like Armfelt, had had checkered relations with the Swedish monarchs. What was in common among these men, however, was a general adherence to the two fundamental laws passed in the reign of the Swedish king Gustavus III, namely the Form of Government of 1772 (q.v.) and the Act of Union and Security of 1789 (q.v.).

In this the Gustavians differed from such members of the Finnish exile group as G. M. Sprengtporten (q.v.), who had fled to Russian service much earlier, and for whom the Gustavian fundamental laws had endangered rather than embodied the old Swedish constitutionalism by granting too much power to the monarch.

In the event, though Alexander I at the Diet of Porvoo (q.v.) confirmed Finland's traditional constitutional laws (those from the Swedish period), these were never specified. The Gustavians simply *understood* this as a reference to the laws of 1772 and 1789.

This outlook fit in well enough with Alexander's views in the period immediately after the incorporation of Finland into the Russian Empire: a strong and wise ruler was to govern with the aid of fundamental law. For the Gustavians, there was another element: the monarch needed wise advisors like themselves.

The Gustavians opposed Speransky's (q.v.) unification schemes and did a great deal to confirm the distinct status of

Finland. Their concept of constitutionalism, however, paid less attention to any need to summon the Diet and stressed more administrative decision making within the framework of law. Until the mid–nineteenth century, therefore, Finland was run by aristocratic administrators, above all by a second-generation Gustavian, Lars Gabriel von Haartman. At least they were Finns.

-H-

HAMINA, PEACE OF. Hamina is a small town on the southeastern coast of Finland. Here peace was concluded between Sweden and Russia after the War of 1808–1809 for the Possession of Finland (q.v.).

The peace made no mention of any autonomy (q.v.) for Finland so that Finnish autonomy could not be said to be guaranteed by an international instrument. On the other hand, the Peace of Hamina was not signed until September 1809, by which time, following the niceties of constitutionalist argumentation, the tsar and his Finnish subjects had made their own "compact" at the Diet of Porvoo (q.v.).

The boundaries of the Finnish state were not drawn at Hamina to accord closely with linguistic considerations. A large number of Finnish-speakers were left in northern Sweden (where there is a native Finnish-speaking minority to this day), while in the south the purely Swedish-speaking Åland Islands (q.v.) were put with the Grand Duchy (q.v.) of Finland, in spite of a strong Swedish wish to retain them. Whatever happened at Porvoo, the inhabitants of these two areas were not consulted.

HATS AND CAPS. These were the names given to the two principal parties that developed in the eighteenth-century Age of Liberty (q.v.).

The term "Hat" derived from the military tricorn hat, which became the symbol of a party dedicated to military adventure, active work for the restoration of the lost lands of the Swedish Empire, the Navigation Act, support of monopolies in foreign trade, manufacturing and mining, and the French alliance.

'The term "Cap" derived from the nightcap, a symbol foisted on the less adventurous party. The Caps had much in common with the Continental Physiocrats in their belief in agriculture and the need to develop domestic trade. They certainly tended to share with the Hats a conviction of the need to have a surplus in foreign trade, but they wished trade to be free and did not believe that such trade was limited in quantity. In foreign politics the Caps would have preferred an alliance with Great Britain; since Great Britain was remote and often uninterested, the Caps tended to want to come to terms with Russia.

Broadly, the Hats were in power from the late 1730s to the mid-1760s, and were followed by a Cap ascendancy until the destruction of the Age of Liberty by the royalist forces around Gustavus III.

The spiritual father of Cap policy was Chancellor Arvid Horn, who was driven from office in 1738 on the formation of a French alliance. Horn had been of the Finnish nobility and, on the whole (with one or two notable exceptions, like Bishop Johan Browallius of Turku) Finnish representation veered toward the policy of the Caps. This was understandable in light of the vulnerable position of Finland vis-à-vis Russia. In this sense (and leaving aside the disgraceful Cap politics in the Swedish-Russian War of 1741–1743 [q.v.]) the Caps were the forerunners of a much later Finnish policy of Compliance.

The Hats were bribed by the French and the Caps by the Russians and, fitfully, by the English. As the Hats, toward the end of the Age of Liberty, turned more and more in the direction of an accommodation with the monarchy, Russian money, funneled to the Caps, tried to uphold Swedish parliamentary constitutionalism: an interesting irony of history.

HELSINKI (Swedish: Helsingfors). This city of just under half a million people, situated on the southern coast, has been the capital of Finland throughout the period of independence (q.v.) and, indeed, was—from 1812—capital of the Grand Duchy (q.v.) of Finland.

When one arrives by sea, the sight of Helsinki is such that it used to be called the "White City of the North." Since

World War II, the famous white shoreline has been to some extent disturbed by what is kindly called "development." Ironically, one of the worst of these modern eyesores is actually a white building, designed by a very famous Finnish architect, Alvar Aalto. His building has succeeded in blocking out the view of half of the Orthodox cathedral, which, to complete the irony, is brick.

Helsinki is a city created by government decree—by the first of the Vasas in 1550. Its first inhabitants (like many subsequently) moved there reluctantly: these were the burghers of Rauma, Pori, and Ulvila, who were ordered by Gustavus I Vasa to live on the original site of Helsinki, at the mouth of the Vantaa River.

The plan of Gustavus Vasa was to found a city that would rival Tallinn as a center of trade with Russia, but the Swedish capture of Tallinn a few years later (a territorially expansionist as well as a commercially expansionist move) rapidly reduced the significance of Helsinki. A few years later Duke John (q.v.) allowed many of the transplanted burghers to go home.

Still Helsinki endured, and in the seventeenth century its development was helped when Governor-General Per Brahe (q.v.) moved the city to its present site.

Helsinki has a very beautiful old center, designed by the German architect and town planner Carl Ludwig Engel, in the 1820s and 1830s. Here may be seen the original buildings of the Imperial Alexander University, established in Helsinki after the university moved from Turku (q.v.) as a result of the destruction caused by the great fire in that city in 1827.

In the main square of the Engel-designed Helsinki center is a statue of a Russian tsar. The statue, neatly fringed with flowers, is of Tsar Alexander II, who recalled the Diet of Four Estates (q.v.) in 1863, thus acknowledging Finnish constitutionalism (q.v.). His statue was unveiled in 1894 as a reminder to his successors to behave similarly.

Helsinki, in spite of the tolerance that should be bred by its bilingualism, is in many respects a symbol of the cut and thrust of modern Finnish life. It is a center to which the rest of Finland has become subordinated as a periphery. Is this going to be symbolic, too, of the whole of Finland's peripheral subordination to another center of the future, situated somewhere in Western Europe?

HENRY, SAINT. This man, perhaps an Englishman or a Scot, became patron saint of Finland, though a Finn murdered him. As far as is known, the circumstances were that Henry, then bishop of Uppsala, followed in the wake of King Eric's crusade into Finland, where, in the province of Satakunta, the bishop spent the night as an unwelcome guest in a peasant household. Shortly after leaving, he was murdered on the ice by the enraged head of the household, one Lalli by name, who possibly suspected the bishop of designs on his wife. These events occurred in the mid–twelfth century.

The saint's remains were ultimately laid to rest in the cathedral of Turku (q.v.), but in 1720, during the Great Northern War (q.v.), the Russians carted them off. The incidents connected with the life, death, and desecration of Saint Henry tell quite a bit about Finnish history.

-I-

INDEPENDENCE. In 1917, after the first Russian Revolution, the Finns could still hardly believe in complete independence for their country; the Activists (q.v.) were an exception in this regard. K. J. Ståhlberg (q.v.) headed a committee which produced a model for a Finnish republic, but still with some connection with Russia. The enabling act, pushed through the legislature by the Social Democrats (q.v.), left external affairs and the questions of Russians in Finland in Russian hands.

It was the Bolshevik Revolution that forced the pace, but with independence once accorded by Bolshevik Russia, the Finnish Whites in power made recognition of the independence of their country in the West more difficult by allying themselves with Germany and abandoning their initial interest in neutrality (q.v.).

Only the defeat of Germany and the triumph of the entente orientation pursued by Mannerheim (q.v.) brought recognition.

INDUSTRIALIZATION. The famine of the late 1860s, when close to 5% of the Finnish population died of starvation and disease and countless thousands were rendered destitute, was a grim token that the Finnish population could not be supported by agriculture alone. The import of foreign wheat was allowed in 1864, but a population that had been living at a subsistence level did not have the wherewithal to buy it. The Bank of Finland (q.v.) under Snellman (q.v.) was reluctant to provide funding to feed the indigent.

Snellman himself believed that the basis of the well-being of the country would remain agriculture; several of the liberalization measures carried through in the post–Crimean War (q.v.) period concerned the maintenance of the rural economy—for example, the granting in 1859 of the right to trade in the countryside. As agriculture slowly moved into the compass of an internal market economy and the population began to expand once more, a surplus labor force of the landless (with the decline of the old slash-and-burn agriculture), the partially employed, and crofters (q.v.) (about one-tenth of the rural population by the early twentieth century) came into being. The effects of the enormous emigration to North America before World War I to some degree offset these rural changes, but the obvious answer was domestic industrialization.

In 1857 the prohibition on establishing sawmills was lifted, and already by the 1830s lumber had begun to replace tar as the country's chief export commodity. Now sawmills began to develop along the banks of the Kymi River, the current of which provided floatage for timber southward to the port of Kotka. From sawmilling it was but a step to papermilling, and by World War I Finland was supplying a vast quantity to the Russian market in spite of certain import restrictions there.

The original prohibition against sawmilling had been motivated by a desire to conserve not only forests but also the livelihood of manual laborers. It can, alas, hardly be argued that the development of industry in Finland was due to a recognition that industrial establishments would provide more work for an expanding population and a rural proletariat. On the contrary, what paternalism remained among the Finnish administrative bodies—and there was plenty, especially in the Senate (q.v.)—was concerned with the protection of the industrialist and then the existing agricultural sector.

In statistical terms, the growth of industrial output in Finland was rapid, helped by a swift electrification due to the use of hydropower in a country unburdened by a previous gaspower era. British visitors to Finland in the 1890s were amazed at the use of the telephone among the elite, while part of the population still lived in primitive cabins or even the unhealthy, smoke-filled *savupirtti* (a chimneyless hut in which the smoke from the stove gradually escaped through a tube or vent in the ceiling or wall).

Here was the rub. The annual growth in industrial output between 1890 and 1913 was 5.3% and, with independence (q.v.), rose between 1920 and 1938 to 7.9%. But the starting point had been low, and much of the industry that did develop (such as the paper industry) was capital-intensive and technology-intensive rather than labor-intensive. Industry, in short, could not absorb all the underemployed of the rural areas.

The problem was complicated by the position of agriculture. Successive governments have favored it. Export bounties began to be paid for agricultural produce in the period of independence. In addition, on grounds of national security, self-sufficiency became a goal for agriculture, a policy justified by the experiences of World War II, when Finland was greatly isolated and its own agriculture managed to produce 80% of the nation's food.

After the war, with the resettlement of the Karelian evacuees on land elsewhere in Finland, and with the strong position of the Agrarian party in Finnish politics, the area of cultivated land grew—and kept on growing: it has been estimated that as late as between 1956 and 1966 approximately 395,000 acres of new land were put under cultivation.

Since all farms in Finland carry some forest acreage, however, farming is in a close relationship with the main industrial branches of the country: paper, pulp, and timber. Until the recent strike of forest-owners, this created a powerful industry-agriculture relationship, another aspect of which was the connection between native agriculture and a carefully protected food-processing industry. Still, behind all this, lies an agriculture whose end food product by the 1980s was three-quarters subsidized. Further, the agricultural sector has never succeeded in eliminating unemployment, but only in concealing it.

Finnish industry has been protected as well. In spite of adhering to GATT in 1950, such forms of protection as a licensing system or limitation of foreign share-ownership have until recently played their part. Conversely, Finland has built up a strong set of exports, much based on the traditional paper, pulp, and timber commodities (more than 40%), but since World War II also consisting of engineering products. Attempts to diversify beyond this have been less successful, especially with the recent near-collapse of Finnish-Soviet trade. Only the high-tech multinational corporation Nokia been very successful in breaking into the international economy. All this notwithstanding, Finland's foreign trading performance has, on the whole, been a highly meritorious one, and the Finnish standard of living has been among the ten highest in the world.

From the mid-1980s onward a further period of liberalization began in the Finnish economy, when capital movements were freed by the Bank of Finland. This went hand in hand with an unaccustomed frenzy of speculation on the stock exchange and within the banking system. Much bank capital flowed abroad, or was invested in real estate that could not be disposed of when the crunch came, or went up in bankruptcies of fly-by-night entrepreneurs. The banking system fell into collapse and was rescued to the tune of well over 40 billion finnmarks (more than $7 billion)—so far—paid for by the Finnish taxpayer, at the command of a government anxious to rebuild a sound banking system as an earnest of good faith for membership in the European Union.

Industry, already hurt by the collapse of Finnish-Soviet trade, gained little from all this, and ordinary taxpayers least of all, seeing the benefits of the welfare state (q.v.) increasingly reduced as their taxes were shorn off to keep up the banking system.

The government trusts the major Finnish export industries (wood, paper, pulp, and the metal industry—some 80% of exports) to help pay off Finland's international debt. The government hamstrings the domestic market and the industries serving it (with the exception of the food-processing industry, so closely related as it is to highly subsidized Finnish agriculture) and continues to pare down the infrastructure (such as universities).

Since much of export industry is capital intensive, growth in exports does not relieve the chronic unemployment rate in the country, which, on the contrary, continues to rise. In February 1992 it was 13.7%, and it was expected in early 1994 to rise to 20%. A fall in purchasing power of 8% was forecast for the same year so that the prospects for domestic industry remain poor. The present Center (Agrarian Union [q.v.])–Conservative (National Coalition Party [q.v.]) government seem deaf to the calls of economists like Jouko Paunio of the University of Helsinki and Veikko Reinikainen of the Turku School of Economics and Business Administration that the domestic economy should now become the focal point of spending and investment.

INGRIA (Finnish: Inkeri; Swedish: Ingermanland). Historically, this area lay between the old pre-1939 Finnish frontier and Estonia, comprising, in other words, the area around Saint Petersburg. In ancient times the area was inhabited by Finnic tribes like the Vatya and the Inkeroiset (who thought of themselves later as part of the Karelian Orthodoxy) and it fell under the sway of Novgorod and Moscow. The original Ingrian language, spoken by the earlier Finnic inhabitants, remains today the language of very few.

In the late sixteenth century the Swedes began to conquer Ingria, and from the Peace of Stolbova in 1617 until the conquests of Peter the Great the region was under the Swedish Crown, linking the Swedish possessions in Finland and Estonia.

Most of the population later known as Ingrians now came in from Finland. Though Peter the Great brought Ingria into the Russian Empire, the Ingrian Finns retained their Finnish language (q.v.) and Lutheran (q.v.) religion. Saint Petersburg was built on their soil. Russians, too, soon moved into many parts of Ingria.

After the Bolshevik Revolution, an independence movement started in northern Ingria, but had little chance of success. In connection with the signing of the Peace of Tartu (q.v.), assurances were given that the cultural autonomy of the Ingrians would be respected. These assurances were dishonored, and the peasant economy of the Ingrians was later wiped out. Deportations occurred, and many families became afraid to use Finnish.

In 1943 the Germans evacuated large numbers of Ingrians, ultimately to Finland. After the Armistice Agreement (q.v.) with the Soviet Union and Great Britain, Finland sent them back to the Soviet Union. Later, President Kolvisto (q.v.) launched a policy of allowing people of Ingrian origin to come to Finland, even though many of the younger generation do not know the Finnish language. Some help is being sent from Finland to those who remain in Ingria.

INTEGRATION. Having for years proclaimed their neutrality (q.v.) and their special relationship with the Soviet Union, the Finns are now rushing into membership in the European Union which, since the ratification of the community's Maastricht Treaty in 1993 has now become the European Union. Most Finnish leaders say that they are afraid of missing the train, but it is as yet by no means certain that the majority of the Finnish people want to be on that train.

What exactly would be involved in membership is something the Finnish politicians themselves are not agreed about. One day the reservation of neutrality as an essential condition for Finnish membership is talked about; the next day a speaker will urge consideration of the possibility of NATO membership alongside EU membership, or will dwell upon the virtues of the future security safeguard known as the Western European Union (the backdoor to NATO), the transition to which is now laid down in the Maastricht Treaty as part of the essential development of the European Union.

WEU and security-policy consideration aside, the main shock in the negotiations for Finnish membership in the European Union has so far been agriculture. Before the negotiations actually started, the leader of the agricultural producers' union—the MTK—twice reversed his position about whether membership would be a good thing for the agricultural interests (though the membership application had then been made by a government whose prime minister was from the Center party, the party nearest to the MTK). The next stage was that in 1993 the MTK leader, Heikki Haavisto, became foreign minister and himself began to conduct the negotiation for EU membership. His mortification was great on finding that the EU was not prepared to give carte blanche to the demands for greater protection of Finnish agriculture than is the norm in even the well-protected EU agricultural sector.

Since January 1, 1994, Finland has been a member of the European Economic Area, a free-trade arrangement between the old European Community countries and the EFTA states (with the exception of Switzerland). In terms of population the EEA is the largest free-trade area in the world: its population of 372 million is 12 million more than the population of NAFTA. Though based upon the free movement of capital, labor, goods, and services, the EEA does not cover agriculture, and customs arrangements with third countries are not its concern. Financial and taxation policy are also, inter alia, matters for the individual country to deal with. Thus the attitude of the Finnish government is to regard EEA membership as a temporary stage on the road to membership in the EU, especially as the EEA does not, of course, touch security policy.

It may well be that all these matters left out of the EEA are matters that the Finnish majority will want kept out of integration. In any case, EU membership, unlike EEA membership, is an issue that is going to be submitted to a national referendum.

INTERNATIONAL CULTURAL ADDRESS TO THE TSAR. This was a Western and Northern European response to the February Manifesto (q.v.) of 1899 of Tsar Nicholas II to abridge Finnish autonomy (q.v.). The response, however, was organized by the Finns themselves—J. N. Reuter, Edvard Westermarck, and Konni Zilliacus (q.v.) playing particularly important roles.

The idea of the address was to shame the tsar by getting up a petition of illustrious names from various branches of cultural and academic life. Then the address was to be taken to Saint Petersburg and presented to the tsar himself. Such an approach related to earlier (and somewhat abortive) endeavors by the Finns and their supporters in Western Europe to embarrass the tsar's initiative at the Hague Peace Conference.

Many renowned personalities signed the International Cultural Address to the Tsar, among them the dramatists Henrik Ibsen and Björnstjerne Björnson from Norway, and the Norwegian explorer Fridtjof Nansen. Among the Swedish names was that of the explorer Adolf Nordenskiöld (q.v.), who had been born a Finn. The Danish literary historian and critic Georg Brandes was prominent among the signatories, as was the historian Theodor Mommsen from Germany, who signed after an initial hesitation. The British signatories included Florence Nightingale and Herbert Spencer.

This collection of names was meant to be nonpolitical, as if to float the Finnish cause above party and the politics of the powers. An approach of this kind also freed the official policy of any particular country from embarrassment, as a Danish foreign office official made clear.

Sometimes it was difficult, however, to draw the line between culture and politics. In what capacity did the notable Dreyfusard senator L. Trarieux, a former minister of justice, sign — as a jurist or prominent political campaigner for justice?

In spite of the professedly nonpolitical nature of the address, several who were approached to sign thought that it was still a piece of political meddling. The Irish historian John Lecky (an anti–Home Ruler, significantly enough) refused on these grounds to sign. So did the explorer H. M. Stanley. While Thomas Hardy signed, the future author of Peter Pan, James Barrie, would not.

Credit for the idea of an address has been given to several people — to Zilliacus, to Peter Kropotkin, to a professor of philosophy at Jena, Rudolf Eucken, and to his aunt, Gertrude Coupland, who was Westermarck's landlady in England. Westermarck certainly had a hand in developing the idea. In

Finland a Great Address (q.v.), signed by over half a million Finnish citizens, had previously been presented to the tsar.

The International Cultural Address was taken to Saint Petersburg, but its bearers did not see the tsar. The court chamberlain was astonished at the "quality of names" in it, but the matter went no further.

The International Address was a reflection of a certain idealism current in Western culture at that time. Many leading Finns had a strong dose of cultural internationalism in their outlook and tended to see international culture as a bulwark against, or at least a counterweight to, Russian pressure.

In broad terms this was not a viable policy, but the galvanizing of international opinion, through a measure like the International Cultural Address, was a boost to Finnish national pride and a training ground for relations with foreign powers, once Finnish independence (q.v.) became conceivable.

INTERVENTION. In Finland after World War I this policy was closely associated with Mannerheim (q.v.), who wanted to take East Karelia (q.v.) away from Russia for Finland and, even more important for him, to capture Petrograd and hand it over to the White Russians. Thus in his concept of intervention there was a mixture of Finnish and Russian aims— the annexation of East Karelia was approved of by many Finns, but most were wary of going on to attack Petrograd. In any case the White Russians had never recognized the severance of Finland from the Russian Empire, so it did not look very alluring to most Finns to put the Whites back in power in Russia. This mood, plus war weariness in Finland, lost Mannerheim the presidential race in 1919.

What complicated matters still further was that the Allies did not see eye to eye with Mannerheim either. If they supported the White Russians, it was no part of Allied policy to see the Russian Empire stripped further away by the loss of East Karelia, which might additionally fall under German influence as a result of Finnish annexationist politics.

Here was the crux of Allied interventionism: its desire to thwart any further advance of German power, whether based on a continuing Russo-German rapprochement or not.

As it worked out, Allied interventionism was itself full of

contradiction. General Sir Hubert Gough, head of the British Military Mission to the Baltic States, came to Finland in 1919 to try to coordinate action between the Finns and the forces of the Russian White general N. N. Yudenich, then attempting an advance on Petrograd from Estonia. The British admiral W. H. Cowan and his subordinate Augustus Agar, operating from Finnish waters, were preparing to sink as much of the Russian fleet at Kronstadt as they could manage. Quite a few vessels were blown up, and the Russian fleet (as in the Crimean War [q.v.]) was scared into keeping inshore. In spite of the professed support for Yudenich, it seems quite clear that the British were thinking more of keeping the Bolsheviks from the Baltic littoral, whether north or south of the Gulf of Finland, than of seriously backing a large-scale military operation against the Bolshevik state. Either way, the British probably overestimated Bolshevik power.

The British were also concerned to prevent the German army in the Baltic States, which was under the command of General Rüdiger von der Goltz (the former commander of the German forces assisting the Whites in the Finnish Civil War [q.v.]), from building up German enclaves in the Baltic lands and thus establishing a physical link between Germany proper and the Russian state. Indirectly, this fear meant that the British (as well as the French) wanted a pro-Entente Finland, free from German influence. In this period Finland and the Baltic States were envisaged as a wedge between Germany and Russia, a conceptualization that certainly gave support to a recognition of Finnish independence (q.v.), but did not pay too much attention to the power alignments that might in the future be needed to back up that independence. Allied intervention was followed by Allied withdrawal, and Finland was exposed without its leaders fully realizing it.

-J-

JAEGER MOVEMENT. Shortly after the outbreak of World War I, the idea was bruited in student circles at the University of Helsinki of securing training in military skills for Finnish volunteers, who would later serve to liberate their land from Russian imperial power.

The *causa proxima* was the publication of a further program of unification measures (in November 1914) from the Russian side, which gave rise to the feeling among many students that no concessions — war or no war — could ever be expected from the Russians. Student dissatisfaction was also shown against sections of big Finnish industry that were profiting from the war, while, equally, the students were convinced that the passive resistance (q.v.) advocated by the older constitutionalists was fruitless.

In seeking military training these Activist (q.v.) students found no support at home among former Finnish officers (most of Finland's own army had been suppressed in 1901, as had the Finnish Guards in 1905). An approach was therefore made for military training in Sweden, but the Swedish authorities cried neutrality.

It was the Germans who were obliging. A training course, in which 182 Finns participated, began at Lockstedt, near Hamburg, in February 1915. The Germans insisted that the training given should not be restricted to students, though the overwhelming majority in the first course were students. In 1916 the young men were formed into the twenty-seventh Royal Prussian Jaeger (Light Infantry) Battalion, which then saw some service on the Latvian front and was stationed for a period at Libau.

Before being brought back to Finland, in February 1918, to play a decisive role in the Civil War (q.v.) on the White side, a total of 1,888 young Finns had been trained through the Jaeger movement in Germany.

Two points need emphasizing. First, the student Activists of 1914 had not planned the involvement of Finland in pro-German policy, but that is what occurred — the forces of history took off from this small opening. Second, the original Jaeger movement was not a determinedly Rightist force. Many young Social Democrats (q.v.), in the tradition of the old alliance between Activism and the Left, joined it. After its role in the Civil War, however, the Jaeger movement was inevitably part of Rightist Finland, even sometimes an extra-constitutional part.

In independent Finland, the Jaegers were important people, but some of them felt that they were not quite important enough. In the mid-1920s they quarreled in the Finnish army about the dominance of officers who had previously served in the tsarist army—General Wilkama, one of the latter, was forced out in 1926.

Some of the Jaegers reached the pinnacle. General A. E. Heinrichs was head of the defense forces in 1945, and General Aarne Sihvo occupied the same position from 1946 to 1953.

The Jaeger movement spawned a romanticism of its own. Sam Sihvo, a Jaeger and brother of the above-mentioned general, wrote a popular operetta called *The Jaeger's Bride*. From this an equally popular film was made by Risto Orko in 1938. It is racist, and in post–World War II Finland it was banned until recently as being offensive to the Russians.

The figure of Ruth Munck, "Schwester Ruth," one of the two Finnish nurses with the Jaegers in Germany, had a certain cult following.

A combination of Jaeger romanticism and professedly hardheaded realism gave rise in World War II to a particularly unpleasant manifestation of the Finnish-German line, the Finnish S.S. battalion (q.v.). Ruth Munck was back in the picture, too. After the break between Finland and Nazi Germany in the fall of 1944, she organized in Germany the training of Finnish girls for spy operations against her own country. For this, she was jailed after the war.

JEWS. There are approximately one thousand Jews in Finland, a number that has remained fairly stationary over the past few years, though after World War II the number was more than double. Emigration to Israel may account for most of this decline.

When Finland was part of the Swedish kingdom, Jews were not allowed to settle in Finland. This was basically due to the fact that Jewish settlement was restricted to a few towns in Sweden proper. Still, one or two, presumably Christianized Jews, entered Finland from Sweden, including the ancestors of the great Swedish-Finnish writer, Zacharias Topelius.

When Finland became a Grand Duchy (q.v.) in the Russian Empire, a few Jews began to come in. Many of them remained in Finland after completing their lengthy military service in the Russian army; a decree of 1858 gave Russian soldiers this right, though voices were immediately raised in Finland that this should not apply to Jews.

The Swedish-Finnish Liberal Leo Mechelin (q.v.) tried to free Jews from legally imposed restrictions by raising the matter in the Diet of Four Estates (q.v.) in 1872. This was the start of a struggle that went on for many decades. Some deportations (of whole families) occurred in 1881, and in 1889 a decree was promulgated limiting the settlement of Jews to only three localities in Finland and further laying down that should their grownup children marry (which was not possible for Jews in Finland), these young Jews of the second generation would have to leave the country for good.

It is to be regretted that in the struggle to emancipate the Jews in Finland the Estate of Clergy in the Diet of Four Estates and the Fennoman movement (q.v.) on the whole opposed emancipation.

In 1908 Georg Brandes, a Danish literary critic who was of Jewish origin, came to Finland to protest the situation. He had, incidentally, in 1899 signed the International Cultural Address to the Tsar (q.v.) in favor of the maintenance of Finnish constitutional autonomy (q.v.).

In the end the unicameral legislature (q.v.) passed an emancipation law (the fate of the Jews in Finland was beginning to embarrass the work of the passive resistance movement [q.v.] abroad, particularly in England). The most active in the promotion of this law were the Social Democrats (q.v.), but all laws required the tsar's signature and this one he was not going to allow. The Jews in Finland had to wait for their emancipation till Finnish independence (q.v.).

In both the Winter War (q.v.) and the Continuation War (q.v.) Jews served in the Finnish armed forces (q.v.), and a field synagogue was set up for them. Marshal Mannerheim (q.v.) as well as several Finnish generals (including Kekoni and Martola) attended services for the Jewish war dead. Considering that Finland was a cobelligerent (q.v.) of Nazi Germany in the Continuation War, this was a remarkable testimony to the Finnish tradition of a state founded on law.

Unfortunately, the situation in regard to foreign Jews was

more complicated. In the summer of 1938 some Jews arrived in Finland from Stettin on the SS *Ariadne*. They were fleeing from the Austrian *Anschluss*. After some hesitation, these Jews were allowed into Finland. They were subsequently known as "Kekkonen's [q.v.] Jews" for the then minister of the interior, Urho Kekkonen, whose final say it was that the Jews could reside in Finland. In the middle of August, however, when the *Ariadne* arrived again with fifty-three Austrian Jews on board, they were turned away and taken back to Germany, where most undoubtedly perished. This group, too, could be called "Kekkonen's Jews," though in a different, more tragic sense. Kekkonen made the final decision.

In the Continuation War many foreign Jews, most of them employed, were nevertheless expelled from Helsinki (q.v.). Most of the able-bodied males were placed in vicious work camps.

In 1942 the head of the state political police, Arno Anthoni, began the deportation of foreign Jews across the Gulf of Finland to Nazi-held Estonia. Thanks to the vigilance and convictions of several leading Social Democrats, and to the watching brief of Marshal Mannerheim, this policy was stopped, though not before eight Jews had been sent over, two of them children and one of the others a volunteer for the Finnish cause in the Winter War. Only one survived.

In 1942 others were deported besides Jews, including a number of foreign Communists. All this was done in close collaboration with the Gestapo, Himmler visiting Finland shortly before the deportations started.

After the war, Anthoni was charged with war crimes, but he was acquitted (the judge was a former chairman of the Finnish-German Society). Anthoni then took his case to a higher court and was awarded compensation for the time he had spent in prison awaiting trial.

Toivo Horelli, a member of the National Coalition party (q.v.), who was minister of the interior in 1942 and therefore Anthoni's superior, was never brought to trial. He continued to refer to the Jews with the contemptuous Finnish word *jutku*. Former president Ryti (q.v.) after the war stated that he remembered having seen a list of Jews (the deportation list), but it did not fall within his jurisdiction.

Historically, the question of Jews in Finland has been one of the battlefields between the liberal and conservative forces, the latter afraid of any impingement upon their identity. There has also been the question of how far one extends the concept of the *Rechtsstaat*.

In recent times Russian Jews have been flown out to Israel from Finland, some of them going to the West Bank. This is a complex rights question which has hardly been aired in Finland. Official Finland takes refuge in the fact that these Jews could also apply for domicile in Finland, instead of flying on, as it were. How well this possibility is communicated to the Jews in question is quite unclear.

JOHN III (1537–1592). John was the son of the first of the Vasas, Gustavus I Vasa; in 1556 his father appointed him to a duchy composed of areas in southwestern Finland, including Åland (q.v.). Historians have subsequently maintained that in the creation of a duchy for his son the father's policy was motivated by the need to control the pretensions of the nobility, which in Finland were particularly strong.

Later, John extended his power over the whole of Finland, holding a splendid court in the castle of Turku (q.v.). He was reasonably popular in Finland, reestablishing the port and city of Rauma, whose inhabitants had been forcibly transported by his father to found a port and city at Helsinki (q.v.).

John's relations with his brother, Eric XIV, who had succeeded their father as king of Sweden in 1560, worsened, and open hostility occurred when John married Catherina Jagellonica, the sister of the Polish king, in 1562. This marriage was to have fateful consequences for Finland.

Initially John and his wife were turned out of Turku by Eric and imprisoned in the castle of Gripsholm. Later the tables were turned and, with the help of his brother Charles, John succeeded in becoming king in 1568, Eric dying in somewhat mysterious circumstances in 1577.

It is a question debated by historians as to whether, without the Polish connection, Sweden would have been so deeply drawn into war with Russia. At any rate, in 1570 began the period known in Finnish history as the Long Wrath (q.v.), a period of extensive warring on the eastern frontier.

At the same time the Polish connection helped to sap the Swedish state from within, for a fractious nobility, both in Sweden and Finland, saw in John's son Sigismund (q.v.) a king who could remain in Poland and be a nominal king of Sweden, while the nobility did what it liked. In the latter years of his reign John desperately tried to get Sigismund to reside in Sweden, but his hopes went unrealized.

John also failed in his effort to unify the realm (and take the Polish connection into account), in spite of the religious compromise between the Lutheran church (q.v.) and Catholicism (q.v.) in the Red Book liturgy (s.v. Lutheran Church). His politics aptly illustrate the dangers of dynastic ambition to the well-being of society as a whole, for what really triumphed in his reign was an avaricious nobility, the likes of which (in the Finn Klaus Fleming [q.v.], to take but one instance) represented the lowest point of military barbarity.

JUSLENIUS, DANIEL (1676–1752). Churchman and scholar. Juslenius, the son of a clergyman, was born in the parish of Mietoinen in southwestern Finland. Though he passed the university entrance examination at the age of fifteen, his studies at the University of Turku were often interrupted by his poverty; at one time he served as a merchant seaman.

Working as a private tutor at the home of Bishop Johannes Gezelius the Younger, Juslenius learned to take pride in the Finnish language (q.v.) and in his Finnish origins. In his dissertation *Aboa vetus et nova* ("Turku: Old and New") Juslenius even maintained that Sweden had historically received its culture from Finland. He subsequently went on to defend the Finns in another dissertation, the *Vindiciae Fennorum*. His views may be seen, in part, as a reaction against the opinions of an earlier, Swedish-born professor at the University of Turku, Israel Nesselius, who had argued that both the Finnish language and sauna should be eradicated.

These arguments—pro and con—were two sides of the same coin. The issue was whether "Finnishness" was a residue of ignorance based on pagan superstition. In championing the Finns, therefore, Juslenius resorted to biblical arguments. In 1712, in his inaugural lecture as professor of Greek and Hebrew, he tried to show that the Finnish language was related to these "holy languages," and he later advanced the view that the Finns were descended from Noah's son Japhet (a view that, strangely enough, surfaced again in England in the writings of Canon F. C. Cook as late as 1885).

In his justification of the Finns, however, Juslenius was driven into ambivalence. On the one hand, he collected folk poetry and produced the first Finnish dictionary, in 1745. On the other hand, he fought strongly against the relics of superstition as if to ensure that the Finns would, after all, become an advanced Christian civilization. This meant that they would be strict adherents to the Lutheran church (q.v.) and, as bishop of Porvoo, Juslenius struggled to suppress the Greek Orthodox churches (q.v.) surviving in the border parishes.

Juslenius had twice to flee Finland for Sweden, both in the Great Wrath (q.v.) and in the Lesser Wrath (q.v.). There is no doubt that he preferred the Swedish connection to the Russian.

The great Finnish scholar H. G. Porthan (q.v.), who shared the enthusiasm of Juslenius for folk poetry and for the cultivation of a sense of place, was the grandson of Daniel Juslenius's nephew. In honor of Juslenius the building housing the Humanities Department of the University of Turku has been named Juslenia.

-K-

KALEVALA. The Finnish national epic. *Kalevala* is actually a place: a country struggling against another, *Pohjola,* or the "Land of the North."

The *Kalevala* was put together by Elias Lönnrot (q.v.), then a country doctor, from folk poetry sung or recited to him by the rune singers (*runo* in Finnish means "poem") of eastern Finland or East Karelia (q.v.). Since Lönnrot transposed the verses to form an epic, he had sometimes to create linking verses of his own, though these comprise only 5% of the total and are often adaptations of folk verses anyway. When Lönnrot was young, he worked with his father as a tailor, and it has been said that his later work on the *Kalevala* was also a piece of tailoring.

Though fighting and slaughter are depicted in the *Kalevala* (an aspect that has been ascribed to Viking influence), a large part of the epic revolves around the use of magic spells—the Italian nineteenth-century folklorist Domenico Comparetti called it, not unreasonably, "the epic of charms." The epic, in short, is shamanistic. Väinämöinen, the leader of his people, communes with the dead—at great risk to himself. His soul travels.

The epic has much in common with other epics. There is in it a myth of creation: a story of how a seabird's egg breaks into pieces from which arise earth, heaven, and the celestial bodies. The heroes, wooing the maid of Pohjola, must submit to impossible tasks—Väinämöinen must knit an egg. The heroes also perform tasks of great value to their people: Väinämöinen, like Prometheus, brings fire to lighten darkness, while Ilmarinen, who ultimately wins the maid of Pohjola, is a smith who learns how to make iron from crude ore (as does Wayland the Smith of English legend).

The basic plan turns on the struggle to possess the mystical Sampo. This has been variously described as a mill, or as the pillar around which the earth rotates, even as identical with the Tree of Life of Eurasian folklore. More recently, it has been given a political interpretation, as a symbol of certain taxation privileges in connection with trade.

The political elements in the *Kalevala* are now being discovered, giving lie to the traditional Western European responses (as, for example, in the writings of Max Müller) that this is a saga of a prepolitical people. Inevitably, perhaps, in the last century the reception of this epic in Western Europe served to emphasize too greatly the difference between a civilized Swedish Finland and an apparently tribal people it imposed upon.

When declaimed (alas, too infrequently, in modern Finland), the *Kalevala* is a work of great power, which comes from alliteration (not rhyme) and from the eight-syllable trochaic line. It is said that Longfellow, in composing "Hiawatha," was influenced both by the themes and meter of the Finnish epic.

KALLIO, KYÖSTI (1873–1940). President of Finland from 1937 to 1940. Kallio was the first president of Finland to have a

Finnish name. He also has the distinction of being the only Finnish president never to have completed senior high school.

Of farming stock, Kallio himself became a successful farmer at Nivala in northern Ostrobothnia, where he promoted a local savings bank and cooperatives and engaged in youth and temperance work. (As president, he was to become notable for never offering his guests a drink.)

Kallio entered politics early as a constitutionalist in the passive resistance movement (q.v.) against measures of Russian unification (q.v.). He sat in the Estate of Peasants in the final period of the unreformed Diet of Four Estates (q.v.) and from 1907 onward, until becoming president, he sat in the unicameral legislature (q.v.) as a member of the Agrarian Union (q.v.).

In the critical time of 1917–1918 Kallio was a member of the Senate (q.v.), but resigned when the Senate drew up a proposal for the legislature in favor of the establishment of a monarchy. In independent Finland one of Kallio's greatest achievements was the passage in 1922 of the "Lex Kallio," by which the detested crofter (q.v.) system was finally extinguished.

In later life of distinctly grandfatherly appearance, Kallio has been called the "peasant president," and there is much that is positive in this designation, for he was a product of an intensely democratic tradition rooted in love for both home district and homeland. His biographer has recounted, on the other hand, that he was glum on his election as president, while his wife was even sorrowful, preferring her modest life in the Nivala farmhouse to entering the presidential palace.

The fact was that Kallio's election was a compromise move, the outcome of strategic voting in the electoral college so as to prevent either the Liberal Progressive K. J. Ståhlberg (q.v.) or the Conservative P. E. Svinhufvud (q.v.) from being elected president.

Kallio's political tragedy was that, though his presidency undoubtedly helped prevent a polarization of Finnish internal politics, he could not cope with the main presidential task, that of directing the foreign policy of the country. This field he left to his foreign ministers, one of whom, Eljas

Erkko (q.v.), told him not to interfere. As it turned out, these ministers were no wiser, and Finland was drawn into the Winter War (q.v.). It is fair to add that recent research has, however, shown that Kallio was, if anything, even more adamant than his ministers on the impossibility of major territorial concessions to the Soviet Union.

The impress of foreign and defense policy, including the prima-donna-like behavior of Marshal Mannerheim (q.v.) before the outbreak of war, seriously disturbed the constitutionalism of which Kallio was a representative. In the Winter War he was not kept closely informed by Foreign Minister Väinö Tanner (q.v.). After the war, when Risto Ryti (q.v.) served as acting president during Kallio's illness, it is uncertain whether Kallio knew anything at all about the tentative approaches to Nazi Germany.

Having signed the Peace of Moscow (q.v.), concluding the Winter War by the concession of one-tenth of Finnish territory to the Soviet Union, Kallio expressed his sense of personal tragedy at the fate of his country by quoting the words of Zechariah (11: 17), "His arm shall be clean dried up." Having resigned the presidency, he was traveling back to Nivala in December 1940 when he was stricken by a seizure at the Helsinki railroad station, and he died in the arms of Marshal Mannerheim.

In his final year of office, however, he had not been entirely powerless, but against the wishes of many influential political figures had insisted that the Finns of the ceded territories be brought back to Finland and resettled rather than remain under Soviet rule.

KALM, PEHR (1716–1779). Natural scientist and geographer. Kalm was born in the province of Ångermanland, Sweden, but his parents were from Finland, having fled to Sweden in the Great Wrath (q.v.). Kalm's father, a clergyman, returned to Finland, and in 1735 the young Pehr Kalm began to study at Turku (q.v.), concentrating especially on natural sciences. Later he studied under Carolus Linnaeus at Uppsala.

Kalm never graduated, but as early as 1745 he was made a member of the Stockholm Academy of Sciences; in 1747 he became first professor of political economy at Turku.

Kalm traveled much, both in the remoter Swedish provinces and in eastern Finland, collecting botanical specimens, particularly with regard to their utility, but taking notes on the manners of the inhabitants, too.

Between 1747 and 1751 Kalm visited England, Canada, and other British North American colonies, bringing back botanical collections of great value for Linnaeus. Kalm has become famous for his perceptions of the New World. He criticized a certain slothfulness and indifference among the inhabitants of the former New Sweden (Delaware), but in general praised the liberal regime of Pennsylvania, especially the separation of Church and State, the low level of taxation prevailing, and the general absence of state superintendence of the economy.

Through observations of this kind Kalm was making oblique criticism of mercantilist Sweden. His own views—of the utilitarian value of knowledge and of the need to utilize the bounty of nature—brought him close to a Physiocratic standpoint. His most famous pupil, Anders Chydenius (q.v.), undoubtedly took much from Kalm's teachings on natural economics.

Kalm took holy orders in 1757, becoming rector of the parish of Maaria, near Turku (its medieval church is still in use). In 1765 Kalm published his *Flora Fennica*. This was the only account of Finnish plant life to appear in the eighteenth century, but Kalm's isolating of Finland as a unit of study was in its way a pointer to the future. Kalm refused the offer of a professorship in botany at the Saint Petersburg Academy of Sciences. In symbolic terms, his refusal was another token of a growing Finnish self-sufficiency.

KALMAR, UNION OF. The Union of Kalmar was established in 1397 as a result of policies pursued by Margaret I of Denmark. It was a union of all Scandinavian states under one monarchy and was directed against German power. It has thus had a symbolic significance for supporters of later Nordic unity and especially for the nineteenth-century Pan-Scandinavians (q.v.).

Sweden (and hence of course Finland, which was then a

part of Sweden) broke away from the union finally in 1521, but as far as Denmark and Norway were concerned, the union can be seen to have endured up to 1814, when Norway was taken from Denmark and joined to Sweden in a joint kingdom.

The original Union of Kalmar was rocked by the growth of the might of Sweden by the early sixteenth century, and Sweden gradually replaced it as the arbiter of Northern European and Baltic affairs.

Finland's participation in the politics of the Union of Kalmar was rather a passive one. No Finns were present at its symbolic inception. Curiously, however, the final spark that lit its development was the intriguing of the lord of Turku Castle, Jeppe Diekn (Djäkn), in 1395 with Albert of Mecklenburg against the interest of the Swedish nobility as a whole.

KARELIAN ISTHMUS. This area, lying between Lake Ladoga and the Gulf of Finland, constituted the greater part of Finnish Karelia, as opposed to East Karelia (q.v.), which has never by right belonged to Finland.

The Karelian Isthmus was taken from Finland by the Soviet Union at the Peace of Moscow (q.v.), which concluded the Winter War (q.v.) in 1940. Being reconquered by the Finns in the Continuation War (q.v.), the isthmus was lost again in 1944.

Most of the inhabitants of the Karelian Isthmus were Finnish-speaking, though a minority spoke the Karelian language akin to that spoken in East Karelia. All left for Finland on both occasions when the area was ceded to the Soviet Union.

Historically, part of the Karelian Isthmus was confirmed to the Swedish Crown by the 1323 Peace of Pähkinäsaari (q.v.). Further areas (including Käkisalmi) were granted to the Swedes by the 1617 Peace of Stolbova (q.v.). Lutheranization was pushed on rapidly—even against the stipulations of the Stolbova treaty. By the eighteenth century, though the isthmus was taken into the tsar's domains by the Peace of Uusikaupunki (q.v.) in 1721, the area remained overwhelmingly Lutheran. As the major part of the so-called

Old Finland (q.v.), the Karelian Isthmus was joined to the Grand Duchy (q.v.) of Finland in 1811.

Resettlement of the Karelian refugees in the rest of Finland after the Armistice Agreement (q.v.) of 1944 was one of the most important acts of social policy of post–World War II Finland. Over 400,000 people had to be resettled.

Some bad feeling arose when certain Swedish-speaking areas in western Finland were unwilling to take Karelians out of fear of a possible Finnicizing of their local district. Another important consequence of the resettlement was the maintenance in strength of Finnish agriculture (and with it the strength of the Agrarian Union [q.v.]), for the evacuees put more fields under cultivation than had been the case on the isthmus.

The loss of the city of Viipuri was felt by all Finland. In other ways, too, the loss of Karelia represented an intangible cultural loss, which has furthered the dominance in the current Finnish national character of the traits that are characteristic of the western Finn, in particular his thrusting inarticulateness.

Stalin justified the taking of the Karelian Isthmus by the need to protect Leningrad, since the old frontier was only some thirty kilometers from that city. Neither the development of modern weapon technology nor the present mood of détente would seem to provide much justification for keeping up Stalin's "defense-in-depth" policy. On the other hand, so far at least, no powerful irredentist movement has arisen in Finland. For one thing, the Russians have left the isthmus in a mess, and much investment will be needed to pull the area up to the Finnish level. For another thing, the Finns are fighting to maintain their own high level of prosperity in the current depression and have few funds to spare. Sectoral cooperation between Finns and Russians may be a gradualist approach to a constructive solution, a good example of which is the already thirty-year-old cooperation over the Saimaa Canal.

KEKKONEN, URHO KALEVA (1900–1986). The longest-serving president of Finland, Kekkonen occupied the post for a quarter of a century, from 1956 to 1981, when, incapacitated, he was compelled to resign before the expiration of his term. Since then, the Kekkonen presidency has been under an increasingly critical scrutiny (often by those who did not dare open their mouths in protest, or could not even conceptualize protest, when the imposing head of state was in full vigor). The continuing scrutiny of what Kekkonen did or did not do, however, has become a part of a doubtlessly healthy reappraisal of Finnish political society as a whole.

Kekkonen was the son of a foreman in the forest industry and came from the poor northeastern part of the country. As a schoolboy, he participated on the White side in the 1918 Civil War (q.v.) and, later in life, confessed that he had had to command an execution squad during this war. From the trauma (as he described it) of such a commission, he was led to work for conciliation between the classes in Finland.

In the beginning, his concept of national unity was a forced one. After toying briefly with the Progressive party (q.v.), Kekkonen soon settled down into the bosom of the Agrarian Union (q.v.), expressing some of the more unpleasant features of this most Finnish party with gusto. In an essay entitled "If I Were a Dictator," he playfully projected a vision of Finland in which all citizens were compelled to have Finnish (not Swedish) names and in which the Orthodox church (q.v.) would be ruled out as "Russian".

Kekkonen graduated in law from the University of Helsinki and took his doctorate there in 1936. He was also a sportsman (a high-jumper), and this got him into the politics of sports, becoming chairman of the bourgeois sports association, SVUL, from 1931 to 1947, as well as being chairman of the Finnish Olympic Committee for seven years.

Determined to win, Kekkonen had found by the 1930s that too close an association with the authoritarian streams in Finnish politics would lessen his own chances, and his power base in Agrarianism would be sapped. He became more of a democrat, disliking the antidemocratism of the Academic Karelia Society (q.v.) and leaving it. He wrote against the People's Patriotic Movement (IKL) (q.v.) and as minister of the interior in A. K. Cajander's government before the Winter War (q.v.) tried to suppress this Finnish fascist organization, taking his own advice about the right of a democracy to defend itself.

But the courts thought differently, and refused to allow his anti-IKL measure. After World War II, Kekkonen gained much credit, particularly in Soviet eyes, for his attempt to suppress the IKL. His motives may have been mixed. The IKL was held to be a competitor to the Agrarian party in many areas. It was anyway a vehicle for a "foreign" ideology—and before World War II Kekkonen was just as adamant against the Communists, another force for "foreign" ideas.

Kekkonen was out of the government in the Winter War and was one of the very few who opposed the Peace of Moscow (q.v.). During the Continuation War (q.v.) he conduced vigorous prowar propaganda under the pseudonym of *Pekka Peitsi,* or "Peter the Lance." He kept writing when he no longer believed in the war and after he had been in Sweden, hinting about peace. In the fall of 1944, still as Pekka Peitsi, he wrote about the postwar convergence of ideas between the West and the Soviet Union (the West would become more "social" and the Soviet Union more "liberal" in outlook).

Many, all over Europe, wanted to believe in this kind of a future. But in Finland, by this time, Kekkonen's shifts of political mood had rather tarnished his image, and he had become known as the "Weather Vane."

Out of this unpromising background, Kekkonen nevertheless emerged in the post–World War II world to be one of the leading figures in Finnish politics and, in the end, to be *the* leading figure. He played a commanding role in the war trials (q.v.) and in the negotiations for the Finnish-Soviet Treaty (q.v.) of 1948. He had a certain flair for keeping in the public spotlight; on the postwar "reconstructed" state radio, he was the dominant nonsocialist politician in the important "miniature Parliament" debates. A degree of isolation within his own party only strengthened his proclivity to find allies in other camps. Since all Finnish governments are coalition governments, adaptability—nay, opportunism—does not come amiss.

For years, to the dislike of the older generation, Kekkonen

had been a professional political survivor. When, in the early 1950s, the Agrarians became alienated from the Social Democrats (q.v.), Kekkonen headed a government without the latter, drawing closer to the trade union movement and the Communists, though neither force was to enter any government for several years. What was already clear was Kekkonen's ability to manipulate faction and rally it behind him.

In 1956 Kekkonen was elected president by 151 votes to 149 in the electoral college, triumphing over his Social Democrat "Western" opponent K. A. Fagerholm. By now Kekkonen had amply proved himself as a "Compliant" (q.v.), an advocate of good and fruitful relations with the Soviet Union. In this he claimed to be continuing the work of the great postwar president, Paasikivi (q.v.) — who had actually at the last moment been persuaded to enter the presidential race once more.

But the official line that was gradually to develop in the twenty-five years of the Kekkonen presidency was something bolder than anything contemplated in the Paasikivi term. In a Europe — in a world — full of dangerous tensions, Kekkonen was to cultivate good relations with the Soviet Union so as to enable Finland to keep its avenues open to the West, as, for example, with the FINEFTA agreement (q.v.) of 1961.

What this policy meant was that Finland would be ready to perform, when the time came, mediating services for the Soviet Union westward — the most important of which was the Finnish promotion of the Soviet idea of a European Security Conference in the early 1970s, a move that spawned the process leading to the Conference on Security and Cooperation in Europe (q.v.).

Thus Finland became, internationally speaking, a small but significant island of sanity in the emotionally overwrought politics of the Cold War, but the pursuit of such rational politics was always held by Kekkonen to require national unity. Dealing with the Soviet Union was never easy, and the 1968 Czechoslovak crisis had made Finnish-Soviet relations somewhat tense. Only later was it realized what strain Kekkonen had to endure in the early 1970s, when, among other things, his request for Soviet recognition of

Finnish neutrality was thwarted, and the candidature of Max Jakobson for the post of U.N. secretary-general was torpedoed by the Russians.

Under these circumstances, and because of earlier experiences, Kekkonen openly bound together a successful handling of the Soviet Union with a successful handling of internal Finnish politics—and he sought to crush initiative in the latter by referring to the overriding imperative of good Soviet-Finnish relations. A politics like this ends up on what the Finns call *Pietarin tie,* or the "road to Saint Petersburg" (q.v.).

No one could get rid of Kekkonen, and the forces around him were afraid of what would crumble if he went. In 1974 he became president by a special law without an election. He did have a campaign in 1978, but his opponents were pilloried by journalists of the state radio and television network.

Then, at the turn of the 1980s, Kekkonen became incapacitated. He was obviously mortally ill. Rumors abounded that a junta was prepared to rule provisionally in his name—this would have included a military man—but Kekkonen was prevailed on to resign.

Kekkonen's successor to the presidency, Mauno Koivisto (q.v.), shot off in the other direction, backing away from issues that Kekkonen would have settled then and there. The style of presidential politics thus exhibited a change.

How far Finnish society can take more fundamental structural changes is still an open question. A famous biography notwithstanding, Kekkonen was no wizard. He was head of a society of a traditionally corporativist nature, of intermingling power groups, of young intellectuals who turned themselves into administrators to serve. Such a system does not depend on the exercise of power by one man, has not been abandoned, and may even fit well into the framework of European integration (q.v.).

KOIVISTO, MAUNO HENRIK (1925–   ). President of Finland from 1982 to 1994. Koivisto, the son of a carpenter, was born in Turku (q.v.). After military service in World War II, during which he engaged in operations behind enemy lines, he worked as a longshoreman, becoming a trade union and Social Democratic party (q.v.) official. It is said that part of his work was keeping Communists out.

At the same time he studied at the University of Turku, taking his M.A. in sociology and in 1956 his doctorate on the subject of industrial relations among harbor workers. (The doctoral defense is a public occasion in Finland, and when Koivisto presented his dissertation there were longshoremen in the audience to give him the support of their opinions.)

His academic and party background enabled him to find a place in the Workers' Savings Bank, and thereafter he rose rapidly. He became head of the Bank of Finland (q.v.) in 1968 and was Finland's representative on the IBRD from 1966 to 1969 and the IMF from 1970 to 1979. These commitments in the banking sphere went hand in hand with political commitments. Koivisto was minister of finance from 1966 to 1967, prime minister from 1968 to 1970, and again prime minister from 1979 to 1981. From the latter post he moved to the presidency in 1982.

In spite of this clear success story, his relations in the 1970s with President Urho Kekkonen (q.v.) were not always the best. Koivisto probably felt betrayed by the collapse of the Nordek (q.v.) project in 1970. Kekkonen, in turn, did not have a very high an opinion of him and tried to thwart Koivisto's second term as prime minister.

Kekkonen's jealousy may have been to some extent motivated by the simple reality that Koivisto was an even better exponent of the politics of consensus (q.v.). What Kekkonen forced and bullied on, Koivisto achieved by mediation.

If any thinker has ever had any influence upon Koivisto, it is allegedly Edvard Bernstein, the gradualist socialist. Koivisto's cautious outlook owes more to gradualism than to socialism. In the late 1960s he supported the Kekkonen policy of integrating the Communists into the governmental system, a policy that was supposed to promote industrial peace. Koivisto's later success was in another direction. As president he helped foster in 1987 the joint government of Social Democrats and the National Coalition party (q.v.)—the Conservatives—a political integration that Kekkonen could not, and would not, have managed.

Thus Koivisto brought "industrial Finland" together, and

before the parliamentary elections of 1991 went somewhat out of his way to praise the merits of the Social Democrat–Conservative combination.

There was a certain ambivalence in Koivisto's presidency. He came into office (elected across the political board by 167 electors out of an electoral college of 301) as a low-profile president, committed to strengthening of both parliamentary and governmental power, in contrast to his predecessor, who tended to intervene all over the place. In 1988 Koivisto was reelected, on the same expressed outlook, by the votes (in the second round) of 189 electors. Behind the scenes, however, Koivisto did exert his influence as a former Bank of Finland man, backing the maintenance of a strong finnmark (high finnmark, lower prices)—a policy that crumbled at the end of 1991.

There was a certain "establishment" quality about Koivisto that led him sometimes to make sudden lurches into policy issues in particular cases. Regarding a widespread case of alleged corporate crime in 1984, he wondered aloud how it was that the charges were so readily brought. A year previously, he had lambasted social scientists for their critique of his presidency. He called investigative journalists "lemmings."

In foreign policy (which in Finland is the ultimate prerogative of presidential power) he declared, as late as January 1991, that it was in the interest of Finland that the Soviet Union be maintained. His attitude to the Baltic States in their struggle for renewed independence was not particularly encouraging.

In contrast, in his New Year's speech of 1992 he refused to give a lead on the question of a Finnish application for European Community membership. This could most certainly be related to his view that Parliament should first make its opinion known, but it also raised the question as to how much longer foreign policy decisions should, by virtue of the constitution (q.v.), continue to be the prerogative of the president. In the event, no one has seemed to want to change this aspect of presidential power.

By 1994 Koivisto had made up his mind about the European Community, now Union. In his New Year's speech of that year he gave the country to understand that it should get into the European Union as quickly as possible.

In office, Koivisto expressed the opinion that in a reform of the constitution two terms of office should be sufficient for any president. It took him quite a long time to decide that he himself would not run for a third term.

KUUSINEN, OTTO WILLE (1881–1964). One of the founders of the Finnish Communist party (q.v.), Comintern official, head of the Soviet-established Finnish Terijoki government (q.v.), and member of the Soviet politburo.

Kuusinen, the son of a tailor, was born near Jyväskylä, educated at the high school there and at the University of Helsinki, where he studied philosophy, literature, and art history. As a youth he wrote poetry and was much under the influence of the national epic, the *Kalevala* (q.v.), and of the patriotic poets J. L. Runeberg (q.v.) and Z. Topelius. Like many other students of his time, he spent his summers lecturing the people of the countryside. In his case his major theme was the work of a philosopher of Finnish nationalism, the Hegelian J. W. Snellman (q.v.). Kuusinen's political views at this period were those of an Old Finn (q.v.).

In the 1905 Great Strike (q.v.) Kuusinen became one of the "November Socialists," though the influence of Sulo Wuolijoki, the inspector of Kuusinen's student corporation (q.v.), was also in the background.

True to the Old Finn outlook of the role of the people as a national regenerative force, Kuusinen, as a socialist, first believed in the possibility of a bloodless revolution in Finland. In spite of his lifelong identification with revolutionary socialism, Kuusinen's convictions about the means of its attainment shifted constantly, however. In personal terms he was, in fact, a calculator, always endeavoring to estimate the consequences.

As a young M.P. in the unicameral legislature (q.v.), he proved himself to be an administrative demon, but was ready enough with denunciations of the fallacy of revisionism. In 1917, however, he came up with a revisionist solution: the creation of a coalition Senate (q.v.) with bourgeois members. In the crucial month of November 1917, a few weeks before the outbreak of the Civil War (q.v.), he first voted against the dictatorship of the proletariat and then for it. He let the proletarian revolutionary impulse burst forth without much of a belief in its success. After all, according to the theory, the revolution should have started in Germany. Kuusinen seemed to be preoccupied by the role of preventing the revolutionary impulse in Finland from degenerating into anarchy. In this, leaving aside his pessimism, he was already approaching the Bolshevik line of controlling, not starting, events.

He was not yet a Bolshevik, however. In the Red government in Finland in 1918 he played a prominent role, producing a draft "Red Constitution," which accorded the legislature great power, in light perhaps of parliamentary aspirations, which, reaching back to the eighteenth-century Age of Liberty (q.v.), had never been adequately satisfied in Finland. The model of the Swiss constitution also had its influence here.

Kuusinen had urged a compromise peace in the Civil War, but it was not to be. Once in Russia, after the defeat of the Finnish Reds, he urged the formation of a Finnish Communist party, separate from the Finnish Social Democratic party (q.v.), which had anyway split over the Civil War. Dissatisfied with the initial program of the Communist party, Kuusinen, temporarily in Stockholm, fostered the development in Finland of a parliamentary Socialist Labor party, which was, however, banned in 1923 after three years of existence.

In the early 1930s Kuusinen opposed the proposals of his Finnish Communist rival Kullervo Manner to move the headquarters of the Finnish Communist party from Moscow to Stockholm, proposals which were to prove fatal for Manner. In the late 1930s Kuusinen gave pronounced support to Popular Front tactics for Finland, which included endorsing the Liberal Progressive presidential candidate K. J. Ståhlberg (q.v.) against the Conservative P. E. Svinhufvud (q.v.). Kuusinen's acceptance in December 1939 of leadership of the puppet Terijoki government sealed forever his fate as persona non grata in Finland. According to his second wife, Aino Kuusinen, he envisaged marching back to Finland under the banner of the Red Army. She, in her turn, spent twenty years in a Soviet concentration camp.

Otto Wille Kuusinen survived the Stalinist and post-Stalinist purges. In 1956 he was awarded the Order of Lenin. He was buried in the Kremlin wall.

-L-

LAPLAND WAR. This was the last of the three wars fought by the Finns between November 1939 and April 1945. In the Winter War (q.v.), they fought alone. In the Continuation War (q.v.), they fought as cobelligerents (q.v.) of the Germans. In the Lapland War, they had to turn against the Germans and expel them from northern Finland.

This was a condition of the second paragraph of the Armistice Agreement (q.v.) of September 19, 1944. Even before the agreement was signed, however, the Russians insisted on this Finnish action, and Molotov may have delayed the agreement because he thought that the Finns were not already driving the Germans out.

The German troops in southern Finland left peaceably by sea on September 6. The Finnish military authorities thereafter tried to come to an understanding with the German forces remaining in Finland, principally the nine-division strong Twentieth German Mountain Army in the north under the command of General Lothar Rendulic. The understanding was that of a phased retreat in which no one would get hurt.

The Germans were more than agreeable to this. Hitler was afraid of an Anglo-American landing in northern Norway and wanted German troops out of Finland. At the same time the Germans were afraid that the Soviet forces would move into northern Finland and divide them. This is what General K. A. Meretshkov wanted to do, but he was restrained by Stalin.

Stalin's decision was probably political, bearing in mind the sensitivity of his allies over Norway and his own resolution not to conquer Finland. This was good. What was bad was that Soviet restraint required, in turn, that the Finnish army harry the Germans out.

The understanding between Finns and Germans (by which, incidentally, German forces had helped evacuate

Finnish civilians from Lapland) was at an end. Hostilities in Lapland broke out—hence the name of the war. The only other conflict had taken place earlier on September 14 and 15 when the German navy had unsuccessfully tried to capture the island of Suursaari in the Gulf of Finland.

Approximately a thousand Finns lost their lives in the Lapland War, many of them young and inexperienced conscripts. The town of Rovaniemi, the capital of the province of Lapland, was burned to the ground by the Germans. In practice most of the fighting was over by January, 1945, though a strong pocket of German troops remained on Finnish soil in the Enontekiö enclave at Kilpisjärvi until April 1945.

By virtue of fighting the Lapland War, some Finnish leaders felt that Finland might get a seat at the U.N. charter meeting in San Francisco in April 1945, but this did not come to pass. The British, in refusing to have a peace treaty with the Finns in September 1944, ensured that Finland would remain an enemy state for the next two and a half years.

LAPPS. There are approximately 4,000 Lapps in the Finnish province of Lapland, where they are vastly outnumbered by Finns. There are considerably more Lapps living in Sweden and Norway than in Finland, but more Lapps in Finland than on the Kola Peninsula.

Since 1975 there has been instruction in the Lapp language in schools, and there is a Nordic Lapp Council, founded in 1956, which in 1979 moved to Utsjoki in Finnish Lapland.

Much of the reindeer herding in Lapland is in the hands of the Finns, but recently it has been officially proposed to restore to the Lapps their ancient rights to fell and forest. Nothing so far seems to have been done about this.

The Finnish Lapps are divided into two groups, and the smaller group of Skolt Lapps belong to the Orthodox church (q.v.).

LAPUA MOVEMENT. This populist movement was named for a small town in southern Ostrobothnia. Lapua is the seat of a bishopric; in November 1929 a group of Young Communists foolishly went there to propagandize openly. They were seized and manhandled by the enraged inhabitants of this deeply religious locality.

A deputation of about twenty left Lapua for Helsinki (q.v.) on December 6—Independence Day—to protest the growing power of the Communists, whose representatives, under the rubric of the Socialist Workers' and Small Farmers' Parliamentary Group, had won 13.5% of the votes in the 1929 elections. The Lapua deputation was welcomed at the Helsinki railroad station by members of the Academic Karelia Society (q.v.) and it ended up at the presidential ball.

Leading politicians, including the prime minister, the Agrarian Kyösti Kallio (q.v.), as well as the president, Lauri Kristian Relander (q.v.), also from the Agrarian Union (q.v.), identified at first with what had rapidly become an Ostrobothnian peasants' movement. A stricter censorship law and a tightening of the law of associations were promised, though Relander, a kindly man, balked at the imposition of a death penalty for treason.

The Lapua movement grew in strength. On July 7, 1930, well over twelve thousand peasants marched in military formation through the streets of the capital (they had been conceded half-price tickets on the state railways to get there). In the course of the march they were fulsomely greeted by the new prime minister, P. E. Svinhufvud (q.v.), General Mannerheim (q.v.), and President Relander.

In fact, the Lapua movement was threatening to become a nationwide conspiracy whose menaces were directed not only against Communism but against a Parliament that was reluctant to pass the strict, repressive laws the men of Lapua demanded. Kallio, a constitutionalist, had long ago turned to oppose them, while Svinhufvud, now that he was prime minister (largely as a result of their pressure), would brook no interference with his power.

The illegalities of the Lapua movement began to shock the nation. Not merely were Communists or suspected Communists beaten up or "taken for a ride" by the movement, but in October 1930 the former president K. J. Ståhlberg (q.v.), who had publicly opposed the Lapua movement, was kidnapped along with his wife.

The Lapua movement as such ultimately expired in the

abortive military revolt at Mäntsälä (q.v.) in February 1932. What had really broken the movement had been the results in the general election of 1930, for in that election the bourgeois parties had gained two-thirds of the seats in Parliament. In 1931 Svinhufvud was elected president. After these events there was no apparent need for an extraparliamentary Right.

Yet something lingered on. Encouraged by Svinhufvud himself, a People's Patriotic Movement (q.v.) — the IKL — was founded in 1932. This was the true heir of the Lapua movement. Its emergence testified that what the Lapua movement had tried to express was more than the socioeconomic tensions of the peasants of southern Ostrobothnia.

In respect of these tensions, however, it is worth asking whether the Ostrobothnian peasants and the Communists they condemned had equal grounds for looking askance at the workings of the international capitalist system on their lives.

LENIN, VLADIMIR (Vladimir Ilyich Ulyanov) (1870–1924). Russian revolutionary, one of the founders of the Soviet state.

Lenin spent almost two years of his life in Finland, though he met his first Finnish acquaintance when he was in exile in Siberia. This was the metalworker Oskar Engberg, who made the wedding rings for Lenin and Nadezhda Konstantinovna Krupskaya and was best man at their wedding.

Lenin did not, however, meet any of the leaders of the Finnish workers' movement till 1905, and it is not without significance that his first contacts with conspiratorial Finnish leaders were with the Activists (q.v.).

Lenin returned to Russia through Finland during the 1905 Revolution, being particularly impressed by the Finnish Great Strike (q.v.). He met Stalin for the first time at the Russian Social Democratic Workers' party conference, which was actually held at Tampere in December 1905 (the same premises are now occupied by the Lenin Museum, which has recently been suggested, somewhat playfully, as a fit resting place for Lenin's embalmed remains).

For most of 1906 and 1907 Lenin resided in Finland; in danger of arrest, he left in December 1907, jumping off the

Turku train at Littoinen to avoid the gendarmes, and later struggling across the ice in the Turku archipelago to pick up the boat for Sweden.

In April 1917 Lenin entered Russia from Finland once more, fled Russia for Finland in August 1917, and then finally returned to Russia on October 8 for the triumph of the Bolshevik Revolution.

At the Tampere conference in the fall of 1906 Lenin had told the Finnish workers' leaders that Finland would gain its national self-determination only through revolution in Russia. Now, as chairman of the Council of People's Commissars, he formalized Finnish independence (q.v.) by an act of recognition on December 31, 1917.

The government in Finland was not a workers' but a bourgeois government, however, and it has often been asked why Lenin and the Council of People's Commissars so readily — almost offhandedly — accorded Finnish independence. For one thing, they had no choice; Russia was too weak to stop it. For another, in light of their own evaluation of the situation, a socialist revolution was about to occur in Finland anyway. This was correct; what went wrong was that in the ensuing Finnish Civil War (q.v.) the Reds lost.

Lenin's role in the Finnish Civil War was devious. Before the outbreak of major hostilities, he sent a consignment of 15,000 rifles to the Finnish Reds, but there was to be no constant help, for this would have upset the Germans with whom Lenin was bent on making peace and whose demands included control over Finland. It has been argued that by making a deal with the Germans at Brest-Litovsk the Russian Revolution was saved at the expense of the Finnish Revolution.

Lenin knew much about Finland, but the country constituted a hard case for his theories. It was, in comparison with tsarist Russia, a more advanced capitalist state, where the high level of literacy and the growing respect for women's rights won Lenin's admiration. As a necessary part of the breakup of the tsarist empire, Finland, as Poland, had a claim to independence, which no Bolshevik should have resisted. Somehow, however, the Finns were also oppressed by the capitalist system that had pulled them ahead of tsarist Russia.

Once the Finnish proletariat was liberated, it would join the Russian proletariat, possibly in a federal-type state. On this count, at least, Lenin was wrong.

LIIKKALA NOTE. Shortly after the outbreak of war between Sweden and Russia in 1788, a handful of serving Finnish officers, fearing the sort of devastation for Finland that had occurred in the Great and Lesser Wraths (q.v.) and apprehensive of a further abandonment by Sweden to Russia of Finnish territory, drew up an appeal for peace to Catherine the Great. In it the officers expressed the hope that in the name of peace Russia would restore the Finnish territory it had gained in 1743 at the Peace of Turku (q.v.).

Bearing the note from the village of Liikkala, the emissary of the officers, Major J. A. Jägerhorn, added at Viipuri a statement calling for the summoning of the Swedish Diet, for a return to the constitution of the Age of Liberty (q.v.), and for a special position for Finland.

These views bore on the constitutionalist conflict in Sweden, arising from the reassertion of monarchical power contained in the Form of Government of 1772 (q.v.). They reflected a degree of acceptance of the interference hitherto of the Russian throne in Swedish affairs, an interference allegedly on the side of liberty. What was more startling was the edging toward the idea of Finland as a buffer zone between Sweden and Russia, though that term was not used.

The Russian empress responded cautiously, making no mention of territorial changes, referring only to the possibility of a Finnish Diet. The king of Sweden, Gustav III, became almost immediately aware of the note.

Indeed, one of his frontline commanders—Major General K. G. Armfelt—was a signatory. Gustav III demanded an oath of loyalty, but in giving it many officers signed a wider protest, the Anjala Covenant (q.v.).

LÖNNROT, ELIAS (1802–1884). Compiler of the Finnish folk epic, the *Kalevala* (q.v.). Lönnrot was born in the village of Sammatti, in southern Finland, the son of the local tailor and fiddler. For periods in Lönnrot's childhood, the family was so poor that they ate birch-bark bread.

By virtue of great diligence, Lönnrot passed the university

entrance examination privately. He graduated in the humanities from the University of Turku, and when the school moved to Helsinki (q.v.) after the disastrous fire of 1827 in Turku (q.v.), he graduated from there in medicine. His doctoral thesis was written on the subject of the magic medicines of the Finns, a topic that bore witness to his greatest interest, the folk wisdom of the Finnish people. His doctorate, with its recognition of psychological elements in healing, was the subject of some scorn: it was ahead of its time.

Lönnrot, though working for several years as a doctor—he was one time district doctor at Kajaani in northeastern Finland—made eleven trips on foot to collect oral folk poetry from the mouths of the "rune-singers," as they were called. Many of these trips were made over the border into East Karelia (q.v.), where the oral tradition survived alongside the Orthodox church (q.v.) in an easier manner than it did alongside the Lutheran church (q.v.) in Finland proper. The Finnish Literature Society was founded to assist Lönnrot in his task, which indicated that he was moving with the spirit of the times.

In 1834 he published an initial version of the *Kalevala;* in 1835 and 1836 appeared the two volumes of the *Old Kalevala,* as it is called; and in 1849 he published the *New Kalevala*. In other words, he had built an epic from this folk poetry, but some of the epic he wrote himself.

Lönnrot was a great believer in the education of the people, whose misery, he thought, was due to their own lack of endeavor and enlightenment. He was consequently a founder of a temperance (q.v.) society, inspired by the example of what was going on in North America. Lönnrot has traditionally been held up as a model of true temperance, for he indulged in the occasional glass of wine, it was said. Recent research has revealed that it was more than occasional.

A press publicist for the Fennoman movement (q.v.), Lönnrot ended up as professor of the Finnish language, being the second holder of the chair—after M. A. Castren (q.v.).

Lönnrot retired to Sammatti. He was a tough, yet modest, man, whose personal life was tragic: most of his children died young and his wife died overwhelmed with despair at the children's fate.

The Swedish-Finnish poet J. L. Runeberg (q.v.), in praising Lönnrot, wondered how such a wise man could have been born of "purely" Finnish parents.

LUTHERAN CHURCH. This church is the first official church in Finland, the second being the Orthodox church (q.v.). More than 90% of the Finnish population belong, by registration, to the Lutheran church and pay taxes to it. The Lutheran church receives three-quarters of its income from taxation, 10% of which comes from its right to tax businesses and other corporations, which means that, indirectly, there are Finns (and some non-Finns) who are not members of the Finnish Lutheran church yet are compelled to contribute to it.

Lutheranism began to penetrate Finland on the return of the young Finnish scholar Petrus Särkilahti in 1523 from the universities of Rostock and Louvain. He arrived in Turku (q.v.) with the doctrines of the Reformation and, to the astonishment of the inhabitants of the city, a wife.

The role played by the new Swedish monarch, Gustavus I Vasa, who had been elected king only in 1523, was also of the utmost significance. At the Diet of Vesterås in 1527 Gustavus secured the authority to get his hands on church lands and thus alleviate the chronic indebtedness of the Swedish State caused by the struggle to overthrow Danish power with the accompanying costly alliance, for the Swedes, of Lübeck. Gustavus would brook the existence of no potential counter-forces to his authority, and so his particular financial needs coincided with a more general desire to reduce the might of the Church. In 1528, for example, he had destroyed the episcopal castle of Kuusisto, near Turku (the ruins can still be seen). Further, wherever possible, Gustavus kept ecclesiastical positions vacant for long periods, taking the revenues for himself and weakening the power of the Church as well.

The Diet of Vesterås had not come out openly for Luther—only for the "purity" of religion. Moreover, it met three years before the Augsburg Confession was drawn up. It is nonetheless remarkable that it took until 1593 for the Synod of the Swedish Church, meeting at Uppsala, to declare for Lutheranism, repudiating at the same time both Calvinism and Catholicism.

What was also repudiated at Uppsala was the attempt at

compromise through the "Red Book." This had been promoted by Duke John, later John III (q.v.), and was intended
as a means of reconciling some of the elements of the Reformation with a mainly Catholic liturgy—priests, for example,
would have been allowed to marry.

The Red Book had a certain following in Finland, but papal intransigence doomed this compromise, and devout
Protestants feared that the Red Book would be Catholicism
through stealth. The political and economic problems attendant upon the reign of Sigismund (q.v.) only served to reinforce a felt need for religious conformity.

Typical of seventeenth-century conformity and uniformity
was the great Ecclesiastical Act of 1686. No other faith but
Lutheranism was to be allowed in the land, and the king was
declared to be the Supreme Bishop.

This identification of Lutheranism with the statepower has
remained strong in Finland—even when, with the creation of
the Grand Duchy (q.v.) of Finland in 1809, the monarchy in
question was Orthodox. In the Years of Oppression (q.v.),
Archbishop Gustaf Johansson could not accept the demands
of the passive resistance movement (q.v.) not to have read
from the Lutheran church pulpits the proclamations for the
call-up of Finnish youth into the Russian army.

In short, the Lutheran church has often been held responsible for indoctrinating the Finnish populace with the virtues
of passivity and obedience to authority. The Psalmist's
words, "The fear of the Lord is the beginning of wisdom,"
are well known in Finland and are given a wide interpretation.

There is another side to the picture, however. Lutherans,
as Protestants, held the staunch conviction that all people
should be able to read the Word of God themselves. This
made the Lutheran church a force for education (q.v.). The
parishioners' ability to read was tested by their clergymen
through the institution of the *lukukinkerit*. Illiterates could
not be confirmed and therefore could not marry.

Clergymen were also chosen by election—even if, by the
eighteenth century, a property qualification had crept in to
determine the right to vote. The measure of a clergyman was
the quality of the test sermon he had to deliver.

Hence Lutheranism in Finland has been a promoter of

knowledge and of the exercise of knowledge, albeit within a conservative framework. The strength of revivalism (q.v.), particularly in the nineteenth century, is a testimony to the persistence of ordinary Finns, inspired by Luther's teachings, to think things out for themselves and not to be overwhelmed by a legitimacy preached in the name of a State-Church relationship.

In recent years occasional opinions have been voiced about deestablishing the Lutheran church. Even President Mauno Koivisto (q.v.), a man not noted for boldness of vision, dropped a few hints about this, though mainly he seems to have been motivated by resentment of the critique of Finland's uncharitable refugee policy launched by Archbishop John Vikström.

More seriously, newspaper polemic has argued that the Church has an undue influence in schools, in the armed forces (q.v.), and in regard to issues like Sunday closing. What is being scrutinized here is the legacy of conformity and uniformity.

-M-

MANNERHEIM, CARL GUSTAF (1867–1951). Soldier and statesman, marshal of Finland (1942) and president of Finland from August 1944 to March 1946.

Mannerheim was born into a famous aristocratic family at Louhisaari (the mansion is now a museum), southwestern Finland, but his father, through business and gambling debts, later lost his property and abandoned his family.

Carl Gustaf Mannerheim was educated at the Hamina Cadet School, from which he was ultimately expelled for trifling misconduct. His aristocratic background and money from his uncle (Albert von Julin, who came from a more recently ennobled family of industrialists) enabled the young Mannerheim nevertheless to enter the Russian Cavalry School in 1887 and subsequently the crack Chevalier Guards, whose elegant uniform fascinated him. Like many a Finnish aristocrat, he thus served the Russian monarch in the most traditional of ways; but it was, significantly, money from the manufacturing class in Finland that paid for the education for this service.

Throughout his life Mannerheim was devoted to the Romanov dynasty. A picture of the last tsar, Nicholas II, in whose coronation procession Mannerheim had walked as an officer of escort, was always over his bed.

Characteristically, when his elder brother, Carl Mannerheim, was expelled from Finland by the Russian authorities in 1903 for his part in the struggle against measures of imperial unification (q.v.), Carl Gustaf Mannerheim did not resign his commission. He simply trusted that in the Russian elite there would be forces that would in the end defend Finnish liberties.

Mannerheim had a successful career in Russia, fighting with distinction both in the Russo-Japanese War and in World War I. His marriage to a Russian noblewoman was a failure, but it brought him money as well as two daughters.

With the changes in Russia in 1917, Mannerheim retired in the fall of that year, shortly before the Bolshevik Revolution. He was even awarded a pension by the authorities of the Bolshevik government in 1918. He retired to Finland shortly before its independence was declared. The breakup of the Russian Empire was the key factor in both cases.

In the Finnish Civil War (q.v.) Mannerheim was given command of the White forces, an aristocrat leading the rescue operation for the bourgeois state. He explained his disarming of the remaining Russian troops in Finland at the beginning of the Civil War as a rescue operation for Europe—saving the Continent from Bolshevism—but these troops were already being repatriated. Only 40,000 out of an earlier force of 125,000 were by that time left in Finland.

In the victory parade of May 16, 1918, Mannerheim on horseback cut quite a figure. He was, however, already quarreling with the government that was thanking him for his services: he did not want German control over the Finnish armed forces. He resigned, but was soon performing valuable tasks for his country by trying to mediate better relations with Great Britain and France, which he had all along argued for.

With the collapse of Germany toward the end of 1918, Parliament elected Mannerheim to be regent of Finland, a post he held from December 1918 to July 1919, when he lost his chance in the presidential stakes, for the Social Democrats (q.v.) were resentful over his role in the Civil War, and the majority of Parliament distrusted his wish to use Finland as a base from which to overthrow Bolshevism in Russia. In this policy of intervention (q.v.) he showed himself to be Russian rather than Finnish in outlook.

Twenty years later the same Russian background enabled Mannerheim to understand the strategic needs of the Soviet state; in 1939, as chairman of the defense council, he urged the Finnish government to make territorial concessions to the Soviet Union. Had his advice been taken, the Winter War (q.v.) might well have been prevented.

Mannerheim twice threatened to resign in 1939, once on the very eve of hostilities. In spite of this temperamental behavior, he led the army well as commander in chief in the Winter War. He was adamant that the offer of intervention from Great Britain and France in the later stages of the war must not be taken up, but only used as a threat to facilitate peace with the USSR.

Mannerheim's role regarding the Continuation War (q.v.) is far more controversial. Before the outbreak of hostilities he helped foster and yet conceal the strengthening connection with Germany. Once hostilities commenced, he sent the Finnish troops beyond the lost territories and into East Karelia (q.v.), an area that had never before belonged to Finland. His refusal to countenance surrender in the face of the strong Soviet offensive of the summer of 1944 cost the country thousands of casualties, and it is far from clear that this stand saved Finnish independence.

Mannerheim was elected president by Parliament in August 1944 and remained in office till March 1946. He was a figurehead around whom the majority of this defeated nation could rally their self-confidence. He had little self-confidence left himself, however. He feared a Soviet takeover of his country. For himself he feared prosecution in the war trials (q.v.). Ignominiously in 1948, at the time of the negotiating of the Finnish-Soviet Treaty (q.v.), he asked the U.S. State Department for $10,000 to get out of Finland. Though then a private citizen, he stated as reason for his request his disinclination to "become another Benes or Masaryk" in the face of Soviet pressure.

He spent his retirement years in Switzerland, where he wrote his memoirs.

MÄNTSÄLÄ REVOLT. This was the last fling of the Lapua movement (q.v.). In February 1932 a Social Democratic meeting was broken up in the village of Mäntsälä, and Civil Guards (q.v.) seized the place preparatory to a nationwide coup in the spirit and with the backing of the Lapua movement.

The immediate aim was to unseat the president, P. E. Svinhufvud (q.v.), who had proved a disappointment to the Lapua movement, and give the real power to Mannerheim (q.v.). Svinhufvud acted swiftly against the conspirators, and the bulk of the army, under General Aarne Sihvo, remained loyal to the constitution (q.v.), which stipulated that in peacetime the president was commander in chief.

The Mäntsälä conspiracy was an attempt to impose unity on Finland by military force. Involved in it was Major General K. M. Wallenius, the former chief of general staff, who had had to resign in 1930 over his participation in the Lapua movement. It is clear that Major General Lauri Malmberg, the commander of the Civil Guards, was prepared initially to support the revolt. In addition, General Rudolf Walden, Mannerheim's sidekick, expressed to President Svinhufvud his wish to become prime minister in a deal that would have given the army over to Mannerheim.

While the failure of the Mäntsälä revolt enabled Svinhufvud to suppress the Lapua movement, a policy of post-Mäntsälä "balancing-up" saved many of the conspirators and, perversely, led to loss of office of some of those who had opposed the Mäntsälä revolt. The role of the National Coalition party (q.v.) in harrying the latter group was shameful. In 1933 even General Sihvo was driven to resign.

MECHELIN, LEO (1839–1914). Finnish statesman, one of the most outstanding figures in the period of autonomy (q.v.), whose main features he struggled to preserve.

The son of a Hamina cadet school inspector, Mechelin

studied in the faculties of humanities and law of the University of Helsinki, becoming professor of administrative law in 1874. In 1872 he had been elected to the Estate of Burghers of the Diet of Four Estates (q.v.) and, being ennobled in 1876 by Tsar Alexander II, he sat thereafter in the Estate of Nobles.

As a member of the legislative organ of the Finnish constitution (q.v.), Mechelin endeavored to strengthen the authority of the Diet over the state budget. His concept of constitutionalism, however, presupposed close cooperation between the Diet and the executive organ of the constitution, the Senate (q.v.), where he himself served, initially from 1882 to 1890.

As a member of the Senate in this period, Mechelin worked on the one hand for the improvement of legal administration and on the other for the development of industry, especially in the field of technical education. A remarkable commercial treaty, negotiated by Mechelin between Finland and Spain (not between the Russian Empire and Spain), was ratified in 1888. This meant a distinct reduction in tariffs for Finnish timber and butter exports to Spain.

Mechelin was careful to avoid any imputation that a treaty of this kind would represent a quiet confirmation of Finnish autonomy; in other respects, however he had by this time become an avowed defender of the autonomous position of his country vis-à-vis the rest of the Russian Empire.

In 1886 he published his *Précis du Droit public du Grand-Duché de Finlande,* which was meant for foreign as well as for Russian readers. Charles Cooke, the British vice-consul in the Finnish capital and an enthusiastic defender of Finnish rights, translated the *Précis* into English and got it published in London. Mechelin prevented him from retitling it with the tendentious rubric of "Home Rule in Finland."

Ordin's Russian edition of the *Précis*, with notes intended to refute most of what Mechelin was arguing, provoked a spirited counterresponse from the Finnish side, Mechelin being defended by the Fennoman (q.v.) J. R. Danielson-Kalmari, whose defense also appeared in English.

In the development of Mechelin's thinking about the autonomous position of his country, two ideas became uppermost. The first of these was that Finland was a state by virtue of having its own fundamental laws, confirmed by Tsar Alexander I at the Diet of Porvoo (q.v.) in 1809, which fundamental laws could not be changed without the consent of the Finnish Diet of Four Estates. The second key idea in Mechelin's thinking was that Finland was in a real union with Russia through the common monarchy (this view recalled the 1867 Austro-Hungarian *Ausgleich*). Here Mechelin, while committing himself to Finnish statehood, could in no way commit himself to independence (q.v.), an outlook that two or three decades later was to constitute a gulf between him and the Activists (q.v.).

Once certain changes had occurred in internal Finnish politics in the late 1860s, through the 1870s, and into the 1880s (such as the regular meetings of the Diet and the liberalizing of trade), the position of Mechelin was bound to be conservative, though he always believed he was a Liberal.

The rigid adherence to the fundamental laws of the Finnish constitution produced a state of mind which made it difficult to accommodate to developments in Russia that were producing demands for unification (q.v.). Equally difficult did it become to adjust to the emergence of new social forces in Finland, which were not going to be content with the maintenance of certain eternal Finnish legal and political verities.

Mechelin's Liberal party, which he tried to promote (and failed) in the early 1880s, was an attempt to bridge the language dispute among the elite. His lack of understanding of the emergent socialist movement was seen in 1899, when the socialist leaders were ignored in the protest activity organized by Mechelin and his followers against the February Manifesto (q.v.).

After the promulgation of the Postal Manifesto (q.v.) in 1890, and with it the threat of further measures of unification, Mechelin resigned from the Senate. By 1899, as a member of the Diet, he was in place to become the natural leader of the passive resistance movement (q.v.) and was exiled to Sweden by Governor-General Bobrikov (q.v.) in 1903.

In December 1904, under the milder regime of Bobrikov's successor, I. M. Obolensky, Mechelin was allowed back and his manipulation of the situation arising from the Great Strike (q.v.) a year later allowed him to return to the Senate.

This victory of the passive resistance forces was soon to reveal its hollow base. Through the last session of the unreformed Diet, through the law codification committee, and through Senate influence, the passive resistance party strove to produce a form of unicameral legislature (q.v.) that would not give rein to the wildest of democratic impulses.

Nothing, however, could controvert the first election results of a 200-member Parliament in which 80 Social Democrats (q.v.) had been elected along with 59 Old Finns (q.v.). A second election failed to bridle these forces. Mechelin, who had come to see the Senate as having a kind of ministerial responsibility to the legislature, was driven in 1908 to resign.

The circumstances were ironic. Mechelin's overriding concern was to oppose the renewed Russian demand for the institution of imperial legislation, but the increasing attacks of the Social Democrats on the Senate were more than he could cope with.

Mechelin was a pacifist at heart, and his favored ambience was the European community of learned men. Most of the passive resistance movement's propaganda in Western Europe, which he tried to direct, was in the style of the detailed argumentation of a letter to *The Times* of London, a newspaper to which, in fact, he did address letters of the fate of Finland.

Developments—both internal and external—passed Mechelin by, but his work and that of the passive resistance movement in general did much to fortify the concept of a Finland founded on law, a *Rechtsstaat,* in short.

MONARCHISTS. On December 6, 1917, the Finns proclaimed their independence (q.v.). Two days previously their constitutional committee, set up by the Senate (q.v.) and under the chairmanship of K. J. Ståhlberg (q.v.), had recommended the establishment of a Republic of Finland. With the outbreak of the Civil War (q.v.) at the end of January 1918, however, and the subsequent intervention of German forces on the White side, the Monarchist party grew in Finland.

For a monarchy to be created, a vote of five-sixths of the members of the legislature was required under traditional Finnish constitutionalist rulings. Even in the rump Parliament after the Civil War, this number of votes could not be mustered.

The Monarchists had another approach for legitimizing their demands, however. They claimed, with justification, that the Form of Government of 1772 (q.v.) from the Swedish times had not been repealed, and that it was *the* constitutional body of rules that had prevailed as fundamental law throughout the period of the Grand Duchy (q.v.). By the Form of Government Finland was a monarchy. What was more, Finland had, as a matter of fact, always been under monarchical rule.

On October 9, 1918, the prince of Hesse, Friedrich Karl, was elected king of Finland by a parliamentary majority (not five-sixths). Previously feelers had been put out to the Swedish royal family and to the family of Kaiser Wilhelm II, but to no avail. Friedrich Karl, who had had some leadership experience as governor of the Cameroons, was to take the name of Väinö I. He had started to learn Finnish. Ten days after acceptance of the Finnish throne, though, he found it prudent to withdraw, as the collapse of imperial Germany made the German connection a hindrance to the recognition of Finnish independence. The fact that the Finnish Monarchists went on, so late in the day, with the project of a German monarchy for Finland was a testimony to their lack of understanding of the course of world events.

Not all the Monarchists were pro-German, however. Enckell (q.v.) and Mannerheim (q.v.) were supporters of the Entente Powers, a consideration that enabled Mannerheim, as regent of Finland, to confirm the Republican Constitution on July 17, 1919.

An important feature of this constitution was a strong presidency, whose occupant was to be indirectly elected. This aspect of the constitution was a consolation for the Monarchists. In another form it was an embodiment of what they always wanted: a strong executive.

The obsession with having a German-style monarchy (which, as far as J. K. Paasikivi (q.v.) for example was concerned, also meant a close relationship with imperial Germany) was part of a basic outlook among many leading Finns that Finland could not stand alone in the world. This outlook did not expire with the aborting of the Finnish monarchy.

MOSCOW, PEACE OF. The Peace of Moscow concluded the Winter War (q.v.) between Finland and the Soviet Union. According to the peace treaty itself, the peace was signed on March 12, 1940. In fact, the signing did not actually occur until one o'clock on the morning of March 13, a delay caused by the consternation of the Finnish delegation at the unwillingness of the Soviet delegates, led by V. M. Molotov, to consider any meaningful alleviation in terms. President Kyösti Kallio (q.v.) was reluctant to make this peace, and two ministers in the government opposed it.

Article 2 of the peace required the ceding to the Soviet Union of the Karelian Isthmus (q.v.), certain islands in the Gulf of Finland (including Suursaari), a large part of Salla, and in the farthest north the Finnish part of Kalastajasaarento (Rybachy), though not the mainland Petsamo (q.v.) area. Finnish naval power was to be severely restricted in the Petsamo area and adjacent waters (Article 5), though this was, in effect, a repetition of the provisions of Article 6 of the 1920 Peace of Tartu (q.v.).

At the mouth of the Gulf of Finland the peninsula of Hanko was to be leased for thirty years for the establishment of a Soviet base there (Article 4). Equally ominous was the Soviet requirement (Article 7) for a railroad to be built from Kandalaksha on the White Sea to Kemijärvi in northern Finland, the Finns having to build the Finnish section (Article 7). The ostensible purpose of this railroad was commercial, but to the Finns it looked like a rapid-transit line for Soviet troops in any future invasion of Finland, or Scandinavia through Finland.

Article 3 of the peace enjoined upon both contracting parties the obligation not to enter into coalitions against each other. By reference to this provision, Molotov was soon able to frustrate any Finnish intentions of adhering to a Nordic Defense Alliance (q.v.), or, somewhat later, of entering a political union with Sweden. Thus the Peace of Moscow became an instrument of control over Finland.

To many Finns the peace treaty seemed only to be the thin edge of the wedge. After it the Soviet government demanded that Soviet troops, traveling to and from the Hanko base, should use the railroad through southern Finland, though the Finns had understood that these transports would occur by sea. Åland (q.v.) had to be demilitarized and a Soviet consulate set up there, while, in regard to the Petsamo region, the Soviet government demanded an increasing share in the nickel deposits (q.v.).

At the Peace of Moscow Finland lost more than one-tenth of its territorial area, and 400,000 people had to be evacuated from the lost lands. Deep resentment and uncertainty were bred.

MURMANSK LEGION. Toward the end of the Finnish Civil War (q.v.) in early April 1918, some of the Finnish Red leaders thought of enlisting British aid in their cause with the proposal that the British forces would help expel the Germans from Finland and overthrow the pro-German Finnish Whites. Though the British Consul in Moscow, Robert Bruce Lockhart, was attracted by the proposal, nothing came of it. In May, the principal Finnish Red leader involved, Oskari Tokoi, further suggested that East Karelia (q.v.) be used as a base by the Allies from which to invade Finland and defeat both Germans and Finnish Whites.

He offered the services of Finnish Red Guards, who were already in East Karelia, for this purpose. Since Allied intervention (q.v.) forces were now in Murmansk to prevent the establishment of German submarine bases there and gradually to advance down the Murmansk railroad, Tokoi's offer was accepted. A force of between one thousand and two thousand Red Guards from Finland was formed into a legion under British command. The Finns were either Red Guards who had crossed the border in the Civil War, coming mainly from the areas of northern Finland that were difficult for the Reds to hold, or they were Finnish lumbermen who were already in East Karelia when the Civil War broke out and had declared themselves for the Red cause.

Tokoi, who was soon to join the Murmansk Legion himself, even wanted to go to the United States and recruit Finnish-Americans, in the name of the Allied cause, for the legion. This proposal was not accepted.

Tokoi claimed that he had discussed the original scheme to found a Finnish Legion with Lenin (q.v.) and that the latter had said he had nothing against the idea, but that, after Brest-Litovsk, could not openly endorse action against the Germans. Tokoi, however, ran foul of many of the Finnish Red leaders in Russia. Eino Rahja came north to Sorokka (Russian: Soroka) to try to take the legion back to the Bolsheviks; the British navy warned him off. In the end Otto Wille Kuusinen (q.v.), Kullervo Manner, Rahja, and others condemned Tokoi to death as a traitor to the cause.

With the armistice between the Allies and Germany of November 11, 1918, the Murmansk Legion, which had engaged in a bit of skirmishing with White forces in East Karelia, had no raison d'être. Painfully, the British pressed a solution upon the Finnish government. Most of the members of the legion and their families would be allowed to return to Finland, each case being investigated there with British representatives present. Those with a grave involvement in the Civil War were not to be allowed to stay. There were thirty-six of these—who were seen off from Turku (q.v.) harbor by the British envoy to Finland, Lord Acton. There was also a proscribed list of those whom the Finnish authorities would under no circumstances consider. On the list was the name of Oskari Tokoi, who went to Canada as a lumberjack, migrating to the United States in 1920 and ultimately becoming editor of the Finnish newspaper *Raivaaja* in Fitchburg, Massachusetts.

British pressure upon the Finnish government in this question was closely connected with Britain's de jure recognition of an independent Finnish state.

-N-

NATIONAL COALITION PARTY (*Kansallinen Kokoomus*). The official name of the Finnish Conservative party. The National Coalition party was formed in December 1918 by a group of prominent Finnish-speaking Finns, most of whom were from the Old Finn (q.v.) party but some of whom had formerly been Young Finns (q.v.). The most notable of the latter was P. E. Svinhufvud (q.v.), who was just about to lose his post as Holder of Supreme Power in Finland.

Perhaps the tightest bond between the different members of the founding group was, apart from their Finnish-language nationalism, a conviction that monarchy was the best form of government for their country (s.v. Monarchists). Since the German candidate for the Finnish throne had withdrawn a few weeks earlier on the collapse of Germany in the World War, the National Coalition party founders were, in this sense, born losers.

In other respects, however, they were far from being losers. The National Coalition party rapidly became the voice of the Finnish-speaking elite, ready to push Finnicization forward as savagely as circumstances, after a vicious Civil War (q.v.) on tougher issues than language, would permit. The party became, and has remained, the political expression of many interlocking conservative-minded elites: of banking and finance, industry, education (q.v.), the Church, and the armed forces (q.v.).

In pre–World War I days the party's demands for the supremacy of the Finnish language (q.v.) alienated the Swedish-speaking elite. Only a few figures in the National Coalition party — but one of them was J. K. Paasikivi (q.v.) — protested against the excess of these demands. So nationalist was the party that in 1933 it even formed an electoral alliance with the People's Patriotic Movement (q.v.) (the IKL), who were fascists.

The identification of the National Coalition party with military patriotism made it suspect after World War II. Yet it was a member of that party, admittedly a very cranky one, who held the trust of the Russians and built up the modus vivendi with them. This was, of course, Paasikivi, a Compliant (q.v.) in the early twentieth century.

The National Coalition party increased its membership rapidly in the early years after the war, partly perhaps because it was so suspect to the Russians that it became a rallying point of a quiet protest. It also began to adopt, as with Conservative parties elsewhere in Europe, programs with a social-policy content.

For most of the Kekkonen (q.v.) period the party was relegated, and Kekkonen came to regard it as the chief forum of his opponents, especially as the National Coalition party had, with the Social Democrats (q.v.), sponsored the candidature of Olavi Honka in the 1961 presidential election campaign as a nonparty contender against Kekkonen. In the 1968 presidential election the National Coalition party again fielded a man against Kekkonen: the banker Matti Virkkunen.

Like the Social Democrats a decade or so earlier, the Conservatives in 1973 came to Canossa and supported the continuance of Kekkonen in office without an election (partly to secure the Free Trade Agreement with the European Economic Community). Still, the National Coalition party continued to be overlooked as far as participation in government was concerned (all governments in Finland are coalition or minority or caretaker governments). An alleged correspondence of interests between Soviet dislike of the party and Center party concern to keep power has been projected as the reason.

In the post-Kekkonen era of the 1980s the National Coalition party came into its own, helping to take the country into the European Community (Union) and ruling the roost with the Center party. Its sterling Finnish patriotism seems to be once more swinging toward Germany. Some would only point to Brussels and argue that this has become the National Coalition party's equivalent to Kekkonen's Moscow.

In or out of the government, the forces around the National Coalition party should never be underestimated. When out of office for years, the party's supporters exerted their power through their other connections—business, cultural, or otherwise. Since the party feels it can handle the international milieu in which it is plunging Finland ever more (while trumpeting patriotism), this party—especially in its role as international mediator—will certainly be around for a long time.

NAZI-SOVIET PACT. On August 23, 1939, Nazi Germany and the Soviet Union signed what was entitled a Nonaggression Pact. This was startling to those Finns who had previously regarded the security of their country in terms of the maintenance of a strict Finnish neutrality (q.v.) alongside the confrontational balance between the latently hostile powers of Nazi Germany and the Soviet Union. Now, not merely had these two totalitarian states become friendly, but in their act of friendship they had cut out the Western states.

In part, the border states (like Finland) had been, albeit unwittingly, a cause of this. In previous discussions with Great Britain and France, the Soviet Union had hammered away at a concept of "indirect aggression," by which was meant the use of the border states as springboards for aggression against the Soviet Union. To prevent this, the Soviet government demanded, in their negotiations with the Western powers, the right to move forward through the territories of the border states to "guarantee" them. This was a great stumbling block to Soviet-Allied accord, as the Western powers upheld the rights of the border states against a concession to Soviet emergency politics of this kind. In the end, too late in the day, the British negotiators, at least, were preparing to give way and include a secret protocol in a treaty with the Soviet Union that would have recognized this Soviet need.

There was certainly a secret protocol to the Nazi-Soviet Pact. By it Poland was divided and Lithuania placed in the German sphere. Besserabia, Latvia, Estonia, and Finland were placed in the Soviet sphere, as was Lithuania shortly afterward, in exchange for extra areas of Poland for Nazi Germany.

Rumors of a secret protocol filtered through to some Finns—Paasikivi (q.v.) is said to have learned of it from information given by the U.S. embassy in Moscow, but no one was sure. Whether the rumors had any effect on Finnish Foreign Minister Eljas Erkko (q.v.) is not known. He certainly made no haste to change his policy and stuck, until far too late, to a policy of rigid neutrality and no territorial concessions.

The behavior of the Soviet Union toward the Baltic States of Estonia, Latvia, and Lithuania has formed the basis of a latter-day folk wisdom in Finland, according to which all Soviet talk about the need to prevent "indirect aggression" against the Soviet Union was only a smoke screen for the aggressions of the Soviet Union itself. No master plan for such aggression has so far turned up in the Soviet archives, however, and later Soviet policy seems to have matched closely German successes in the West—it was not until the fall of France in June 1940 that the Baltic States were finally taken over by the Soviet Union. Above all, there is also an important point in the difference in geopolitical importance between the Baltic States and Finland.

What can be deduced is a certain correspondence between the Nazi-Soviet Pact and the 1938 Munich agreement between Nazi Germany and the Western powers: border states were, where necessary, suitable pawns between hostile powers.

The mystery of the Nazi-Soviet Nonagression Pact remains. Prima facie, the powers took up forward positions against one another, and *agreed* to do so. Yet the Nazi invasion of the Soviet Union in 1941 caught Stalin off guard. Had he taken the Nonaggression Pact as an act of reassurance? Was it a safeguard, in his eyes, against the old Soviet fear of Western interventionism?

One solution to the mystery which has recently surfaced in Russia is that the pact unleashed war in the West, and with it the prospect of European revolution. In this context, the Terijoki government (q.v.), established by the Russians on Finnish soil at the beginning of the Winter War (q.v.), becomes a revolutionary government—a first stage for Europe, as it were.

Little concrete evidence has been advanced for this kind of a theory. It is surely (to some extent, at least) contradicted by the patience with which the Soviet negotiators in the fall of 1939 tried to make a deal with the Finns.

NEUTRALITY. The Finns would like to be neutral, but their history seems to show that it has not always been possible to found their security upon a strict neutrality alone. In this the position of Finland has differed from that of Switzerland—and even from that of Sweden.

In historical terms, the institution of neutrality has arisen from two general situations: the desire to protect cargoes at sea from the depredations of the belligerents and the desire to keep one's territory free from war. In both situations the concept of an inviolate space has to prevail.

Both these aspects of neutrality have had their significance for the Finns. To their consternation, their mercantile fleet, an important source of foreign exchange for the whole country and source of livelihood for the peasant farmers who engaged in summer navigation, was seized and destroyed by the British in the Crimean War (q.v.). The Finnish mercantile fleet, of course, flew the Russian mercantile flag.

After the war, this gave rise for demands for a distinct Finnish mercantile flag. The Liberals associated with the newspaper the *Helsingfors Dagblad* even discussed an extension of the neutrality of Åland (q.v.), guaranteed in Paris in 1856, to cover the whole of Finland. Thus neutrality at sea and territorial neutrality became fused in this school of Finnish thinking. It is also worth noting that neutrality reasoning coincided with an emerging sense of statehood—"separatism," the Russians were to call it.

The dissident Finn Becker Bey (q.v.) drew the natural conclusion from this: an independent and neutral Finland guaranteed by the powers. His contemporaries, back home in Finland, were aghast, but in 1885, when danger of war between Great Britain and Russia was again threatening, a Finnish emissary, Robert Runeberg (son of the national poet J. L. Runeberg [q.v.]), appeared at the British embassy in Saint Petersburg to plead for the neutrality of Finland should war break out. And behind Runeberg was the respected Finnish senator H. W. Zilliacus.

Even in autonomous Finland, therefore, neutrality had been seen as a means for avoiding getting trapped in the confrontation between the West and Russia. Since this confrontational situation has endured into the twentieth century, it is hardly surprising that independent Finland has also been drawn to neutrality, though it has been difficult to convince other states of its worth. In the mid-1930s, when Finland proclaimed an identification with Nordic neutrality, the Soviet Union felt that this would be too weak a bulwark against the pressure of Nazi Germany.

Independent Finland has often, therefore, chosen a modus vivendi with one of the sides in the confrontation. In 1941, after the Soviet denial of Finland's neutrality in the Winter War (q.v.), Finland chose cobelligerency (q.v.) with Nazi

Germany, while since 1944 it has had to lean to the Soviet side.

In the Finnish-Soviet Treaty (q.v.) of 1948, neutrality was expressed as an aspiration (though the term "neutrality" was not used), but a great deal of labor was also put into showing that the treaty itself did not really contradict Finnish neutrality.

In the sense of the aspiration to neutrality, mentioned in the preamble to the 1948 treaty, President Urho Kekkonen (q.v.) developed a creative line of "neutrality policy," the key to which was the promotion of conditions that would prevent a conflagration ever arising. This policy aimed at reducing the weight of the confrontation between the powers, refusing to accept the precepts of Cold War thinking. Hence was born one of the most valuable moments in Finnish foreign policy, expressed through the attempt to promote the Nordic Nuclear-Weapon-Free Zone (q.v.), the process leading to the Conference on Security and Cooperation in Europe (q.v.), and the candidature of Max Jakobson for the post of U.N. secretary-general. Yet deep down, Kekkonen always cherished the hope of recognition of a Finnish neutrality in the most traditional sense.

The Finns' almost obsessive interest in neutrality could be seen even quite recently in respect of their initial reaction to integration (q.v.) politics. Carl Bildt, then Swedish Prime Minister, expressed the view that integration overrode his country's traditional neutrality, but the Finnish Foreign Minister of the early 1990s, Paavo Väyrynen, clung doggedly to neutrality for Finland. Some believed that neutrality represented a kind of independence alongside integration, like having your cake and eating it, too. Others had not forgotten the seemingly eternal confrontation between the West and Russia, which might have been only temporarily in respite. Today, with the downgrading of Russia in the world and with a supposedly multilateral solution to Finland's security problem being brought by Finnish membership in the European Union, the case for neutrality seems to be slipping a bit.

NICKEL DEPOSITS. These were found in the Petsamo (q.v.) region in 1922, only two years after the area had been ceded by

Soviet Russia to Finland by the Peace of Tartu (q.v.). There was insufficient capital in Finland for their exploitation, so the concession was given to the Canadian-British Mond Nickel Company.

During the Winter War (q.v.) the Russians occupied the mining and industrial area, but did not demand its cession as a condition of the Peace of Moscow (q.v.). In the period between the Winter War and the Continuation War (q.v.) the Germans, desperately short of nickel for their own war effort, and cut off now from Canadian nickel, began to take an interest in securing nickel from Finland. The British were expelled, and in the summer of 1940, when Finland was still neutral, a deal was made under the shadow of the Nazi-Soviet Pact (q.v.) by which Germany gained 60% of the nickel ore production and the Soviet Union 40%. Recent research has shown that Finland's willingness to agree to German demands on this question was a factor that brought the German leadership to stand up for Finland against Molotov in November 1940.

After the Continuation War the mines (and, indeed, the whole Petsamo region) were ceded to the Soviet Union. This industrial area is now a major source of pollution for Finnish Lapland.

NONAGGRESSION TREATY WITH THE SOVIET UNION. This treaty was signed in 1932 for a three-year period, but was renewed before its expiration for a further period of ten years. Article 2 of the treaty bound Finland to neutrality (q.v.) should the Soviet Union be attacked by another state.

Similar treaties were made by the Soviet Union with other border states, but the rise of Nazi Germany worsened the picture for the Soviet leaders. Nonaggression treaties were no longer enough; the Soviet Union, now ready to enter the League of Nations, planned with France the creation of an Eastern Locarno security system.

The Finns thought that such a tighter security system, far from protecting them, would draw them either into conflict or more tightly into the embrace of the Soviet Union, whose troops, once on Finnish territory to safeguard it, would never be gotten to leave.

No Nordic state showed itself particularly joyful at the entry of the Soviet Union into the League of Nations, but for Finland a cool Nordic neutrality went hand in hand with a torpedoing of the whole idea of an Eastern Locarno.

Later in the 1930s Soviet diplomats Erik Assmus, Boris Stein (q.v.), and Boris Yartsev (q.v.) tried to interest Finland in bilateral security arrangements, but these were also nonstarters. The country drifted, unknowingly, toward the Winter War (q.v.).

NORDEK. This is one of the unresearched—and hence largely unwritten—chapters in the complex and fitful history of Nordic cooperation (q.v.).

The core of the Nordek project was to be the creation of a customs union among the Nordic states. In addition, certain common institutions—notably a Nordic Investment Bank (q.v.)—were to be set up. The latter institution came into being, but not the customs union itself. The failure of the project is often cited as an example of the strains that always emerge when firmer schemes for Nordic cooperation are mooted. Some particular aspects are, however, worth recalling.

All five Nordic states were EFTA states, Finland through the FINEFTA agreement (q.v.). By the end of the 1960s, however, it had become clear that Great Britain, the prime force in EFTA, again intended to seek membership in the EEC, leaving its EFTA companions adrift. As early as the spring of 1968, therefore, the Danish prime minister, Hilmar Baunsgaard, began to talk in the Nordic Council (q.v.) of the possibility of a customs union among the Nordic states. Two years later, however, he definitely changed his tune and tried to persuade the Swedish prime minister, Olof Palme, to take Sweden into the EEC—for EEC membership was what Baunsgaard now apparently wanted for Denmark.

The projected Nordek market of twenty million thus gave way before an EEC market over ten times larger. Indeed, suspicions soon arose that Denmark (as well as manufacturing interests in Sweden) had all along seen the Nordek project as either a stopgap or as a lever for an EEC arrangement. In the event, Denmark entered the EEC, while the other Nordic states concluded free-trade agreements with the EEC, Finland's free trade agreement (q.v.) being ratified in 1973.

While undoubtedly the major factor in the case, the fate of Nordek cannot entirely be laid at the door of the EEC. In Finland Prime Minister Mauno Koivisto (q.v.) was an enthusiastic advocate of the Nordek project, so much so that President Urho Kekkonen (q.v.), quite characteristically, accused Koivisto and government officials of rushing ahead with the project and keeping the presidency somewhat uninformed of what was occurring.

Kekkonen was, in part at least, playing the innocent. He had originally appeared to support the Nordek project as a shield against an EEC penetration of Northern Europe. After his visit to Moscow in February 1970, he discovered that Nordek would permit not merely a desirable flow of Nordic capital into Finland but would serve as a backdoor through which *international* capital would flow into the country so that Finnish economic life would be dominated by Western European or even global capitalist forces.

So, in March 1970, Finland withdrew, blaming the other Nordic states for being lured by the EEC. The prime minister of Sweden, Olof Palme, blamed Finland and especially Urho Kekkonen himself.

NORDENSKIÖLD, NILS ADOLF ERIK (1832–1901). Mineralogist, historian of science, explorer, and public figure. Always claiming to be "a Swede by descent", Nordenskiöld was born in Helsinki (q.v.) of a noble family and educated at the Porvoo Lyceum under the cane-swinging J. L. Runeberg (q.v.) and later at the University of Helsinki.

As the son of the head of the Finnish mining administration, Nordenskiöld, when a university student, was able to make a trip to the mines of the Urals with his father, as well as a study trip to Berlin. A combination of trips of this kind was not unusual for Finnish savants, eastward signifying untapped knowledge and westward a confirmation of the principles of science.

All hopes of preferment for the young Nordenskiöld, whether in Finland or elsewhere in he Russian Empire, were soon blighted by his own behavior in openly identifying on festive occasions during and after the Crimean War (q.v.) with "the free and sane land of Sweden." These expressions of Scandinavianism were characteristic of those who, during the Crimean War, had hoped for the restoration of Finland to Sweden.

Nordenskiöld went into exile in Sweden, becoming a Swedish citizen, and even sitting in the Swedish Estate of Nobles until its abolition in 1865. He was appointed professor of mineralogy at the Swedish Academy of Sciences. His ambivalent attitude toward his original homeland was seen in his application for the post of professor of geology at the University of Helsinki only a decade after he had gone into exile.

Had he been appointed, he would have sought to promote the name of Finland by organizing scientific expeditions, backed by government financing (each expedition would have cost the equivalent of the upkeep of only one hundred soldiers). This brilliant scheme was frustrated by the opposition of Count Nikolai Adlerberg, governor-general of the Grand Duchy (q.v.), to the appointment of Nordenskiöld.

So instead he became one of Sweden's most famous explorers. Following in the footsteps of the Swedish scientists Sven Lovén and Otto Torell, he first became engaged in expeditions to Spitsbergen, then unclaimed territory. With Torell, he even harbored hopes of striking out to the North Pole.

By the early 1870s Nordenskiöld was already turning his attention to the Northeast Passage—the sea route from the Atlantic along the northern shores of Eurasia and through the Bering Strait to the Pacific. Apart from the obvious connection between an industrialized Europe and the markets of China and Japan, Nordenskiöld also envisaged the establishment of ports at the mouths of the great Siberian rivers and the opening up thereby of the Siberian interior.

Optimistically hoping for official Russian backing, he had to rely instead on the support of the Russian merchant Alexander Sibiriakov, of Oscar Dickson of the Scottish-Swedish Gothenberg trading house, of the Swedish monarch Oscar II, and of the Swedish government. His successful voyage in the *Vega* (1878–1880) through the passage and home by way of Asian waters and the Mediterranean brought him the Order of Saint Vladimir of the Russian Empire as well as a Dutch prize of 25,000 guilders, first offered as an inducement for this feat of seamanship in 1596.

Alas, Nordenskiöld's epic voyage did not signify the development of a great avenue of commerce along the waters of the Eurasian northern rim. This was partly due to the prospect of opening up Siberia and the northern China markets by the Trans-Siberian railway and its extensions, which began construction in 1891. It was left to the Soviet Union to try to utilize the northern sea route, with the aid of Finnish icebreakers.

Nordenskiöld's later career involved the exploration of the Greenland interior in 1883, proving fairly conclusively (and contrary to his own expectations) that the interior was a gigantic ice cap.

Nordenskiöld's last significant act was to join the deputation bearing the International Cultural Address (q.v.) to Tsar Nicholas II, a petition of protest against the abrogation of Finnish constitutional rights through the tsar's 1899 February Manifesto (q.v.).

In 1863 Nordenskiöld married Anna Mannerheim, a Finnish noblewoman, whose future nephew, Carl Gustaf Mannerheim (q.v.), was to become marshal and president of Finland.

NORDIC BALANCE. A concept of interstate relations worked out largely by the Norwegian security policy expert, Arne Olav Brundtland. In spite of there being no formal alliance among the Nordic states as a group, Brundtland argued that their security policies had dovetailed into each other, had been in their moderation a factor of stability in the north, and had ultimately constituted a source of mutual support.

The concept started with the fact that Norway and Denmark had never had a maximum input in their NATO membership (a no-base policy, no nuclear weapons on their soil in peacetime, no troop concentrations in the outlying regions of Finmark and Bornholm). Finland, for its part, had only a limited military relationship with the Soviet Union, expressed in a Finnish-Soviet Treaty (q.v.) and not in Warsaw

Pact membership. In between lay neutral Sweden, the pivot of the balance.

Pressure by a power, or power bloc, on one Nordic country (so the theory ran) stimulated elsewhere in the north a matching input from the other side. Thus, if the Soviet Union had pressed Finland, then NATO might have been able to persuade Sweden to abandon its neutrality. Alternatively, Norway and Denmark might have abandoned the limitations on the NATO presence in their countries. The threat of the latter step, argued Norwegian and Danish political leaders in the 1960s, was a factor enabling Finland to resist Soviet pressure at the time of the 1961 Note Crisis (q.v.).

In Finland the concept of the Nordic Balance was not much liked. It seemed to make of Finland a passive pawn, unable to handle successfully its own relations with the Soviet Union.

In general, the Nordic Balance concept was too "Western." It did not explain how the growing NATO influence in Denmark and Norway in the late 1950s (through the BALTAP arrangements) was hardly countered by successful Soviet pressure on Finland. On the contrary, in the Note Crisis the Soviet Union was alleged to have given way in Finland, refraining from military talks. In fact, the Soviet Union just went on expanding its Murmansk base. Herein lay the real weakness of the Nordic Balance scenario. It was excessively "political," seeing interaction between states and ignoring the global, military dimension.

NORDIC COOPERATION. Three of the Nordic states (Sweden, Norway, and Denmark) are monarchies, and two (Iceland and Finland) are republics. Three of the Nordic states gained their independence, or had it restored, only this century (Norway in 1905, Finland in 1917, and Iceland in 1944). Yet to a very great degree these five states share a common political culture, and what emerges from their history is an aspiration toward a rational politics.

These states have a parliamentary tradition, though in Finland it has been tempered by a strong presidency. In terms of the human rights laid down in the 1948 United Nations Universal Declaration of Human Rights the Nordic states do well.

In all the Nordic states the official religion is that of the Lutheran church (q.v.), though in Finland there is a second state religion, the Orthodox church (q.v.). Lutheranism has its authoritarian side, but its emphasis on literacy and its acceptance of the election of the clergy have probably helped strengthen the common trend toward democracy in the north.

The political—and to some extent, cultural—dominance of Sweden, whether over Finland or over Norway, as well as the historical reminders of the late-medieval Union of Kalmar (q.v.), also contribute to the joint heritage. Great importance should also be attached to the closely related nature of three of the Nordic languages (Swedish, Danish, and Norwegian), while in Finland there is a Swedish-speaking minority and the land is officially bilingual. All over the Nordic area it should be possible to communicate in the modified form of Swedish known as *Skandinaviska*.

Politically, Nordic cooperation owes much to the mid-nineteenth-century current of opinion called Pan-Scandinavianism (q.v.). In 1872 Denmark, Norway, and Sweden formed a currency union, and in the same year the first uniform legislation emerged—the bill-of-exchange legislation. These steps were not difficult to attain at that time, with the existence of the Joint Kingdom of Sweden and Norway and a Kingdom of Denmark that controlled its dependency of Iceland. Finland, a Grand Duchy (q.v.) in the Russian Empire, fell outside all such arrangements.

Yet this was the start of a continuing process of harmonization of Nordic legislation, a process Finland joined after 1918. Finland never adhered to the currency union, which in any case disappeared finally in 1931 in the upheavals resulting from the abandonment of the gold standard.

After World War II, the first great achievement of Nordic cooperation was the abolition in 1952 of passport control for citizens of Nordic states visiting other Nordic states; this abolition took place even before the formation of the Nordic Council (q.v.), established in 1952, which introduced a common Nordic labor market in 1954—a matter of immense import for Finland, which joined the Nordic Council at the end of 1955.

In spite of the different security arrangements entered into by the Nordic states after World War II, a common penchant—even nostalgia—for neutrality (q.v.) has existed in them all (this may be seen in the reservations on NATO membership made by Norway and Denmark). The inhabitants of these states have been described as "reluctant Europeans." The attitude to Western European integration (q.v.) in at least four of the Nordic states has been hesitant.

It must still be said that, although voluntary associations like Pohjola-Norden, devoted to the promotion of cultural links among the Nordic states, have tried to further a consciousness of Nordic cooperation, no particularly dynamic Nordic ethos has been engendered. However reluctantly, eyes are being focused on more distant horizons.

NORDIC COUNCIL. Founded in 1952, the Nordic Council constitutes the structural framework for Nordic cooperation (q.v.). Finland joined the council at the end of 1955 with the proviso that foreign policy, security policy, and military issues were not to be dealt with there. Only recently has Finland lifted the ban it imposed on foreign policy discussions.

The Nordic Council comprises 87 members elected by the national parliaments or, in the case of the autonomous units, by the local representative bodies. Sweden has 20 representatives, Norway has 20, Finland has 18, Denmark has 16, Iceland has 7, while the Faroe Islands, Greenland, and the Åland Islands (q.v.) each send 2 representatives. This structure and representation recalls the ancestry of the Nordic Council, which stems from the Nordic Inter-Parliamentary Union (1907–1957), though lacking that association's concern for the solving of thorny international problems by means of arbitration.

Nevertheless, bearing in mind the cooperation of the Nordic states in the United Nations, and the fact that from 1971 onward a Nordic Council of Ministers has regularly met, it can be said that a certain wider, internationally oriented ethos often permeates these Nordic discussions. Still, the Nordic Council has been faulted on just this point in recent times, when it fended off requests from the Baltic States for membership or some form of participation in its work. A separate Baltic Sea Council, of the Scandinavian and Baltic States and Russia, Germany, and Poland was set up in Copenhagen in 1992.

The Nordic Council is not a supranational body, and it can only make recommendations to the national governments. In the Nordic Council of Ministers the consensus principle operates.

Under the auspices of the Nordic Council, many basic reforms, meaningful for the ordinary citizens of the Nordic lands, have been attained. Mention should be made of the common labor market and reciprocity in social security benefits, though in respect of the former Finland continued to impose restrictions on the employment of Nordic teachers and researchers until quite recently.

The greater hopes for economic cooperation envisaged in Nordic Council planning—Nordic Customs Union (q.v.) of the late 1950s, the ideas laid down in the Helsinki Agreement of 1962, the Nordek (q.v.) project of the late 1960s—have not been realized. External forces have been stronger.

NORDIC CUSTOMS UNION. The economic dimensions of Nordic cooperation (q.v.) reach back into the second half of the nineteenth century, but only after World War II were serious plans discussed for a Nordic Customs Union.

In 1948 a Joint Scandinavian Committee for Economic Cooperation was set up by the Danish, Icelandic, Norwegian, and Swedish governments. In 1954 the Nordic Council (q.v.) gave preliminary approval to a plan for the establishment of a common external Nordic customs tariff and for the removal of internal barriers to trade among the Nordic lands. At this time Finland was not yet a member of the Nordic Council.

It had already become clear that there were problems enough among the above-mentioned four Nordic states. In particular, tension arose between Denmark and Norway, and the Norwegian Right became expressly concerned about the need to protect many Norwegian industries. At the Harpsund discussions, therefore, a cautious, sectoral approach was recommended.

With the onset of negotiations for a common market elsewhere in Europe, which swiftly bore fruit in the 1957 Rome treaty, the Nordic states redoubled their efforts to find some kind of joint solution for their own economic future. Their position was complicated by the fact that Great Britain, which remained out of the Common Market, had sought to build up a free-trade area nonetheless associated with the Common Market. When this project was repulsed by the Rome treaty states, there still endured the possibility of a Nordic Customs Union as part of a wider free-trade area, dominated by the British.

Unfortunately, by the late 1950s, the Soviet authorities, egged on by even more strident representations from the Finnish Communist party (q.v.), had become suspicious of the idea of a Nordic Customs Union tied, in devious ways, to Western economic interests. By 1959, however, the idea of a separate Nordic Customs Union began to appear acceptable to the Soviet Union—and was, indeed, briefly suggested by the Finns to their Nordic partners.

In the same year EFTA was founded, and its pull was too strong to be resisted by the Nordic states, who joined it—a classic illustration once again of how external forces thwart purely Nordic solutions. Finland made its own—very successful—accommodation with EFTA by the FINEFTA Agreement (q.v.) signed in 1961.

The fate of Nordek in 1970 was much of a repeat of what had occurred in the late 1950s.

NORDIC DEFENSE ALLIANCE. The prime mover in this abortive proposal made in 1948 and 1949 was Sweden. The Soviet Union was deeply hostile, regarding the whole idea as one by which a North Atlantic alliance would, under the thinnest of disguises, penetrate Northern Europe. Sweden was anyway non grata to the Soviet Union for having accepted, though a neutral state, Marshall Plan aid.

The projected Nordic Defense Alliance would have been composed of Norway, Sweden, and Denmark. Finland, with the Finnish-Soviet Treaty (q.v.) signed in April 1948, would not have joined, though there was a favorable reference to the idea in Kekkonen's (q.v.) "Pajama-Pocket Speech" (q.v.) of January 23, 1952. In any case, the Nordic Defense Alliance project could not resist the Norwegians' compulsive yearning for a direct Atlantic connection, nor could it staunch the Danes' qualms that the United States would not willingly provide arms for a purely Nordic alliance. In April 1949 NATO was created, and Sweden, with its dreams of being a dominant state in the North once again thwarted, was left to nurse its traditional neutrality.

Thus the Swedes did no better than the Finns had done, when, after the conclusion of the Winter War (q.v.) in 1940, they too had dreamed of a Nordic Defense Alliance outside the protection of the great powers.

NORDIC INVESTMENT BANK. The creation of a bank of this kind was discussed in the late 1950s in connection with the proposals for a Nordic Customs Union (q.v.). The Nordek (q.v.) project of the late 1960s also envisaged the creation of a Nordic Investment Bank. In fact, the foundation of this bank in Helsinki in 1976 is practically all that has survived from the aborted Nordek project.

Basically, the function of the bank is to grant credits for investments that concern at least two Nordic lands or would promote collaboration between Nordic firms in export markets outside the Nordic area. The Nordic Investment Bank may also mediate foreign loans for projects of regional development in the Nordic lands.

Finland contributed 17% of the initial capital of the bank, Norway 19.2%, Denmark 21.3%, Sweden 41.4%, and Iceland 1.1%.

It is noteworthy that a recent Nordic proposal to found a Baltic Bank, for the channeling of Nordic investments into the Baltic States, was rejected by the Nordic finance ministers at a Helsinki meeting. They referred to the growing economic difficulties in the Nordic states and rejected it in favor of the IMF, or the World Bank—a sad comment on the inability of Northern Europe to get in at the ground level as new opportunities begin to occur on the other side of the Baltic.

NORDIC NUCLEAR-WEAPON-FREE ZONE. The creation of such a zone (originally called the Nordic Nuclear-Free Zone) has been on the agenda of Finnish foreign policy since President Urho Kekkonen (q.v.) first proposed it in a Paasikivi Society meeting in May 1963.

His plan was closely connected with the proposal of the former Swedish foreign minister, Östen Undén, for the establishment in Europe of a "club" of states that would not have nuclear weapons on their territory. Kekkonen also referred with approval to Latin American attempts (ultimately successful) to set up a nuclear-weapon-free zone for their continent. In Europe proposals for such zones grew (like the Polish Rapacki plan) out of thinking about geographical disengagement in Central Europe and fear of a revanchist Germany, armed with nuclear weapons.

Since, to the West, there appeared to be no dramatic confrontation in the North between NATO and the Warsaw Pact, the utility of a Nordic nuclear-weapon-free zone seemed questionable to the Americans and Western Europeans. Ironically, the biggest nuclear arsenal in Europe, if not in the world, lay in the Kola Peninsula, adjacent to the proposed zone, yet the Kekkonen plan would not have put Soviet territory into the zone. To add to the West's suspicions, Nikita Khrushchev had been advocating the creation of a Nordic and Baltic Sea nuclear-weapon-free zone for several years. No nuclear weapons were sited in the Nordic states anyway. What then was afoot in the Kekkonen proposal?

In the proposal itself Kekkonen explained that in this matter the Nordic states had made only a unilateral, self-denying ordinance. He referred to the Cuban missile crisis of 1962 as a horrifying example of how rapidly events can escalate anywhere in the world. His proposal undoubtedly also reflected some of the elements of the 1961 Finnish Note Crisis (q.v.), particularly in connection with the growing NATO naval interest in Denmark and Norway, which had retained their option of having nuclear weapons on their territories in wartime (the continuing wish to retain this option was to be one of the obstacles to the creation of the zone).

As to the role of the Soviet Union, it was left to later Finnish commentators to underline the need for superpower guarantees and that a state cannot guarantee itself by including its own territory in such a zone. What this argument led to—and it was implicit in the original Kekkonen proposal—was the acceptance of an overarching, superpower nuclear balance in the world. The problem lay in the danger of proliferation.

It could therefore be argued that the 1968 Nonproliferation Treaty, which the Nordic countries signed and ratified, cut the ground out from under the Kekkonen plan.

The development of weapon technology, as Kekkonen pointed out in May 1978 in speaking before the Swedish Institute for International Affairs, gave a new relevance to his basic idea, however. Thus, with the renewed stress on cruise missiles, Kekkonen saw that the position of the Nordic states had worsened. Wherever these weapons were sited, the territorial airspace of the Nordic states might be infringed upon once they were used.

In spite of global weapons-reduction policies, projects for regional disengagement have not lost their significance in actuality. For example, the work of dismantling the nuclear frontier in Germany has been an essential part of the global deals.

It is interesting to note that, in an interview in *Aftenposten* of September 5, 1991, J. J. Holst, the Norwegian Minister of Defense, proclaimed his belief in the virtues of a Nordic-Baltic nuclear-weapon-free zone for the security of the Baltic States. In addition, the question of nuclear weaponry in the Barents and Norwegian seas still awaits solution.

NORTH KARELIA. This is the area around Joensuu, which in 1960 became an administrative unit—a province—the capital of which is Joensuu. In light of later enthusiasm to trim the public-sector budget, a proposal was mooted for the abolition of the province and its fusion into something bigger, like a Savo-Karelia province.

The proposal was not adopted, and it would have been a pity if it had been, for North Karelia had become famous in the 1970s as a result of the North Karelia Project, a sociomedical program of investigation and controlled behavior, the aim of which was to reduce cardiovascular and other diseases. In this investigation, great attention was paid to environmental and dietary factors; part of a way of life was under scrutiny. Far from producing a picture of a basically healthy rural life, the project turned up many disquieting features of life in the countryside.

NOTE CRISIS. This is one of the most important, and at the same time most tantalizing, episodes of the Kekkonen (q.v.) era.

In 1961 President Urho Kekkonen paid several visits to the West—to Great Britain, Austria, Canada, and the United

States. At the height of his U.S. visit, the Soviet government, on October 30, 1961, delivered a note to the Finnish embassy in Moscow. The note asked for military consultations under Article 2 of the Finnish-Soviet Treaty (q.v.).

The main burden of the note was the growing power of the West German *Bundeswehr* and especially its increasing influence on Norway and Denmark. West German naval might in the Baltic (a consequence, in fact, of the BALTAP arrangements of NATO that had been under way for some time) and the West German desire for the hydrogen bomb were heavily underscored in the note.

What was also mentioned was the alleged sympathy of certain circles in Sweden and Finland for these developments. Since a presidential election was shortly to be held in Finland, this particular part of the note looked like a distinct interference in Finnish internal politics, contrary to the express wording of Article 6 of the Finnish-Soviet Treaty.

The opposition candidate in the election, Olavi Honka, believing that his candidature was liable to endanger the security of the country, withdrew as a patriotic act, though the Social Democrats (q.v.) alone ran another candidate, Rafael Paasio. Urho Kekkonen, having previously traveled to Novosibirsk to meet Khrushchev and get the military consultations put off, was duly reelected. No military consultations were subsequently ever held.

Though the Finnish military, because of the second Berlin crisis in the late summer of 1961, had thought that a Soviet note to Finland might be dispatched, and though Andrei Gromyko later let it be known that the Soviet military really had wanted consultations, there were (and are) those in Finland who take the view that Kekkonen himself engineered the whole episode to secure his reelection. No clear evidence for this has so far emerged, though the Soviet embassy in Helsinki seems to have been concocting something in Kekkonen's favor.

It is clear that the Soviet government did want Kekkonen reelected. Nevertheless, since his trips westward, especially to the United States, were quite successful, there might also have been an element in the Soviet attitude of calling to the attention of their anchorman the direction in which the prime security interests of his country lay.

The successful denouement of the Note Crisis gave rise to excessive claims on the part of Kekkonen and other Finnish commentators that henceforth it was Finland's responsibility to take the initiative on whether Article 2 of the Finnish-Soviet Treaty was to be activated. These claims were sternly refuted by Soviet experts later in the decade.

As far as military consequences were concerned, the commander of the Finnish armed forces (q.v.), General Sakari Simelius, had argued all along that the note might never have been sent if Finnish military preparedness had been more reassuring to the Soviet Union. After the note, therefore, the defense of Lapland was taken more seriously in hand. Additionally, Article 17 of the Peace Treaty of February 10, 1947 (q.v.) was alleviated, and guided missiles were procured for the Finnish defense forces (without much urgency: it took fifteen years for the antiaircraft arm to get ground-to-air missiles).

Politically, the main internal effect was the enforcement of consensus (q.v.). No one could beat Kekkonen.

NOVEMBER MANIFESTO. This proclamation by Tsar Nicholas II, issued on November 4, 1905, formally put an end to the first period of the Years of Oppression (q.v.). It was issued a few days after the start of the Great Strike (q.v.) in Finland and may be seen as an attempt to undercut the power of the more extreme elements, especially of the workers' movement, in that event.

From several points of view, the November Manifesto was an apparent triumph for the Finnish constitutionalists' leader, Leo Mechelin (q.v.). For one thing, the manifesto was based on a draft he had sent to Saint Petersburg. For another, it called upon the traditional Finnish Senate (q.v.)—and not any kind of national assembly—to draw up a proposal for a new legislative organ, based on universal suffrage. The proposal was to be put to the last meeting of the old Diet of Four Estates (q.v.).

Thus, when Finland got its new unicameral legislature (q.v.) in 1906, the procedure for its creation had been in proper constitutional form. And above the legislature, the Senate remained. This so antagonized the Social Democrats (q.v.) that they expelled one of their members, J. K. Kari, who joined it.

What was important for Mechelin, too, was that shortly after the issuing of the November Manifesto he himself rejoined the Senate, from which he had been dismissed in 1903 by the Russian governor-general of Finland, N. I. Bobrikov (q.v.). The Compliants (q.v.) had now to clear out, and Mechelin felt he could restore the rule of constitutionalism.

Expressly set forth in the November Manifesto was the abrogation of many of the unification (q.v.) measures imposed on Finland in the first Years of Oppression. One of these was the decree of July 12, 1901, which introduced the draft into the Russian imperial army for young Finnish men, but the regulations for the introduction of the Russian language into the higher administrative echelons were not abolished.

It was thought at the time that the November Manifesto meant the abandonment of the principles of the February Manifesto (q.v.) of 1899, which had been the serious beginning of unification. A careful reading of the November Manifesto, however, shows only that the "basic rules" of the February Manifesto would not be observed in order that "the matters concerned could be dealt with through legislative action."

This, within a brief space of time, opened the way for imperial legislation, passed in a Russian Duma. Mechelin was to be sidestepped.

-O-

OLD FINLAND. This was the name given to the areas taken by Russia from Finland at the 1721 Peace of Uusikaupunki (q.v.) and the 1743 Peace of Turku (q.v.). The territories lost at Uusikaupunki were on the Karelian Isthmus (q.v.), including the city of Viipuri (now Vyborg), and on the northern shores of Lake Ladoga. At the Peace of Turku territory stretching westward from the Karelian Isthmus to the Kymi River was ceded.

The cession of these lands disturbed the economy of Finland, since the export of tar from the eastern forests could no longer go through Viipuri. On the other hand, as far as the isthmus and particularly Viipuri itself were concerned, the proximity of Saint Petersburg was a stimulus to trade.

Old Finland remained Finnish and Lutheran (q.v.) in character; indeed, the areas ceded in 1743 continued to be under the spiritual jurisdiction of the bishop of Porvoo. Viipuri retained, even strengthened, its cosmopolitan character, however, and received some positive influences from Saint Petersburg, especially in respect of female education.

The most negative aspect in the possession of these territories by Russia lay in the creation of the "donation estates"—lands granted by the Russian monarchs to Russian aristocrats. Serfdom had not been characteristic of Finland, but the conditions on the donation estates resembled serfdom for the peasants working there.

At the very end of 1811, Tsar Alexander I, under the influence of G. M. Armfelt (q.v.) and other Finns who were backed by the tsar's advisor M. M. Speransky (q.v.), decreed the reincorporation of Old Finland with the rest of Finland. This immeasurably strengthened the concept of Finland as a state (in spite of Speransky's deeper, unitary visions). But the problem of the donation estates remained.

In 1826, in desperation, Robert Rehbinder, the state secretary of the Committee of Finnish Affairs, suggested that the areas in which the donation estates lay should be put back into Russia. Fortunately his view was not acted upon. A few years later conditions on the estates were attacked in Snellman's (q.v.) paper, *Saima*. Not until 1867 (six years after the abolition of serfdom in Russia) was the Finnish Diet, now beginning to meet regularly, able to start on the work of redeeming the estates for the peasants who lived upon them.

OLD FINNS. The Old Finns were those who still followed the main lines laid down by the Fennoman party leaders, in contrast to a Young Finn (q.v.) group, which was in clear formation by 1894.

The tenets of belief of the Old Finn group in the last decade of the nineteenth century and the early years of the twentieth century were decreed unwaveringly by Yrjö Sakari Yrjö-Koskinen: a continuing hostility to the use of Swedish in official and cultural life, with which went a deeper concern that only a nation unified in the Finnish language could hope to withstand Russian imperial unification (q.v.) pressures. This outlook did not rule out the possibility of making a deal with the Russians. On the contrary, the modus vivendi was implicitly there, since the Russians need not fear the nonliberal, non-Western Fennoman.

The national unity posited by the Old Finns derived a philosophical and political justification from the Hegelian philosophy of J. W. Snellman (q.v.), but the tactics of seeking to attain a modus vivendi with the Russians led easily into a situation in which the Old Finns became Compliants (q.v.). National unity had been meant to be a source of strength, thus enabling negotiations to take place. Instead, it became something to be desperately maintained at the cost of making one concession after another. Swiftly, indeed, the very concept of national unity became hollow, a mere Hegelian fiction. The Young Finn group and nearly all the Swedish-speakers chose the path of passive resistance (q.v.), and the Social Democrats (q.v.) emerged, some of them from the ranks of the Old Finns, and having a very different set of concepts in regard to both unity and resistance.

The Old Finns did not oppose the promulgation of the tsar's 1899 February Manifesto (q.v.) and thereafter Yrjö-Koskinen succeeded in securing measures that brought parity for Finnish with Swedish as an official language. At the same time, Russian was introduced into the higher ranks of the administration. The Hegelian ethos was not working in the sense Yrjö-Koskinen and his followers had wanted. Before his death in 1903, Yrjö-Koskinen was increasingly isolated within his own party.

J. R. Danielson-Kalmari, who took over leadership, established compliance more in terms of pragmatic politics to which there were limits. In the first period of the Years of Oppression (q.v.) the Old Finns clung to senatorial office long after the constitutionalists had left, but in the second period the Old Finns resigned (in the fall of 1909) only a few months after the constitutionalists. Henceforth a national unity was seen in opposition to all future measures of unification from the Russian side. How fragile this unity, in its turn, was came out less than a decade later in the Finnish Civil War (q.v.).

The Old Finns supplied one president to independent Finland, J. K. Paasikivi (q.v.), whose post–World War II foreign policy of friendship with Russia greatly reflected Old Finn political concepts.

OPPRESSION, YEARS OF (Finnish: *sortovuodet,* Swedish: *ofärdsåren*). These years, when measures of imperial unification (q.v.) were imposed on Finland to the detriment of its autonomy (q.v.), lasted from 1899 to 1917. The years fall into three distinct periods of oppression, with a brief spell of alleviation between the first and second periods.

The first period lasted from the promulgation of the February Manifesto (q.v.) in 1899 until the Russian Revolution of 1905 and the Finnish Great Strike (q.v.) of the same year. During this period a number of imposing measures of unification (including in 1901 the abolition of the separate Finnish army and the subsequent calling up of young Finns into the Russian imperial forces) were brought about by decrees of the tsar.

When these measures were largely set aside by the 1905 November Manifesto (q.v.), Finland began to enjoy a brief period of real autonomy once more under a completely new unicameral legislature (q.v.).

Unfortunately for the Finns, the wording of the November Manifesto had left open the question of imperial legislation, which was the bone of contention between Finns and Russians. When, under the direction of P. A. Stolypin, imperial Russia began once more to reorganize itself, the question of imperial legislation came up again, but this time it was to go through a Russian constitutional organ—the Duma.

A new, second period of oppression began for the Finns, lasting from 1908 to 1914. Because Russian measures were now being adopted in a kind of Parliament—the Duma—it became very difficult for many of Finland's friends in the West to make a case against a Russian "arbitrary oppression" of Finland. In the British Parliament, the foreign secretary, Sir Edward Grey, argued in 1908 for an understanding of the "change in the constitution of Finland" because it had been "made by legislation, introduced and justified in public before the Duma."

While Stolypin certainly did not attempt, through the Duma or otherwise, to again impose Russian military service on Finnish youth, nevertheless the Finns had to pay financially for this privilege, and additional measures of unification (in regard to the pilot service) were gradually brought in. By 1909 even the Compliants (q.v.) had left the Finnish Senate, to be replaced largely by Russians born in Finland or, simply, Russians. The tsar continued to refuse to sign many of the reform proposals coming from the Finnish unicameral legislature, so that many valuable measures of social legislation were frustrated. When the Russian law for imperial legislation had finally passed through the Duma in 1910, the quality of the debate on Finland had disgusted even Sir Edward Grey.

The third period of oppression lasted from the outbreak of World War I until the March Revolution in Russia in 1917. Immediately after the outbreak of war, Finland was placed under military rule, which enabled the reactionary governor-general, F. A. Steyn, to intensify his police measures. In November 1914 the tsar imposed further restrictions—the volunteering of a few hundred Finns for service in the Russian army had had no alleviating effect. The Finnish Parliament was not summoned, though elections for a new Parliament were held in 1916. No change came from this until the Finns were able to form a coalition Senate (q.v.) of their own after the March Revolution in Russia.

After this, they staggered toward independence (q.v.) and the bloody horror of quarreling among themselves—in the Finnish Civil War (q.v.) and its aftermath killing thousands of their own, whereas the Russians, during the eighteen Years of Oppression, had hardly killed a Finn.

ORTHODOX CHURCH. One of the two state churches in Finland (which means, inter alia, that it has the right to tax its members).

Orthodox Christianity from Novgorod began to spread among the Karelian Finns at the time the western Finns were becoming Roman Catholic—in the eleventh and twelfth centuries. Both forms of Christianity were contending with paganism until well into the sixteenth century.

Since religion defined identity in past times, these two forms of Christianity also contended with each other. The crusade, under Bishop Thomas, of the western Finns and Swedes against the Karelians was checked at the Neva by Alexander Nevsky in 1240. In 1323 by the Peace of Pähkinäsaari (q.v.) Karelia, including the isthmus, was divided, and in the eastern half, which went to Novgorod, Orthodoxy strengthened. In 1617 by the Peace of Stolbova (q.v.) most of the Karelian Isthmus (q.v.) and Ingria (q.v.) were ceded to Sweden, however. The practice of Orthodoxy was guaranteed in the ceded territories, but this guarantee was not honored and conflict broke out. The upshot was that Lutheran settlers were introduced, part of the inhabitants were forcibly converted, while many others (such as the Finns of Tver), wishing to retain their Orthodoxy, fled to Russia. By 1721, at the end of the Great Northern War (q.v.), when Karelia and Ingria were again in Russian hands, the population of these territories was Lutheran and was to remain so.

Thus Orthodoxy became the religion of a small minority in Finland. The transfer of Finland to the Russian Empire in 1809 did not significantly alter this situation, for the Lutheran church (q.v.) kept its position as the sole state church. The tsar himself, in the mid-1820s, had to decree the rights of the Orthodox to posts in the Finnish administration. In spite of the gradual introduction, from 1865 onward, of a Finnish liturgy in Orthodox services, the religion was considered by most Finns to be foreign.

At first glance it is somewhat surprising, therefore, that the Orthodox church became a state church in 1918, shortly after the independence of Finland. This was not due to the development of a new spirit of tolerance. Rather the zealous minister of education, E. N. Setälä, saw the act as a means of controlling a potentially subversive element in the new state, especially in regard to the border parishes. Later Setälä became interested in incorporating the Orthodox of East Karelia (q.v.), especially through the creation of an autocephalic "Orthodox Church of the Finnic Peoples" (Finns, East Karelians, and Estonians), but for political reasons nothing came of this.

In the time of the First Republic the important monasteries of Valamo and Konevitsa, on islands in Lake Ladoga, remained in Finland. The former, dating originally from the twelfth century, was of great importance in the history of Russian Orthodoxy. From there missionary enterprises went forth in the fifteenth century to found the White Sea monastery of Solovetsk, in the sixteenth century to convert the Lapps (q.v.), called Skolt Lapps, and in the eighteenth century to bring Christianity to Alaska. After World War II the monastic communities of Valamo and Konevitsa, as well as the nunnery of Kivennapa, were reestablished at Heinävesi in Finland.

There are at present some 55,000 members of the Orthodox church in Finland, comprising 1.2% of the population. The church is autonomous but not autocephalic. From 1923, when the church broke away from the Moscow Patriarchate, it has been under Constantinople.

OUTPOST OF THE WEST. This phrase, often on the lips of right-wing Finns in the early years of independence (q.v.), represented an attempt to find a destiny for their country. It was a kind of justification for being a border country—between a backward, Bolsehvik Russia and an allegedly civilized Western Europe. (Incidentally, the expression "the great cultural lands," which was current among the nineteenth-century Finnish university-trained elite, never included the Russian Empire.)

The "outpost of the west" image was given a suitable historical pedigree in that Finnish history was seen as a confrontation against an eastern barbarism. The image also had a useful function in internal politics: it was yet another way of condemning Communism as alien, a penetration from the East, something that could not possibly be understood as having native roots.

Even if Finland were a borderland, that borderland might be crossed, by the promotion (when opportunity arose) of a Greater Finland (q.v.) among the Finnic peoples on Russian territory. Thus, outpost ideology could take on an aggressive as well as a defensive connotation.

It was characteristic of Mannerheim's (q.v.) confused outlook toward Russia that as regent of Finland in 1919 he saw Finland as a sentinel against the darkness of the East, though in other respects he had admired traditional Russian hierarchical society, topped by a picturesque monarchy, all of which had somehow engendered more darkness than light.

In his powerful address to the Finnish armed forces (q.v.) on March 13, 1940, the day the Winter War (q.v.) ended, Mannerheim returned to the same theme. He said then that Finland had had a historical vocation to defend Western civilization; this vocation it had again fulfilled by fighting the Russians in the Winter War (as if, in short, by attacking Finland, the Soviet Union had really been planning an attack on the West). Mannerheim said that by its sacrifices in the Winter War Finland had paid its debt to the West—a view that would seem to see Finland as having been culturally colonized by the West, to the evident advantage of the Finnish nation.

In the Continuation War (q.v.), an even more lurid form of the "outpost of the west" idea became current in certain circles. In the German New Order, Finland was to become, according to some Finns and Germans, the leading state of Northern Europe, and once again a bulwark against the East. In fact, as Risto Ryti's (q.v.) discussions with the German minister revealed, the Finnish government would have been delighted if a wedge of German-occupied territory had been created to separate Finland forever from its troublesome Russian neighbor.

Post–World War II Finnish foreign policy has been founded upon a rejection of the "outpost of the west" outlook. As the Finns have now moved into membership of the European Union, in theory, as a consequence of the security-political ambitions of the Maastricht Treaty, Finland's position as a Western European outpost might pop into the picture again—provided, that is, the Union itself does not reach a firm understanding with Russia. The positive prospect would be that of an umbrella of multilateralism covering Russia and preventing at the same time the exposure of Finland.

-P-

PAASIKIVI, JUHO KUSTI (1870–1956). President of Finland from 1946 to 1956. As president, Paasikivi inaugurated a policy that subsequently became known as the "Paasikivi line," based on the view that by showing an understanding of Russian strategic concerns Finland could escape maximalist demands on her independence (q.v.).

Paasikivi was the son of a country huckster who established a business of his own at Lahti and prospered there. The young Paasikivi graduated from the high school in Hämeenlinna and then went on to study history and law at the University of Helsinki. After studying further in Sweden and Germany, he took his doctorate in law at Helsinki with a thesis on taxation history.

To the end of his life, Paasikivi remained proud of his historical studies and knowledge of the history of many lands. He read avidly, in many languages, works on history, politics, and economics; his extensive library may be seen at the University of Turku. He looked down on those who were "mere lawyers" by training.

Paasikivi was truly a conservative by inclination. Originally, he was an Old Finn (q.v.) in politics; throughout, he was afraid of what might befall his country. The future worried him, but he always strove to find a way out of the thicket. The picture of him as an irascible figure, hurling imprecations at all and sundry, has been too easily formed. Paasikivi wanted to discuss politics with men of equal caliber and to find political rather than military solutions. If with no one else, he discussed politics with himself, as his copious diaries and memoirs—great sources of Finnish history—reveal.

As an Old Finn, Paasikivi, before World War I, followed the politics of Compliance. But he, too, became disillusioned and left the civil service for the world of private banking. Fortunately—for Finland's future—Paasikivi never entirely lost the basic outlook of the Compliants that at some level it should be possible to reach an accommodation with the Russians.

In 1918, though, with the breakup of the Russian Empire and Finland's independence, Paasikivi was a monarchist (q.v.) who favored a German prince on a Finnish throne. Here he underestimated the strength of the Allies, as Mannerheim (q.v.), another monarchist by conviction, was quick to remind him.

In this erroneous policy Paasikivi was trying to establish legitimacy for a Finnish state and nation. He was also trying to lean on German strength. This, for Paasikivi, was not just a consequence of the role the Germans had played in the Finnish Civil War (q.v.)—a role that Mannerheim continued to feel was vastly overestimated—but in the Paasikivi outlook there was something else that was always characteristic of him. He believed that Finland could never survive in complete political isolation; the country had to be associated, in one form or another (a crucial point—how?), with a power or set of forces external to itself. If necessary, Finland had to make concessions ("Compliance"), as when Prime Minister Paasikivi made commercial concessions to Germany in the summer of 1918.

With the collapse of Germany, Paasikivi lost his premiership; shortly afterward, President Ståhlberg (q.v.) appointed him one of the negotiators at Tartu, in the peace negotiations with Soviet Russia.

Paasikivi, so the Activist (q.v.) Right was ready to allege, made concessions to Russia (his Compliant past was thrown up against him). It was argued that far more than Petsamo (q.v.) could have been gotten for Finland had Paasikivi and one of his fellow negotiators, Väinö Tanner (q.v.), been firmer with the Russians.

While it cannot seriously be argued that, for Paasikivi, Soviet Russia stood in 1920 where imperial Germany had stood in 1918, yet it was a fact that he brooded later on the mistakes made by the Finns at Tartu. Far from thinking that the Finns had given too much away, he tended to think that they had not given enough. Had Russia had better borders, pressure on Finland to make border adjustments in the late 1930s would not have occurred.

Continuing his career in private banking, serving his country at the League of Nations in 1927, Paasikivi became chairman of the National Coalition party (q.v.) in the years 1934–1936. He then helped to steer the party clear of any further involvement with extraparliamentary extreme right-wing activity.

In 1936 he was appointed Finnish minister in Stockholm. In some ways this was a demotion, but in that position he

178 / Paasikivi, Juho Kusti

tried to argue for a joint Nordic security policy. Once again, his conviction of the dangers of a too isolated Finnish position came out.

Paasikivi was not informed of the proposals made to the Finnish government by the Soviet emissaries Boris Yartsev (q.v.) and Boris Stein (q.v.) for joint security arrangements and territorial concessions (a Soviet leasing of strategically placed Finnish islands in the Gulf of Finland, for instance). In the fall of 1939, however, the task of negotiating with the Russians in regard to their demands for part of the Karelian Isthmus (q.v.) and strategic points on the Gulf of Finland was placed upon the shoulders of Paasikivi and Tanner, who were in favor of concessions. Had their policy been heeded by the home government, the Winter War (q.v.) might have been avoided and, at least, further time gained for a strengthening of the Finnish military arm.

In the difficult period after the Winter War Paasikivi was Finnish minister in Moscow, having played a leading role in negotiating the Peace of Moscow (q.v.). There he did his best to rebuild relations with the Soviet Union, but he was not kept informed of his own government's growing orientation toward Nazi Germany.

He had, however, come more and more to the conclusion that Nazi Germany would smash the Soviet Union and, back once more in Finland, endorsed—even publicly—the government's policy of entering the war and his government action in the first year of the war.

Thus, in the early days of this Continuation War (q.v.), he felt that Finland would get Lebensroum of its own alongside and in cooperation with the German lebensraum policy. As noted, this was all of a piece with his fundamental conviction that Finland could survive only in some kind of a relationship to an external power.

This could not be the Western Allies—they were too remote. When, toward the end of 1942, Paasikivi began to have doubts about the war, he came to see the problem of extricating Finland from hostilities as basically one of restoring trust with the Soviet Union. He had no sympathy for the military's plans to cling to East Karelia (q.v.) and none for fantasies about a breakdown in relations between the West and the Soviet Union, though the question of a separate peace between Germany and the Soviet Union occasionally crossed his mind. He knew the Peace Opposition (q.v.) group but never really joined them. They were Western oriented.

After the hostilities ceased, Paasikivi became both the symbol and the directing force of the new accommodation with the Soviet Union. Before becoming president in March 1946, he served as prime minister, and during much of the time of the Mannerheim presidency it was Paasikivi who served as acting president, in the periods of illness and despair that gripped the marshal.

Paasikivi ruled. He saw to it that the Allied Control Commission (q.v.) dealt directly with him and was in no danger of constituting a kind of alternative administration. As far as the internal dimensions of Finnish politics were concerned, Paasikivi played politics with any forces he could utilize. Immediately after the war, he leaned much on the Communists and the Finnish People's Democratic League, while between July 1948 and March 1950 he gave support to a minority government of the Social Democrats (q.v.), a government detested by Communists and Agrarians alike. After 1950, he came to rely more and more on the Agrarian politician Urho Kekkonen (q.v.), a man who was persona grata to the Russians, in part for his role of helping negotiate, with Paasikivi's backing, the 1948 Finnish-Soviet Treaty (q.v.).

Paasikivi and Kekkonen were in collaboration with regard to the first important demarche of post–World War II Finnish foreign policy, that contained in Kekkonen's so-called Pajama-Pocket Speech (q.v.) of January 1952. The two men worked together to secure the return of the leased Porkkala enclave at the end of 1955.

Paasikivi, who sought to reassure the Russians by unilateral statements about the willingness of the Finns to prevent aggression against the Soviet Union through Finland, never wanted the Finnish-Soviet Treaty (and he was advised by former president Ståhlberg not to have it). Aware of foreign political realities, however, he forced acceptance of the treaty upon Parliament and nation.

His strong presidency compelled him to restrain and inhibit internal political forces. This tradition was continued by

President Kekkonen, who developed a more ambitious policy vis-à-vis the Soviet Union, while for Paasikivi the 1948 treaty was the final accommodation. Admittedly in different fashions and contexts, both presidents thought that foreign policy demands had often to override internal political party considerations. It all went back to the failure of parliamentary politics to prevent the slide into the Winter War.

While Paasikivi, as Kekkonen, had no trust in the possibility of a security guarantee from the West for Finland and no conviction in the worth of such a guarantee anyway, he, as Kekkonen, aimed to keep open and expanding Finland's trading links with the West. Paasikivi even laid down a rough-and-ready rule that Soviet trade should cover no more than 25% of Finnish exports. Though Finland, for political security reasons, did not accept Marshall Plan aid, both the U.S. and Sweden supplied considerable credits to Finland in the early years of the Paasikivi presidency—up to 1952 the Americans had granted directly more than $150 million worth.

In 1956, Paasikivi was prevailed upon to run in the presidential stakes as a last-minute candidate, but his candidature this time had no significance. Kekkonen was elected by a clever piece of strategic voting.

PAASO, DIET OF. Somewhat grandiloquently called a "diet," this was a meeting of the local Finnish gentry in a section of the border region with Russia held in December 1789, at the height of the Swedish-Russian War of 1788–1790 (q.v.).

The meeting made a declaration of Finnish independence (q.v.) and requested armed assistance from the empress Catherine. It elected the renegade Georg Magnus Sprengtporten (q.v.) as its leader.

The Diet of Paaso should be seen as a more desperate expression of the mood of the Liikkala Note (q.v.) and the Anjala Covenant (q.v.), a desperation engendered by the sufferings in war of the border areas of Finland. The gentry assembled at Paaso had lost their faith in the ability of the Swedish Crown to defend Finland.

These "Eastern" views thus constitute part of the continuing debate in Finnish society between the partisans of the

Western connection and those who believe that Finland cannot avoid having to come to terms with Russia.

PÄHKINÄSAARI, PEACE OF. The peace, concluded in 1323 between the Swedes and Novgorod, was the decisive instrument in relations between Sweden and Russia until the Peace of Täyssinä (q.v.) of 1595. The Peace of Pähkinäsaari was the first written document in which the border between Swedish and Novgorod domains was defined, albeit not with much precision in respect of some areas.

The border ran, in broad terms, from the Karelian Isthmus (q.v.) through North Karelia (q.v.) and Savo to the Gulf of Bothnia. Not all the Karelian Isthmus fell, however, under the Swedish Crown, while Russian domains extended in theory to the northern end of the Gulf of Bothnia. This was to ensure fishing rights in the rivers of the north for the Orthodox Karelians who owed allegiance to Novgorod. It is true that, though documented, the Peace of Pähkinäsaari did not ensure the end of raiding in the areas through which the border ran, but in disputes the document drawing up the peace was inevitably the point of reference.

Several factors, symbolized by the making of the peace, are worthy of attention. The peace signified the end of the Swedish crusading impulse. The boundary drawn was to be a cultural one between Roman Catholic and Orthodox, an issue of identity not essentially disturbed until the 1617 Peace of Stolbova (q.v.) and its consequences—most importantly, the persecution of Orthodox by Lutheran.

The making of peace at Pähkinäsaari owed quite a lot to commercial pressures. Just as at Stolbova nearly three hundred years later, foreign merchants (at Pähkinäsaari the German traders of Gothland) intrigued for peace—yet another example of the triumph of the commercial over the territorial interest.

PAJAMA-POCKET SPEECH. This speech was written by the then prime minister Urho Kekkonen (q.v.), but never delivered. Being convalescent, Kekkonen drew the speech out of his pajama pocket and saw that it was printed in the Agrarian Union (q.v.) newspaper *Maakansa* on January 23, 1952.

The speech, discussed beforehand with President Paasikivi (q.v.) and known to the Soviet ambassador, V. Z. Lebedev, was the first important demarche of postwar Finnish foreign policy. Its author expressed his worry at the threat of a global escalation of the Korean War. He stressed the common neutrality (q.v.) tradition of all the Nordic states and in this connection even distorted the text of the preamble of the 1948 Finnish-Soviet Treaty (q.v.) by avowing that it gave Finland a "right" to stay "outside the conflicting interest of the Great Powers," whereas the treaty actually spoke only of a Finnish "desire."

What is important in the speech is the positive tone taken about the idea of a Nordic Defense Alliance (q.v.), a project mooted in 1948 and 1949 and then torpedoed by, among other things, the opposition of the Soviet Union. Now once again Soviet policy was shifting—and again, too late in the day. In the Pajama-Pocket Speech, however, Kekkonen tried to associate the Finnish-Soviet Treaty with a de facto Nordic security system based on a low military input (it should be remembered that Norway and Denmark, though NATO member states, would not have NATO bases on their soil). On the whole, Kekkonen saw the North as taking a minimalist, near-neutral position, and he put Finnish neutrality alongside the traditional neutrality of Sweden.

Though Finland later repudiated Nordic balance (q.v.) thinking, there is an element of it in the underlying structure presented by Kekkonen in the Pajama-Pocket Speech as being the essence of the Nordic political security reality. His speech created nothing specifically new, but it was probably welcome to Swedish Prime Minister Tage Erlander as helping him resist pressure on Sweden (from Denmark and Norway, inter alia) to abandon neutrality and join NATO.

The Pajama-Pocket Speech has been titled in English "The Common Neutrality of the Nordic Countries."

It has been revealed that at a sauna session in the summer of 1952 Urho Kekkonen admitted to U.N. Secretary-General Trygve Lie that he would sleep better at night if there were NATO bases (U.S. troops and planes) on Norwegian soil. Coming so soon after the Pajama-Pocket Speech, this avowal of Finnish duplicity astonished the Norwegian.

PAN-SCANDINAVIANISM. This romantic movement emerged in the mid–nineteenth century and was a Scandinavian equivalent to the unification movements in German-speaking and Italian-speaking Europe. Several issues of practical politics nonetheless inspired the Pan-Scandinavians, most important of all perhaps the need to shore up Denmark against the German states and German nationalism. The failure of other Scandinavian states to help Denmark in 1864 sounded the death knell to political Pan-Scandinavianism.

As far as Finland was concerned, a Pan-Scandinavian interest had arisen vis-à-vis that land a decade earlier during the Baltic operations of the Crimean War (q.v.). In Sweden the Finnish poet Emil von Qvanten had argued for a separation of Finland from the Russian Empire and a new statehood under the Swedish Crown. Norwegian reactions were hostile to the whole idea; it was thought—with great distrust on the Norwegian side—that Finland, once under the Swedish Crown, would be able to play Sweden off against Norway. What seemed to remain, therefore, was only a possible incorporation of Finland into Sweden.

The Fennoman leader J. W. Snellman (q.v.) forcibly argued that Finland had, in fact, got more "statehood" out of the Russian connection. When Tsar Alexander I had restored Old Finland (q.v.) to the rest of Finland in 1811, Snellman said, Finland's boundaries as a state had been extended.

In spite of Sweden's failure to act during the Crimean War, Pan-Scandinavianism continued for some time to have supporters among certain student circles in Finland. These were largely Swedish orientated, for though Qvanten had been sympathetic to the Fennoman movement (q.v.) and had tried to explain its significance to the Swedes in his writings, the Fennoman attack upon his views was decisive. By the late 1850s it was becoming evident that for the "Scandinavians" there were two choices—exile, which Nordenskiöld (q.v.) took, or the formation of a Svecoman movement (q.v.) in Finland to counter Fennomanism.

PASSIVE RESISTANCE MOVEMENT. Finland was once cited as a sterling example of the virtues of passive resistance, though to look at the present fascination of the country with military service one might never believe this.

On a significant scale the passive resistance movement started in 1899 with protests against the imperial legislation foreshadowed in the February Manifesto (q.v.) of that year of Tsar Nicholas II. The key figure behind the resistance was undoubtedly Leo Mechelin (q.v.), who, even as early as 1892, had been trying to interest the French minister in Stockholm, René Millet, in the potential threats to Finnish autonomy (q.v.).

In the beginning the passive resistance movement tried to work by petitions to the tsar, like the Great Address (q.v.) from Finland and the International Cultural Address to the Tsar (q.v.) from Western, Central, and Northern Europe. The idea was, whether fiction or conviction, that the tsar was being misled by his advisors. Throughout, the passive resistance movement made great use of foreign newspapers and foreign journalists, men such as John Gilmour of the London *Morning Post*.

In 1901, however, with the first attempt to conscript Finnish youth into the imperial army, a coordinating committee called the Kagal was set up. The word is Hebrew and had been used by clandestine Jewish political organizations in Russia to refer to their own conspiratorial groups. The Kagal, with decreasing success, tried to institute resistance to the draft. By the fall of 1903, to some extent under the inspiration of Konni Zilliacus (q.v.), an Activist (q.v.) party emerged, dissatisfied with the caution and constitutionalism (q.v.) of the passive resistance leaders, and prepared to cooperate with such Russian revolutionary groups as the Social Revolutionaries.

When, after the Russian Revolution of 1905, a quasi-constitutionalist system developed in Russia from 1906 onward, the Finnish passive resistance network found further work in opposing the subordination to this system of any of the institutions of autonomous Finland. Statements were gotten from internationally renowned jurists, British chambers of commerce were prevailed upon to protest against an allegedly threatening imposition of the higher Russian tariff on Finland; in London, Liberal, Labour, and Irish Nationalist backbenchers signed an admonitory memorial to the Duma.

Even though basic improvements in the position of Finland came only with the revolutions in Russia, there was still something to be said for Finnish passive resistance. Among other things, its original opposition to the imperial draft kept Finnish youth out of the holocaust of World War I.

PEACE OPPOSITION. This very unstructured movement began to emerge toward the end of 1942; its aim was to work for the disentanglement of Finland from the Continuation War (q.v.). By this time Marshal Mannerheim (q.v.), the Finnish commander in chief, as well as many members of the government, were also having their doubts about Finland's involvement with Germany.

A first move of the Peace Opposition, therefore, was to try to secure the election of Mannerheim to the presidency in the elections of February 1943. His possible candidacy was probably initially promoted by his alter ego in the Finnish cabinet, the minister of defense, Rudolf Waldén. Waldén did not belong to the Peace Opposition, but had, like Mannerheim himself, come to the conclusion that Finland should endeavor to extricate itself from the war.

In the determined opinion of the Peace Opposition a renewal of the presidency of Risto Ryti (q.v.) would be considered by the Allies as a demonstration of loyalty to Germany, but without overwhelming backing Mannerheim refused to run. Ryti was reelected.

In August 1943 a peace petition, with thirty-three names attached, was forwarded to President Ryti. The petitioners were mainly members of Parliament, and they urged on Ryti the necessity of upholding relations of trust with the United States.

Unlike Great Britain, which had declared war on Finland on December 6, 1941 (Finnish Independence Day), the United States had neither declared war nor, as yet, broken off diplomatic relations. The Peace Opposition regarded the U.S. connection as a lifeline for Finland and, indeed, the very existence of this group had a positive effect in the United States.

The Peace Opposition was Western oriented, a characteristic that has been held against it, since the main factor in the peace process was the Soviet Union. In 1944 the Soviet minister to Stockholm, Alexandra Kollontay, who was personally sympathetic to the Finns, refused to treat with the Peace Opposition. Their importance, however, lay in the fact that having a pro-Allied outlook and having important links with U.S. officials (through the contracts cultivated by Laurin Zilliacus), they helped convince the United States government that a growing section of Finnish opinion was for peace. This, in turn, enabled the U.S. to speak more favorably of Finland with Moscow, though in any case the Soviet Union was continually sounding out the Finns for peace.

There were many overlapping circles connecting with the work of the Peace Opposition. Its core was, however, a group of liberal-minded Swedish-speaking academics and politicians, with a smaller group of Social Democrats (q.v.). By the spring of 1943 the Swedish People's party (q.v.) was mainly supportive of the Peace Opposition, but the Social Democrats were split—their leader, Väinö Tanner (q.v.), regarding the Peace Opposition as an embarrassment to the government's quieter attempts to further peace.

In this connection, it is worth recalling that Ryti had tried, in February 1943, to communicate to President Roosevelt a proposal that Finnish troops should withdraw to the 1939 borders as a first step toward peace. Soviet insistence on the borders of the Peace of Moscow (q.v.) rendered such proposals fruitless, of course.

The existence of a Peace Opposition in Finland in World War II testified, through the very fact of its public dissent, to a certain quality of constitutionalism in the land. In Nazi Germany members of the Peace Opposition would have been executed. It is equally worth emphasizing that the goals of the Peace Opposition and the Finnish government were not, by 1943, essentially dissimilar.

PEACE TREATIES. *See* HAMINA, PEACE OF; MOSCOW, PEACE OF, PÄHKINÄSAARI, PEACE OF; PEACE

TREATY OF FEBRUARY 10, 1947; STOLBOVA, PEACE OF; TARTU, PEACE OF; TÄYSSINÄ, PEACE OF; TURKU, PEACE OF; UUSIKAUPUNKI, PEACE OF

PEACE TREATY OF FEBRUARY 10, 1947. This treaty, signed in Paris, ended the state of war between Finland and the Allies (principally the Soviet Union and Great Britain—the United States had never declared war on Finland). Most of the provisions of the Peace Treaty were a repetition of those of the Armistice Agreement (q.v.) of September 19, 1944. But for British insistence to the contrary, this would have formed the core of a Peace Treaty, since the Soviet government then did not want to bother with an interim armistice agreement.

The main changes were in regard to the Finnish armed forces (q.v.). By Article 4 of the Armistice Agreement Finland had to undertake "to place her army on a peace footing within two and a half months." Because of the Lapland War (q.v.)—to expel German troops from Finnish soil, the Finns had been unable to fulfill this requirement, but after the Lapland War military reductions had taken place.

Now, by Article 13 of the Peace Treaty, the total strength of the Finnish armed forces was set at slightly under 43,000 men. These are primarily armed forces of trainee soldiers; but in wartime (when the restrictions on personnel are held not to apply) the Finns, by calling up their reserves, can field an army of several hundred thousand men.

By the same Article 13 Finland was not allowed to possess bomber aircraft, and Article 17 forbade guided missiles, atomic weapons, torpedoes, MTBs, and submarines. In short, the idea was to prohibit offensive weaponry.

As a result of the Note Crisis (q.v.) of 1961, the prohibition on guided missiles was raised in 1962. In consequence of changes in the Soviet Union, statements were made from the Finnish side in 1990 to indicate that the Finnish armed forces would no longer be bound by the Peace Treaty restrictions. This does not apply to nuclear weapons (Finland has loyally abided by the Nonproliferation Treaty of 1968) and cannot be construed as a change from purely defensive thinking, but it hardly indicates that Finland is going along with the general European trend toward disarmament.

It is not commonly realized that the original Peace Treaty restrictions on Finnish weaponry were not made at the insistence of the Soviet Union. It was the British who imposed them, and it was to be the British who were to make the fuss in 1962 when the Finns wanted guided missiles for their armed forces. In the tortuous negotiations among the Allies in 1946 and 1947, some of the restrictions on the Finnish armed forces—as on those of the three Eastern European former enemy countries (Hungary, Romania, and Bulgaria)—arose in part out of the wrangling between the Western powers and the Soviet Union over the conditions to be imposed on Italy, by this time a ward of the West.

The Finns did not really seem to care very much about their armed forces in this period. Not until several decades later was the Finnish army able to begin to restore its image as the ultimate guardian of the Finnish soul.

What the Finnish delegation cared about in 1946 and 1947 was the possibility of getting some of the lost lands back and of reducing the amount of war reparations (q.v.). A Finnish delegation to Moscow in 1946 had presented both issues to Stalin as economic questions. He had been sympathetic only about the reparations, indicating a chance of reducing them by $100 million.

At Paris it was not to be, however, and Molotov dismissed the faintest of Finnish hints about a return of part of the lands and did not hold out at that point any hope of reparations reductions, which did not occur until June 1948.

On the whole the position of the Finnish delegation in Paris was a fairly humiliating one. The Allies discussed the issues among themselves; when, at one public session, some of the Finnish delegation were seen in the public gallery, they were asked to leave. Back home, the rising Communist star, Hertta Kuusinen (the daughter of Otto Willie Kuusinen [q.v.]) criticized the delegation for its refusal to acknowledge the defeat of Finland in the Continuation War (q.v.). This she did in spite of the fact that among the delegation were two members of the Finnish People's Democratic League, or SKDL, of which the Finnish Communist party was a constituent part. These delegates were Mauri Pekkala, the prime minister, and Yrjö Leino, the minister of the interior and her husband.

In connection with the signing of the Peace Treaty, President Paasikivi (q.v.) gave a unilateral promise that Finland would always repel an attack on the Soviet Union if the attack were attempted through Finnish territory. This was insufficient, and the next year a Finnish-Soviet Treaty (q.v.) was made.

PEOPLE'S PATRIOTIC MOVEMENT (*Isänmaallinen kansanliike,* or IKL). This extreme nationalist movement grew up immediately after the demise of the Lapua movement (q.v.) and the failure of the Mäntsälä revolt (q.v.). Present and influential at the preliminary negotiations leading to the setting-up of the People's Patriotic Movement was President P. E. Svinhufvud (q.v.).

The movement had close links with Svinhufvud's party, the National Coalition party (q.v.) (Conservatives). In November 1932 the Central Committee of the National Coalition party affirmed that the great majority of party members endorsed unconditionally the goals of the People's Patriotic Movement.

A certain parting of the ways soon occurred, particularly when the movement's pronounced antiparliamentarism led it to adopt the fascist concept of the corporate state. The movement was avowedly anticapitalist, a stand that alienated the Conservative bourgeoisie. Being against the political parties (it was a "movement"), the People's Patriotic Movement reached across party and class lines. Unlike the Lapua movement, repentant former Communists were welcomed—if there were any.

In short, the People's Patriotic Movement was seeking to establish a working, unitary ethos for Finland. They soon alienated any potential Swedish-speaking supporters by preaching the necessity of a unilingual society, and their views recalled the old Fennomanism of Ahlqvist-Oksanen (*Yksi kieli, yksi mieli*: "One language, one mind"). Behind their fascism was a simplified form of the Hegelianism that had found fertile ground in Fennomanism. Hence, in spite of Svinhufvud's retreat, many Conservatives, especially in the teaching profession, were drawn to the ideals of the People's Patriotic Movement.

In 1938 Urho Kekkonen (q.v.), then minister of the interior, tried to get the movement banned (probably because he thought it was "foreign" and a threat in any case to the Agrarians). The courts threw out his ban.

In the election of 1939 the movement won only eight seats. Its leader, Vilho Annala, served in the first government of the Continuation War (q.v.), but the movement was finally banned by the 1944 Armistice Agreement (q.v.).

With the breakup of the Soviet Union, the movement was revived in 1993.

PETSAMO (Russian: Pechenga). The Petsamo area, now in the Russian Murmansk oblast, belonged to Finland from 1920 to 1944. It is the possession of this area, bordering on the Barents Sea, that gives Russia a joint frontier with northern Norway. Since Finland lost this territory, it has been cut off from access to the northern seas.

The Petsamo area is large, comprising over four thousand square miles in all and containing the town of Petsamo, the outport of Liinahamari, and the mining and refining center of Nikkeli (using here the Finnish names).

According to Finnish tradition, the Petsamo area was promised to the Grand Duchy (q.v.) of Finland by the imperial Russian authorities in 1864 in exchange for the miniscule area of Siestarjoki (Russian: Sestroretsk) on the Karelian Isthmus (q.v.). In the event, the Russians gained Siestarjoki but the Finns did not gain Petsamo.

It was not until the 1920 Peace of Tartu (q.v.) that the Finns secured Petsamo. This enabled them to have an ice-free port on the northern seas, thanks to the Gulf Stream, and Liinahamari (previously of little significance) was gradually developed.

It was in the tense period of 1940 and 1941, between the Winter War (q.v.) and the Continuation War (q.v.), when 60% of Finnish merchant shipping was bottled up in the Baltic, that Liinahamari boomed. The Polar-Sea Road from Rovaniemi to Liinahamari often witnessed a bumper-to-bumper stream of trucks, Swedish and sometimes Norwegian as well as Finnish. The accident rate was comparatively high, and there was some lawlessness, including the siphoning off of such valuable cargo as coffee.

Overshadowing in historical significance these colorful aspects of Finnish Petsamo was, however, the fact that before World War II nickel deposits (q.v.) had been discovered in the region; the concession was given to the Canadian-British Mond Nickel Company. In 1940 pressure on Finland both from the Soviet Union and from Germany arose over the nickel question. Historical research has revealed that this issue was a prime factor in the development of closer relations between Germany and Finland in this period.

The geographical position of Petsamo, lying between German-occupied Norway and the Soviet Union, helped encourage the Germans, as they contemplated an invasion of the Soviet Union, to think in terms of a German-Finnish military arrangement. In fact, the *Silberfuchs* plan of striking at the port of Murmansk and its railroad soon petered out, partly because the Germans, fearful of British raids on Norway, were unable to spare enough troops.

Petsamo was lost to Finland as a condition of the Armistice Agreement (q.v.) of September 19, 1944, a condition confirmed in the Peace Treaty of February 10, 1947 (q.v.). The Soviet Union greatly exploited the nickel deposits of the area, which is one source of the pollution of adjacent Finnish territory. A plan by the Outokumpu Corporation of Finland to deal with this pollution at its source has been resisted by the local industrial complex concerned. A later suggestion by the Finnish Center party M.P., later minister, Hannele Pokka, by which Finland should lease the Petsamo area in return for financing the reduction of the pollution coming from the whole Kola Peninsula, has not met with a positive response either in Russia or Finland.

POLITICAL UNION WITH SWEDEN. This question arose out of the thwarted debate on a Nordic Defense Alliance (q.v.) in March 1940, shortly after the signing of the Peace of Moscow (q.v.), which ended the Winter War (q.v.) between Finland and the Soviet Union. Molotov had rapidly torpedoed the idea of a Nordic Defense Alliance, but throughout

1940 the question of a closer union between Sweden and Finland at the political level was fitfully in the air. As Molotov divined, such a structure would have afforded opportunity for military cooperation. He therefore condemned it, claiming to be an upholder of the strictest form of traditional neutrality for both Finland and Sweden.

For Finland a political union with Sweden in 1940 might have alleviated, in a certain way, the slow trend toward Nazi Germany. So argued Jarl Wasastjerna, the Finnish minister in Stockholm. On the other hand, such a union would have been unthinkable without German endorsement. Some Finns, including General P. J. Talvela, Mannerheim's (q.v.) emissary to Germany, even broached the idea as a means of getting closer to Germany.

The Germans refused to endorse this project, maintaining punctilious relations with the Soviet Union, while preparing for a war against that country—a war into which Finland was to be drawn.

In this question of political union with Finland the Swedes were torn between a fear of being isolated and a fear, should they join the union, of being dragged by the Finns, at the heels of Germany, into a revanchist war with the Soviet Union for the recovery of the Finnish territories lost at the Peace of Moscow.

The idea of a political union (with at least a common foreign, defense, and customs policy) seems to have been Finnish in origin, a belated fling of the Activists (q.v.), especially Rafael Erich. Yet from the Swedish side important figures were, for brief moments, drawn to the idea. Among these was the Swedish foreign minister, Christian Günther.

True to form, the Soviet Union woke up late in the day on this issue. At the end of April 1941, the new minister to Finland, Pavel Orlov, told the Finns that the Soviet government had now nothing against the union plan. By this time, though, the Finns had already begun to enter Nazi Germany's fatal embrace.

PORTHAN, HENRIK GABRIEL (1739–1804). One of Finland's greatest scholars, Porthan was born in the parish of Viitasaari in the heart of Finnish-speaking Finland. His father was a clergyman, while his grandfather on his mother's side was a nephew of the historian Daniel Juslenius (q.v.).

Porthan studied at the University of Turku, becoming a docent in rhetoric (Greek and Roman literature) in 1762 and professor of rhetoric in 1777. Meanwhile, in his work as university librarian, he had more than trebled the number of volumes in the library, though most of these books were destroyed in the fire of 1827.

Though sometimes superficial in his approach, Porthan was one of the last scholars in Europe to whom the term *uomo universale* might be applied. Through the broad scope permitted by his lectures on rhetoric, he dealt with topics ranging from health education to classical archaeology. His interest in the latter stemmed in part from his championship of the "new humanism" based on a revitalization of classical culture. Here Porthan's work exerted an influence on the culture of his own land long after his death, as, for example, when J. L. Runeberg (q.v.) began to portray the Finns as northern Greeks.

Porthan helped launch the Aurora Society, a debating club on the Swedish model, which in addition published the first newspapers in Finland. He was also one of the founders of the Suomen Talousseura (whose building still stands in Turku), a society devoted to the propagation of useful knowledge and the stimulation of enterprise in agriculture and related branches of the Finnish national economy.

In spite of these extramural involvements, Porthan never left the ivory tower for long. Yet the ivory tower of the University of Turku was not quite high enough for the realization of all his dreams. He sought to link the hitherto somewhat isolated academic life of Finland with a wider world than that represented by the sister universities of Sweden.

In 1779 he made a study trip to Göttingen, where he became acquainted with a fuller expression of the new humanism. Porthan brought to Göttingen publications from his own university for reproduction in the Göttingen *Gelehrte Anzeigen*. There, with the German scholar A. L. Schlözer, he developed the idea of Finland as a European Canada, destined to be fought over by Sweden and Russia for its untapped natural resources, just as France and Great Britain had fought over Canada.

In any case, in spite of this comparison with Canada, Porthan (both during his Göttingen stay and otherwise) tried to convey a picture of the distinctiveness of Finland and its inhabitants. He found a ready listener in Schlözer, who knew the Finnic peoples from his own travels in the Russian Empire.

An important part of Porthan's life was his work to focus attention upon the rich oral poetic tradition of the Finnish-speaking Finns. On the one hand, this had a wide scholarly significance: his doctorate, *De Poësi Fennica,* can be regarded with some justification as one of the pioneer studies in folklore. On the other hand, the study of the Finnish language and culture was an illustration of Porthan's conviction of the need to investigate the local.

Either way his inspiration was hardly that of a political nationalism, and there were times when he thought that the Finnish language would ultimately die out. His determined concentration upon Finnish studies (as well as his interest in the work of the Suomen Talousseura), coupled with his need to advance the knowledge of Finnish matters at Göttingen, show a clear consciousness of a Finnish identity distinct from that of Sweden.

Porthan wanted to retain the Swedish connection, but disliked the dragging of his country into the Swedish-Russian War of 1788–1790 (q.v.) and in general the court politics of Gustavus III, which undoubtedly diminished the significance of Finland's voice in Sweden.

As a scholar, Porthan was the proponent of the Aufklärung in Finland. He broke the academic world free from the narrower interpretations forced upon it by a strict Lutheran orthodoxy—he dismantled, for example, the mythic explanations of Juslenius, who derived the Finnish language and the origin of the Finnish race from biblical stories.

Though preaching the necessity of a rationalist approach to learning, Porthan drew the line at conduct based solely on reason (and was thus anti-Kantian). He opposed the doctrines of the French Revolution, believing in God and trying to believe in the Swedish monarchy (q.v.), hoping it would cease its dissipation in war and luxury.

Porthan died unmarried, five years before his country fell under the Russian scepter. He is commemorated in Turku by C. E. Sjöstrand's statue, erected in 1864, and by the Porthan Society, established in 1936, which is publishing under the rubric *Opera Omnia* the collected writings of Porthan in the original Latin or Swedish versions (so far eight volumes have been issued).

PORVOO, DIET OF. Summoned by Tsar Alexander I to ensure the loyalty of his new Finnish subjects, this Diet met at the little town of Porvoo, seat of a bishopric, to the east of Helsinki. The Diet sat from March to September 1809.

The Diet, in the ancient Swedish form of a Diet of Four Estates (q.v.), was not part of a regular parliamentary process, for it was not summoned again (in Helsinki) till 1863, when Alexander II was tsar–grand duke.

Still, the Diet of Porvoo has had an immense significance for Finnish history. At Porvoo the Estates swore loyalty to the tsar and he promised to uphold the fundamental laws of the land—those inherited from the recent Swedish time—though they were not specified by name.

In the decades after the Diet of Porvoo, a kind of a contract theory was developed out of what happened there. The point was first strongly made by Israel Hwasser, a Swede, who had been professor of medicine in Helsinki. Hwasser argued that this "contract" was the basis of a Finnish statehood and that Sweden should never attempt to recover Finland.

In spite of some initial astonishment in Finland, Hwasser's views, put forward in 1838, gained ever more adherents among the Finns. Leo Mechelin (q.v.) was inspired by them, and the view that a "breach of contract" on the part of the tsar had occurred with the February Manifesto (q.v.) in 1899 was a basic tenet in passive resistance (q.v.) ideology.

Actually, what had probably occurred at Porvoo in 1809 was a simple act of assurance (Swedish: *forsäkringsakt*) on the part of Alexander I without the intention of a contract (though it sounds somewhat like the sort of thing known to Anglo-Saxon law as a "special contract").

In any case, the fundamental laws confirmed at Porvoo gave the monarch great power—and they were the very laws of the Gustavian period that were then being overthrown, along with King Gustavus IV Adolphus, in Sweden. By these laws the Diet had to give its consent to new laws and taxation, but it still proved possible for the tsars to have Finland run administratively and without a Diet for the subsequent fifty-six years. A Finnish administrative elite, dominated by aristocrats, did the work through an organ called the Senate (q.v.). The country gave no trouble, and the Russian authorities, occasionally disturbed by grass-roots Finnish revivalism (q.v.), remained on the whole content that Finland was so quiet.

As both states began to modernize in the latter part of the nineteenth century, however, they clashed. Russian publicists began to look into the matter of the Diet of Porvoo, to find that it was summoned after a Russian conquest of Finland (might makes right), that Finnish officials had sworn oaths of allegiance to Alexander before the summoning of the Diet (no contract therefore), and that the whole matter of Finland was regulated by an international act, the Peace of Hamina (q.v.), between Sweden and Russia above the heads of the Finns.

POSTAL MANIFESTO. By this decree, promulgated in 1890, the independent postal service of the Grand Duchy (q.v.) was placed under the control of the Russian ministry of the interior.

The measure was, in itself, a comparatively small one. Russian-type stamps with the double eagle on them were introduced, but Finnish stamps of the traditional kind — featuring the Finnish lion — continued to be used for a decade, until Bobrikov (q.v.) forbade them, when Finnish protest stamps were placed by patriots alongside the Russian stamp issues.

Administratively, what the 1890 Postal Manifesto achieved was the placing of foreign post within the imperial postal system. Symbolically, however, this was not a pleasant development for those Finns who wished to emphasize the character of Finland as a state with its own relations to other states.

Tsar Alexander III certainly envisaged other measures of unification (q.v.), and it was ominous that he put through the

Postal Manifesto after reading K. F. Ordin's work, published the year previously, entitled *The Subjugation of Finland*.

In 1890 the great Finnish constitutionalist, Senator Leo Mechelin (q.v.), resigned from the Senate (q.v.). He most certainly regarded the Postal Manifesto as an illegal measure, but his resignation was undoubtedly motivated even more by the prospect of further acts, in particular the unifying of the customs between Finland and Russia. In the event, this did not occur.

With the promulgation of the Postal Manifesto, many of the younger Finnish academics with foreign contacts, like the orientalist J. N. Reuter and the sociologist Edvard Westermarck, began seriously to work for the maintenance of Finnish autonomy (q.v.) through the publicizing of the Finnish cause abroad.

PROGRESSIVE PARTY (*Edistyspuolue*). This party, founded in 1918, exerted an influence in Finnish politics out of all proportion to its numbers (it had only 26 seats in 1919 and had fallen to 11 in 1930). The Progressive party (or National Progressive party, as it was officially styled) grew out of the party known as the Young Finns (q.v.), itself a product of the liberal wing of the Fennoman movement (q.v.).

The foundation of the Progressive party after independence (q.v.) was due to the fact that a few young Finns, notably P. E. Svinhufvud (q.v.), had become monarchists (q.v.), a development that ran quite counter to the professed political radicalism of the rest.

The Progressive party supplied the first real president of Finland in the person of K. J. Ståhlberg (q.v.). The party was generally Western oriented; this could be seen clearly in the early postindependence foreign policy of Rudolf Holsti. It was a tragedy for their second president, Risto Ryti (q.v.), president during the Continuation War (q.v.), that this Anglophile felt he had to align his country with Nazi Germany. Knowledgeable as a true Progressive party man about the ways of the West, in 1941 Ryti warned the British that they, in their turn, were falling under the sway of the United States.

After World War II the Progressive party declined and in 1951 dissolved itself. A set of smaller liberal parties thereupon emerged. They were even less fitted than the Progressive party had been to defend the liberal outlook: mainly they seemed to concentrate on getting their leading members ministerial posts.

-R-

REED, JOHN (1887–1920). Revolutionary and recorder of revolutions. Reed was born in Portland, Oregon, and came from a well-connected family — his father, an admirer of Theodore Roosevelt, being active in the West Coast Progressive movement.

John Reed, after a Harvard education, became a Greenwich Village journalist. Far from developing into a dilettante, he wrote powerfully about the great textile workers' strike in Paterson, New Jersey, in 1913. In this way he got to know both the rank and file and the leadership of the IWW forces that organized the strike.

Then he went to Mexico, riding for several months with Pancho Villa's men. In 1914 his book *Insurgent Mexico* appeared, expressing warm sympathies with the rural proletariat of Mexico, including Emiliano Zapata and his followers. These Mexican experiences — and their public recounting — severed Reed's relationship with his father.

In World War I, Reed, who took a socialist-pacifist line against the war, came to Europe, visiting the German lines in the West and theaters of war in the Balkans. He wrote against the war, which he had already dubbed a "businessmen's war," and when the United States entered, Reed regarded Wilson as having betrayed those who worked for his election.

In September 1917 Reed was in Russia, where he was soon to witness a fight he could approve of: the Bolshevik Revolution. Reed, who did not leave Russia until February 1918, had a first-class view of this event and published, in 1918, his famous account of it, *Ten Days That Shook the World*. Lenin (q.v.) liked the book so much he later wrote a foreword to it.

Back in the United States, Reed became involved in the wranglings within the Socialist party and helped found a rival Communist party to the hard-line one that was founded and dominated by immigrants. The party Reed put himself behind was the Communist Labor party, which had some reflections in it of IWW thinking.

In the fall of 1919 Reed traveled (once more through Finland) to Russia in order to seek the recognition of the Third International for the Communist Labor party. The matter was held in abeyance; in March Reed, furnished with diamonds obviously given by the Soviet authorities to be sold for the promotion of Communist agitation abroad, traveled back clandestinely through Finland.

To get from Finland to Sweden, he had to use the normal means favored by Bolshevik couriers—a hiding-place in the coal bunker. Already on the boat in Turku (q.v.), he was arrested, probably on a tip-off.

Reed spent the next three months in a prison cell in Turku (the cell can still be seen in the old police station in the center of the city). After a month, Reed was convicted of smuggling (the diamonds), but was able to pay the fine. He was kept for a further two months in disgusting conditions, the Finnish authorities suspecting him of being involved in the founding of the new Socialist Labor party in Finland and of acting as a courier for the Finnish Reds in exile.

Nothing could be proved against him. Thanks to the efforts of the Wuolijoki (q.v.) circle, especially Aino Malmberg, Reed was released, got to Estonia, and from there he was able to travel to Soviet Russia. He died a few weeks later—he had earlier suffered from serious kidney trouble and his privations in the Turku prison cell had worsened his general health.

Reed's treatment at the hands of the Finnish authorities was characteristic of the suspicious atmosphere prevailing in the early decades of Finnish independence (q.v.). The authorities believed themselves constantly under internal and external threat, and a distrust of foreign influence was rampant.

The Finnish authorities, incidentally, confiscated the original of Lenin's foreword to *Ten Days That Shook the World*. It was never retrieved, but somewhere another copy existed.

RELANDER, LAURI KRISTIAN (1883–1942). President of Finland from 1925 to 1931. Relander, the second president of Finland, was undoubtedly the most colorless. He was elected as a compromise candidate, since his own party, the Agrarian Union (q.v.), would not endorse the candidate of the National Coalition party (q.v.), the former monarchist P. E. Svinhufvud (q.v.), while the National Coalition party would not accept Risto Ryti (q.v.), the candidate of the Progressive party (q.v.). Relander's wife was Swedish-speaking, and this helped ensure the votes of the Swedish People's party (q.v.): "We voted for her, not him."

Notwithstanding his personal hesitancy, Relander's election illustrated the political power of the Agrarians as a balancing element between the bourgeois parties.

Relander was born in Karelia, the son of an agricultural college teacher of Fennoman (q.v.) outlook. He started his professional life as a teacher of agricultural subjects, writing a guide to rabbit breeding, before going on to produce a Helsinki University dissertation, written in German, on the subject of agricultural chemistry. Relander's subsequent combined career as a parliamentarian and public official followed a path that many leaders in the Agrarian Union were to take, but the presidency was unexpected, and his wife and daughter moaned about it.

Relander was known to his contemporaries as "Traveling Relander" from his habit of making state visits to neighboring countries (though not the Soviet Union). Nothing much emerged out of these trips, certainly not the "Nordic Locarno" that had fitfully crossed his and some Finnish diplomats' minds. Unlike post–World War II presidents, Relander left foreign policy mainly to his foreign ministers. In the latter period of the presidency the foreign minister, Hjalmar Procopé, pursued a policy he called "splendid isolation"; Relander and Procopé were as one in fending off Soviet attempts for a nonaggression treaty (q.v.). It was parochial, not splendid.

Within Finland storms burst. Relander was quite unable to resist extraparliamentary pressures. As far as the armed forces (q.v.) were concerned, Relander gave way, as President K. J. Ståhlberg (q.v.) had not, to the demands of the

Jaegers (q.v.) for the removal of General K. F. Wilkama. Above all Relander caved in to the Lapua movement (q.v.). Many others did, too, but he was president.

RESISTANCE TO THE CONTINUATION WAR. In the Continuation War (q.v.) of 1941–1944, 532 opponents of the war are known to have been executed. Some of these were pacifists or near-pacifists. Arndt Pekurinen was shot on the front lines in 1941 for refusing to take part in anything to do with the war. He had previously served for several years as chairman of the Finnish branch of the War Resisters' International, and his prewar persecution had roused international attention—among others, Albert Einstein had tried to intervene on his behalf.

Not all pacifists who came into the hands of the authorities were shot. The actor Tarmo Manni was given forced labor, kept on short rations, and was beaten at night by the camp guards.

Of those executed, more than eighty were Communists. The Communist party was illegal in Finland, but many of those executed had taken part openly in the activities of the Finnish-Soviet Friendship Society, which flourished legitimately—to the anger of much of the Finnish establishment—in the period between the ending of the Winter War (q.v.) and the commencement of the Continuation War.

The Communists engaged in sabotage, trying to hinder the flow of German war matériel. Granaries were also destroyed. The Communists encouraged young men to desert from the Finnish armed forces (q.v.) or to resist the draft. Forest hideouts were set up for these men.

It is impossible to speak of a resistance movement in Finland in the sense that it was known in many other European lands. Nonetheless the saboteurs were an extreme expression of a wider minority dissatisfaction with the denial by the Finnish system of Communist representation within it as well as an unease in several quarters about the real aims of the war.

The Communists went to their deaths proclaiming their belief in world revolution. They also hurled abuse at the Finnish alignment with Nazi Germany. They believed they were opposing fascism and like the Communists elsewhere in Europe at this time were undoubtedly on the side of the Allies.

These people seemed to have had no contacts with the sophisticated literati of the Peace Opposition (q.v.).

A seamstress, Martta Koskinen, who was known both to Hella Wuolijoki (q.v.) and Hertta Kuusinen, was convicted of spying. She continued this activity in prison, reporting to her comrades outside the probability that antiaircraft guns were placed near the prison. President Ryti (q.v.) turned down an appeal for clemency. Before being shot against the cemetery wall at Malmi, near Helsinki, she was struck in the mouth by a guard for singing the "Internationale." Olav Laiho, a spirited speaker and debater, was shot after hostilities had ceased between Finland and the Soviet Union in September 1944.

When, after the war, the remains of the executed Communists were taken from Oulu prison through the streets of the town, written on the walls were the words, "We speak from the grave." Among other things, what was spoken about was a denial of the political rights of an important minority of the Finnish population. These rights were restored by the Allies, in the name of the United Nations, and through the Armistice Agreement (q.v.). In this manner both Finland and its Communists were impelled, ever more strongly, into the devious politics of parliamentary democracy.

REVIVALISM. After the occupation of Finland and its devastation during the Great Wrath (q.v.) of the Great Northern War (q.v.), a Pietistic movement developed in Finland, coming through Sweden from Germany. What this represented in part was the breakdown of a political culture, especially in its critique of the close identification of Church and State, the legitimacy of which the wars and accompanying distress had seemed to set at naught.

The authorities responded to the Pietist challenge in 1726 by forbidding prayer meetings outside church services, meetings which were often led by laymen. Nonetheless waves of revivalism continued in the eighteenth century to be a feature of both Finland and Sweden. In Finland the regions of the southwest and Ostrobothnia were particularly affected.

The accommodation of the Finnish Lutheran church (q.v.) in 1808 and 1809 to the Orthodox tsar—especially the ease with which Bishop Jakob Tengström, as early as May 1808, swore loyalty—may have been a factor further weakening the legitimacy of the hierarchical church.

Undoubtedly for many reasons, the early nineteenth century witnessed a spread of revivalism in many regions of Finland. Some of the leading lights were clergymen (like Henrik Renqvist in North Karelia [q.v.]), others were laymen (like Paavo Ruotsalainen in Savo), but both these men were the sons of independent peasants. The official church (and the followers of the revivalists did not leave it) was disturbed, and it and civil authorities punished revivalist preachers when they could. Behind this reaction was the state power, the Russian authorities being afraid of the "democracy" in the movements and wanting to hear no whispers of anything from Finland.

Basically, the revivalist movements were a manifestation of a class-conscious peasantry, for whom, in the end, all were equal before God. This egalitarianism also embodied a protest from the periphery against an official culture imposed from the center.

The Fennoman movement (q.v.) looked askance at revivalism, and Lönnrot (q.v.) was troubled by the revivalist condemnation of the ancient, pagan rune-singing. This was the other side of revivalism: a disturbing, all-embracing, and often authoritarian moralism.

The influence of revivalism has remained strong in many parts of Finland. It is reflected in much of the literature of the land, as in the modern novels of Timo Mukka.

ROAD TO SAINT PETERSBURG (Finnish: *Pietarin tie*). This image is used when referring to the cultivation of relations with Russia or Russian authorities by interested parties in Finland for their own ends.

The phenomenon emerged in nineteenth-century autonomous Finland. It did not necessarily mean that the interested party traveled to Saint Petersburg. A classic example is the behavior of the Fennoman (q.v.) leader J. W. Snellman (q.v.) in 1863. The Diet of Four Estates (q.v.) was meeting that year for the first time since 1809. Snellman secured a language edict, decreeing that Finnish was to have equal status with Swedish in courts and offices when dealings with the public were concerned. He did this by meeting Tsar Alexander II at the military encampment at Parola, thus getting the matter solved by a direct appeal to the monarch.

Often tactics of this kind meant entering into a cosy relationship with the Russian governor-general. The Svecoman (q.v.) party got on better with Governor-General N. V. Adlerberg (1866–1881), who helped them frustrate Fennoman education plans. In turn, the Fennoman party worked with Governor-General F. L. Heiden (1881–1897) to see that the 1863 language edict (which had been given a period of twenty years for its gradual enforcement) really was being implemented.

The politics was understandable in a system in which the Diet was often immobilized by a Fennoman (Peasants and Clergy) and Svecoman (Nobles and Burghers) tie, while on the other hand, the Senate (q.v.), Finland's executive, was appointed by the monarch and not responsible by law to the Diet anyway.

The mass politics of the twentieth century ran counter to behavior of this kind, though it continued to occur. Though it embarrassed his own party, the Fennoman leader Y. S. Yrjö-Koskinen tried after the promulgation of the February Manifesto (q.v.) to get further language rights for Finnish-speakers by truckling to Governor-General Bobrikov (q.v.). In the summer of 1917, to take a striking example, the last Finnish minister state-secretary in Saint Petersburg, C. J. A. Enckell (q.v.), ran to Kerensky to get the Finnish unicameral legislature dissolved because he disagreed with the enabling act put through by the Social Democrat (q.v.) majority.

In the period of Finnish independence (q.v.) up to 1944, relations with Russia were latently and actively hostile, so that the "road to Saint Petersburg" was not being trod. The post–World War II development of good relations with the Soviet Union brought out this phenomenon again. Indeed, in the period when the Allied Control Commission (q.v.) was in Finland there was no alternative. But the question arose with the Kekkonen (q.v.) era—which, after all, lasted twenty-five years—of how far the internal quality of Finnish politics was being damaged by the Soviet reliance on "favorites" within the Finnish system. The Center party, in particular, has been accused of blackening other Finnish parties in Soviet eyes during this period.

In the run-up to the presidential election of 1982 a would-be Center party contender for office, Ahti Karjalainen, was asked by the Soviet authorities whether they could do anything to help him. A supporter, Paavo Väyrynen, chairman of the Center party and foreign minister of Finland, suggested (in his chairman's capacity) to the Soviet go-between that the Soviet Union might promise to increase its oil exports to Finland, for Karjalainen was the Finnish head of the Finnish-Soviet Trade Commission.

Karjalainen did not get the Center party presidential nomination. Further, the winner in the presidential election was Mauno Koivisto (q.v.). Not everyone lost through this Soviet bungling, however. Paavo Väyrynen was taken into the Aho government as foreign minister in 1991 and remained in office till 1993, resigning to contest the presidential election.

RUNEBERG, JOHAN LUDVIG (1804–1877). Swedish-Finnish poet. Born in Pietarsaari, in the predominantly Swedish-speaking area of the northeastern littoral, Runeberg was the son of a sea captain and on his mother's side was descended from a clerical family.

He studied at the University of Turku, supporting himself in part by private tutoring, which took him to the interior of Finland, where he became acquainted with the Finnish-speaking majority. In him was bred a deep respect for the ordinary Finnish people, who figure (particularly in the person of "Saarijärven Paavo") as stoical heroes in his poems, embodying some of the classical virtues he had absorbed in his learning.

It is difficult to overestimate the importance of the poetry of Runeberg upon the Finnish psyche. His poems were rapidly translated into Finnish and later served as a staple of elementary and high school indoctrination. He made articulate the inarticulate Finns. By Runeberg's time most Finns had forgotten the wealth of oral poetry that Elias Lönnrot (q.v.) was frantically trying to put together into the *Kalevala* (q.v.), trudging around the obscurest parts of the country and over into East Karelia (q.v.) to collect it.

The impact of Runeberg has had its curious side. By reciting his poems, the Finns were drilled into a kind of articulation; but the hero of the poems was often an inarticulate man, seen clearest of all in the person of the humble soldier Sven Dufva, who knows how to do his duty. Thus there is an ambivalence in Runeberg: the wisdom is that of the folk, but it is a folk that is drawn to serve, not to think.

Out of this material a nation had to be made. Runeberg's *Tales of Ensign Stål* breathe the rejection of Finland by Sweden, in spite of the sacrifices made by the Finns for the Swedish Crown. Since the battles are fought against the Russian invader, the upshot is that the Finns are alone and must rely on themselves—a prophetic belief if ever there was one. The *Tales of Ensign Stål* deal, of course, with the War of 1808–1809 for the Possession of Finland (q.v.), as recounted by a veteran of the war.

It has been said of Runeberg himself that "his life was happy and uneventful." He was a schoolmaster and rector at Porvoo, yet he seems to have been seething with martial vigor, the nearest physical expression of which was his passion for hunting, out of which came the poem, "The Elk Hunters".

His poems often contain exhortations about how you "hot with youth, in battle strife, die for your land." Women die with shame when their loved ones are not found dead on the field of battle. Hardly surprisingly Runeberg's poems were read, long after World War II, to trainees at the Reserve Officers' School at Hamina.

Apart from his martial vigor, Runeberg also seems to have been seething with sexual vigor, exerting a magnetism upon a number of lovesick females. In the twentieth century all this was turned into a famous Finnish film, improbably entitled *The King of Poetry and the Migratory Bird*.

Runeberg was in holy orders and wrote the words for over sixty Finnish hymns. In 1832 he married Fredrika Tengström, his second cousin and niece of Archbishop Jakob Tengström. She was a writer, too, dreaming of women's social emancipation. Of her it was reported that Runeberg once said she was to be honored as the mother of his children. Runeberg also wrote the words for the Finnish national anthem.

RYTI, RISTO (1889–1956). President of Finland from 1940 to 1944. Ryti was born of farming stock at Huittinen in the Finnish-speaking province of Satakunta in southwestern Finland. He studied law at the University of Helsinki. His marriage, in 1916, to Gerda Serlachius allied him to one of the most influential of the Swedish-speaking industrial families in Finland.

Ryti became head of the Bank of Finland (q.v.) in 1923 and was soon a familiar figure in the international banking world. As early as 1919, he had been elected to Parliament on the Progressive party (q.v.) ticket and in the 1925 presidential stakes was ultimately runner-up to Lauri Relander (q.v.)—many being surprised that Ryti did not win on the final ballot.

Ryti often showed a certain reluctance to enter the political fray, and sometimes claimed to be primarily a banker—a significant comment on Finnish political life if ever there was one. It therefore took the insistence of President Kyösti Kallio (q.v.) to make Ryti accept the post of prime minister of the war cabinet formed in December 1939 at the outbreak of the Winter War (q.v.). This post Ryti continued to hold after the Peace of Moscow (q.v.), but due to Kallio's illness he also served for periods as acting president.

In December 1940, on the death of Kallio, Ryti was elected president almost unanimously, and was reelected by an overwhelming number of votes of the electoral college in February 1943. He served until August 1944, then giving way to the emergency presidency of Marshal Gustaf Mannerheim (q.v.).

There was much in the Ryti persona that spoke for a man of liberal disposition and Liberal principles. So Anglophilic was he that he was dubbed in Finland "Sir Risto." And, before World War II, he opposed the pretensions of the Academic Karelia Society (q.v.) for the possession of vast tracts of territory in the Soviet Union.

Yet, in the vital period of 1940 to 1941, Ryti allowed the military command in Finland, under the leadership of Marshal Mannerheim, carte blanche to enter into relations with Nazi Germany. The extent of these relations was unknown to Parliament, and unknown, indeed, to most members of the government. It was these relations that helped draw Finland, as a cobelligerent (q.v.), into the invasion of the Soviet Union in June 1941, the start of what the Finns call the Continuation War (q.v.), an enterprise conducted without stated war aims and without a political discussion of alternative courses of action.

Soon after hostilities began, Ryti was made aware of the German plan to raze Leningrad to the ground. No Finnish troops were to be involved in this dirty work, but Ryti asked for the creation of a strip of German-occupied territory to separate forever the Finnish conquests in Russia from what would be left of the truncated Russian state.

Among many Finns, Risto Ryti, in whose memory a modernistic monument has been erected ("his second crucifixion") was considered a patriot of the deepest order. In particular, his action in June 1944, when he swore to the Nazi leadership not to make a separate peace with the Soviet Union and thus gained additional German military aid to stem the Russian summer offensive, is regarded by many commentators and by a strong section of opinion as a sacrifice made by a man of honor. This action of Ryti's, so runs the argument, enabled the Finns to keep the Russians out of Helsinki. Additionally, some would say, it maintained Finnish independence (q.v.), the Finns, in any case, then being able to make their separate peace (for Ryti lied) from a stronger position.

Among the several issues overlooked by this pro-Ryti argumentation is that the unconditional surrender first demanded by the Russians in the summer of 1944 was not the same as occupation or loss of independence (and the Americans could have told Ryti this). While, on the other hand, stemming the Soviet offensive cost Finland one-third of the casualties of the whole Continuation War.

When peace came, Risto Ryti was arraigned in the war trials (q.v.) as a war criminal. He was sentenced to ten years' imprisonment for, among other things, allowing the military discussions with Nazi Germany in May 1941, leading Great Britain to declare war on Finland, stalling peace negotiations, and making the Ribbentrop agreement (i.e., the 1944 pledge to Nazi Germany for additional arms).

Part of his defense—for example, the claim that he had not known the extent of the military discussions with Nazi Germany—was weak. The general line of his defense statement, however, the associating of the Continuation War with the problems arising from the Winter War, was intelligently set forth. But it was disallowed.

On medical grounds (he suffered from cancer) Ryti was released after serving only three years of his sentence.

- S -

SENATE. The Finnish Senate grew out of the Governing Council, whose regulations were confirmed by Tsar Alexander I on August 18, 1809. This was the executive body within Finland, while in Saint Petersburg a Committee for Finnish Affairs, headed by a state-secretary—after 1834 minister state-secretary—reported directly to the tsar.

The Governing Council in Finland was given the title of Senate in 1816. It was wholly composed of Finns, with the exception that the chairman was the Russian governor-general. Since, from 1809 to 1863, the Finnish Diet of Four Estates (q.v.) was not summoned after the Diet of Porvoo (q.v.), which had ended in September 1809, the Senate was not part of any Finnish Montesquieu-type constitutional system. The senators were, in any case, nominated by the tsar.

Still, in the latter part of the century, there were senators—like Leo Mechelin (q.v.)—who thought that the Senate should be responsible to the legislative organ (the Diet).

The fact remains that Finland was largely an administered country, albeit by the Finns themselves, at least up to 1909, when, in the latter part of the Years of Oppression (q.v.), Russians became nominated for senatorial posts. In essence the creation of a Governing Council, subsequently Senate, was a continuation of Swedish collegial administration, which provided plum appointments for leading members of the Finnish elite, thus binding them—until the February Manifesto (q.v.) of 1899—firmly to the Romanov dynasty.

The Senate was divided into an economic division and a judicial division. Many subordinate organs grew up. In the first half of the century the system was run by aristocrats, but in the second half by men who were more responsive to the bourgeois forces. When socialism emerged in the early twentieth century, its focal point, as far as constitutionalism (q.v.) was concerned, was the legislature. In 1906 the Social Democratic party (q.v.) even expelled a would-be senator from its ranks.

An understanding of this difference in outlook is vital for appreciation of the events of 1917–1918 in Finland. Though the Social Democrats entered a coalition Senate in March 1917 (after the bourgeois Russian Revolution), this was an unwelcome decision for many members of the party; by August and September of the same year the Social Democratic senators had withdrawn.

SIBELIUS, JEAN (1865–1957). Composer. Sibelius was born in Hämeenlinna, the son of a doctor who died when the boy was two years old. Throughout his life Jean Sibelius behaved more like a scion of the aristocracy—or perhaps he sought to embody the aristocratic concept of the lone artist, an image so dear to bourgeois culture. He was born Johan, but like his seafaring uncle Johan he changed his name to Jean.

Sibelius began studying law at the University of Helsinki, but the music school soon took over. By 1896 he was the favorite for a post in music at the university, but a jealous friend, the conductor Robert Kajanus, intervened to take it for himself. Instead Sibelius received a modest state pension, and his future as a composer seemed to be assured, but he always managed to overspend his income, having expensive tastes in clothes and drink.

He was bailed out by his friends, especially by Axel Carpelan, who sacrificed himself for Sibelius, often receiving scant consideration in return. Sibelius could also be inconsiderate to his own family. His wife, Aino Järnefelt, a person of intelligence, came from an aristocratic family; her modesty contrasted with the self-centeredness of "Jean" Sibelius. Aino herself had much to put up with, but Sibelius expressed his love for her, naming his permanent home at Järvenpää in southern Finland for her. The house is called Ainola, and Sibelius is buried on its grounds.

Sibelius, who was educated in both Swedish-language and Finnish-language schools, hovered in politics somewhere between the Young Finns (q.v.) and Svecoman (q.v.) position. During the Years of Oppression (q.v.) he was the staunchest of patriots. In the Civil War (q.v.) he was, naturally, White and had already written the "Jaeger (q.v.) March."

Though this has sometimes been disputed, even by the composer himself, the influence of Wagner can be heard in his music as well as in the choice of legend as a theme. His early work was also certainly influenced by Tchaikovsky, and it was once cruelly said that the Sibelius violin concerto is "the best thing Tchaikovsky ever wrote."

Outside the world of music, Sibelius was inspired by the historical works of the dramatist Strindberg. His deepest source of creative inspiration was, however, the Finnish national epic, the *Kalevala* (q.v.), as it was for his friend, the painter Axel Gallen-Kalela.

It was significant that the first major work of Sibelius, conducted by him in Helsinki (q.v.) in 1892, was the *Kullervo* Symphony, as it was called. The Kullervo stories, from the *Kalevala,* constitute a grim saga of intrafamily feuding; they have been compared to the Hamlet theme.

In this connection, it may be of interest to note that the Finnish Communist leader Otto Wille Kuusinen (q.v.) described, late in his life, the Finnish working class as "of the family of Kullervo."

In a manner too little appreciated by his fellow countrymen, who tend to restrict their acquaintanceship to formal patriotic occasions or to mild chamber music recitals, Sibelius brought the Finnish genius universal recognition through his tone poems and symphonies. With him the Finnish experience becomes embodied in a series of episodic works, all of which relate to mankind's quest for destiny. The *Kalevala,* compiled by Lönnrot (q.v.) as the Finns rose to national consciousness, is a poetic form of the same quest.

SIGISMUND (1566–1632). King of Poland from 1587 to 1632 and king of Sweden from 1594 to 1604. Sigismund was the son of John III of Sweden and Catherina Jagellonica, and he was brought up by his mother to be a devout Catholic. His father, who had furthered his election to the Polish throne, wanted him back in Sweden two years later so as to ensure his succession to the Swedish throne. This move failed, but on his father's death in 1592 the Swedish prospect opened before Sigismund again.

He seemed to accept the Lutheranism pronounced at the Uppsala Synod in 1593 and in consequence was crowned king of Sweden in 1594. In fact, he never lost either his Catholicism or his Polish commitment. It did, however, suit a section of the Swedish nobility to have a king across the sea and out of the way. This was even more the case in Klaus Fleming's (q.v.) Finland.

While Sigismund's uncle, Duke Charles, a son of Gustavus I Vasa, succeeded in becoming regent in 1595 and steered the realm against Sigismund, the latter retained, under Klaus Fleming's leadership, a powerful base in Finland.

The truth was that Fleming wanted to run the place, and the name of Sigismund provided cover for this. Fleming died in 1597, however, with the regency of Charles already working against him and the Sigismund monarchy. In 1604 Charles became king of Sweden as Charles IX, finally putting paid to Sigismund's hopes. The Swedish realm, though united, was now involved in war with Poland, while drawing ever deeper into the politics of military intervention in Russia.

SNELLMAN, JOHAN WILHELM (1806–1881). Philosopher of Finnish nationalism. Snellman, the son of a Swedenborgian sea captain, was born in Stockholm, but brought up in the Finnish coastal town of Kokkola after 1813. He studied at the University of Turku and then at Helsinki when the university was reestablished there in 1828. Becoming docent in philosophy, he claimed the right to lecture on "academic freedom," a bold step in the reactionary reign of Nicholas I.

Snellman's liberalism made him an admirer of England, a country he visited in 1847. Before this, however, he had spent some time in Sweden and Germany, and was already a declared Hegelian prior to his visit to Germany.

His Hegelianism demanded the recognition of the Finnish language as the language of the Finnish state, a state which had come into being with the separation from Sweden in 1809. This separation gave scope to the emergence of a national spirit whose "Finnish" (i.e., Finnish-language) character had to be recognized.

By this somewhat tautologous line of reasoning Snellman sought to persuade the upper class of the Grand Duchy (q.v.) to Finnicize itself and thus find a bulwark in the common people.

The Janus face of Fennomanism was discernible in Snellman. It was anti-Western in seeking to replace the Swedish language and cultural connection—an aspect that made Fennomanism attractive to the Russian imperial authorities. On the other hand, Fennomanism was Western in its aim of cherishing and developing traditional Finnish institutions and thus forestalling the imposition of the Russian language, culture, and politics. The beginnings of an isolationism were also present in this outlook of Snellman.

Snellman argued forcefully that Finland could maintain itself by establishing a modus vivendi with Russia. He openly opposed those who believed that Finland could win its independence in the midst of a war between the powers. Thus Snellman laid the foundations for the thinking known as "Compliance" in Finland.

In 1856 he became professor of ethics and the system of knowledge (receiving, in fact, a chair of philosophy, but the word "philosophy" was suspect). Later Snellman became a senator and was ennobled. This did not stop him from quarreling with the imperial authorities over the railroad question—he disliked the proposal of Governor-General Adlerberg to link the Finnish railroad system with Saint Petersburg—and the place of Finnish in schools. Harsh and awkward, he was prepared to compromise with authority only on condition that he could share in it, as a true Finn.

SOCIAL DEMOCRATIC PARTY. Having broken out of the paternalist workers' associations charitably formed by Finnish patricians, a group of class-conscious Finnish workers founded the Workers' party in Turku (q.v.) in 1899. At the Forssa meeting in 1903 this party changed its name to the Social Democratic party and adopted a Marxist program.

With the establishment of a unicameral legislature (q.v.), after the Great Strike (q.v.) of 1905, the SDP became a parliamentary party. In fact, it did extremely well in the 1907 elections, gaining 80 out of the 200 seats in the legislature, thus becoming the largest party. It did not have even a simple majority, though, a goal not attained until the wartime elections of 1916, when, on a low turnout throughout the country, it won 103 seats. It was this Parliament that was dissolved as a result of Enckell's (q.v.) and Kerensky's action in July 1917.

For a party officially committed to Marxism, this parliamentary experience was, to say the least, frustrating, especially as several of the reforms that been adopted by the legislature during the Years of Oppression (q.v.) had never been entered into the statute book, for the tsar had refused to append his signature.

In January 1918, therefore, a large section of the party went for revolution. Organizationally, the Social Democratic party did not split, but an important group, under the leadership of Väinö Tanner (q.v.) refused to take arms.

Thus the Social Democratic party was kept within the constitutional system; in the elections of 1919, with the Civil War (q.v.) only a year behind, it still won 80 seats. Between December 1926 and December 1927 Tanner headed a Social Democrat government in Finland, taking the salute as the White Civil Guard (q.v.) marched past him.

In this accommodation with what was a conservative constitutional regime, the SDP concentrated on securing measures of social welfare. This did not conflict with a certain strain of thought on the Right of the political spectrum, according to which the nation should cherish its young. Welfare measures were also a politics that the Agrarian Union (q.v.) could understand. In 1937 the Social Democrats entered a "Red Earth" (Social Democrats and Agrarians) government, in which there were also important members of the Progressive party (q.v.).

One of the keys to understanding the position of the Social Democratic party in Finnish politics is studying their relations with the Agrarians, for the great tripartite political division has been along the lines of Social Democrats–Agrarian Union–and National Coalition party (q.v.)—the Right, in other words.

From the point of view of its class antagonism toward industrialists and financiers, the alliance between the SDP and the Agrarians would seem natural enough. From the point of view of an industrial interest versus an agrarian interest, then, a coalition of Left and Right might occur. Since, after the Civil War, the Agrarian Union captured a large part of the former SDP rural vote, this town/country polarization has been a prominent feature of the politics of independent Finland.

After World War II, the draining off of so much of Finland's wealth into agricultural subsidies and the monopolizing of relations with the Soviet Union by the Agrarians gradually drove the SDP closer to the Conservative industrial interests. An opening occurred with the aborted candidature of Olavi Honka in the 1961 presidential election, but Kekkonen's (q.v.) bringing back Communists and the SDP into government in 1966 scotched this development. In 1987, however, a coalition government was at last formed between the SDP and the National Coalition party—a clear expression of industrialized Finland.

Lo and behold, in the 1991 election a sufficient proportion of bourgeois voters turned out to support the Center party (the Agrarian Union by another name) so that the SDP-Right coalition could not be reconstituted. Still, in comparison with political constellations in Sweden, Finnish politics has been popping up with strange bedfellows for quite a time, and the ever-shifting alignments of consensual politics do not end here.

SOVIET PRISONERS OF WAR. The treatment of Soviet prisoners of war by the Finns in World War II does not redound to their credit. In the Winter War (q.v.) prisoners were supervised by the Civil Guards (q.v.). There were often no trained nurses for the sick and wounded in the camps. In one camp, at least, bandages were washed and used again. In part, conditions in the camps in the Winter War can be put down to the unpreparedness of the Finns for the conflict with the Soviet Union.

In the Continuation War (q.v.) the Finns took 64,188 prisoners, of whom 44,453 were returned at the end of hostilities. Most of the rest had died, a mortality rate of 29%. The Civil Guards, as part of the Home Forces, did most of the guarding until Marshal Mannerheim (q.v.) intervened in 1943 and removed the camps from their superintendence.

The worst period was 1941 and 1942, when more than 80% of the deaths occurred, mainly from malnutrition, disease, and neglect. At Nastola, in southern Finland, there is a memorial to the Soviet prisoners of war who died in the camp there. The harsh attitude of the military authorities was the main reason for the dreadful conditions in these camps. The Finnish Red Cross did its best, while the American Red Cross protested the treatment meted out to the prisoners and by the end of 1943 was sending food parcels to them.

While conditions in the Finnish camps were better than in the German camps (some prisoners tried to escape from the German camps to the Finnish camps; they were returned by the Finns and shot by the Germans), racism was also characteristic of the Finnish military authorities' outlook. Prisoners who came from peoples related to the Finns were given better rations and lighter work. Russians and Communists fared worse. Jews were counted with the Russians. Colonel A. E. Martola, who, a decade and a half later, was to be one of the originators of the U.N. peacekeeping forces, was instrumental in drafting the lines for this racism: the Cheremis were too distantly related to the Finns to count for favored treatment, he argued.

Corporal punishment, inflicted as a public spectacle with rubber truncheons or metal-reinforced rods, was a form of discipline used in the camps. In general, the treatment of the prisoners reflected the racist norms of behavior typical of the military authorities in other contexts—for example, in the administration of occupied East Karelia (q.v.).

To alleviate this grim picture, mention should first be made of the kindness (including extra food) received by Soviet prisoners who were allowed out to work on Finnish farms. Second, some prisoners, Karelians and Ingrians, had joined the Finnish forces and by the 1944 Armistice Agreement (q.v.) had to be returned to a nasty fate in the Soviet Union. Many of these men were, however, assisted to escape to Sweden.

SOVIET TRADE. Until recently trade between Finland and Russia has been an important pillar of the Finnish economy, Finland gaining a distinct advantage in a situation in which the United States put pressure on Western Europe not to trade with the Soviet Union.

In fact, however, Finnish trade with the Soviet Union arose out of the war reparations (q.v.) paid to the Russians between 1944 and 1952. President Paasikivi (q.v.) always argued that Soviet trade should not exceed 20–25% of the total of Finnish foreign trade. In 1953 it was 23.5%, declining somewhat thereafter, but it began to rise again after 1974, and by 1982 had reached the barrier level of 25%.

The trade occurred through a clearing system. In principle the system was one of an exchange of goods—a barter trade—by which allegedly both countries exchanged goods in the same amount. The central banks of both countries operated a clearing account in which the transactions were recorded and assessed. Through this form of trade Finland saved on vital foreign exchange, especially in regard to oil imports, even though the Soviet trade authorities used in their valuations the fluctuating Rotterdam prices. The trade with the Soviet Union was a distinct boost to the diversification of the Finnish economy, more particularly in regard to the engineering industry (thus following the trend laid down in the war reparations) but also serving to stimulate Finland's textile and footwear industry as well as to prop up its agriculture, whose recurrent surpluses could readily be dumped on the Soviet consumer.

As was pointed out by Lev Voronkov and other Soviet experts, this trade gave Finland a certain economic stability that its trade with the capitalist economy did not—for one thing, Soviet-Finnish trade was planned over five-year periods.

All this began to collapse in 1990, when trade between

Finland and the Soviet Union fell rapidly to under 12% and in 1991 was only a few percent. The clearing trade was abandoned on the Russian side, leaving 7.5 billion finnmarks worth of debts unpaid by the Russians.

Hopes rest with the development of trade between Finland and the border regions, especially with Russian Karelia. European Union spokesmen have seen Finland as a future, vital component in the expansion of trade with the Saint Petersburg area, where there is a market much larger than the population of Finland itself. Since the old Finnish-Soviet trade took place under a Finnish-Soviet Trade Commission, it has often been argued that Finnish businessmen have not yet been able to adapt to the conditions of a freer system of enterprise. On the other hand, trade between Finland and Russia now runs the risk of a "Russian Mafia" involvement. It may, indeed, be better for the Finns to work hand in hand with larger foreign consortia, who can take advantage of the Finns' undoubted special knowledge of Russian conditions while protecting any investment that is to be made.

SPERANSKY, MIKHAIL MIKHAILOVICH (1772–1839). Advisor to Tsar Alexander I. Speransky was born in the Vladimir region, the son of a village priest. In spite of a limited seminary education, he became a civil servant and by 1807 was secretary of state. The surname "Speransky" had been given him in anticipation of the hopes raised by his brilliance. His own hopes were founded on his knowledge of the doctrines of the Western European Enlightenment, which he absorbed from his reading of French literature.

Speransky was present at the Diet of Porvoo (q.v.), where he worked with Robert Rehbinder and was thus, in one sense, an upholder of Finnish constitutionalism. A little later Speransky helped establish the Committee for Finnish Affairs in Saint Petersburg, which reported directly to the tsar without going through the imperial ministers. Speransky also supported the restoration of Old Finland (q.v.) to the Grand Duchy (q.v.). In this way Speransky may be said to have strengthened the concept of Finland as a state and not a province.

Speransky ran afoul of the imperious Finnish aristocrat Gustaf Mauritz Armfelt (q.v.), a Gustavian (q.v.), who, as late as 1811, discovered a loyalty to the Russian tsar. In his quarrel with Speransky, Armfelt sought to protect the privilege of aristocratic rule in Finland, but there was also a more basic point of difference between the two men.

Speransky's constitutionalism was that of a tsar who ruled by law (*zakonnost:* "conformity with the law"), but this did not imply a constitutionalism in the Swedish sense of a balanced working between constitutional parts, let alone in the sense meant by Montesquieu of a separation of powers. Speransky's admiration for constitutionalism was that it would make the autocracy more efficient by being less arbitrary. Speransky's enthusiasm for Napoleon, which was the cause of his downfall in 1812 when Alexander broke with the French emperor, was part of this.

Armfelt had divined that Speransky cherished aspirations toward an administrative and legal unification of the Russian Empire—always a menacing issue for an avowed Finnish patriot. Thus, Speransky had wanted Russians to serve on the Committee for Finnish Affairs and had been lukewarm about Armfelt's proposal to establish a Finnish army.

SPRENGTPORTEN, GEORG MAGNUS (1740–1918). Soldier and political activist. Sprengtporten, the son of an untitled officer, was born in the province of Uusimaa. In 1772 he assisted his elder half-brother, Jakob Magnus Sprengtporten, in the revolt at Sveaborg (Suomenlinna, q.v.), which was an important part of the coup for the restoration of royal power.

The Sprengtportens—a jealous lot—remained dissatisfied with the rewards they got from Gustavus III. In the case of Georg Magnus his personal rancor became fused with his concern for Finnish military preparedness. He founded the first cadet school in Finland in 1779 and wanted to built up in the northeast a mobile force of lightly armed troops, able to take advantage of the difficult terrain. This proposal did not meet with the approval of Gustavus III, nor did the king go along with Sprengtporten's aspiration to be commander of the military forces in Finland.

Sprengtporten developed the idea that Finland would be better off as a client state of Russia. Since the threat to Saint Petersburg would thereby be removed, Finland could then live in peace. Sweden could be compensated for the loss of

Finland by taking Norway from Denmark (a view held by Gustavus III which became a reality in 1814).

Impressed by political developments in the Netherlands (where he lived briefly) and in the United States (he had wanted to go and fight there against the British), Sprengtporten produced a federal constitution for his projected Finnish state. His constitution would have allowed plenty of power for enlightened, upstart aristocrats like himself.

Sprengtporten entered Russian service in 1786 and fought in the Russo-Swedish War on the Russian side. The so-called Diet of Paaso (q.v.) elected him as its leader.

In December 1808 he was appointed by Alexander I governor-general of Finland, but his tenure lasted only a few months. Nonetheless he undoubtedly helped the transition of Finland into the Russian Empire as a constitutionalist state, playing an important part at the Diet of Porvoo (q.v.). In Russia he had previously argued for a constitutionalist, autonomous Poland.

S.S. BATTALION. In August 1940, when Finland was at peace, certain Finnish military men began to discuss among themselves the possibility of founding a Finnish fighting force to serve the German cause—this would, so their idea ran, be a re-creation of the Jaeger movement (q.v.) of World War I.

The Finnish arrière-pensée was now, however, a little different. It was not the gaining of Finnish independence (q.v.), but its maintenance, through good relations with Germany, that the military men were of course thinking of. This was the period in which Colonel J. Veltjens came to Finland to make, among other things, transit arrangements for German troops going to Norway. On his second visit in October he heard about the Finnish proposal for a Finnish fighting force on the German side—and warmed to the idea.

When the proposal was implemented, however, in the spring of 1941, it was discovered that the Finnish troops would be expected to serve in the Waffen-S.S. and not, as World War I Jaegers had served, in the *Wehrmacht*. The Finnish foreign office seemed to go along with this, though from the side of the Finnish military it was still hoped—in vain—to have the troops in the regular German army.

The matter seemed to have some urgency, for in January and February 1941 the Finnish government came under Soviet pressure once more—this time about the Petsamo (q.v.) nickel deposits (q.v.). It was precisely to counter Soviet pressure of this kind that the Finns had thought of using German support, and the means to gain this was the creation of a force of Finnish volunteers under German command.

No sooner were the men sent to Germany than Finland itself was in the war on the German side. The purpose the Finnish S.S. battalion ultimately served was in the act of its creation: to bind Finland closer to Germany in order that Finland and Germany might engage in the same war. The true background to this was the Nazi-Soviet Pact (q.v.) of August 1939, which had put Finland into the Soviet sphere, against which fate the Finns claimed to be struggling all the time.

Just over 1,400 men served in the battalion, of whom over 200 were killed in action, the battalion seeing heavy fighting on the Caucasus front. Finns of Nazi sympathies were not intentionally recruited into the battalion; it was intended to be consciously "nonpolitical" in character, but some Finnish Nazis got in.

The best that can be said is that its members were politically naive. So, too, were the Finnish leaders who helped create the battalion. The battalion became an embarrassment to the Finnish claim that Finland was not an ally of Nazi Germany, but only a cobelligerent (q.v.). And while the Finnish S.S. battalion comprised battle troops, some of them were also ordered to round up Russian Jews.

In the spring of 1943, as the Americans again began to put pressure on the Finns to get out of the war, the S.S. battalion had to be gotten home. Fortunately, the men had made two-year engagements only and this, plus Marshal Mannerheim's (q.v.) insistence that they were needed to defend Finland, persuaded the Germans to give way. A handful still went back to fight for the Nazis. During the Lapland War (q.v.) between the Finns and the Germans in 1944 and 1945, the Germans even planned to build up a Finnish S.S. force in Norway for future resistance in Finland (a mere 150 Finns were involved in this inchoate plan).

In Finland important names had been associated with the

original S.S. battalion's recruitment, as if, indeed, it was the Jaeger movement all over again. One such name was the famous mathematician Rolf Nevanlinna, rector of the University of Helsinki. Another was "Schwester Ruth," Ruth Munck, the nursing sister of the Jaegers in World War I, who went out to nurse the S.S. men, too.

STÅHLBERG, KAARLO JUHO (1865–1952). President of Finland from 1919 to 1925. Ståhlberg was the first officially styled president of his land, though in order of time he was the third head of state. Preceding him had been Carl Gustaf Mannerheim (q.v.), who was given a title generally translated into English as "Regent," and before him Pehr Evind Svinhufvud (q.v.) who had been termed "Holder of Supreme Power."

Ståhlberg, the son of a clergyman, went to a Finnish school in Oulu and was a Fennoman (q.v.) from his earliest days. Studying law at the University of Helsinki, he went on to write his dissertation on the laws of vagrancy. A certain social liberalism remained characteristic of him always, but it was subordinated to a prime concern for upholding the law and its procedure.

Becoming a university teacher and then an official in the Senate (q.v.), Ståhlberg had been aghast at the promulgation of the 1890 Postal Manifesto (q.v.), which seemed to foreshadow further measures of unification (q.v.) with the rest of the Russian Empire. Ståhlberg distanced himself from the old Fennoman leadership and adopted the principles of the Young Finn (q.v.) movement, which, while disagreeing with the Svecoman movement (q.v.) on the language issue, was at one with the Svecoman majority in wanting to resist Russian encroachments on Finnish constitutional rights.

For Ståhlberg this resistance had always to be passive resistance (q.v.). In 1903 he was dismissed from his post in the Senate for refusing to draft measures relating to the conscription of Finnish youth into the Russian armed forces, but he never became an Activist (q.v.), and in World War I was quite unsympathetic to the Jaeger movement (q.v.). Resentment thus festered about him among a section of the Right, and this proved dangerous to him later.

In the tense year of 1917 Ståhlberg strove for reconciliation with the Social Democrats (q.v.), whose militancy grew as the connection with Russia began to break down and economic conditions deteriorated in Finland. Ståhlberg was far from being opposed to many of the Social Democratic demands for a reform of the local government franchise and a change in the tenure conditions of the crofters (q.v.), to take but two examples. Like nearly all bourgeois politicians of this time, however, he failed to appreciate the urgency of these demands and the pressures from below upon the Social Democratic leadership.

As Finland drifted toward the confrontation of the classes which broke out the following year into a Civil War (q.v.), Ståhlberg concerned himself with the constitutional regulation of relations between Finland and Russia—like most Finnish leaders, including for a long time the Social Democrats themselves, he could not quite bring himself to believe in a complete severance of connection between the two states.

In the tortuous negotiations and differences of opinion between the Finnish political parties in 1917, however, on one other major issue Ståhlberg drew away from the Social Democrats. He could not adopt their view of the supremacy of Parliament. And his concern for regulating, in a constitutional form, relations between Finland and Russia was essentially bound up with a desire to fix the supreme, sovereign power in the state in a clear, executive-level arrangement. A necessary tripartite division of the constitution (q.v.) would then ensue, but there would be a certain overlapping of function in which the legislative power would be shared between legislature and, as it turned out, president.

It was Ståhlberg who was to be the main force in the drafting of the constitution of independent Finland, where he followed the broad lines set down by Leo Mechelin (q.v.) in 1905.

Ståhlberg had become a Republican, however. After the defeat of the Reds in the Civil War, he saw republicanism as a means of binding a partially suppressed Social Democracy back into Finnish political society. Those Social Democrats remaining in Parliament voted for him in the 1919 presidential election, which was conducted through Parliament.

As president, Ståhlberg was not above using presidential

power. Though he is often contrasted with the rival presidential candidate Mannherheim, who was in favor of intervention (q.v.) in Russia, Ståhlberg was not averse to territorial annexation in principle. Thus he sent Finnish troops into Petsamo (q.v.) in early 1920 (they were kicked out by the Russians) and secured Petsamo at the Peace of Tartu (q.v.) later in the year. His main opposition to intervention was that the Allies would not countenance it. All other hope of territorial adjustment foundered upon his refusal to consider any trading of Finnish territory for vaster areas in, say, East Karelia (q.v.).

The right-wing Activist element in the country hated him—additionally—for not having *demanded* more at Tartu. As time went on, he believed the forces of the Right were becoming more representative of the country's mood. Always, he claimed, a reluctant politician, he decided not to contest the presidential election. From the point of view of the maintenance of a liberal constitutionalism, this was regrettable. His successor, L. K. Relander (q.v.), was weak; toward the end of the Relander presidency the forces of rightist, extraparliamentary action, such as the Lapua movement (q.v.), gained strength.

In 1930 Ståhlberg and his wife were kidnapped by members of the Lapua movement, the intention being to dump Dr. and Mrs. Ståhlberg over the Soviet border. The kidnappers were fortunately not men of firm resolve, however, and they left the former president and his wife at Joensuu in eastern Finland.

In 1931 Ståhlberg, nothing daunted, did contest the presidential election. He lost to Svinhufvud by 2 votes (149 versus 151 in the electoral college). Again, one can only regret this, for Svinhufvud's pro-German sympathies were well known to the Soviet Union.

Ståhlberg failed in the presidential election of 1937. His policy of conciliation, though, understood by all except the extreme Right, probably represented the best that could be expected in a society which, after the horrors of its Civil War, chose to live in a rather conservative mold. Ståhlberg, who was a founding member of the Progressive party (q.v.) in December 1918, bore his Progressivism in a different way from that of, for instance, Risto Ryti (q.v.).

STEIN, BORIS. Stein was Soviet minister to Finland in 1934 and 1935. He then tried fruitlessly to persuade the Finns to take part in an eastern Locarno-type of collective security pact.

Stein, later Soviet ambassador to Italy, suddenly turned up in Finland once more, in March 1939, when he attempted to continue the failed negotiations for a military security understanding with Finland. He suggested, with the defense of Leningrad in mind, that Finland should lease Suursaari and four other islands in the Gulf of Finland, while in return the Soviet Union would grant a stretch of territory in East Karelia (q.v.).

Unlike the previous proposals made by Boris Yartsev (q.v.), Stein's proposal was brought to the attention of the Defense Council and therefore of Mannerheim (q.v.). Mannerheim seemed inclined to view the proposal favorably, but the civilians were adamant: Finnish territory was "inviolate."

This way of thinking enabled the government to avoid, inter alia, trouble with the public (who, with a refusal, did not have to be told about Stein and his predecessor Yartsev anyway). The actual price of territorial inviolability was nonetheless to be paid by the public (or rather, the younger male members of it) a few months later when the Winter War (q.v.) broke out.

STELLA POLARIS. In September 1944 radio equipment, information about decoding, and intelligence personnel and their families were sent from Finland to Sweden. The whole operation had been planned many months earlier and behind it was collusion between the Finnish minister of defense, General Rudolf Waldén, and the Swedish minister of defense, Edvin Sköld. The general name for this operation was "Stella Polaris," or Northern Star.

For many of the people who went to Sweden, it was a question of escaping the vengeance they thought was coming to them. Some were undoubtedly in panic. After a time in Sweden, many returned to Finland, where they were never charged for desertion or anything else. Some remained in Sweden and were employed by Swedish military intelligence; others, like Colonel Aladar Paasonen, seem to have ended up in the service of U.S. intelligence.

The equipment and information was sold to Sweden, and

the Stella Polaris archives have never been fully recovered by the Finns. The whole connection was said to have been an embarrassment to the Swedish government from 1944 to 1945, but the Swedish military and defense ministry had their way.

As far as the Finns were concerned, the issue was yet another aspect of the alternative policies for Finland worked out by the Finnish military. While it is difficult to tie all the ends together (the matter is largely unresearched), the Stella Polaris scheme and the arms caching (q.v.) in Finland were interconnected. The intelligence that was transferred to Sweden was to be used in case of a worsening of relations between the West and the Soviet Union, which, many in the Finnish military thought, might lead to open war and the turning of Finland into a battlefield.

From what is known of the Stella Polaris operation, the Germans were cognizant of it and even supplied it with cash. What effect all this had on modifying the breakdown in Finnish-German relations that was given expression in the Lapland War (q.v.) is unknown.

The most astonishing recent revelation is that much of the decoding material (especially for Soviet transmissions) was sold to the Japanese intelligence services.

STOLBOVA, PEACE OF. This peace agreement between Sweden and Russia, signed in a small village in Ingria (q.v.) in 1617, concluded for some time Swedish intervention in Russia. The phase of Swedish intervention that led to the Peace of Stolbova had arisen out of rivalry with Poland and, in particular, from the complex politics of the Sigismund (q.v.) era. Sigismund had been unable to maintain a joint Swedish-Polish state, and Poland became Sweden's prey, with tempting lands on the Baltic, and also a threat, due to Polish ambitions to control the Russian state.

In the Time of the Troubles in Russia (1604–1613) Vasili Shuisky called in Swedish help against the pretender to the throne, the second False Dmitri, who, like the first False Dmitri, was backed by Poland. The election of Mikhail Romanov as tsar in 1613 was a prelude to the withdrawal of Sweden and the end of Swedish hopes to found a client state of Novgorod, ruled over by a member of the Swedish royal family.

At Stolbova Sweden gave up Novgorod (for a payment), but retained Ingria and the province of Kåkisalmi on the Karelian Isthmus (q.v.). The possession of Ingria, which afforded a tenuous link with Swedish Estonia, was the farthest eastward the Finnish frontier was ever to go (though Ingria was never incorporated into the Swedish realm as Finland was).

The new frontier satisfied the needs of the Finns for a safer border—a consideration which had led many of them to support Sigismund in the late sixteenth century. Sweden now became one of the biggest states in Europe. Yet, as far as Russia was concerned, Sweden was henceforth restricted to the Baltic littoral. Sweden's treatment of the Karelian population of the new lands, who belonged to the Orthodox church (q.v.) and who, in subsequent years, began to flee to Russia, showed how unable the Lutheran Swedes and Finns were to rule over a population of alien culture. It was in this century that the Karelian Isthmus and Ingria were Lutheranized by force or settlement.

It is interesting to note that the making of peace at Stolbova owed something to the pressure of English and Dutch commercial interests, sick of the dynastic struggles affecting the Russian and East Baltic areas.

STUDENT CORPORATIONS. Finland inherited this medieval, and in the postmedieval world, Germanic tradition of having its university students recruited into corporations based on locality. In the Middle Ages Finnish students at the University of Paris were placed, as northerners, in the English corporation, it was said. In Finland the locality for the corporation has been the region or province.

The student corporations have been famous features of Finnish history, and it has been regarded as an honor for an academic (generally a professor) to be appointed inspector of such a corporation. They have never been dueling clubs. These corporations have engaged in voluntary and often patriotic work, sending their members out to rural areas to teach the people or collect folk poetry in the period before independence. In previous decades, too, they were sometimes an important source of ideas, a forum for intimate debate—the Communist leader O. W. Kuusinen (q.v.) is said to have learned much about socialism from the inspector of his corporation, Sulo Wuolijoki (later the husband of Hella Wuolijoki, q.v.).

So fascinating was life in the student corporations for many members that they tried to prolong it by creating associations of former members. One such association, an extended arm of the Satakunta Corporation, drank toasts to Saint Henry (q.v.): *In nomine Sancti Henrici bibamus.* The saint was murdered in Satakunta.

While student corporations still exist, much of their glory has gone. Study-subject organizations, like the law student's association of the University of Turku, called Lex, play more important roles. Above all, students are now directly represented in the university assemblies. In the University of Turku they have one-third of the seats in such organs, and even the ever-resistant University of Helsinki has at last moved toward a student-representative system.

These changes draw energetic spirits away from the activities of the student corporations, though the results are not especially radical, even if the whole concept of student activism derives its origin on these planes from the student radicalism of the late 1960s.

SUOMENLINNA. Historically, this was a fortified island complex off the coast of Helsinki (q.v.), and was once dubbed by the poet J. L. Runeberg (q.v.) a "Gibraltar of the North." Suomenlinna is a brief ferry trip from the southern harbor of Helsinki. Its proud title means the "Castle of Finland," but the fortifications were originally built as Sveaborg, the "Castle of Svea" (the poetic name for Sweden), from which was derived its first Finnish name of Viapori. The name was changed to Suomenlinna in 1918 to mark the newly gained independence (q.v.) of Finland.

Fortifications in this area were laid down as early as 1555 by Gustavus I Vasa, but the present fortifications were started in 1748 in light of the broad plans drawn up by the Swedish military and naval commander Augustin Ehrensvärd, who is buried in the island church. In spite of the aggressive Swedish-Russian War of 1788–1790 (q.v.) forty years later, the fortifications at Sveaborg—and the even wider, unrealized plans for the mainland coast—represented a change in Swedish policy, a move back to defensive positioning.

In the construction of the fortifications, granite hewn from the island itself was used, as well as sandstone brought from the Swedish islands of Gothland and Öland.

Under mysterious circumstances in May 1808, the island fortress was yielded to Russia in the War for the Possession of Finland of 1808–1809 (q.v.). The culprit was the commandant himself, whose deed later provided J. L. Runeberg with the melancholy satisfaction of pillorying him obliquely: "Mention not his name." His name was C. O. Cronstedt, and he appears to have suffered much in spirit after his action.

The Russians extended the fortifications of the island complex, and it became an important feature of the defenses both of Helsinki and of the approaches to Saint Petersburg. In 1855, during the Crimean War (q.v.), the fortress was bombarded by the combined British and French fleets, a spectacle viewed by the burghers of Helsinki and their wives from the hilltop park of Kaivopuisto on the mainland shore.

In 1906 a mutiny occurred among part of the Russian garrison, and Sveaborg was briefly in the hands of the revolutionaries (Social Revolutionaries and Anarchists as well as Bolsheviks) assisted, to the consternation of the official Finnish Social Democratic (q.v.) leadership, by some Finnish Red Guards. The Russian ringleaders were executed there.

In the 1918 Civil War (q.v.) Russian forces and Finnish Red Guards collaborated for a period in garrisoning the fortress. As a result, however, of the Hanko agreement of April 5, by which the Russian forces declared their neutrality to the invading German troops, the Russian commandant of Sveaborg threw out the Finnish Red Guards.

On the defeat of the Reds in the Civil War, large numbers of them were imprisoned in Sveaborg and many executed there. As was the case with the writer Maiju Lassila (Algoth Untola), who was shot on the boat journey to Sveaborg, the executed were buried on the neighboring island of Santahamina, where, in 1925, the Finnish army built a pigsty on their graves.

Since independence Suomenlinna has served both as a

naval station and as a garrison (a submarine from World War II may be inspected there). The military and naval contingents have now been removed, and current plans for the island complex include the building of more private houses. At present the area has just under 900 permanent inhabitants.

SVECOMAN MOVEMENT. By the mid–nineteenth century the bureaucracy in Finland had long been Svedicized. Their opposition to the Fennoman movement (q.v.) broadly derived from an unwillingness to learn Finnish, which was not considered to be a language of a developed culture, and a fear that promoting the language of the people was a revolutionary act. Snellman (q.v.) was called, quaintly, a "Communist."

When, by the early 1860s, Fennomanism threatened to become a popular political force in reality and not just in aspiration, a parallel movement was developed among the Swedish-speaking population. A Swedish nationality was discovered to exist in Finland, and an identity of interests somewhat clumsily emerged among Swedish-speaking bureaucrats, urban Swedish-speakers, and the Swedish-speaking peasantry and fisher folk of the southern and western littoral and archipelagoes.

Though such scholars and jurists as A. O. Freudenthal tried to weld these rather diverse elements into a political force, the Swedish elements in Finland did not blend together very readily. The bureaucrats kept their power more easily than they had previously thought possible, and Mechelin's (q.v.) attempt to form a Liberal party reaching across linguistic boundaries was repulsed as much by Svecoman bureaucrats, fortified for years ahead by Swedish control of the Estate of Nobility and Estate of Burghers, as by the leaders of the Fennoman movement. It may with some truth be argued that a true Swedish party came into being only as a result of the disturbances of 1905 and the subsequent establishment of a unicameral legislature (q.v.).

The advent of democratism thus compelled the creation of a Svenska folkparti—a Swedish People's party (q.v.), and the name is significant. It was definite proof that the bond of party was now avowedly the language interest, and the ethnic overtones that had haunted Freudenthal and his associates were fading.

SVINHUFVUD, PEHR EVIND (1861–1944). Holder of Supreme Power in Finland from May to December 1918; president of Finland from 1931 to 1937.

Svinhufvud came of a noble family. They farmed, but his father also went to sea, as a trading captain. He was drowned in the Mediterranean when Pehr Evind Svinhufvud was two years old.

The young Svinhufvud went to the leading Finnish-speaking school in Helsinki (q.v.) and then on to graduate both in the humanities and in law from the University of Helsinki, but unlike several of Finland's future presidents, Svinhufvud was no legal scholar. What he had imbibed, however, was a fundamental belief in the worth of the Finnish legal and constitutional system and its basic norms. Thus, in 1903, in the Years of Oppression (q.v.), he was dismissed from his post in the Turku (q.v.) High Court for refusing to abide by Senate (q.v.) directives he considered at variance with traditional Finnish legal norms.

In politics, Svinhufvud was a Young Finn (q.v.); when he took his seat in the House of Nobles of the Diet of Four Estates (q.v.) in 1894, he was one of the few Finnish-speaking members of that house.

In 1901 Svinhufvud became one of the founding members of the secret society known as Kagal, which directed passive resistance (q.v.). In fact—unlike the great passive resistance leader Lee Mechelin (q.v.)—Svinhufvud later cultivated relations with the Activists (q.v.), too.

After the Great Strike (q.v.) of 1905, with the establishment of a unicameral legislature (q.v.), Svinhufvud became its speaker, but his opening addresses and other remarks were offensive to the tsar and imperial power. The work of the legislature was difficult enough, due to internal dissension as well as the refusal of the tsar to sign many laws. In 1913 Svinhufvud was not reelected speaker.

At the end of 1914, as chairman of the regional court at Luumäki in eastern Finland, Svinhufvud challenged the jurisdiction of the Russian procurator, K. Kasanski, in a matter concerning the Equality Law (a law imposed on Finland which granted equal rights for Russian citizens in the Grand Duchy [q.v.], including the right to trade).

Svinhufvud was, in consequence, exiled to Siberia, whence he said he would be freed only by the power of "Heaven and Hindenburg" (as the years went by, Svinhufvud grew to resemble Hindenburg, and he had always liked guns).

So, with World War I pursuing its course, Svinhufvud rightly saw that Finland's problems would take a new turn with the defeat of Russia by Germany. Back from his exile, he was successfully pushing, by the end of 1917, for a declaration of independence (q.v.), endorsement for which he himself got from Lenin (q.v.).

Unfortunately, Svinhufvud's vision of international relations was, like Paasikivi's (q.v.), correct only up to a certain point. Having called in German troops—against the wishes of Mannerheim (q.v.)—to help suppress the Reds in the Civil War (q.v.), Svinhufvud was convinced of a future German hegemony in Europe. He failed—unlike Mannerheim—to estimate the power of the Western Allies. As Holder of Supreme Power in Finland after the collapse of the Reds in the Civil War, Svinhufvud, as late as October 1918, was still urging upon Finland a monarchist (q.v.) solution for its problems of legitimacy, and the monarch was to be a German prince. So Svinhufvud had to go, to be replaced by Mannerheim, who was pro-Allied.

It was the extraparliamentary right-wing agitation of the late 1920s and early 1930s that brought Svinhufvud to the political fore again, now as a member of the conservative National Coalition party. At first he sympathized with the Lapua movement (q.v.), but becoming prime minister in 1930 and president in 1931, he gradually asserted the strength of a constitutionalism (q.v.) in which he had, at heart, always believed. Anyway, with Svinhufvud in power, the Right could get what it wanted by constitutional means. The rank and file among the men of Lapua trusted him, and when the Mäntsälä Revolt (q.v.) broke out in 1932, Svinhufvud was able to stop both army units and further units of Civil Guards (q.v.) from joining it. It collapsed.

While the election of Svinhufvud to the presidency undoubtedly damped the ardor of the Right to take the law into its own hands, Svinhufvud continued to alienate the Left, including the constitutional Left of the Social Democrats (q.v.), whom he refused to have in government. He had never gotten over the fact that a large section of the old Social Democratic party had tried to effect a revolution in 1918 (he had been convinced in 1917 that they would not do this) and remained obstinately blind to the constitutionalism of those Social Democrats—like Väinö Tanner (q.v.)—who had opposed taking up arms in 1918.

In 1937, though a candidate again for the presidency, Svinhufvud lost. A deeper national unity than he could conceive of had to be created through the emergence of a "Red Earth" politics: a coalition between the Social Democrats and Agrarian Union (q.v.).

In the sphere of foreign relations the Svinhufvud presidency was not a remarkable one. A Nonaggression Treaty (q.v.) was signed with the Soviet Union in 1932 and renewed in 1934 until 1945. From the Finnish side, this was pro forma, and Finland fended off all Soviet feelers for an Eastern Locarno and took with bad grace the Soviet admission to the League of Nations.

Svinhufvud, though unsympathetic to Nazi ideas, was still pro-German. The image he projected of Finland's international position in Soviet eyes had less to do with the weak Nordic line the Finns claimed to be associating with and more to do with the lure of growing German power. In any case, by appointing Mannerheim to be chairman of the Defense Council in 1931, Svinhufvud showed clearly in which direction he thought Finnish security policy should be strengthened. Mannerheim's role in the Defense Council was the beginning of an alternative source of power in Finland, one that ultimately came to fruition in the years 1940 and 1941 when the military took Finland into preparations for belligerency alongside Nazi Germany.

Events passed Svinhufvud by. In 1939 and 1940, on two separate occasions, he was involved in attempts to get German help for Finland, but these matters were now on a different plane.

In a sense, what happened in 1941 when Finland became a cobelligerent (q.v.) of Nazi Germany was a confirmation of his own outlook on how to protect Finland's place in Europe.

Once again he underestimated the potentiality of the West, nor was he alone.

He died of cancer in 1944, still believing that Finland could retain its East Karelian conquests (q.v.); he had always upheld Finland's right to that region. His last words to a political colleague from the Agrarian party were, "Never trust the Russians."

SWEDISH LANGUAGE. One of the two official languages in Finland, guaranteed by Article 14 of the constitution (q.v.). Historically, Swedish has been as important as Finnish in the development of the country. Nowadays, as a mother tongue, Swedish is in decline in Finland: in 1910 it was spoken by 11.6% of the population, while today the figure is a little over 6%.

In Finland the term "Swede" is used to denote people whose mother tongue is Swedish, but reveals nothing necessarily about their ethnic background, except in the case of the people of Åland (q.v.), who are mainly descended from early Swedish settlers and do not consider that they are Finns anyway. In addition to Scandinavian settlers on the mainland of Finland, the Swedish kings also transferred population from central Sweden to Ostrobothnia and Häme in the early Middle Ages, but in all these cases varying degrees of admixture with the Finns occurred. Later many boys of pure Finnish origin were swedicized in the course of their education, being given Swedish names if they went to high school.

Swedish and Finnish ran together for many centuries, but with the tightening of the administrative system and the gradual replacement of Latin by Swedish as the language of higher education, Swedish became the language of the upper class.

Though Snellman (q.v.) demanded in the nineteenth century that this class Finnicize itself, even he recognized the complexity of the linguistic pattern in Finland by accepting Swedish as the natural language of the peasantry in some coastal areas. Early in the twentieth century the Social Democratic party (q.v.) in Finland had to come to terms with the fact that some of its most ardent supporters were actually to be found among the Swedish-speaking urban proletariat.

Still, the upper-class tinge of Swedish-speaking has remained long into this century a resented element for many ordinary Finns. An extreme example is furnished by the baron in Väinö Linna's novel *Here Under the Pole Star*: the baron gives orders to his estate workers in a Finnish he can hardly speak. Nowadays, however, a fluent bilingualism is more likely to be found among Swedish-speakers than among Finnish-speakers.

Nevertheless, all Finnish-speaking high school pupils study six years of Swedish and must pass an examination in the language in order to graduate. Apart from the cultural inheritance of Swedish, this is also justified on grounds of Nordic cooperation (q.v.). An opinion is gaining strength against compulsory Swedish in the schools for Finnish-speakers. It is argued that European integration (q.v.) pressures require a shift of emphasis to other languages or even to nonlinguistic subjects.

There is an enormous volume of literature written in Swedish in Finland. The patriotic writers J. L. Runeberg (q.v.) and Z. Topelius wrote in Swedish. Swedish was also the mother tongue of the composer Jean Sibelius (q.v.) and of the military and political leader Marshal Mannerheim (q.v.). In general, the outlook of the Swedish-speaking minority in Finland may be characterized as Western but by no means necessarily tied up with the interests of Sweden.

In contrast to many countries there is no acrimonious language conflict in Finland; the last open conflict was seen in the 1930s over the allegedly excessive dominance of Swedish at the University of Helsinki. Swedish-speakers have their own schools and a large share in higher education, including their own university in Turku (q.v.), Åbo Akademi. By the Language Law of 1922 Swedish-speakers (just as Finnish-speakers) have been confirmed in their right to receive official documentation, including anything relating to their own court cases, in their own language. The formal aspects of bilingual peace in Finland have been the object of favorable scrutiny by Canada. Much of this peace is undoubtedly due to the fact that from the second half of the nineteenth century a section of the upper class began to Finnicize itself.

SWEDISH MONARCHY. Since Finland was an integral part of the Swedish state till 1809, the influence of the Swedish monarchy upon its development has been of prime significance.

Traditionally, the Swedish monarchy was elective. A ruler's compact, called *härskarfördrag,* if not exactly a contract, was felt to be evident in the fourteenth and fifteenth centuries. The citizens and those in positions of trust in the realm swore allegiance, while the monarch undertook to administer law with the consent of the people, not to take property without legal right, and to maintain the privileges of the Estates.

Though the monarchy became hereditary in the Vasa line in 1544, an Accession Charter was forced on Sigismund (q.v.) in 1594. In 1611 the monarch had to agree that the Estates should share legislative power.

The requirements forced on the monarchy during the eighteenth-century Age of Liberty (q.v.) ensured, after the absolutism of Charles XII, the emergence of a mixed monarchy à la Pufendorf. Though much royal power was restored in the coup d'état of Gustavus III in 1772, the two principal constitutional documents of his reign—the Form of Government of 1772 (q.v.) and the Act of Union and Security of 1789 (q.v.)—though they accorded the monarch much power, were nonetheless fundamental laws of a constitutionalist state.

When Finland was lost to the Russian Empire in 1809, this Swedish legacy endured, for Alexander I at the Diet of Porvoo (q.v.) confirmed the fundamental laws of Finland. These were never specified, but were understood as the Form of Government and the Act of Union and Security.

A less happy consequence for Finland of Swedish monarchical power was the futile wars into which the country had been plunged, especially the eighteenth-century attempts to get back the lost lands and the concomitant inability to defend Finland against Russian counterassaults. This legacy made Finnish acceptance of Alexander I that much easier.

SWEDISH PEOPLE'S PARTY (Svenska Folkpartiet). This party, founded in 1906 in preparation for elections to the unicameral legislature (q.v.), arose out of the Svecoman movement's (q.v.) Swedish party, which had been dominant in two of the states of the old Diet of Four Estates (q.v.): the Estate of Nobles and the Estate of Burghers. In the first elections for the unicameral legislature, based as they were on universal suffrage, the Swedish People's party received only 24 out of the 200 seats.

Since the days of entrenched political privilege were over, the Swedish People's party endeavored to become a party representative of a broad coalition of interests sharing in common a perceived need to protect the status of the Swedish language (q.v.) in Finland. Many Swedish-speaking workers, however, have voted for the Social Democratic party (q.v.), which has been neutral in the language question.

In 1918 the Swedish People's party was full of monarchists (q.v.). It clung to demands for regional autonomy—realized only in the case of the Åland Islands (q.v.)—until the early 1920s. Then these demands were abandoned and the party settled down gradually to being a component in coalition governments, from which vantage point it could protect the Swedish language. In the devious politics of Finnish presidential elections it has sometimes played an important role.

The Swedish People's party has often had a liberal, progressive side to it. Thus in the Continuation War (q.v.) a surprising number of the members of the Peace Opposition (q.v.) were from this party. In general the attitude of this party toward the refugee question is more liberal than that of many Finnish parties.

SWEDISH-RUSSIAN WAR OF 1741–1743. This war was a colossal blunder on the part of Sweden, and its ill effects, particularly for Finland, have been summed up in the designation of these years as the Lesser Wrath (q.v.), an unmerited supplement to the Great Wrath (q.v.) of 1713–1721.

In the background to the war of 1741–1743 were the intrigues of the Swedish party known as the Hats (s.v. Hats and Caps) with the future Russian empress Elizabeth. The daughter of Peter the Great, her succession to the throne was being thwarted by the existence of the infant tsar Ivan VI. The

Swedish leaders decided to help promote Elizabeth's bid for power by starting an invasion of Russia in return for which they foolishly expected Elizabeth to restore the lands lost by Sweden in 1721 by the Peace of Uusikaupunki (q.v.).

The rival Swedish party of the Caps (s.v. Hats and Caps) behaved no better. They were prepared to see the hardships and costs of war, and even, if necessary, a Russian occupation of Finland, so as to unseat the Hats by the emergent popular discontent.

These disastrous politics were but one example of the manipulation of foreign policy in eighteenth-century Sweden for the pursuit of domestic political gains. The same politics was also an expression of the illusion that Sweden was still a great power.

In the event, what Elizabeth did was issue a proclamation on March 8, 1742, offering the Finns an independent duchy of Finland should they support the Russians. Nothing came of her proposal, even though two local Finnish assemblies endorsed it by suggesting that her relative, Karl Peter Ulrik, duke of Holstein, should take over a Grand Duchy (q.v.) of Finland. Elizabeth already had other plans for him—succession to the Russian throne (he was to reign briefly as Peter III)—so the minor issue of Finland dropped away.

In the war the Russians occupied Finland, and after it were called to Sweden to protect the country from a threatened Danish invasion. The humiliation of Sweden was completed, at the Peace of Turku (q.v.), by further territorial losses in and for Finland, this time from the Karelian Isthmus (q.v.) boundary to the Kymi River.

This war is sometimes known as the War of the Hats.

SWEDISH-RUSSIAN WAR OF 1788–1790. This conflict was initiated by Gustavus III without the consent of the Diet of Four Estates (q.v.), though halfway through the war, with the passage of the Act of Union and Security (q.v.), Gustavus gained for himself the right to start a war on his own initiative.

Ostensibly, Gustavus embarked on hostilities with Russia to effect the restoration of the Finnish lands lost at the 1721 Peace of Uusikaupunki (q.v.) and the 1743 Peace of Turku (q.v.). The war of 1788–1790 was not unconnected with the worrying fate of Poland. Above all, through these hostilities

and hoped-for conquests, Gustavus aimed to regain his pop-
ularity and strengthen even further monarchical power. He
thus snubbed the nobility in the adoption of the Act of Union
and Security, while enhancing the peasants' rights to redeem
their lands from the Crown.

With the exception of the great Swedish naval victory at
the second Battle of Ruotsinsalmi (off Kotka) in 1790, most
of the hostilities involved ineffectual engagements in Savo
and the southeast. The lost lands were not restored, though
Catherine willingly made peace so as to be able to deal with
her Turkish foes.

Certainly the upshot of the war was to free Sweden from
Russian interference in its internal affairs, for by the Peace
of Värälä the obnoxious Section 7 of the Peace of Uusikaupunki was abrogated, but the Swedish-Russian conflict
itself was not ended in 1790.

While most Finns remained loyal to the Swedish monarchy during the war of 1788–1790, the discontent of a number of Finnish officers and estate owners was seen in such
manifestations as the Liikkala Note (q.v.), the Anjala
Covenant (q.v.), and the Diet of Paaso (q.v.). Those who
were involved in these events asked themselves whether
Finnish security might be better maintained by coming to
terms with Russian power. Apart from the spread of epi-
demics like dysentery, Finland suffered during the hostilities
from severe inflation. This was caused by Gustavus's printing of his own notes (in which tender the soldiers were paid)
through a specially constituted State Debt Office, which enabled him to avoid control of his finances by the Diet.

All in all, the Swedish-Russian War of 1788–1790 did not
strengthen the position of Gustavus himself, and a section of
his jealous nobility were soon to bring him down.

-T-

TANNER, VÄINÖ (1881–1966). Social Democratic party (q.v.)
leader. The son of a brakeman, Väinö Tanner secured a law
degree while already active in the Finnish cooperative movement, a force with which he was identified all his life. Tanner refused to take part in the revolutionary government of

the Reds in the 1918 Civil War (q.v.) and became an embodiment of that section of the Finnish Social Democratic party which had never wanted to capture the state by violence. His subsequent leadership held the party together as a legitimate element in the traditional political system, but at the price of the alienation of the more radical left wing.

As early as 1920 Tanner was sufficiently trusted by the Finnish establishment to be appointed to the Peace of Tartu (q.v.) delegation. He became prime minister for a year in December 1926 and was acting president during the illness of President Relander (q.v.). He was one of the Finnish negotiators with the Soviet Union in the autumn of 1939 and was in favor of making minimal territorial concessions that might have prevented the outbreak of the Winter War (q.v.). It has been averred that in June 1941, just before the Continuation War (q.v.) began, Tanner suggested to a limited audience that it was enough for the Finnish army to mobilize, or that, if hostilities were to be engaged in, they should be limited to an attack on the Hanko Peninsula. Since Tanner was not then a member of the government, he did not need to express these views very strongly.

When the war broke out, Tanner became a member of the government, serving first as minister of trade and industry and then as minister of finance. At one time he seemed to be attracted to the German New Order in Europe. Later he came to dislike the Peace Opposition (q.v.) for spoiling the "real chances" of making a separate peace.

After the war, Tanner was convicted in the war trials (q.v.) and jailed as a "war criminal." He returned to Parliament thereafter, his leadership of the Social Democratic party thus helping to compromise that party in Soviet eyes.

TARTU (DORPAT), PEACE OF. By this treaty, signed at Tartu, Estonia, on October 14, 1920, the state of war between Finland and the Soviet Union was brought to an end. Though Lenin (q.v.), on December 31, 1917, had accorded the Bolshevik recognition of Finnish independence (q.v.), hostilities between Finland and Russia had—even after the Finnish Civil War (q.v.) of 1918—endured. Finnish irregulars had moved into East Karelia (q.v.), while Mannerheim (q.v.) had favored intervention (q.v.) against Petrograd.

Mannerheim's defeat in the presidential election of 1919 removed the latter threat—at least from the Finnish side. A new danger arose for the Bolsheviks in 1920, however, with the military successes of the Poles against them and the apparent menace of a wider Baltic alliance, which for the Finnish foreign minister, Rudolf Holsti, was not without its attractions provided it could be gotten in suitable form.

As Holsti was to discover, however, the Finnish public was inclined to leave Russia to its own devices. The exception to this mood, particularly in rightist circles, was the need to adjust the frontier of the Karelian Isthmus (q.v.) and to grab as much of East Karelia as possible.

Here the Peace of Tartu was gravely disappointing. During the lengthy negotiations preceding its signing, the military position of the Bolsheviks vis-à-vis the Poles improved. This stiffened the attitude of the Soviet negotiators at Tartu.

The large East Karelian parishes of Repola and Porajärvi, which had been taken into Finland, were restored to Russia, though Article 10 of the peace, which sanctioned this, also referred to the self-determination of East Karelia. What Finland gained by the second article of the peace treaty was the Petsamo (q.v.) area in the north, which had originally been promised to the Grand Duchy (q.v.) in 1864. Article 6 of the Tartu peace treaty nevertheless imposed considerable restrictions upon a Finnish naval and military presence in the Petsamo area.

The chief Finnish negotiators at Tartu, J. K. Paasikivi (q.v.) and Väinö Tanner (q.v.), were blamed by the Finnish Right for having demanded too little from Russia. The subsequent failure of the Soviet government to honor, in terms understood by the Finns, the self-determination of East Karelia laid down in Article 10, as well as the ignoring of the additional assurances given by the Soviet delegates when signing the peace about the rights of the east Karelians and Ingrians, soon began to stimulate resentment in Finland. The stage was set for further military action in East Karelia and (when that failed) for the establishment of one of the most powerful Finnish political lobbies ever, the Academic Karelia Society (q.v.).

TÄYSSINÄ (TÄYSINÄ), PEACE OF. This was concluded in a village in Ingria (q.v.) in May 1595 and was meant to end the twenty-five years of hostilities between Sweden and Russia known in Finland as the Long Wrath (q.v.).

Sweden renounced possession of the fortress and district of Käkisalmi on the Karelian Isthmus (q.v.) and Ladoga shores, but in return the frontier between Finland and the Russian domains was demarcated in a way more favorable to the Finns. What this meant was that the Orthodox Karelians were henceforth denied the right to use the lands to the north of the Ostrobothnian river of Pyhäjoki. These lands were now behind the Finnish eastern border.

On the other hand, though this long-awaited adjustment of the Swedish-Russian border in the Finns' interest guaranteed in theory a Finnish border running up to the Arctic Ocean, the last stretch of this was never finally demarcated. Not all of the Peace of Pähkinäsaari (q.v.) was thus set aside, and in the farthest north Russian tax collectors and Karelians continued to harass the Lapps (q.v.) in territory that should rightly have been within the Swedish realm.

Savo and Kainuu, however, were now clearly within that realm, since the Swedes in their turn renounced any claims to the Viena and Aunus areas in what later became known as East Karelia (q.v.). Most important of all, Sweden gained the city and port of Narva and Northern Estonia, so that only Ingria (q.v.) still cut off the Swedes from a complete possession of the shores of the Gulf of Finland. Ingria was not attained until the Peace of Stolbova (q.v.) in 1617.

The Peace of Täyssinä had thus given only a temporary respite. Sweden's eastward expansion was to continue, though in the next stage it was to become involved, through the dynastic quarrels between Charles and Sigismund (q.v.), in a Swedish-Polish conflict. As a part of that conflict, the Swedes tried to control the politics of the Muscovite state, even dreaming of the imposition upon the unhappy Muscovites (and the more willing inhabitants of Novgorod) of a Swedish tsar. So the Swedes and Finns, only a few years after Täyssinä, were once more fighting the Russians.

TEMPERANCE MOVEMENT. As early as the 1850s, concern was being shown among certain Finnish reformers about the excessive drinking habits of their fellow countrymen. In 1853 the first committee was set up in the Finnish capital (though under a Russian professor) to deal with this problem, particularly at the level of home distilling, which was banned in 1866. By the 1880s temperance societies with a program of rigid abstinence began to arise, with some inspiration from the rest of Scandinavia and from the Good Templar movement in the United States.

Before World War I some temperance work was being carried on in the Finnish elementary schools, a well-known teacher called Alli Trygg-Helenius employing for this purpose a doll with a diseased liver. Temperance had, by this time, also become a part of Finland's political regeneration; the temperance movement was represented at the foundation of the Social Democratic party (q.v.) at Forssa in 1903.

The high point of the temperance movement was the attainment of prohibition in 1919. This ran until 1932 and produced its own crime—the smuggling of spirits from Estonia and illicit distilling. After prohibition ended, a state alcohol monopoly was set up, called Alko. How long this will survived now that Finland, on January 1, 1994, joined the European Economic Area—in apparent preparation for European Union (formerly European Community) membership—is difficult to say. Both the EEA and the EU are based upon opposition to monopoly.

TERIJOKI GOVERNMENT. This was the puppet government set up by the Soviet Union on December 1, 1939, a day after the hostilities of the Winter War (q.v.) had commenced. It takes its name from its seat, the border town of Terijoki (now Zelenogorsk) on the Karelian Isthmus (q.v.).

Of this government of seven ministers, the only remarkable figure was Otto Wille Kuusinen (q.v.), then secretary of the Executive Committee of Comintern, who became both prime minister and foreign minister. Aksel Anttila, the minister of defense, was named Commander of a Finnish People's Army. Recent research has shown that there really was such an army—composed of Finnish Reds in the Soviet Union.

The Terijoki government served the purpose of allowing

the Soviet government to claim that it was not at war with Finland, but only with a clique of rulers in Helsinki. Finland, as the Soviet Union argued before the League of Nations, meant the Terijoki government, with which the USSR concluded on December 2 a Treaty of Friendship and Cooperation and exchanged the vast East Karelian (q.v.) lands for the areas it wanted on the Karelian Isthmus and at the mouth of the Gulf of Finland.

It should be stressed that the Terijoki government was a provisional government. Elections for a new government were to be held once the Soviet army reached Helsinki (q.v.). It did not reach Helsinki, however. The resistance of the Finns slowed down the advance of the Red Army, and by the end of January 1940 the USSR was prepared to treat with the constitutionally elected government of Finland and to forget about the Terijoki government. It had been impossible for the Soviet Union to conjure up the ghosts of the Finnish Civil War (q.v.) to its aid.

Care should be taken in evaluating the significance of the Terijoki government. It was part of the Soviet maximalist solution for Finland—conquest. So far as is known, this arose out of the frustrations of the years 1935–1939 when Soviet minimalist solutions were fended off by the Finns.

TURKU (Swedish: Åbo). Turku is a city of somewhat under 160,000 inhabitants in southwestern Finland, in the area from which the whole country has taken its name. Turku is a port, and several passenger ships a day leave from there for Stockholm, sailing through the beautiful archipelago between Turku and Åland (q.v.).

Turku is often described as the old capital of Finland. This is correct to the extent that, when Finland became a Grand Duchy (q.v.) under the tsars in 1809, the administration of the country was carried on for the first three years from Turku, though in 1812 Helsinki (q.v.) became the capital.

After the great fire of Turku in 1827, the university, which had been founded there by Governor-General Per Brahe (q.v.) in 1640, was also moved to Helsinki, being reestablished there in 1828 as the Imperial Alexander University. Turku did not get back its university-city status until 1919 when the Swedish-language Åbo Akademi was founded, followed by the Finnish-language University of Turku in 1922.

Though Finland was a part of Sweden up to 1809, and not a separate state under a Swedish king, in certain periods of history there are grounds for claiming that Turku served as a kind of Finnish capital. In the mid–sixteenth century Duke John (q.v.) held court in Turku castle, and in the seventeenth century Turku was the center of Per Brahe's administration, though for the first few years of his governor-generalship of Finland, the concept of Finland excluded Ostrobothnia, which was left outside his original jurisdiction.

As a settlement, Turku is much older than its cathedral (of the present Archdiocese of Finland), as its castle—both buildings of which were started in the thirteenth century— would indicate. A bishop earlier had his seat, it is presumed, at Koroinen, higher up the Aura River, but still within the Turku area. This was also a center for inland trade with Häme and for maritime trade.

The name Turku is customarily derived from the word *torg* (a word found both in the Scandinavian and in the Russian languages, but probably in origin from the former) meaning "market." Some scholars see Turku as having been an important commercial center on the very boundary between two seagoing empires, the one based on Lake Mälaren in Sweden and the other on the islands of western Estonia. Even before this, however, there was an Iron Age settlement at the mouth of the Aura.

Many of the present-day inhabitants of Turku appear fascinated by this ancient lineage, turning out in droves to listen to lectures by the Turku Society on the past of the city. They are not fascinated enough, though, to stop the destruction of the old buildings in the city center—Turku having become notorious for this form of modern vandalism.

Turku has also become notorious—in this connection— for a wider malaise, summed up by Professor Hannu Klami as the "Turku disease" (in Finnish, *Turun tauti*): a spreading pattern of corruption, starting with deals made between building contractors, eager to get their hands on valuable plots of land, and politicians, eager to get campaign funding.

Ancient monuments are but one of the casualties of the evil face of a politics without an ideal.

TURKU, PEACE OF. This was signed on the riverside in Turku (q.v.) on August 8, 1743, and brought to an end the Swedish-Russian War of 1741–1743 (q.v.), a war sometimes known as the War of the Hats. Large tracts of eastern Finland, beyond the Kymi River and south of Lake Saimaa (but including the island fortress of Olavinlinna), were lost. These areas were joined to the lands lost at the Peace of Uusikaupunki (q.v.) in 1721 and came to constitute a region known as Old Finland (q.v.), which was not restored until 1811.

-U-

UNICAMERAL LEGISLATURE. This legislature, unique in the Europe of its time, first sat in 1907, when it replaced the ancient Diet of Four Estates (q.v.). The change was made possible by the Russian Revolution of 1905: the Russians thus facilitated the development of democracy in Finland. Actually, the Finnish Social Democrats (q.v.) during the Finnish Great Strike (q.v.) in the autumn of 1905 demanded the summoning of a national assembly, and they were fobbed off instead with a unicameral legislature by the swift machinations of the Finnish bourgeois forces.

From its outset the unicameral legislature was based on universal suffrage (the grant of the franchise to women as well as men), but the voting age was set at twenty-four. Typical of a certain conservative streak in the Finns, this was not reduced to twenty-one until 1944. Following international trends, the voting age was reduced to twenty in 1969 and eighteen in 1972.

The unicameral legislature was retained at independence (q.v.) and has survived to this day. In looking at its work and powers, some commentators have argued that the legislature's own Grand Committee of Parliament in practice forms a second revisory chamber. Another limitation upon the power of the legislature has been the delaying power of the president in legislative matters. It is quite clear, both from writings and constitutional behavior, that the unicameral legislature of independent Finland can never become an executive—as the Social Democrats wanted in 1917 and 1918.

As for the fear of majoritarian tyranny, that has been almost dispelled by making permanent legislation depend on a two-thirds majority and constitutional change on a five-sixths majority of parliamentary votes. The striving for consensus (q.v.) replaces the verdict of the majority, and with it the horse-trading of the parties has full play.

UNIFICATION. A policy of unifying the institutions of the Grand Duchy (q.v.) of Finland with Russian imperial institutions began in earnest in the 1890s with the 1890 Postal Manifesto (q.v.) and the 1899 February Manifesto (q.v.), which lay down the main lines for future imperial legislation.

Such legislation had already been discussed by the Bunge Commission, set up during the reign of Alexander III, but his hesitancy, and then his death in 1894, had delayed fulfillment of this goal.

The bond hitherto between Finland and Russia had been monarchical. A Finnish minister state-secretary in Saint Petersburg had presented issues concerning Finland directly to the tsar, without reporting to any imperial ministers. This had now to be changed.

In considering why the change occurred, the Finns (then and since) have rushed to explain the whole phenomenon as an act, or series of acts, of Russification—in short, as an irrational politics, motivated by old-style chauvinism and jealousy. Since the first measure secured by Governor-General Bobrikov (q.v.) in 1900 was a decree authorizing the use of Russian in the higher government offices in Finland, an explanation in terms of Russification has a specious justification. And, it might be argued, the outcome of all the various measures proposed might well have been, in due time, a Russified Finland.

The matter looked obvious when, after the 1905 Revolution, Russia developed a quasi-constitutionalist system of its own with an imperial Duma in which the Finns would have been in an insignificant minority—and where, by 1910, the cry "Finis Finlandiae" was heard. There was, however, a rationale in imperial politics, and it was a grim one, reaching down to a level few Finns then understood. The Russian Empire needed to tighten its security against the growing efficiency of another empire, the German. Bobrikov feared Sweden as an instrument of Germany (and consequently disliked the role of the Swedish language and the Swedish-language elite in Finnish administrative life).

Having been for centuries trapped between a Swedish-Russian confrontation, Finland, in the official Russian perception, was now a dangerous area of weakness in the potential axis of German-Russian antagonism. This problem was to continue once tsarism fell.

The tragedy was that both Finland and Russia were struggling with a process of modernization that was comprehended on both sides too narrowly and inflexibly. The politics of modernization should have been reasonable, but it was this politics that brought the conflict. The ultimate blame must lie with the European state system, where modernization, territorialism, and military security were associated inextricably with one another. In contrast, the Finns, for the most part, during their Years of Oppression (q.v.), remained obstinate believers in a kind of international pacifism.

UUSIKAUPUNKI, PEACE OF. This peace, signed at a small town north of Turku (q.v.) in 1721, concluded the Great Northern War (q.v.). Peace negotiations had been taking place between Sweden and Russia on and off since 1718, mainly in the Åland Islands (q.v.). It was a regrettable feature of Charles XII's policy that the advice of his Holsteiner minister of foreign affairs and finance, Baron G. H. von Görtz, had strengthened his interest in the conquest of Norway from Denmark. In pursuit of this goal Charles was prepared to come to terms with Russia and even seek Russian aid; what was being offered was part of Finland.

Even after the death in battle of Charles XII in 1718 and the subsequent execution of the hated von Görtz, Swedish policy did not change. At Uusikaupunki Finland lost the Karelian Isthmus (q.v.), including the city of Viipuri, and additionally all the lands around the northern and northeastern shore of Lake Ladoga. This upset the trade of eastern Finland, particularly the tar and timber export from the Savo hinterland, which had previously gone through Viipuri.

The borders drawn at Uusikaupunki were broadly the same—as far as southeastern Finland was concerned—as those imposed by the Soviet Union on the Finns in 1940 and 1944.

-W-

WAR OF 1808–1809 FOR THE POSSESSION OF FINLAND. The war was an outcome of the meeting between Napoleon and Tsar Alexander I on a raft in the river Niemen in June 1807. In coming to terms with Napoleon, Tsar Alexander agreed to try to mediate peace between France and England and, if that failed (and it did), to coerce with the French the countries of Sweden, Denmark, and Portugal to break off diplomatic and commercial relations with Great Britain.

In this way, as a consequence of European high politics, Finland came into the Russian Empire. As a matter of fact, the massing of the tsar's troops on the Finnish border and the subsequent invasion of Finland in February 1808 were originally meant only to be acts of pressure on Sweden to change its foreign policy and commercial alignments.

Alexander's starting point does not therefore say much for the theory that explains Russian policy toward Finland as being motivated, throughout modern times, by the overwhelming need to safeguard the approaches to Saint Petersburg. His rather limited initial goal seems to have had something in common with the earlier attitudes of Empress Catherine and Empress Elizabeth, both of whom do not appear to have been able to make up their minds as to whether they really wanted Finland.

In a proclamation issued on March 28, 1808, Alexander declared that he intended to unite Finland with the Russian Empire, and from then on the war was consequently one of conquest. Perhaps what was in question was the high politics of Europe. The French were now triumphing in Spain, and Alexander might well have felt a need to strengthen his empire, wherever he could, against his overbearing ally. In any case Napoleon, later in the year at his Erfurt meeting with Alexander, accepted Russian possession of Finland.

In the hostilities both Finns and Swedes fought bravely against the Russians, but there were defects in leadership, a matter that subsequently enabled the Finnish patriotic poet J. L. Runeberg (q.v.) to indulge in his talent for censure (the Swedish commanding general, W. M. Klingspor, had "only half a heart").

Mysterious things happened. The great fortress of Sveaborg (Suomenlinna, q.v.), guarding Helsinki, gave up with hardly a fight. Perhaps this was because its commandant was in some way involved in the intrigues of Duke Charles of Södermanland, who, as Charles XIII, was soon to replace his nephew, Gustavus IV Adolphus, on the Swedish throne.

Before the war was over, Alexander summoned the Finnish Estates to swear loyalty to him. This took place at the Diet of Porvoo (q.v.), which met from March to July 1809. As the century wore on, the Diet of Porvoo came to be regarded by most members of the Finnish elite as the source of legitimacy of Finland's position in the Russian Empire.

WAR REPARATIONS. In the peace feelers of the spring of 1944 the Soviet Union advocated that the Finns should pay a war indemnity of $600 million. This was considered by the Finnish government an impossible sum. The British worked to get the Soviet Union to scale the amount down to $300 million. In the negotiations that occurred between the cease-fire of the Continuation War (q.v.) and the actual signing of the Armistice Agreement (q.v.) on September 19, 1944, the British also managed to persuade the Soviet government not to insist on an extra $20 million to be paid to the Mond Nickel Company, which lost the nickel deposits (q.v.) of Petsamo (q.v.). The Russians agreed that the sum would be paid out of the $300 million.

That sum was steep enough for the Finns, especially as the goods that made up the reparations were to be assessed at 1938 prices. It has been estimated that, if a comparison be made with two other former enemy states—Hungary and Romania—than the amount paid by Finland worked out to 80 gold dollars per inhabitant, but only 30 gold dollars per inhabitant for Hungary, and 15 gold dollars in the case of every Romanian.

It can honestly be said that in fixing the prices at the 1938 level the Soviet Union went back on what had been agreed in the annex to Article 11 of the Armistice Agreement. The change was finalized in December 1944.

In the first year of reparations, deliveries to the Soviet Union rose to 15% of the Finnish national income, and in the second year were still at the very high figure of 11% of the national income. Small wonder that the Finnish government tried to gain a reduction in the total amount to be paid and a lengthening of the period during which it was to be paid (initially, by Article 11 of the Armistice Agreement, this was fixed at six years).

In October 1945 the Soviet Union extended the payment period to eight years, and in June 1948 the remaining amount of reparations was reduced 50%. This enabled the Finns to pay off all reparations by September 1952.

Finland's difficulties in fulfilling its reparations obligations were also due to the fact that, to the amazement of the Finns, when the first official breakdown of goods required came from the Soviet Union, it was seen to contain a demand that 33.6% of the goods was to be composed of machines and factory installations. A further 20.1% was to be made up of brand-new shipping. To many Finnish politicians and leaders of industry, these demands seemed to be way beyond the capacity of Finland's comparatively modest engineering industry.

At Teheran in 1943, when the question of Finnish war reparations had come up, Churchill had suggested to Stalin that the Finns should "chop down a few trees" for the Russians. At the end of 1944, when the first reparations list came, the share of the wood and paper industry was only 33.4% — well below that of metal-industry products.

Yet the Finns, helped by credits from Sweden and the United States, triumphed over these difficulties. Indeed, in the end, the burden of reparations to the Soviet Union formed the core of a developing trade. As early as April 1946 a Finnish government delegation that had gone to ask Stalin for a reduction in the amount of reparations payments came away with a trade agreement for $30 million. By this Finland received Soviet grain in return for sending prefabricated houses and cellulose.

Soviet trade (q.v.), which undoubtedly grew out of reparations deliveries, became so important an element in Finland's foreign economy that its loss was a significant factor in a Finnish recession in the 1990s.

WAR TRIALS. In accordance with Article 13 of the 1944 Armistice Agreement (q.v.) Finland had to undertake "to collaborate with the Allied powers in the apprehension of persons accused of war crimes and in their trial."

What exactly these crimes were had not, at this time, been more closely defined by the Allies. The appropriate definitions were not finalized until the U.N. charter meeting in San Francisco in April 1945 and, even more important, the London meeting in the summer of that year. By then it had become clear that "war guilt"—meaning by this the starting of a war and conspiracy to this end—was the first of the crimes.

It was distinctly the resolution of all the Allies (and not just a one-sided policy on the part of the Soviet Union) that "war guilt" should concern also the leaders of states that had been fighting alongside Nazi Germany. This was a general resolution, but strongly upheld in principle by the Americans, even though, in the particular case of Finland, the United States had never actually declared war. Thus the Finnish war trials, when they did take place, were officially a response to Allied policy and not simply to Soviet diktat.

J. K. Paasikivi (q.v.), who had become prime minister on November 17, 1944, had had a shrewd idea nonetheless about the Finnish wartime leaders whom the Soviet government would wish to try, but typically he held for some time the view that the mere withdrawal of these leaders from political and public life might be sufficient.

Pressure from radical Left forces in the Finnish Parliament soon joined with Soviet pressure to remind the Finnish government, and especially Prime Minister Paasikivi, of the requirement of Article 13. Paasikivi thus instituted a small committee under the chairmanship of jurist Dr. Eirik Hornborg to look into this question. Since Hornborg had been a member of the Peace Opposition (q.v.), his credentials, in the eyes of both the Soviet authorities and the Finnish radical Left, should have been of the very best. On July 17, 1945, however, the Hornborg report came out with the view that there was no case to answer. At this point Andrei Zhdanov and the Allied Control Commission made their most decisive intervention yet: there had to be a trial.

Thus were arraigned Risto Ryti (q.v.), the former president of Finland, of the Progressive party (q.v.); Väinö Tanner (q.v.), minister of finance from 1942 to 1944, of the Social Democratic party (q.v.); J.W. Rangell, prime minister from 1941 to 1943, of the Progressive party; Edvin Linkomies, prime minister from 1943 to 1944, of the National Coalition party (q.v.); C. H. W. Ramsay, minister of supply in 1942, of the Swedish People's party (q.v.); Tyko Reinikka, second minister of finance from 1943 to 1944, of the Agrarian Union (q.v.); and Anssi Kukkonen, minister of education until 1943, also of the Agrarian Union. In addition, T. M. Kivimäki, who was Finnish minister in Berlin from 1940 to 1944, and had a Progressive party background, was arrainged with the politicians.

It will at once be noted that several of these politicians were not in the government that had made the declaration of war on the Soviet Union in 1941. They were accused, however, of hindering efforts to make peace once other Finns had realized that the Continuation War (q.v.) could not be won.

When the sentences (all of them imprisonment) were handed down by the court, Zhdanov made another intervention, claiming that the sentences were too light. In February 1946 the court reviewed these sentences, stiffening them. Instead of eight years, Ryti, for example, got ten (though because of ill-health he served only three).

The trials and sentencing provoked concern among a section of the Finnish public. There were riots outside the court sessions, and in the then small market town of Kouvola pictures of the sentenced leaders appeared in the window of a local watchmaker under the heading "They Served Finland."

As a matter of fact, the Finnish war trials revealed in many ways the exceptional position of Finland. In Romania, Bulgaria, and Hungary, the Russians behaved ruthlessly—

running the trials in fact—the sentences meted out often being death sentences. In Finland the court was made up of Finns. While it was indeed a special tribunal, its members were chosen through the parliamentary system, and included a member each from the National Coalition party, the Progressive party, and the Swedish People's party, and three members each from the Agrarians, the Social Democrats, and the SKDL, or the Finnish People's Democratic League. The chairman and other members were professional judges.

What the war trials represented was a repudiation in each party of the anti-Russian line that had brought on the Continuation War. The war trials did not represent an attempt to crush the parties—on the contrary, however crassly Zhdanov behaved, the spirit of the trials was embodied in the principles laid down by the Allies.

Looked at from the strictly political point of view of Soviet interests, the composition and the work of the court reflected a Soviet conviction of that time: in the genuinely parliamentary states of Europe a "progressive" politics could emerge.

What is also interesting is that the Finnish war trials did not include any member of the Finnish armed forces (q.v.), and President Mannerheim (q.v.), though personally afraid of being placed on trial, was assured of immunity. Yet the military and their arrangements with Nazi Germany had led the country into war.

Mannerheim was now an essential figurehead for the Russians, enabling a smoother Finnish transition to the postwar world. Still, in March 1946, Mannerheim could take no more and resigned the presidency. In sum, the war trials themselves showed the limited ambitions of the Soviet Union toward Finland, and with them a desire to reach an accommodation with the Finns.

War crimes trials concerning the perpetration of specific acts of cruelty were also held in Finland. The most famous—and astonishing—of these was the case that fell through against the former head of the state political police, Arno Anthoni, in respect of the handing over to the Nazis of several foreign-born Jews (q.v.), a group of eight, which included a baby born in Finland.

WELFARE STATE. Like the other states of the Nordic area, Finland has been, and still largely is, a welfare state in the sense of a state that tries to ensure a high degree of social security for its inhabitants. In Finland, the rate of infant mortality, for example, is one of the lowest in the world and, hardly surprisingly, the country's clinics and day-care system are among the best in the world. A maternity allowance is paid for a period of 105 workdays before and after the birth. Subsequently, an additional parental allowance, for a slightly longer period than the maternity allowance, is payable to the spouse who stays home to look after the child. The father rather than the mother may receive this parental allowance, but in any case the father is entitled to have from 6 to 18 days off from work to help the mother look after the new baby and any other children in the family.

Children's allowances are paid to every family in Finland with children. The payments in 1994 were 570 finnmarks (approximately $100) per month for the first child and 720 finnmarks for the second child, with increases in the amount paid for each subsequent child. Single-parent families receive an extra 200 finnmarks per month per child.

It is regrettable that these magnificent social benefits and services are now under attack, largely owing to the fact that a considerable part of Finnish income taxation is now being used to bail out the banking system and to support the increasing number of unemployed in the country (s.v. Industrialization). In consequence, for example, visits of expectant mothers to clinics are being reduced and many day-care institutions are being closed—in Turku (q.v.) in 1994 five are scheduled for closure. And while single-parents have, as noted, received an increase in their children's allowance payments (which are tax-free for all), it should also be borne in mind that as far as the taxable income of single-parents is concerned, the rate has risen over 13% in the last three years.

WINTER WAR. This war occurred between Finland and the Soviet Union from November 30, 1939, when Soviet troops marched over the Finnish frontier, to March 13, 1940, when the Peace of Moscow (q.v.) was signed. The cause of the war lay in Soviet demands for the cession of Finnish territory from the Karelian Isthmus (q.v.) and for the lease of some Finnish territory at the mouth of the Gulf of Finland (the Hanko Peninsula or even islands adjacent to the southwestern shore).

The Soviet Union was prepared in return to grant Finland vast areas of territory in East Karelia (q.v.), where the population spoke Finnish or the closely related Karelian language. In terms of sheer amount of territory, this exchange would have led to a substantial increase in the area of the Finnish state, for the East Karelian lands offered were twice as large as the areas to be conceded by Finland. The movement of population from the Karelian Isthmus (or a part of it) could not be contemplated by the Finnish government of the day, which feared a gradual takeover of the country through these concessions.

From the Soviet side these demands on Finland may be seen as part of a minimalist program for ensuring the security of Leningrad. From 1935 onward the Soviet Union, after the Anglo-German naval agreement of that year, became much exercised by the fear that Finland would cave in to Nazi Germany. Soviet demands for a security treaty with Finland or for base concessions, as contained in the proposals of Boris Yartsev (q.v.) and Boris Stein (q.v.), made in April 1938 and March 1939, should be seen in this light.

For many Finns therefore it was surprising that, within a few weeks of the conclusion in August 1939 of the Nazi-Soviet Pact (q.v.), Soviet demands on Finnish territory were again made. Not until early October did knowledge about the secret protocol, putting Finland into the Soviet sphere of influence, finally penetrate from Berlin. Even this knowledge did not substantially alter the stance of Foreign Minister Eljas Erkko (q.v.). The Finns were certainly prepared to go on negotiating, but by mid-November the Soviet government had already decided on the maximalist solution of hostilities.

The day after the Winter War broke out, the Soviet government set up, just over the Finnish border, the puppet Terijoki government (q.v.) of Finland, headed by the old Finnish Communist leader, Otto Wille Kuusinen (q.v.). Far from reopening the wounds of the Finnish Civil War (q.v.), the establishment of this puppet government helped to heal them. The Finns fought to a man.

The epic of the Winter War is that of the Finns fighting alone. They were offered help—not merely material help, which they took, from Sweden, Great Britain, and France, but in January the Allies began to make plans for intervention. These plans would have involved a thrust to Finland through Norway and Sweden, but the latter, fearful of being dragged into the World War, righteously proclaimed their neutrality. The Allies were motivated by a desire to control Swedish iron-ore supplies, and helping Finland was only an excuse to get to northern Sweden. This was one of the most harebrained schemes of World War II, for it put Great Britain and France at risk of taking on Nazi Germany and the Soviet Union together. Fortunately the Allies were to wait in vain for the call from the Finns, though this Finnish wisdom could not save Norway from becoming a battlefield between the Allies and the Germans a few weeks later.

Undoubtedly the Allied interest in Finland encouraged the Russians to make peace with the Finns and to forget the Terijoki government and plans to conquer Finland. In any case the Finnish armed forces had repelled the Soviet army's attempt to cut Finland in two.

In the Winter War 25,000 Finns, soldiers and civilians, were killed. The terms of the Peace of Moscow were onerous: one-tenth of the area of Finland was lost. The seeds of bitterness were sown for the revanchist war of restitution—the Continuation War (q.v.), as it was aptly called.

In Finland the Winter War has been alternately viewed as a tragedy caused by the mismanagement of a Finnish civilian leadership unable to appreciate Russia's enduring strategic needs, or simply as a heroic tragedy, showing the unity of the nation in adversity and almost compensating for the frightful disunity of the Civil War. The current mood has swung back to blaming the Russians.

WOMEN. In one sense, Finland has been a pioneer in women's rights, in 1906 being the first country in Europe to grant women parliamentary suffrage. This was a result of the need for national unity in the face of a previous half decade of

Russian unification (q.v.) measures (a few years before this, in 1895, the old Finnish Diet of Four Estates [q.v.] had refused to grant women even the municipal franchise). Now, when the parliamentary franchise came, it took several of the leaders of the Finnish women's movement, the Union, as it was called, by surprise.

Having once gotten the vote, the women's movement suffered from a similar letdown to that experienced by the suffragette movement in Great Britain after 1918. At the foundation of the Union, in 1892, a wide range of equality measures, including that of equal pay for equal work, had been proposed.

The Union itself was an outcome of the significance of education (q.v.) in Finnish society. The Lutheran church (q.v.), deeply conservative as it was on many issues, had emphasized for both sexes the necessity of literacy for the sacrament of marriage. In the second half of the nineteenth century Finland developed from being a state dominated by the aristocracy into a bourgeois state in which women received higher education—in 1878, for example, Rosina Heikel became the first woman to gain the right to practice as a physician. Political rights were thus a corollary to educational progress.

Nowadays in Finland there is evidence of a greater trend toward equality. Out of 200 members of Parliament, 77 are women; there are 6 women ministers in the cabinet, including the minister of defense. Sometimes, however, it is argued that in a corporate state, which Finland certainly is, the power is elsewhere than in Parliament (hence Parliament can tolerate so high a proportion of women).

In spite of the Equal Pay Act of 1962, women's pay is on average 2,000 finnmarks (approximately $460) a month less than that of men's, even though the women today represent a well-qualified labor force—often better qualified than the men. In practice, therefore, subtle divisions of labor exist, often within the same profession. Since performance in the Finnish economy is very much based upon an input of education, and women in Finland do better in the educational system than the men, this trend may be reversed in the future.

There is a certain level of frustration in the women's movement that has something to do with a lack of sense of direction. A few years ago, in the proposal for a new law on surnames, the suggestion was made that children should automatically take the mother's surname unless they expressly wished otherwise. Instead, Parliament changed the tone of the bill on the assumption that normally the husband's surname would be indicated by the spouses, and only when this was not indicated or when they expressly wished to have the wife's surname would the child receive the mother's surname—all this for the protection of the family.

The tension is there. A women's movement may be stifling in so small a society. Small may be beautiful, and the periphery as important as the center, but feminists in Finland seem to be unable to convince themselves or their society that this might be the case. The apparently inexorable process of European integration may thus bring both challenges and opportunities. It could even bring a threat in the form of well-trained, imported foreign male labor.

WRATH, THE GREAT. In the latter part of the Great Northern War (q.v.) Finland was occupied and devastated by Russian troops. This period, known as the Great Wrath, ran roughly from 1713 to the close of the war in 1721.

The period was preceded by a decade and a half of suffering. At the end of the 1690s the harvests failed both in Sweden and Finland, and famine—especially in Finland—was a reality by 1697. After this, in 1700, the Great Northern War broke out and, during its course of over twenty years, roughly sixty thousand able-bodied Finns were compelled into the army of the Swedish king Charles XII; of these, only ten thousand returned to Finland.

In 1710 the Russians captured Viipuri, but not until 1713 did they succeed in taking Porvoo, Helsinki (q.v.), and Turku (q.v.). As they spread throughout large parts of the country, the educated class fled to Sweden. Many of the clergy abandoned their parishioners, though the Luthern church (q.v.) tried to keep up a semblance of its system by employing "students" (those who had passed the university entrance examination) to perform clerical functions in many parishes.

The Russians, from the taking of Viipuri onward, enslaved thousands of Finns. Whole families were deported from Ostrobothnia — some five thousand people in all. The Russians even conscripted Finns into the Russian armed forces for service on the Persian frontier; of 1,500 men taken, a third returned.

Charles XII urged the inhabitants of both Finland and Ingria (q.v.) to continue partisan warfare, which many did to their own detriment, for no help came from Sweden.

Though most of Finland was restored to Sweden at the Peace of Uusikaupunki (q.v.) in 1721, a lurking dread remained among the Finns that at some future time they might be abandoned for good by Sweden. What was also disturbed was the conviction of the safeguarding of a society through a triumphant State and Church legitimacy. Pietism began to emerge.

WRATH, THE LESSER. The term refers to the devastation caused to the Finns by the Swedish-Russian War of 1741–1743 (q.v.). While most of Finland was occupied by the Russians, the suffering of the inhabitants was worse in eastern Finland. When Lappeenranta fell after bitter fighting, its population was taken captive and sold into slavery in Russia. The same happened in many of the rural border parishes.

The Lesser Wrath is nevertheless contrasted with the Great Wrath (q.v.) of 1713–1721 since it was, as its designation implies, somewhat less severe. For one thing, the Swedish government encouraged officials and clergy to remain in occupied Finland, though some of them had to take an oath of allegiance to Empress Elizabeth.

The Lesser Wrath proved the consequences once more of the inability of the Swedish government to defend Finland. Discontent in Finland did not end with the signing of the Peace of Turku (q.v.) in 1743. The Finnish deputation to the Diet of 1746–1747 pointed out that in the seven hundred years of the Swedish connection Finland had enjoyed only twenty-five years of peace.

WRATH, THE LONG. The period in Finnish history known as the Long Wrath ran from 1570 to 1595 and is a reference to an important stage in the constant warfare between Sweden and Russia. Much of the warfare waged during the Long Wrath occurred on Finnish soil, or on the Finnish frontier, or with Finnish arms.

The quarter of a century covered by the term actually included two long periods of truce—from 1573 to 1577 and from 1583 to 1590. These periods, however, did not necessarily mean a cessation of the guerilla warfare between Finns and Karelians (meaning thereby the Orthodox Karelians who owed allegiance to the Russian scepter).

There were really two wars going on. The major, spectacular war was between Sweden and Russia for possession of the Baltic littoral, the opportunity for conquest being provided by the loosening of the hold of the Teutonic Knights on the area as the Reformation sapped their power. On the other hand, the Swedish advance into this region was challenged not merely by Ivan the Terrible but also by the Poles and even by the attempt of the Danes to reestablish their authority in the eastern Baltic.

There were strong commercial interests in these conquests, especially the lure of possessing the eastern Baltic ports which controlled the export of grain from the hinterland. In this war, however, the prizes of military conquest alone, entangled with overriding considerations of dynastic rivalry, tended to assume ever greater weight. These aspects were aggravated by the fact that the Finnish nobility (for instance, Klaus Fleming [q.v.]), and the aspirant nobility among the higher ranks of the fighting men, often saw in hostilities of this kind a chance to enhance their own political and economic power.

A second war in this period has been summed up by the Finnish term *Rappasota,* which is a reference to the Karelian guerrilla fighters known as *rapparit,* or "robbers." The warfare in this case ranged over vast areas of present-day northern Finland and East Karelia.

The circumstances behind this type of fighting had emerged with the changes occurring after the settlement laid down in the 1323 Peace of Pähkinäsaari (q.v.). At that time it had been vaguely decreed that the lands north and east of the Ostrobothnian river of Pyhäjoki should be reserved for the use of the Karelians. Over the centuries, though, the Finns had moved across this line, and the conflict during the Long Wrath was bitter in this region.

The Peace of Täyssinä (q.v.), which brought the Long Wrath formally to an end, should have determined these issues, but it was to prove inconclusive and temporary.

WUOLIJOKI, HELLA (1886–1954). Writer and political figure. She was born Ella Murrik in the province of Viljandi, Estonia. She came from a rural middle-class family of liberal-minded persuasion, and her father brought her up to admire the Finns, a sister nation to the Estonians, but fortunate in the possession of an autonomy (q.v.) the Estonians had not enjoyed.

Against a family and national background of this kind, it is understandable that Ella Murrik, having taken the student examination in Tartu, came to study at the University of Helsinki in 1904. In 1908 she took her M.A. degree in languages, literature, and folk poetry, becoming the first Estonian woman to earn an M.A. degree.

In Helsinki Ella Murrik became radicalized, shedding her liberalism for a vague kind of socialism, some of the tenets of which she had picked up in the student corporation (q.v.). She married a socialist M.P., Sulo Wuolijoki—intelligent, though an alcoholic and a womanizer—from whom she was divorced in 1923. But from her marriage to the end of her life, she remained Hella Wuolijoki.

She identified with Finland, but as a young student had noticed the sense of smug isolation that Finnish nationalism sometimes brought to her companions. When discussing the turmoil in the rest of the Russian Empire, or, indeed, international questions in general, the common Finnish response, *Mitä se kuuluu meille?* or, "What has it to do with us?" began to irritate and haunt her.

She thus came to represent a kind of internationalism that become even more distrusted once Finland gained its independence (q.v.). After the Civil War (q.v.), she ran a salon in Helsinki for several years, where progressive American and English visitors could be met by their Finnish counterparts. Here John Reed (q.v.) made his contact with her. In the end, according to the Social Democratic leader Väinö Tanner (q.v.), who at one time went to the salon, Communist influence became ever more obvious there. Hella Wuolijoki certainly knew that the Communist leader Otto Wille Kuusinen (q.v.) was in hiding in Finland even if she might not have assisted in his sheltering.

She was a complex personality. In spite of her socialism, she prospered in business, at one time running a sawmill utilizing timber bought from over the border, where, in Soviet East Karelia (q.v.), Edvard Gylling was trying to establish another "Red" Finland. Gylling's acquaintanceship with her was probably fatal for him. She met him in Moscow in 1937, and he was picked up by the Soviet secret police soon after. These warped individuals doubtlessly regarded Hella Wuolijoki as a Western agent—in much the same manner their Finnish counterparts regarded her as a Soviet agent.

In the meantime, Hella Wuolijoki had become an estate owner in Finland and was producing, in the Niskavuori series of plays, some of the best portrayals of Finnish agrarian property that have seen the light of day. These were turned into popular films in Finland, and in 1947 one was produced in Hollywood under the title of *The Farmer's Daughter*.

Hella Wuolijoki had not forgotten her politics, which was the politics of internationalism. As the dreadful weeks of the Winter War (q.v.) took their toll, one of her finest moments was to come. She volunteered to go to Sweden to speak with her old friend Alexandra Kollontay, the Soviet minister to Sweden, about the possibility of opening peace talks. Väinö Tanner took advantage of this offer, and the first contacts with the Soviet Union were established.

In between the Winter War and the Continuation War (q.v.), Hella Wuolijoki hosted Bertolt Brecht on her estate, and the play *Herr Puntila und sein Knecht Matti* was a product of their collaboration, though in subsequent years the Brechtians forgot her share in it. Brecht claimed to have his own special insight into the Finns; it was presumably in this period that he coined the bon mot about the Finns being silent in two languages.

Before the outbreak of the Continuation War, Hella Wuolijoki was visited by Soviet diplomats seeking a means

of keeping Finland at peace. She immediately contacted Tanner, who agreed to meet with the diplomats, but then drew
back.

Once the Continuation War started, Hella Wuolijoki got
into deep trouble. Visiting Stockholm, she met with the Soviet diplomat Boris Yartsev (q.v.), while on her new estate
she gave shelter to a Finnish Red, Kerttu Nuorteva, who was
parachuted into Finland from the Soviet Union. She was informed upon, jailed, and sentenced to life imprisonment, being fortunate to escape the death penalty (the vote of the
judges was three to two).

After the Continuation War, she was released from
prison—and thought she had come into her own. The world
looked to her as if it was turning progressive. In 1945, at the
insistence of President Paasikivi (q.v.), she was appointed to
head the state radio. She inaugurated a series of spirited programs, like the "miniature parliament" series, all of which
had a progressive tinge to them. She was also elected to Parliament as a member of the Finnish People's Democratic
League.

In the election of 1948 she lost her seat, and in 1949 Parliament ousted her from the state radio. Paasikivi did not object—the Finnish-Soviet Treaty (q.v.) was already signed,
and Finnish institutional life could be stabilized. Overall, the
progressive world had not emerged, but the Cold War had.

By 1950 Hella Wuolijoki appeared to be a survivor from
a bygone era. But so, too, in a different way, was President
Paasikivi. Even in a nation with such a craving for uniformity
as Finland, individuals of this kind, constant to the ideals of
their youth, may turn out to have a distinct use.

-Y-

YARTSEV, BORIS. Yartsev's real name was Boris Nikolayevich
Rybkin, and he was an NKVD agent. In the late 1930s he occupied the humble post of second secretary at the Soviet
legation in Helsinki, while his wife, also an NKVD agent, ran
the Helsinki Intourist office.

Yartsev's importance lay in the fact that he was entrusted

with the task of negotiating a military security agreement with the Finnish government. He approached, to this end, both Foreign Minister Rudolf Holsti and Finance Minister Väinö Tanner (q.v.).

In April 1938 he made an offer of Soviet military help against a possible German invasion of Finland (in 1935 the Soviet minister to Finland, Erik Assmus, had warned that should war break out in Central Europe, the Soviet Union might be obliged to occupy parts or the whole of Finland). In August, however, Yartsev abandoned the idea of a treaty permitting the entry of Soviet troops into Finland and instead asked for a quiet Soviet supervision of the remilitarization of Åland (q.v.) and a naval and air base on the Finnish island of Suursaari in the Gulf of Finland. In return, Soviet naval forces would guarantee to safeguard Finnish shores and the integrity of Finnish borders would be recognized by the Soviet Union in general.

In October Yartsev reduced still further Soviet requirements; now all the Soviet Union wanted was to use Suursaari, not fortify it. He failed to budge the Finns, who felt that the involvement of their country in security arrangements against Nazi Germany might be the shortest road to involvement in war.

Boris Stein (q.v.) tried to carry on where Boris Yartsev left off, but the latter still had a couple of roles to play in regard to Finland. Yartsev is said to have reassured the Kremlin that the Finnish working class would follow the Terijoki government (q.v.). In the early days of the Continuation War (q.v.) he tried to exercise a more positive role, meeting with Hella Wuolijoki (q.v.) in Stockholm to talk about Finland's making peace.

YOUNG FINNS. This group crystallized within the Fennoman movement (q.v.) in 1894, being critical of the older leadership. On the one hand, the Young Finns demanded a more effective realization of the language program (in particular with respect to the use of Finnish in the central governmental offices); on the other hand, the Young Finns also felt that a concentration on language politics alone was an inadequate response to Finland's needs.

In the years immediately after the promulgation of the 1890 Postal Manifesto (q.v.), the first of the concrete unification (q.v.) measures, many of the younger members of the Fennoman movement believed that it was essential to take a stand in defense of the Finnish constitution (q.v.). Since this was also the Svecoman (q.v.) viewpoint, the barriers created by language politics were at this point breached. This was a shock to the older members of the Fennoman movement— the Old Finns (q.v.), as they came to be called—for whom the cultivation of a Finnish-language nationalism had been the comprehensive solution for all problems.

One of the more prominent of the Young Finns, K. J. Ståhlberg (q.v.), argued on the contrary that the Fennoman movement should be not merely national in outlook, but democratic and liberal as well. The Young Finns, therefore, in defending the constitution against an attack from without, also wanted to make a change in the constitution from within. They especially wanted to reduce the total number of votes (twenty-five was the maximum then allowed) an individual voter could cast (according to his wealth) in the elections for the Estate of Burghers, in respect of urban representation in the Diet of Four Estates (q.v.). This brought the Young Finns back into conflict with much of the Svecoman movement, which then still controlled the Estate of Burghers.

In their liberalism, the Young Finns did not overlook social issues and made statements about improving the prospects of the landless and smallholders. In some way, however, their liberalism prevented them from fully confronting these issues. The existence of a Young Finn movement failed to hinder the emergence in 1906 of an Agrarian Union (q.v.) and formed no alternative to socialism either for the rural or urban proletariat. Indeed, in their concept of a benevolent, patriarchal state, it was the Old Finns who came closer—as, for example, was seen in the Great Strike (q.v.) of 1905—to understanding the Social Democrats (q.v.).

The Young Finns formed an important part of the passive resistance movement (q.v.) to Russian unification measures. Once Finland gained independence (q.v.), five former Young Finns served as presidents of Finland: K. J. Ståhlberg, L. K.

Relander (q.v.), P. E. Svinhufvud (q.v.), Kyösti Kallio (q.v.), and Risto Ryti (q.v.)—the first five of the officially entitled presidents of the Finnish state, in fact.

The heir to the Young Finns in independent Finland was the (National) Progressive party (q.v.), but only Ståhlberg and Ryti made the transition to membership; Svinhufvud joined the National Coalition party (q.v.) at its foundation in 1918, while Relander and Kallio had been among the earliest members of the Agrarian Union.

-Z-

ZAVIDOVO. In August 1972 President Urho Kekkonen (q.v.) went to the Soviet Union, where, at the country house of Leonid S. Brezhnev, at Zavidovo, he had confidential talks about Finland's forthcoming relationship with the European Economic Community. Finland was planning to make a free-trade agreement with the community, which it did indeed make in 1973.

The Soviet leaders had for some time entertained disquiet about Finland's position. To a degree, this Soviet concern was connected with the troubles of the Finnish Communists (q.v.). More important, perhaps, were the ambitions of Kekkonen himself. In 1970 he had wanted a statement of neutrality written into the renewed Finnish-Soviet Treaty (q.v.); he failed to get this. A year later the Soviet Union vetoed the candidature of Max Jakobson for the post of U.N. secretary-general. Writing under a pseudonym, Kekkonen had had to say that the candidature had not constituted a Finnish attempt "to join the West and disengage itself from the East."

Returning home from Zavidovo, where he had tried to reassure the Soviet leaders that Finland, in spite of an EEC free-trade agreement, would maintain its policy of friendship with the Soviet Union, Kekkonen drew up a memorandum of his visit on August 18, 1972.

This was leaked to the press, being worked into a series of articles by the Swedish journalist Tor Högnäs, which appeared on October 31, 1972, in the Finnish-Swedish newspaper *Vasabladet,* the Swedish newspaper *Dagens Nyheter,* and the Norwegian newspaper *Dagbladet.*

An inquiry was held, but Högnäs refused to reveal his source. Court action followed. Kekkonen's head of chancery had already resigned, but was convicted by the court and fined for a breach of confidentiality in office, even though it was not clear who actually got the memorandum—or talked about it—to the Swedish journalist. Others were also convicted and fined. In the fall of 1993 the Social Democratic (q.v.) politician Erkki Tuomioja admitted that he had been the one who had passed on the memorandum to Högnäs, but where Tuomioja got it has not been revealed.

It had generally been assumed all along that the leak of information had been instigated by left-wing forces in Finland, anxious to thwart an agreement with the EEC. There may also have been, in the background, forces wanting to embarrass Kekkonen's own foreign policy so that he would be unable to serve another term of office (he did, in the event, serve another term, through by a special law, without an election). A certain rumor has it that Mauno Koivisto (q.v.), frustrated over Kekkonen's reversal of policy in 1970 on Nordek (q.v.), was not far away on this.

The full story of the Zavidovo episode remains to be told.

ZILLIACUS, KONNI (1855–1924). Political activist and writer. Born in Helsinki, the son of Senator Henrik Zilliacus, Konni Zilliacus was one of the more colorful figures of the struggle for Finnish independence (q.v.).

Having graduated in law from the University of Helsinki, he engaged in several enterprises, but he left Finland in 1889 in order to recoup his fortunes. He worked in railroad construction in Costa Rica and then became a journalist in the United States, writing books about both immigrants and Indians.

Zilliacus lived three years in Japan—a matter of some import for his later career as a political activist—and in 1896 he published an informative work about Japan entitled *Japanesiska studier och skizzer.*

Returning to Finland in the year preceding the promulgation of the February Manifesto (q.v.), Zilliacus from 1899 onward devoted much of his energy to resistance work. He became one of the contestants for the honor of having thought up the idea of an International Cultural Address (q.v.) on Finland's behalf.

Zilliacus soon became impatient with the cautious approach of the passive resistance (q.v.) leadership, however. By the summer of 1899 he was planning an extensive Finnish migration to Canada, though one of his contact men, James Mavor, a Scottish-Canadian economic historian who came to Helsinki, found him "a humbug." Zilliacus, with his friend Arthur Travers-Borgström, went to Canada, but did not like the lay of the land, Zilliacus describing Newfoundland as "waterlogged."

Much more important were the contacts Zilliacus cultivated with the Russian revolutionary movement, on which he published two significant works, in 1902 and 1912. These contacts put Zilliacus squarely into the Activist (q.v.) camp. Indeed, both as an organizer and a propagandist (the latter, for example, through his clandestine paper, *Fria Ord,* "Free Speech"), Zilliacus could lay claim to being the leading Activist of the early twentieth century. He brought copies of *Fria Ord* in from Sweden on his own yacht, also being prepared to smuggle in with them material for the revolutionary movements in Russia.

Soon after the outbreak of the Russo-Japanese War in 1904, Zilliacus made contact in Stockholm with Colonel Motojiro Akashi, the former Japanese military attaché at Saint Petersburg. With Japanese backing Zilliacus helped organize two congresses of opposition groups within the Russian Empire, the first being held in Paris in October 1904 and the second in Geneva in April 1905. With Akashi he also helped to arrange the desertion of Polish troops in Manchuria.

His most spectacular feat, backed by Japanese money, was an attempt to smuggle arms into Finland, some destined for Finnish Activists and the rest for the Russian revolutionary movement. The arms were shipped on two yachts and a steamer, the *John Grafton.* After unloading some of its cargo, the *John Grafton* was wrecked on a reef off the northern Ostrobothnian town of Pietarsaari. One of the Finnish Activists in the crew (most of the crew were Letts), was John

Nylander, a man who had earlier fought for the Greeks against the Turks and taken part in unsuccessful attempts to blow up Bobrikov (q.v.). Characteristically, Nylander now blew up the *John Grafton* and, equally characteristically, did not do the job very thoroughly.

While Zilliacus largely failed in this enterprise, and his line of policy petered out later in the decade, his importance lies in the fact that, like Becker Bey (q.v.), he was one of the first Finns to feel that Finland could get free only by exploiting international conflagration (in his case the Russo-Japanese War and the apparent breakup of the Russian Empire).

His son, also named Konni Zilliacus, was a member of the British Parliament, representing Gateshead for the Labour party.

SELECTED BIBLIOGRAPHY

INTRODUCTION

This bibliography is chiefly composed of English-language works on Finnish history, ethnography, geography, and current affairs. Where I have judged them to be of particular relevance, works in German, French, and Italian have also been listed.

It is necessary to emphasize that this bibliography is, indeed, selective. A vast literature in English has appeared on Finnish themes. Much of it is produced in Finland, especially by academic presses and research institutes, but also by the government. Under these circumstances, the character of a bibliography such as this cannot but be indicatory, not inclusive.

I have nevertheless tried to list works of value in diverse fields, and because this volume is a history, literature that is indicative of the mood of a particular time is also included.

The division into sections in the bibliography is not meant to be a rigid one. Readers looking for works on, say, Marshal Mannerheim, may thus find relevant references in several sections. The sections on this century's political history and international relations have been divided by period; otherwise the division is by subject matter (as, for example, economic history).

Finland was part of Sweden until 1809, and much material on the earlier periods of Finnish history can thus be found in histories of Sweden. These works are not listed here as a general rule, though where Finland is mentioned in works on more recent times covering Scandinavia as a whole, mention may be made of them.

With the exception of the *Kalevala,* the author has not dealt with translations of Finnish literature, many of which may be found in the excellent bibliographies, listed below, compiled by Hilkka Aaltonen (1964) and John Screen (1981).

BIBLIOGRAPHIES AND GENERAL WORKS

The following bibliographies may be found useful:

Aaltonen, Hilkka. *Books in English on Finland: A Bibliographical List of Publications Concerning Finland Until 1960, Including Finnish Literature in English Translation.* Appendix: *A Selected List of Books Published from 1961 to 1963, Inclusive.* Turku: University of Turku, Publications of Turku University Library, No. 8, 1964.

Hoerder, Dirk, ed. *Migrants from Northern Europe.* Vol. 1. *The Immigrant Labor Press in North America: An Annotated Bibliography.* New York: Greenwood, 1987.

Julkunen, Martti, and Lehikoinen, Anja. *A Select List of Books and Articles in English, French and German on Finnish Politics in the Nineteenth and Twentieth Century.* Turku: University of Turku, Institute of Political History, No. B:1, 1967.

Koivukangas, Olavi, and Toivonen, Simo. *A Bibliography of Finnish Emigration and Internal Migration.* Turku: Institute for Migration, 1978.

Kolehmainen, John I. *The Finns in America and Finland: A Bibliography of the Writings of John I. Kolehmainen, 1936–1987.* 3rd rev. ed. New York Mills, MN: Parta Printers, 1988.

Neuvonen, Eero. *A Short Bibliography on Finland.* Turku: University of Turku, Publications of Turku University Library, 1955.

Screen, J. E. O. *Finland.* Oxford: Clio Press, World Bibliographical Series, No. 31, 1981.

There are innumerable works on Finland of a general nature, purveying information, or personal reminiscences, or both. Many of these works communicate something of the character of the country. Worth singling out are:

Bacon, Walter. *Highway to the Wilderness.* London: Hale, 1961.

Hall, Wendy. *Green Gold and Granite: A Background to Finland.* London: Parrish, 1957. Revised edition published as *The Finns and Their Country.* London: Parrish, 1967.

Irwin, John L. *The Finns and the Lapps: How They Live and Work.* Newton Abbot, Eng.: David and Charles, 1978.

Nickels, Sylvie. *Travellers' Guide: Finland.* London: Cape, 1977.

In its own class (in spite of its tincture of Neo-Darwinism) is:

Jakobson, Max. *Finland: Myth and Reality.* Helsinki: Otava, 1988.

Finally, mention should be made of three interesting surveys:

Engman, Max, and Kirby, David, eds. *Finland: People, Nation, State.* London: Hurst, 1989.

Nordstrom, Byron, ed. *Dictionary of Scandinavian History.* Westport, CT: Greenwood, 1986.

Rinehart, R., ed. *Beneath the Northern Star: Reflections of Finland.* Boulder, CO: Westview, 1992.

Since Finland had to change under the impact of the economic recession of the early 1990s, the integration furor, and the breakup of the Soviet Union (which has meant, inter alia, the dwindling away of the important, stabilizing Finnish-Soviet trade, as well as the deterioration of RBMK nuclear power stations in close proximity to Finnish territory), great care should be taken in drawing conclusions from all works of a general nature on the country.

GEOGRAPHY AND ENVIRONMENTAL QUESTIONS

Activities of the Commission, 1986. Helsinki: Baltic Sea Environmental Proceedings, No. 23, 1987.

Asp, Erkki, et al. *The Social Consequences of Regulating the Water Courses in Lapland.* Turku: University of Turku, Department of Sociology and Political Research, Sociological Studies, No. A5, 1980.

Bärlund, K. "Finland's International Environmental Policy." *Yearbook of Finnish Foreign Policy* (1990), 8–11.

Derby, W. L. A. *The Tall Ships Pass: The Story of the Last Years of*

Deepwater Square-Rigged Sail Embodying Therein the History and Detailed Description of the Finnish Four-Masted Steel Barque "Herzogin Cecilie." London: Cape, 1937. Reprint. Newton Abbot, Eng.: David and Charles, 1970.

Fullerton, Brian, and Williams, Alan F. *Scandinavia.* 2nd ed. London: Chatto and Windus, 1975.

Governor-General v. Rosen's Map of Finland, 1747. Helsinki: Geographical Society of Finland, 1969.

Häkkilä, Matti. "Geographical Aspects of the Development and Utilisation of Arable Land Area in Finland." *Fennia,* 162:2 (1984).

―――. "Geographical Aspects of Forest Returns on Finnish Farms." *Fennia,* 152 (1977).

Helle, R. *An Investigation into Reindeer Husbandry.* Oulu: University of Oulu, Publications of the Department of Geography, 1966.

―――. "Reindeer Husbandry in Finland." *Geographical Journal,* 145:2 (1979).

Jaatinen, Stig. "The Glacial Morphology of the Åland Islands, with Special Reference to the Superficial Deposits." *Fennia,* 84:1 (1960).

Jaatinen, Stig, and Mead, W. R. "The Intensification of Finnish Farming." *Economic Geography,* 33:1 (1957).

Jones, Michael. *Finland: Daughter of the Sea.* Folkestone, Eng.: Dawson, 1977.

―――. "A Model of Human Response to Land Emergence in the Vasa Area, Finland." *Terra,* 82 (1970), 1–9.

Kääriäinen, E. "On the Recent Uplift of the Earth's Crust in Finland." *Fennia,* 77:2 (1953).

Kampp, Å. H., and Rikkinen, K. "Farms in a Finnish Village, 1787–1916." *Geografiskt Tidskrift,* 73 (1973).

Kaukiainen, Yrjö. *Microdemographic Studies of Social and Geographic Mobility in Finland: Methods and Problems.* Helsinki: University of Helsinki, Communications of the Department of Economic and Social History, No. 6, 1978.

――――. *Social Structure and Demographic Development in a Southern Finnish Parish (Lohja), 1810–1850.* Helsinki: Finnish Academy of Sciences, Annales scientiarum Fennica B204, 1979.

――――. "Variations in Fertility in Nineteenth-Century Finland." In *Chance and Change: Social-Economic Studies in Historical Demography in the Baltic Area,* ed. Sune Åkerman. Odense: Odense University Studies in History and Social Sciences, No. 52, 1978.

Kish, George. *North-East Passage: Adolf Erik Nordenskiöld, His Life and Times.* Amsterdam: Israel, 1973.

Kuokkanen, Tuomas. "Some Aspects of Environmental Cooperation in the Baltic Sea and the Great Lakes of North America." *ELSA* [European Law Students' Association] *Law Review,* 1:1 (Winter 1989), 61–70.

Mäkinen, Jaakko. *Fenno-Scandian Uplift Gravity Between 1966 and 1984.* Helsinki: Geodeettinen laitos, Government Printing Centre, 1986.

Man and the Baltic Sea. Helsinki: Finnish Baltic Sea Committee, Ministry of the Interior, 1977.

Mead, W. R. "The Cold-Farm in Finland." *Geographical Review,* 41:4 (1951).

――――. "The Delineation of Finland: A Review of an Early Source of Knowledge About Finland in Britain." *Fennia,* 97:3 (1968).

――――. *An Economic Geography of the Scandinavian States.* Aylesbury, Eng.: University of London Press, 1958.

――――. "The Eighteenth Military Reconnaissance of Finland: A Neglected Chapter in the History of Finnish Geography." *Acta geographica,* 20:18 (1968), 255–271.

Mead, W. R., and Jaatinen, Stig. *The Åland Islands.* Newton Abbot, Eng.: David and Charles, 1975.

Mead, W. R., and Smeds, H. *Winter in Finland*. London: Hugh Evelyn, 1967.

Newby, Eric. *The Last Grain Race*. London: Secker and Warburg, 1956.

Paukkunen, Marika. "On Finnish Common Environmental Law." *ELSA Law Review*, I:1 (1989), 71–78.

Perttunen, Marjatta, ed. *Fenno-Scandian Land Uplift: Proceedings of a Symposium at Tvärminne arranged by the Finnish National Committee for Quaternary Research*. Helsinki: Espoon Geologian Tutkimuskeskus, Publications no. 61, Government Printing Centre, 1987.

————, ed. *Transport of Glacial Drift in Finland: Proceedings of a Symposium at Lammi, April 12–13 1988, arranged by the Finnish National Committee for Quaternary Research*. Vammala: Espoon Geologian Tutkimuskeskus, Special Paper, Geological Survey of Finland, 1989.

Pitkänen, Heikki et al. *Pollution Load on the Gulf of Finland in 1982–1984: A Report of Studies under the Finnish-Soviet Working Group on the Protection of the Gulf of Finland*. Helsinki: Vesi-ja ympäristöhallitus, Vesi-ja ympäristöhallinnon julkaisuja no. 22, 1988.

Platt, Raye R, ed. *Finland and Its Geography: An American Geographical Society Handbook*. New York: Duell, Sloan and Pearce. Boston and Toronto: Little, Brown and Co., 1955.

————. *Farming in Finland*. London: Athlone Press, 1953.

————. "Frontier Themes in Finland." *Geography*, 44 (1959).

————. *The Geographical Tradition in Finland*. Edinburgh: Lewis, 1963.

————. *An Historical Geography of Scandinavia*. New York: Academic Press, 1981.

————. "Pehr Kalm in the Chilterns." *Acta geographica*, 17:1 (1963).

————. "Finnish Karelia: An International Borderland." *Geographical Journal*, 118:1 (1952), 40–57.

————. *Land Use in Early Nineteenth-Century Finland*. Turku: University of Turku Publications, No. A13:2, 1953.

————. "Recent Developments in Human Geography in Finland." *Progress in Human Geography,* 1:3 (1977), 361–375.

————. *The Scandinavian Northlands*. London: Oxford University Press, 1974.

————. "Viipuri: Its Importance in the Political and Economic Geography of Finland." *Scottish Geographical Magazine,* 57 (Nov. 1941).

Rotkirch, Holger. *Ten Years of Environmental Cooperation in the Baltic Sea: An Evaluation and a Look Ahead*. Helsinki: Vesiyhdistys, Aqua Fennica, No. 14, 1984.

Saltvik: Studies from an Åland Parish by W. R. Mead and Members of the Geographical Field Group. Nottingham, Eng.: Geographical Field Group Regional Studies, No. 10, 1964.

Saurio, Simo. *Two-Region Input-Output Study for Core-Ring Relationships in Turku City Region*. Turku: University of Turku, Annales Universitatis Turkuensis B190, 1990.

Siren, A. "On Computing the Land Uplift from the Lake-Water Level Records in Finland." *Fennia,* 73:5 (1951).

Siuruiainen, Eino. *On the History of Rural Settlement in Finland*. Oulu: University of Oulu, Acta Universitatis Ouluensis, A63, 1978.

Smeds, H. "Finland." In *A Geography of Norden,* ed. A. Sømme. Oslo: Cappelen, 1968.

Varjo, Uuno. "The Finnish Farm." *Fennia,* 92:7 (1965).

————. *Forestry on State-Owned Lands*. Oulu: Societas geographica Fenniae nordicae, 1978.

Varjo, Uuno, and Huttunen, M-L. *The Founding of the University of Oulu and Its Effects upon Regional Development*. Oulu: University of Oulu, Publications of the Department of Geography, No. 58, 1976.

Väyrynen, Raimo. "The Environment and Development: The Greatest Challenges Facing 'Policy and Humankind.' " *Yearbook of Finnish Foreign Policy* (1988–1989), 3–4.

ETHNOGRAPHY AND PREHISTORY

Abercromby, J. "The Kalevala." *Athenaeum,* 1 (Feb. 18, 1888), 213.

―――. *The Pre- and Proto-Historic Finns Both Eastern and Western, with the Magic Songs of the West Finns.* London: Grimm Library, Nos. 9–10, 1898.

Atlas of Finnish Folk Culture, ed. Toivo Vuorela. Helsinki: Publications of the Finnish Literature Society, No. 325, 1976.

Billson, C. J. *The Popular Poetry of the Finns.* London: Nutt, Popular Studies in Mythology, Romance and Folklore, No. 5, 1900.

Borrow, George. *Targum; or, Metrical Translations from Thirty Languages and Dialects.* St. Petersburg, 1835.

Bowring, J. "On the Runes of Finland." *Westminster Review,* 14:7 (Apr. 1827), 317–341.

Branch, Michael. *A. J. Sjögren.* Helsinki: Suomalais-Ugrilaisen Seuran toimituksia 152, 1973.

Burnham, R. E. *Who Are the Finns? A Study in Pre-History.* London: Faber and Faber, 1946.

Collinder, Björn. *Fenno-Ugric Vocabulary: An Etymological Dictionary of the Ural Languages.* Hamburg: Buske, 1977.

―――. *An Introduction to the Uralic Languages.* Berkeley: University of California Press, 1965.

―――. "The Kalevala and Its Background." *ARV: Journal of Scandinavian Folklore,* 20 (1964), 5–111.

―――. *The Kalevala and Its Background.* Stockholm: Almqvist and Wiksell, 1964.

Collinder, B., et al. *A Survey of the Uralic Languages.* Stockholm: Almqvist and Wiksell, 1969.

Comparetti, Domenico. *The Traditional Poetry of the Finns.* London: Longmans, Green, 1898 (original Italian version published in 1891).

Cook, F. C. "The Kalevala." *Contemporary Review,* 47 (May 1885), 683–702.

Eriksson, Alder W. "Genetic Polymorphism in Finno-Ugric Populations." *Israel Journal of Medical Sciences,* 9:9–10 (1973).

Forsten, Ann. *The Refuse Fauna of the Mesolitic Suomusjärui Period in Finland.* Helsinki: Finskt Museum, 1972.

Fromm, Hans. *Zwischen Parodie und Mythos. Kalevalische Betrachtungen.* Cologne: Schriften aus dem Finnland-Institut in Köln, 1974.

Fromm, Hans, and Groenke, Ulrich. *Kalevala-Kanteletar. Zwei Vorträge.* Cologne: Schriften aus dem Finnland-Institut in Köln, 1974.

Gosse, Edmund. "The Kalevala." *Athenaeum,* 1 (Feb. 4, 1888), 147.

Groenke, Ulrich. *Kanteletar. Poetisches Kunsthandwerk und sein sprachliches Material.* Cologne: Schriften aus dem Finnland-Institut in Köln, 1974.

Haavio, Martti. *Essais folkloriques.* Helsinki: Finnish Literature Society, Studia Fennica 8, 1959.

———. *Väinämöinen: Eternal Sage.* Helsinki: Finnish Academy of Sciences, Folklore Fellows Communications, No. 144, 1952.

Hajdú, Péter, ed. *Ancient Cultures of the Uralian Peoples.* Budapest: Corvina, 1976.

———. *Finno-Ugrian Languages and Peoples.* London: Deutsch, 1975.

Hautala, Jouko. *Finnish Folklore Research, 1828–1918.* Helsinki: Societas Scientiarum Fennica, History of Learning and Science in Finland, 1828–1918, No. 12, 1969.

Hildén, Kaarlo. *The Racial Composition of the Finnish Nation.* Helsinki: Government Printing Office, 1932.

Holmberg, Uno. "Finno-Ugric: Siberian (Mythology)." In *The Mythology of All Races,* ed. C. J. A. MacCulloch. Reprint. New York: Cooper Square Publishers, 1964.

Honko, Lauri. "Baltic-Finnic Lament Poetry." *Studia Fennica,* 17 (1974), 23–58.

———. *Religion, Myth and Folklore in the World's Epics: The Kalevala and Its Predecessors.* New York: Mouton de Gruyter, Religion and Society Series, No. 30, 1990.

The Kalevala: Epic of the Finnish people, trans. Eino Friberg; ed. and intro. George C. Schoolfield. Helsinki: Otava, 1988.

Kalevala, trans. Lore Fromm and Hans Fromm. Munich: Hanser, 1967.

Kalevala, trans. (prose) Aili Kolehmainen Johnson. Hancock, MI: Book Concern, 1950.

Kalevala: The Land of Heroes. Vols. 1–2, trans. W. F. Kirby. 1907. Reprint New York: Dutton, 1961.

Kalevala: The land of the Heroes, trans. W. F. Kirby; intro. M. A. Branch. London: Athlone Press, 1985.

The Kalevala; or, Poems of the Kaleva District Compiled by Elias Lönnrot. A prose translation with foreword and appendices by Francis Peabody Magoun. Cambridge, MA: Harvard University Press, 1985.

Kalevala et traditions orales du monde. Colloques internationaux du Centre National de la Recherche Scientifique. Paris 18–22 mars 1985, ed. M. M. Jocelyne Fernandez-West. Paris: Centre nationale de la Recherche Scientifique, 1987.

Kirby, W. F. "Hiawatha and the Kalevala." *Archaeological Review,* 1 (July 1888), 376–384.

———. "The Kalevala." *Athenaeum* (Feb.–Mar. 1888), 147, 212–213, 276.

Kivikoski, Ella. *Die Eisenzeit Finnlands. Bilderatlas und Text.* Helsinki: Finnlands Altertumsgesellschaft, 1973 (Neuerausgabe).

———. *Finland.* London: Thames and Hudson, Ancient Peoples and Places Series, No. 53, 1967.

———. *Kvarnbacken. Ein Gräberfeld der jüngeren Eisenzeit auf Åland.* Helsinki: Finnische Altertumsgesellschaft, 1963.

Kohlemainen, John I. "Antti Jalava: Hungarian-Finnish Rapprochement." *Slavonic and East European Review,* 21:2 (1943).

———. *Epic of the North: The Story of Finland's Kalevala.* New York Mills, MN: Northern Publishing Co., 1973.

Kuusi, Matti. "The Bridge and the Church." *Studia Fennica,* 18:2 (1975), 37–75.

Kuusi, Matti; Bosley, Keith; and Branch, Michael, comps. *Finnish Folk Poetry-Epic: An Anthology in Finnish and English.* Helsinki: Publications of the Finnish Literature Society, No. 329, 1977.

Lang, Andrew. "The Kalevala." *Athenaeum,* 2 (Oct. 27, 1888), 556.

Lehtipuro, Outi. "Trends in Finnish Folkloristics." *Studia Fennica,* 18 (1974), 7–36.

Léouzon Le Duc, Louis-Antoine. *La Finlande. Son histoire primitive, sa mythologie, sa poesie épique avec la traduction complete de sa grande epopée, Le Kalewala.* Paris: Lafitte, 1845.

Loimu, Keijo. "The Finno-Ugrian Populations in Soviet Russia." *Contemporary Russia and Her Relations with Her Neighbours,* 1:2 (Jan. 1937), 183–198.

Luho, Ville. *Die kammkeramische Kultur und die finne-ugrische Frage.* Helsinki: Congressus secundus internationalis Fenno-Ugristarum, Part 2, 1968.

Mark, Karin. *Zur Herkunft der finnisch-ugrischen Völker vom Standpunkt der Anthropologie.* Tartu: Akademie der Wissenschaften der Estnischen SSR. Institut für Geschichtsforschung, 1970.

Mead, W. R. "The Finn in Fact and Fiction." *Norseman,* 16 (1958), 1–14.

Meinander, C. F. "The Problem of the Finno-Ugrian Peoples' Origin on the Base of Archeological Data." In *Studies in the Anthropology of the Finno-Ugrian Peoples.* Helsinki: University of Helsinki, arkeologian laitos, Moniste 7, 1973.

Müller, Max. *The Languages of the Seat of War in the East, with a Survey of the Three Families of Language: Semitic, Arian, and Turanian.* London: Williams and Norgate, 1855.

Nevanlinna, H. R. "The Distribution of Different Genetic Markers in Finland and Their Occurrence in Estonia and Hungary." In *Studies in the Anthropology of the Finno-Ugrian Peoples.* Helsinki: University of Helsinki, arkeologian laitos, Moniste 7, 1973.

Nordman, Carl Axel. *Archeology in Finland Before 1920.* Helsinki: Societas Scientiarum Fennica, History of Learning and Science in Finland, 1828–1918, No. 14a, 1968.

Oinas, Felix J. *Studies in Finnic Folklore: Homage to the Kalevala.* Bloomington: Indiana University Press, Indiana University Uralic and Altaic Series, No. 147, 1985. Helsinki: Finnish Literature Society, Publication No. 387, 1985.

————. *Studies in Finnic-Slavic Folklore Relations.* Helsinki: Suomalainen tiedeakatemia, 1969.

Puranen, Rauni. *The Kalevala Abroad: Translations and Foreign Language Adaptations of the Kaleva Compiled by Rauni Puranen.* Helsinki: Finnish Literature Society, 1985.

Sauvageot, Aurélien. *Les anciens finnois.* Paris: Librairie C. Klincksieck, 1961.

Sihvo, Pirkko. *Tradition und Volkskunst in Finnland.* Helsinki: Museovirasto, 1978.

Siiriäinen, Ari. *Studies Relating to Shore Displacement and Stone Age Chronology in Finland.* Helsinki: University of Helsinki, arkeologian laitos, Moniste 10, 1974.

Virtanen, Leea, et al. *Arvoitukset: Finnish Riddles.* Helsinki: Finnish Literature Society, 1977.

Vuorela, Toivo. *Ethnology in Finland Before 1920*. Helsinki: Societas Scientiarum Fennica, History of Learning and Science in Finland, 1828–1918, No. 145, 1977.

————. *The Finno-Ugrian Peoples*. Bloomington: Indiana University Press, Indiana University Ural and Altaic Series, No. 39, 1964.

FINLAND BEFORE INDEPENDENCE

Acerbi, Joseph. *Travels Through Sweden, Finland and Lapland to the North Cape in the Years 1798 and 1799*. Vols. 1–2. London, 1802.

Alapuro, Risto. "Nineteenth Century Nationalism in Finland: A Comparative Perspective." *Scandinavian Political Studies* (1979), 19–29.

Apunen, Osmo. "Continuity and Change in Finnish Foreign Policy from the period of autonomy to the Kekkonen Era." (1984), 19–31.

Arter, David. *On the Emergence of a Strong Peasant Party in Finland*. Helsinki: University of Helsinki, Valtio-opin laitoksen tutikimuksia A43, 1976.

Becker, Colonel G. W. [Becker Bey] (*see also* Ilmarinen). *La Finlande indépendante et neutre*. Paris: Extrait du Contemporain, 1880.

Borodkine, M. *Condition juridique de la Finlande*. Paris: Société d'Editions Scientifiques, 1902.

Bowring, L. B. *Autobiographical Recollections of Sir John Bowring with a Brief Memoir by His Son*. London: King, 1877.

Clarke, Edward. *Travels in Various Countries of Europe, Asia and Africa*. Vols. 1–2. London, 1819, and 1823.

Clive-Bayley, A. M. *Vignettes from Finland; or, Twelve Months in Strawberry Land*. London: Sampson Low, Marsden, 1895.

Copeland, W. R. *The Uneasy Alliance: Collaboration Between the Finnish Opposition and the Russian Underground, 1899–1904*. Helsinki: Annales Academiae Scientiarum Fennicae B179, 1973.

The Crisis in Finland. London: Parliamentary Russian Committee, 1909.

Danielson, J. R. [Danielson-Kalmari, J. R.]. *Finland's Union with the Russian Empire, with Reference to M. K. Ordin's "Finland's Subjugation."* Porvoo: Söderström, 1891.

Deck, Jean. *Pour la Finlande. Mémoire et documents.* Paris: Cahiers de la Quinzaine, 1902.

Despagnet, Frantz. *La question finlandaise au point de vue juridique. Avec l'adhésion de treize professeurs français de droit international et de droit constitutionel.* Paris: Librairie de la société du recueil géneral des lois et des arrêts, 1901.

Erich, Rafael. *Das Staatscrecht des Grossfürstentums Finnland.* Tübingen: Morh, 1912.

Feodoroff, Eugene [Kanninen, V. L.]. *The Finnish Revolution in Preparation, 1899–1905, as Disclosed by Secret Documents.* St. Petersburg, 1911.

Finland and Russia: International Conference in London Feb. 26–March 1, 1910. Translated from the French with an Appendix on the Law of 1910. London: Harrison and Sons, 1911.

The Finnish Party in Finland and Their Present Programme Together with a Short Introduction. Helsinki, 1907.

Fisher, J. F. *Finland and the Tsars.* London: Edward Arnold, 1899.

Fredriksen, N. C. *Finland: Its Public and Private Economy.* London: Edward Arnold, 1902.

Freeman, E.A. "Finland." *Macmillan's Magazine,* 65 (Mar. 1892), 321–328.

Fry, Edward. "Finlande et Russie. Déliberation internationale de Londres 26 février–ler mars 1910." *Revue de droit international et de législation comparée,* 2:12 (1910), 375–396, 505–551.

Futrell, Michael. *Northern Underground: Episodes of Russian Revolutionary Transport and Communications Through Scandinavia and Finland, 1863–1917.* London: Faber and Faber, 1963.

Gallen, Jarl. "La Finlande militaire au temps du Grand-Duché, 1809–1917." In *Revue Internationale d'Historie Militaire.* Helsinki: Edition finlandaise, 1961.

Gallenga, Antonio. "Finland." *Fortnightly Review,* n.s. 31 (May 1882), 602–611.

———. *A Summer Tour in Russia.* London, 1882.

Greenhill, Basil, and Giffard, Ann. *The British Assault on Finland, 1854–1855: A Forgotten Naval War.* Bath, Eng.: Bath Press, 1988.

Hennigsen, C. F. *Eastern Europe and the Emperor Nicholas.* Vol. 2. London, 1846.

———. *Revelations of Russia; or, The Emperor Nicholas and His Empire.* Vol. 2. London, 1844.

Henry, René. *La question de Finlande au point de vue juridique. Conférence faite à Paris le 28 janvier 1910 et suivie d'une discussion à laquelle ont prit part (L.) Mechelin, (W.) van der Vlugt et (A.) de Lapradelle.* Paris: Colin, 1910.

Hietala, Marjatta. "The Diffusion of Innovations: Some Examples of Finnish Civil Servants' Professional Tours in Europe." *Scandinavian Journal of History,* 8 (1983), 23–36.

Hodgson, John H. "Finland's Position in the Russian Empire, 1905–1910." *Journal of Central European Affairs,* 20:11 (1960), 158–173.

Holmberg, Åke. "On the Practicability of Scandinavianism: Mid-Nineteenth-Century Debate and Aspirations." *Scandinavian Journal of History,* 9:3 (1984), 171–182.

Huxley, Steve Duncan. *Constitutionalist Insurgency in Finland: Finnish "Passive Resistance" Against Russification as a Case of Nonmilitary Struggle in the European Resistance Tradition.* Helsinki: Suomen Historiallinen Seura, Studia Historica 38, 1990.

Hwasser, Israel, et al. *Finnlands Gegenwart und Zukunft. Eine Sammlung politischer Streitschriften.* 2nd ed. Stockholm, 1854.

Ilmarinen [Becker, E. G. W.]. *La question finlandaise*. Rome: Extrait de la Rivista politica e letteraria, Apr. 1901.

————. *La Russie, son passée, son présent*. Naples: Libreria Detken e Rocholl, 1906.

————. *La russification et la résistance passive en Finlande*. Rome: Estratto dalla Rivista moderna politica e letteraria, Feb. 15, 1903.

Jussila, Osmo. "Finland's Progress to National Statehood with the Development of the Russian Empire's Administrative System." In *Nationality and Nationalism in Italy and Finland from the Mid-Nineteenth Century to 1918*. Helsinki: Suomen Historiallinen Seura, Studia Historica 18, 1984.

————. "Nationalism and Revolution: Political Dividing Lines in the Grand Duchy of Finland During the Last Years of Russian Rule." *Scandinavian Journal of History*, 2:4 (1977), 289–309.

————. "From Province to State: Finland and the Baltic Provinces (1720–1920)—A Comparative Survey." In *Les Petits Etats face aux changements culturels, politiques et économiques de 1750 à 1914*, ed. D. Kosáry. Sixteenth International Congress of the Historical Sciences, Stuttgart, Aug. 25–Sept. 1, 1985. Lausanne, 1985.

Jutikkala, Eino. *An Atlas of Finnish History*. Helsinki: Söderström, 1959.

————. "Die Veränderungen in der Agrargesellschaft Finnlands in der ersten Hälfte des 17. Jahrhunderts." In *Die Bauerngesellschaft im Osterseeraum und im Norden um 1600*. Uppsala: Acta Visbyensia 2, 1966.

————. *Die Bevölkerung Finnlands in den Jahren 1721–1749*. Helsinki: Annales Academiae Scientiarum Fennicae, B:55:4, 1945.

————. "A Survey of Finland's History." In *Finnish Yearbook*. Helsinki, 1936.

Jutikkala, Eino, with Pirinen, Kauko. *A History of Finland*. New York: Praeger, 1962.

Kanerva, Jukka, and Palonen, Kari, eds. *Transformation of Ideas on a*

Periphery: Political Studies in Finnish History. Helsinki: Finnish Political Science Association, 1987.

Kirby, D. G. *Finland and Russia, 1808–1920: From Autonomy to Independence—A Selection of Documents Edited and Translated by D. G. Kirby.* London: Macmillan, in association with the School of Slavonic and East European Studies, University of London, 1975.

————. *Finland in the Twentieth Century: A History and an Interpretation.* London: Hurst, 1979.

————. *Northern Europe in the Early Modern Period: The Baltic World, 1492–1772.* New York: Longmans, 1990.

Kirkinen, H. "Finland in Russian Sources up to the Year 1323." *Scandinavian Journal of History,* 7 (1982), 254–275.

Klami, Hannu Tapani. *The Legalists: Finnish Legal Science in the Period of Autonomy, 1809–1917.* Helsinki: Societas Scientiarum Fennica, History of Learning and Science in Finland, 1828–1918, No. 2, 1981.

Klinge, Matti. *A Brief History of Finland.* Helsinki: Otava, 1981 (also in French, German, Swedish, and Finnish).

Korewo, N. N. *La question finlandaise.* Paris: Librairie Welter, 1912.

Korhonen, Keijo. *Autonomous Finland in the Political Thought of Nineteenth Century Russia.* Turku: University of Turku, Turun Yliopiston Julkaisuja B 105, 1967.

Krasiński, V. *Is the Power of Russia to Be Reduced or Increased by the Present War?* London, 1855.

————. *Russia and Europe; or, The Probable Consequences of the Present War.* London, 1854.

Kropotkin, P. "Finland: A Rising Nationality." *Nineteenth Century and After,* 17 (Mar. 1885), 527–546.

Krusius-Ahrenberg, Lolo. *Der Durchbruch des Nationalismus und Liberalismus im politischen Leben Finnlands 1856–1863.* Helsinki: Annales Academiae Scientiarum Finnicae B33, 1934.

————. "Finnischer Separatismus und russischer imperialismus im vorigen Jahrhundert." *Historische Zeitschrift,* 187 (1959), 249–288.

Lanin, E. B. [Dillon, E. J.]. "Finland." *Fortnightly Review,* n.s. 49 (Jan. 1891), 38–68.

Lauermaa, Matti. *General History Research in Finland.* Turku: University of Turku, Publications of the Institute of General History, No. 1:7, 1967.

Léouzon Le Duc, Louis-Antoine. *La Baltique.* Paris, 1855.

————. *L' empereur Alexandre II. Souvenirs personnels.* Paris, 1855.

————. *Les îles d'Aland.* Paris, 1854.

————. *Souvenirs et impressions de voyage dans les pays du Nord de l'Europe. Suède-Finlande-Danemark-Russie.* Paris: Librairie Ch. Delagrave, 1886, 1896.

Lindberg, Folke. *Scandinavia in Great Power Politics, 1905–1908.* Stockholm: University of Stockholm, Stockholm Studies in History, No. 1, 1958.

Low, Sidney. "The Hypocrisies of the Peace Conference." *Nineteenth Century and After,* 267:45 (May 1899), 689–698.

Luntinen, Pertti. "The Åland Question During the Last Years of the Russian Empire." *Slavonic and East European Review,* 54:4 (Oct. 1976).

————. *The Baltic Question, 1903–1908.* Helsinki: Annales Academiae Scientiarum Fennica B195, 1975.

————. *F. A. Seyn, 1862–1918: A Political Biography of a Tsarist Imperialist as Administrator of Finland.* Helsinki: Suomen Historiallinen Seura, Studia Historica 19, 1985.

Mannerheim, C. G. *Across Asia from West to East in 1906–1908.* Vols. 1–2. Helsinki:Suomalais-ugrilainen Seura, 1940.

Marmier, Xavier. "En Finlande." *Revue brittanique,* 7 (1884), 65–86.

————. *Lettres sur la Finlande et al Pologne.* Vols. 1–2. Paris, 1843, 1851.

Martin, W. C., and Hopkins, Karen. "Cleavage Cystallization and Party Linkages in Finland, 1900–1918." In *Political Parties and Linkages,* ed. Kay Lawson. New Haven, CT: Yale University Press, 1981.

Maude, George. "Finland in Anglo-Russian Relations, 1899–1910." *Slavonic and East European Review* (Oct. 1970).

————. "The Finnish Question in British Political Life, 1899–1914." *Turun Historiallinen Arkisto,* 28 (1973), 325–345.

Mead, W. R. "The Delineation of Finland: A Review of an Early Source of Popular Knowledge About Finland in Britain." *Fennia,* 97:3 (1968).

————. "The Discovery of Finland by the British." *Norseman,* 7:4 (July–Aug. 1949), 3–6.

————. "The Birth of the British Consular System in Finland." *Norseman,* 15 (1957), 101–111.

Mechelin, Leo, ed. *Finland in the Nineteenth Century.* Helsinki: Tilgmann, 1894 (also in French, German, Swedish, and Finnish).

————. *Précis du droit publique du Grand-Duché de* Finlande. Helsinki:Frenckell, 1886 (also in English as *A Précis of the Public Law of Finland.* London: Chapman and Hall, 1891).

Michoud, Léon, and de Lapradelle, Antoine. *La Question finlandaise.* Paris: Librarie Marescq, 1901.

Minzes, Boris. *Russia's Treatment of Finland and Its Bearing on Present World Politics.* Brooklyn: Finnish-American Publishing Co., 1900.

Mosse, Werner E. *Alexander II and the Modernization of Russia.* New York: Colliers, 1962.

Murray's Handbook for Northern Europe. Part 2. London, 1848–1849.

[Murray's] Handbook for Travellers in Russia, Poland and Finland. London, 1893.

Napier, C. *The History of the Baltic Campaign of 1854, from Documents and Other Materials,* ed. G. B. Earp. London: 1857.

Niitemaa, V. *J. V. Snellman und die Schweiz.* Turku: University of Turku, Publications of the Institute of General History, No. 2, 1970.

―――. *Das Strandrecht in Nordeuropa im Mittelalter.* Helsinki: Annales Academiae Scientiarum Fennicae B94, 1955.

―――. "Untersuchungen über die Siedlungsgeschichte Hämes im Mittelalter." In *Studia historica in honorem Hans Kruus.* Tallinn: Eesti NSV teaduste akadeemia ajaloo instituut, 1971.

Nys, Ernest. "Le gouvernement russe et la Finlande." *Revue de droit international et de législation comparée* (1909), 499–515.

Oppenheim, I.; Lauter, I.; et al. "Die finnische Frage." *Archiv für öffentliches Recht* (1900), 435–447.

Osten-Sacken, Wolf von der. *Russland und Finnland.* St. Petersburg, 1910.

Paasivirta, Juhani. *Finland and Europe: International Crises in the Period of Autonomy, 1808–1914.* Minneapolis: University of Minnesota Press, Nordic Series, No. 7, 1981.

―――. *Plans for Commercial Agents and Consuls of Autonomous Finland.* Turku: University of Turku, Annales Universitatis Turkuensis B89, 1962.

Pesonen, Pertti. "Finland: The 'One Man–One Vote' Issue." In *Universities, Politicians and Bureaucrats: Europe and the United States,* Ed. Hans Daalder and Edward Shils. Cambridge, Eng.: Cambridge University Press, 1982.

Plehwe, V. K. von. *Le manifeste impérial du 3 février 1899 et la Finlande.* St. Petersburg, 1899.

―――. "La Russie et la Finlande. Par un russe." *La nouvelle revue,* 20 (1903), 201–216.

Polvinen, Tuomo. *Die finnischen Eisenbahnen in den militärischen und politischen Plänen Russlands vor den ersten Weltkrieg.* Helsinki: Suomen Historiallinen Seura, Studia historia 4, 1962.

Pro Finlandia, 1899. Les adresses internationales à S. M. l'Empereur-Grand-Duc Nicolas II. Fasc. Ed. Stockholm: Tullberg, 1899.

Puaux, René. *La Finlande: Sa Crise Actuelle. Avec une Préface de Anatole France.* Paris: Stock, 1899.

————. *Les Manifestations du Sentiment Nationale en Finlande.* Paris: Lamy, 1901.

La Question finlandaise en 1911. Par un Deputé finlandais (Arvid Neovius). Preface de Frédéric Passy. Paris: Librairie Schleicher Frères, 1912.

Ramsay, August. *Finland; or, The Land of a Thousand Lakes: A Short Description of a Voyage and Sojourn There.* Helsinki: Finnish Tourist Association, 1894.

Raun, Toivo. "The Revolution of 1905 in the Baltic Provinces and Finland." *Slavic Review,* 43 (1984), 453–467.

Raun, Toivo, ed. *Finland and the Baltic Provinces in the Russian Empire.* Mahwah, NJ: Association for the Advancement of Baltic Studies (Special issue of the *Journal of Baltic Studies,* 15:2/3 [1984]).

Reuter, J. N. "Russia in Finland." *Nineteenth Century and After,* 45 (May 1899), 699–715.

Rosny, Leon de. *Le pays des dix-mille lacs. Quelques jours de voyage en Finlande.* Paris: E. Jorel, 1886.

Russian War, 1854. London: Navy Records Society, 1943.

Russian War, 1855. London: Navy Records Society, 1944.

The Russo-Finnish Conflict: The Russian Case, as Stated by Representatives of the Russian Government. London: Harrison and Sons, 1910.

Salomaa, Erkki. "Die deutschen Einflüsse auf die finnische Arbeiterbewegung während ihrer Entstehung im 19. Jahrhundert." *Wissenschaftliche Zeitschrift der Ernst-Moritiz-Arndt-Universität Greifswald. Gesellschafts und sprachwissenschaftliche Reihe* (1961), 101–105.

Scheffer, John. *The History of Lapland (Plus Material by Olof Rudbeck)*. London: Newborough and Parker, 1704.

Schweitzer, Robert. *Autonomie und Autokratie. Die Stellung die Grossfürstentums Finnland im russischen Reich in der zweiten Hälfte des 19. Jahrhunderts (1863–1899)*. Giessen: Schmitz, 1978.

Screen, J. E. O. *The Entry of Finnish Officers into Russian Military Service, 1809–1917*. London: University of London, School of Slavonic and East European Studies, 1976.

————. *The Helsinki Yunker School, 1846–1879: A Case Study of Officer Training in the Russian Army*. Helsinki: Suomen Historiallinen Seura, Studia Historica 22, 1986.

————. "The Helsinki Yunker School and the Finnish Senate: The Fate of the Preparatory Class Proposal of 1877." *Turun Historiallinen Arkisto*, 30 (1985), 183–204.

————. *Mannerheim: The Years of Preparation*. London: Hurst, 1970.

————. *Vårå Landsmän"—Finnish Officers in Russian Service, 1809–1917: A Selection of Documents, Compiled by J. E. O. Screen*. Turku: Åbo Akademi, Publications of the Research Institute of the Åbo Akademi Foundation, 1983.

————. "Russian Officer Training in the 1860s and 1870s: The Helsinki Yunker School." *Slavonic and East European Review*, 65:2 (Apr. 1987), 201–218.

Singleton, F. *A Short History of Finland*. Cambridge, Eng.: Cambridge University Press, 1989.

Soikkanen, H. "Revisionism, Reformism and the Finnish Labour Movement Before the First World War." *Scandinavian Journal of History*, 3:4 (1978), 347–360.

Soovoroff, P. *The Finnish Question: Equal Rights—The Position of Russians in Finland and Finns in the Rest of the Russian Empire*. St. Petersburg: Imprimerie Russo-Française, 1910.

Stead, W. T. "Russia's Policy in Finland: An Open Letter to His Excellency M. de Plehve." *Review of Reviews*, 28 (1903), 142–145.

Stolypine, P. A. *La question finlandaise. Discours prononcé dans la séance du 5/12 mai 1908 à la Douma d'Empire.* Paris: Giard et Brière, 1908.

Thaden, Edward C. *Russia's Western Borderlands, 1710–1870.* Princeton, NJ: Princeton University Press, 1984.

Tommila, Päiviö. *La Finlande dans la Politique Européenne en 1809–1815.* Helsinki, 1962.

Travers, Rosalind. *Letters from Finland, August 1908–March 1909.* London: Kegan Paul, 1911.

Tweedie, Mrs. Alec. *Through Finland in Carts.* London: Adam and Charles Black, 1897.

Wahlroos, Helmer J. "The Finnish Diet of Estates Becomes a Single-Chamber Assembly." In *Scandinavia Past and Present,* vol. 2. Odense: Odense University Press, 1959.

Warner, Oliver. *The Sea and the Sword: The Baltic, 1630–1945.* London: Cape, 1965.

Westermarck, E. *Memories of My Life.* London: Allen and Unwin, 1929.

Westlake, John. "The Case of Finland." *National Review,* 35 (Mar. 1900), 111–121.

Wuorinen, John H. "Scandinavia and the Rise of Modern National Consciousness." In *Nationalism and Internationalism: Essays Inscribed to Carlton J. H. Hayes,* Ed. Edward Mead Earle. New York: Columbia University Press, 1950.

———. *A History of Finland.* New York: Columbia University Press for the American-Scandinavian Foundation, 1965.

Ylikangas, Heikki. "The Historical Connections of European Peasant Revolts." *Scandinavian Journal of History,* 16:2 (1991), 85–104.

Zilliacus, Konni. *The Russian Revolutionary Movement.* New York: Dutton, 1905.

————. *Revolution und Gegenrevolution in Russland und Finnland.* Munich: Müller, 1912.

WORLD WAR I, INDEPENDENCE, AND CIVIL WAR

Agar, Augustus. *Baltic Episode: A Classic of Secret Service in Russian Waters.* London: Hodder and Stoughton, 1963.

Alapuro, Risto. *State and Revolution in Finland.* Berkeley: University of California Press, 1988.

Bell, Henry McGrady. *Land of Lakes: Memories Keep Me Company.* Preface by Sir Paul Dukes. London: Hale, 1950.

Bennett, Geoffrey. *Cowan's War: The Story of British Naval Operations in the Baltic, 1918–1920.* London: Collins, 1964.

Beyer, Franz "War die deutsche Intervention 1918 völkerrechtlich und politisch gerechtfertigt?" *Nordische Rundschau* (1928), 150–154.

Blomstedt, Kaarlo., ed. *Finland: Its Country and People—A Short Survey.* Helsinki, 1919.

Butler, R. *The New Eastern Europe.* London, 1919.

Conférence Politique Russe. *Mémoire sur la Question finlandaise.* Paris: Fournier, 1919.

Coonrod, R. W. "The Duma's Attitude Toward War-time Problems of Minority Groups." *American Slavic and East European Review,* 13 (Feb. 1954), 29–46.

Eliel, John. *Der Klassenkrieg in Finnland. Die finnische Sozialdemokratie im Kampfe gegen die Reaktion 1905–1918.* Copenhagen, 1918.

Elviken, Andreas. "Sweden and Finland, 1914–1918." In *War as a Social Institution: The Historian's Perspective,* ed. J. D. Clarkson and T. C. Cochran. New York: Columbia University Press, 1941.

Erich, Rafael. *Die finnische Frage vor und nach der russischen Revolution.* Frankfurt am Main: Rütten und Loening, 1918.

———. "La question de la Carélie orientale." *Revue de droit internationale et de législation comparée,* 1 (1922).

———. "Schweden, Aland und das unabhängige Finnland." *Deutsche Politik. Wochenschrift für Welt- und Kultur-politik* (1918), 39–44.

Fol, Jean-Jacques. *Accession de la Finlande à l'indépendance. 1917–1919.* Lille: Atelier de Reproduction de Thèse (Université de Lille III), 1977.

Goltz, Rüdiger von der. *Als politischer General im Osten (Finnland und Baltikum) 1918 und 1919.* 2. völlig neubearb. Aufl. Leipzig: Koehler, 1936.

———. *Meine Sendung in Finnland und im Baltikum.* Leipzig: Koehler, 1920.

Graham, Malbone Watson. *The Diplomatic Recognition of the Border States.* Vol. 1: *Finland.* Berkeley: University of California Press, 1935.

———. *New Governments of Eastern Europe.* New York, 1928.

Gummerus, Herman. *Deutschland und die Befreiung Finnlands.* Greifswald: Berichte aus dem Institut für Finnlandkunde der Universität Greifswald, no. 10, 1938.

Hamalainen, Pekka Kalevi. *In Time of Storm: Revolution, Civil War and the Ethnolinguistic Issue in Finland.* Albany: State University of New York Press, 1979.

Hannula, J. O. *Finland's War of Independence.* Intro. General Sir Walter Kirke. London: Faber and Faber, 1939.

Hedengren, Torsten. *Save Finland from Germany and Starvation.* New York: Finland Constitutional League of America. nd. (1918?)

Heinrichs, Erik. "Un tournant dans la vie de Mannerheim." In *Revue internationale d'histoire militaire.* Helsinki: Edition finlandaise, 1961.

Hennig, R. "Deutschlands Interessen an einer Selbständigkeit der Ukraine und Finnlands." *Das grössere Deutschland,* 4 (1917), 1643–1649.

Holsti, Rudolf. "M. Herbert Hoover et la naissance de la république finlandaise." *Bulletin du centre européen de la donation Carnegie* (1934), 783–813.

Hovi, Kalervo. *Cordon sanitaire or barrière de l'est? The Emergence of the New French Eastern European Alliance Policy, 1917–1919.* Turku: University of Turku, Annales Universitatis Turkuensis B 135, 1975.

————. "The Winning of Finnish Independence as an Issue in International Relations." *Scandinavian Journal of History,* 3:1 (1978), 47–73.

Hovi, Olavi. *The Baltic Area in British Policy, 1918–1921.* Helsinki: Suomen Historiallinen Seura, Studia Historica 11, 1980.

Hubatsch, Walther. *Unruhe des Nordens. Studien zur deutschskandinavischen Geschichte.* Göttingen: Musterschmidt-Verlag, 1956.

Jääskeläinen, Mauno. *Die ostkarelische Frage. Die Entstehung eines nationalen Expansionsprogramms und die Versuch zu seiner Verwirklichung in der Aussenpolitik Finnlands in den Jahren 1918–1920.* Helsinki: Suomen Historiallinen Seura, Studia historica 6, 1965.

Jackson, J. Hampden. "German Intervention in Finland, 1918." *Slavonic and East European Review,* 18 (July 1939), 93–101.

Kataja, S. A. *Der Terror der Bourgeoisie in Finnland.* Amsterdam: Görlitz, 1920.

King, J. *Three Bloody Men: Mannerheim the "Butcher," Denikin the KCB, Koltchak the "Bloody One."* Glasgow, Scot.: Reformers' Series, No. 34, 1919.

Kirby, D. G. "The Finnish Social Democratic Party and the Bolsheviks." *Journal of Contemporary History,* 11:2–3 (1976), 99–113.

————. "Revolutionary Ferment in Finland and the Origins of the Civil War." *Scandinavian Economic History Review,* 26:1 (1978), 15–35.

Kuusinen, O. W. *The Finnish Revolution: A Self-Criticism.* London, 1919.

————. "The Finnish Revolution." *Labour Monthly* 22 (1940), 115–124, 173–184.

————. *Die Revolution in Finnland.* Hamburg: Bibliothek der Kommunistischen Internationale, 15, 1921.

Long, Robert Crozier. "Finland's Independence: A Letter from Helsingfors." *Fortnightly Review,* n.s. no. 611 (Nov. 1, 1917), 646–663.

Lyytinen, Eino. *Finland in British Politics in the First World War.* Helsinki: Annales Academiae Scientiarum Fennicae, 1980.

Manninen, Ohto. "Red, White and Blue in Finland, 1918: A Survey of interpretations of the Civil War." *Scandinavian Journal of History,* 3:3 (1978), 229–249.

Menger, Manfred. *Die Finnlandpolitik des deutschen Imperialismus 1917–1918.* Berlin: Akademie Verlag, 1974.

Munck, Ruth. *Mit den finnischen Jägern an der deutschen Ostfront.* Leipzig: Schwarzhäupter Verlag, 1939.

Nuorteva, Santeri. *An Open Letter to American Liberals with a Note on Recent Documents.* New York: Socialist Publication Society, 1918.

Nurmio, Yrjö. "Das königlich preussische Jägerbataillon Nr. 27." In *Waffenbrüder Finnland.* Berlin, 1942.

Passivirta, Juhani. *The Victors in World War I and Finland: Finland's Relations with the British, French and United States Governments in 1918–1919.* Helsinki: Suomen Historiallinen Seura, Studia Historica 7, 1965.

Polvinen, Tuomo. "Lenin's Nationality Policy and Finland." *Yearbook of Finnish Foreign Policy* (1977), 3–8.

Rasila, V. "The Finnish Civil War and the Land-Lease Problem." *Scandinavian Economic History Review,* 17:1 (1969), 115–135.

Reuter, J. N. "Finland's Independence and Its Recognition." *Contemporary Review,* 115 (1919), 511–516.

Simpson, T. Y. "The Recognition of the Baltic States: Finland." In *His-*

tory of the Peace Conference of Paris, vol. 6, ed. H. W. V. Temperley. London, 1924.

Smith, C. Jay, Jr. *Finland and the Russian Revolution, 1917–1922.* Athens: University of Georgia Press, 1958.

————. "Russia and the Origin of the Finnish Civil War of 1918." *American Slavic and East European Review,* 14:4 (Dec. 1955), 481–502.

Söderhjelm, Henning. *The Red Insurrection in Finland in 1918: A Study Based on Documentary Evidence.* London: Harrison and Sons, n.d.

Soderhjelm [*sic*], Werner, "Finland and Germany During the War." *Current History,* 10:2:1 (July 1919), 94–98.

Stenberg, Herman. *The Greater Finland.* Helsinki: Ahjo, 1919.

Stenius, Henrik. "The Breakthrough of the Principle of Mass Organization in Finland." *Scandinavian Journal of History,* 5 (1980), 197–217.

Tokoi, Oskari. *Sisu: "Even Through a Stone Wall"—The Autobiography of Oskari Tokoi.* New York: Speller and Sons, 1957.

Travers, Rosalind H. "Politics in Finland." *New Europe,* 8 (July and Aug. 1918), 31–34, 60–63.

Turpeinen, Oiva. "Auffassungen der russischen Behörden über die Jägerbewegung und die Deutsche Finnlandpolitik in den Jahren 1914–1916." *Scandia,* 53:2 (1987).

United States Department of State. *Texts of the Finland "Peace."* Washington, DC: Government Printing Office, 1918.

Upton, Anthony F. *The Finnish Revolution, 1917–1918.* Minneapolis: University of Minnesota Press, 1980.

Wright, H. G. "The Revolution in Finland: Its Causes and Results." *Quarterly Review,* 231 (Jan. 1919), 149–168.

Wuorinen, John H. "Finland's War of Independence, 1918." *American-Scandinavian Review,* 51 (1963), 389–395.

Yarmolinsky, A. "The Republic of Finland: Finnish Separatism Since the Revolution." *Current History,* 7 (1918), 437–441.

Zilliacus, Konni. *Russland und Finnland.* Berlin: Puttkamer und Mühlbrecht, 1916.

FINLAND BETWEEN THE WORLD WARS

The Åland Question and the Rights of Finland: A Memorandum by a Number of Finnish Jurists and Historians. Helsinki: Finnish Literary Society, 1920.

Les Ålandais sur la question d'Åland. Uppsala, 1918.

Alapuro, Risto. "Students and National Politics: A Comparative Study of the Finnish Student Movement in the Inter-War Period." *Scandinavian Political Studies,* 8 (1973), 113–140.

Alapuro, Risto, and Allardt, Erik. "The Lapua Movement: The Threat of Rightist Takeover in Finland." In *The Breakdown of Democratic Regimes,* ed. Juan Linz and Alfred Stepan. Baltimore, MD: Johns Hopkins University Press, 1978.

Barros, James. *The Aland Islands Question: Its Settlement by the League of Nations.* New Haven, CT: Yale University Press, 1968.

Bellquist, E. C. "Finland's Treaties for the Peaceful Settlement of International Disputes." *American Journal of International Law,* 26 (Jan. 1932), 70–86.

———. *Some Aspects of the Recent Foreign Policy of Sweden.* Berkeley: University of California Press, 1929.

Braunschweig, Albert. *Deutschland und der Norden 1933–1945.* Stuttgart: Fleischauer und Spohn, 1935.

East Carelia: A Survey of the Country and Its Population and a Review of the Carelian Question. Helsinki: Akateeminen Karjala-Seura, 1934.

Finland's Territorial Forces, 1935. Helsinki: Territorial General Staff, 1936.

Gummerus, H. "Die Lappobewegung in Finnland." *Nordische Rund-schau,* 1 (1931), 1–9.

Headlam-Morely, A. *The New Democratic Constitutions of Europe.* London: Oxford University Press, 1928.

Heinonen, Reijo E. "From People's Movement to Minor Party: The People's Patriotic Movement (IKL) in Finland, 1932–1944." In *Who Were the Fascists: The Social Roots of European Fascism,* ed. Stein Ugelvik et al. Oslo: Universitetsforlaget, 1980.

Hovi, Kalervo. *Interessensphären im Baltikum. Finnland im Rahmen der Ostpolitik Polens 1919–1922.* Helsinki: Suomen Historiallinen Seura, Studia Historica 13, 1984.

————. *Le point de vue du ministre de Finlande à Paris sur la nature de l'occupation de la Ruhr.* Turku: University of Turku, Publications of the Institute of General History, No. 3:4, 1971.

Jackson, J. Hampden. *Finland.* London: Allen and Unwin, 1938.

Kalela, Jorma. "Right-Wing Radicalism in Finland During the Inter-War Period: Perspectives from and an Appraisal of Recent Literature." *Scandinavian Journal of History,* 1:1–2 (1976), 105–124.

Kaukiainen, Leena. "From Reluctancy to Activity: Finland's Way to the Nordic Family During the 1920's and 1930's." *Scandinavian Journal of History,* 9:3 (1984), 201–219.

Kirby, D. G. "New Wine in Old Vessels? The Finnish Socialist Workers' Party, 1919–1923." *Slavonic and East European Review,* 66:3 (July 1988), 426–446.

Macartney, C. A. *National States and National Minorities.* London: Oxford University Press, 1934.

Macartney, C. A., et al. *Survey of International Affairs, 1925.* London: Oxford University Press, 1928.

Manner, Kullervo. "Die Streikbewegung in Finnland." *Die kommunistische Internationale,* 2 (1920), 225–232.

Munch-Petersen, Thomas. "Great Britain and the Revision of the Åland Convention, 1938–39." *Scandia,* 41:1 (1975).

Munck, Ruth. "Lotta Svärd—eine anti-kommunistische Frauenorganisation in Finnland." *Contra Komintern* (1937), 173–176.

Myhrman, Anders Mattson. *The Swedish Nationality Movement in Finland.* Chicago: University of Chicago Libraries, 1939.

Newman, E. W. Polson. *Britain and the Baltic.* London: Methuen, 1930.

Ørvik, Nils. "From Collective Security to Neutrality: The Nordic Powers, the League of Nations, Britain and the Approach of War, 1935–1939." In *Studies in International History: Essays Presented to W. N. Medlicott,* ed. K. Bourne and D. C. Watt. London: Longmans, 1967.

―――. *The Decline of Neutrality: With Special Reference to the United States and the Northern Neutrals.* 1st ed. Oslo: Johan Grundt Tanum Forlang, 1953. 2nd ed., with a new foreword and supplementary chapter on nonalignment and neutrality since 1952. London: Cass, 1971.

Paasivirta, Juhani. *L'administration des affaires étrangères et la politique extérieure de la Finlande. Depuis le début de l'indépendance nationale en 1917 jusqu'à la guerre russo-finlandaise de 1939–1940.* Turku: University of Turku, Annales Universitatis Turkuensis B99, 1966.

―――. *Finland and Europe: The Early Years of Independence.* Helsinki: Suomen Historiallinen Seura, Studia Historica 29, 1989.

Pollitt, Harry. "The Political Background of the Antikainen Trial." *Labour Monthly,* 18 (1936), 569–573.

Prothero, G. W. *The Åland Islands.* London: Handbook Prepared Under the Historical Section of the Foreign Office, 1920.

―――. *Finland.* London: Handbook Prepared Under the Historical Section of the Foreign Office, 1920.

Puntila, L. A., ed., et al. *Finland, 1917–1967: An Assessment of Independence.* Helsinki: Kirjayhtymä, 1967.

Räikkönen, E. *Svinhufvud, the Builder of Finland: An Adventure in Statecraft.* London: Wilmer, 1938.

Rintala, Marvin. "Finland." In *The European Right: A Historical Profile,* ed. Hans Rogger and Eugen Weber. London: Weidenfeld and Nicolson, 1965.

———. "Finnish Students in Politics. The Academic Karelia Society." *Eastern European Questions,* 6 192–205.

———. *Four Finns: Political Profiles.* Berkeley: University of California Press, 1969.

———. "An Image of European Politics: The People's Patriotic Movement." *Journal of Central European Affairs,* 12:3 (Oct. 1962), 308–316.

———. *Three Generations: The Extreme Right-Wing in Finnish Politics.* Bloomington: Indiana University Publications, Russian and East European Series, No. 22, 1962.

———. "Väinö Tanner in Finnish Politics." *American Slavic and East European Review,* 20:1 (Feb. 1961), 84–98.

Rintala, Marvin, and Hodgson, John H. "Gustaf Mannerheim and Otto W. Kuusinen in Russia." *Slavonic and East European Review,* 56:3 (July 1978), 371–386.

Rothery, A. *Finland, the New Nation.* London: Faber, 1936.

Sandler, Rickard. "Neutralité Nordique." *Le Nord,* 1 (1938), 29–36.

Scott, A. MacCallum. *Suomi, the Land of the Finns.* London: Thornton Butterworth, 1926.

Sederholm, J. J. *The Aland Question from a Swedish Finlander's Point of View.* Helsinki: Government Printing Office, 1920.

Setälä, E. N. *La Lutte des Langues en Finlande.* Paris: Collection linguistique publiée par la societé de linguistique de Paris, 1920.

Söderhjelm, J. O. *L'Autonomie de la Province d'Aland et son application pratique.* Helsinki: Publications du Ministère des affaires étrangères de Finlande, 1930.

Stover, W. J. "Finnish Military Politics Between the Two World Wars." *Journal of Contemporary History,* 12:4 (1977), 741–757.

Wuorinen, John H. *Nationalism in Modern Finland*. New York: Columbia University Press, 1931.

————. "Suppression of Communism in Finland." *Current History,* 33 (Jan. 1931), 623–624.

WORLD WAR II

Aspelmeier, Dieter. *Deutschland und Finnland während der beiden Weltkriege*. Cologne: Schriften aus dem Finnland-Institut in Köln no. 7, 1967.

Auer, Väinö, und Jutikkala, Eino. *Finnlands Lebensraum. Das geographische und Geschichtliche Finnland*. Berlin: Alfred Metzner Verlag, 1941.

Bayer, James A., and Ørvik, Nils. *The Scandinavian Flank as History, 1939–1940*. Kingston, Ont.: Center for International Relations, Queen's University, National Security Series, No. 1/84, 1984.

Bell, Henry (Mc Grady). *British Relief to Finland, February-October 1940*. Helsinki: Frenckell's Printing Office, 1941.

Beranek, August. *Mannerheim*. Berlin: Luken und Luken, 1942.

Berry, Michael. *American Foreign Policy and the Finnish Exception: Ideological Preferences and Wartime Realities*. Helsinki: Finnish Historical Society, Studia Historica 24, 1987.

Blücher, Wipert von. *Gesandter zwischen Diktatur und Demokratie*. Wiesbaden: Limes Verlag, 1951.

Borenius, Tancred. *Field-Marshal Mannerheim*. London: Hutchinson, 1940.

Bourcet, C. de. *Le baron Mannerheim, maréchal de Finlande*. Paris: Sorlot, 1940.

Burns, Emile. *The Soviet Union and Finland*. London: Communist Party of Great Britain, War Library, No. 3, 1940.

Chew, Allen F. *The White Death: The Epic of the Soviet-Finnish Winter War*. East Lansing: Michigan State University Press, 1971.

Citrine, Walter. *My Finnish Diary*. London: Penguin, 1940.

Citrine, Walter; Noel-Baker, Philip; and Downie, J. *Finland: Interim Report*. London: Labour Party, 1940.

Clark, Douglas. *Three Days to Catastrophe*. London: Hammond, 1966.

Coates, W. P., and Coates, Zelda K. *The Soviet-Finnish Campaign, 1939–1940*. London: Eldon Press, 1942.

————. *Russia, Finland and the Baltic*. London: Lawrence and Wishart, 1940.

Condon, Richard W. *The Winter War: Russia Against Finland*. London: Pan/Ballantine Illustrated History of World War II, 1972.

Deutschland und Norden. Gemeinsame Wege zur Kontinental Wirtschaft. Lübeck, 1941.

The Development of Finnish-Soviet Relations During the Autumn of 1939, Including the Official Documents. London: Harrap, 1940.

Dilks, David. "Great Britain and Scandinavia in the Phoney War." *Scandinavian Journal of History*, 2:1 (1977), 29–51.

Erfurth, Waldemar. *Der finnische Krieg 1941–1944*. 1st ed. Wiesbaden: Limes Verlag, 1950. 2nd ed., 1977. In English (abridged) as *The Last Finnish War*. Washington, DC: University Productions of America, Classified Studies in Twentieth-Century Diplomatic and Military History, 1979.

Finland Reveals Her Secret Documents on Soviet Policy, March 1940–June 1941: Official Blue-White Book of Finland, with a Preface by Hj. J. Procopé, Minister of Finland to the United States. New York: Funk, 1941.

The Finnish Red Cross: The Main Features of the Work During the Decade 1938–1948. Helsinki: Published by the Finnish Red Cross for the XVII International Red Cross Conference in Stockholm, 1948.

Forster, Kent. "Finland's Foreign Policy, 1940–1941: An Ongoing Historiographic Controversy." *Scandinavian Studies*, 51:2 (1979), 109–123.

Fox, Annette Baker. *The Power of Small States: Diplomacy in World War II*. Chicago: University of Chicago Press, 1959.

Garvin, V. G. "Finland: Its Land and People." *Scottish Geographical Magazine,* 56 (May 1940), 49–58.

Gebhardt, James F. *The Petsamo-Kirkenes Operation: Soviet Breakthrough and Pursuit in the Arctic, October 1944*. Fort Leavenworth, KS: Combat Studies Institute, Leavenworth Papers, No. 17, 1990.

Graham, Malbone W. "Stability in the Baltic States: Finland." In *New Governments in Europe: the Trend Toward Dictatorship,* ed. Vera Micheles Dean et al. New York: Columbia University Press, 1941.

Gripenberg, G. A. *Finland and the Great Powers: Memoirs of a Diplomat*. Lincoln: University of Nebraska Press, 1965.

Hooper, Arthur Sanderson. *The Soviet-Finnish Campaign*. Watford, Eng.: Odhams, 1940.

Jaakkola, Jalmari. *The Finnish Eastern Question*. Porvoo: Söderström, 1942.

Jakobson, Max. *The Diplomacy of the Winter War: An Account of the Russo-Finnish War, 1939–1940*. Cambridge, MA: Harvard University Press, 1961.

Jalanti, Heikki. *La Finlands dans l'étau germano-soviétique 1940–1941*. Neuchâtel, Switz.: Editions de la Baconnière, 1966.

Jokipii, Mauno. "Finland's Entrance into the Continuation War." *Yearbook of Finnish Foreign Policy* (1977), 8–19.

Julkunen, Martti. *Helsinki or Terijoki: Foreign Comments for the Early Days of December 1939*. Turku: University of Turku, Institute of General History, No. 1:6, 1967.

Kanninen, Ermei, et al., eds. *Aspects of Security: The Case of Independent Finland*. Helsinki: Finnish Military History Commission, 1985.

Kirby, David G. "Conflict in the North: Recent Writings on the Winter War (1939–1940)." *Books from Finland,* 10:3, 4 (1976), 59–63.

Kolehmainen, John I. *Täällä Amerikka—The Voice of America Calling Finland: An Essay on U.S. Shortwave Broadcasting to Finland, 1942–1945 and 1951–1953.* New York Mills, MN: Parta Printers, 1985.

Krosby, H. Peter. *Finland, Germany and the Soviet Union, 1940–1941: The Petsamo Dispute.* Madison: University of Wisconsin Press, 1968.

Ludlow, Peter. "Britain and Northern Europe, 1940–1945." *Scandinavian Journal of History,* 4 (1979), 123–162.

Lundin, C. Leonard. *Finland in the Second World War.* Bloomington: Indiana University Press, Indiana University Publications, Slavic and East European Series, No. 6, 1957.

Mannerheim, C. G. E. *The Memoirs of Marshal Mannerheim.* London: Cassell, 1953; New York: Dutton, 1954.

Meister, Jürg. *Der Seekrieg in den osteuropäischen Gewässern 1941–1945.* Munich: Lehmann, 1958.

Menger, Manfred. "Das militärpolitische Verhältnis zwischen Deutschland und Finnland im Herbst 1944." *Militärgeschichte,* no. 3 (1979), 297–309.

Meretškov, Kirill. *Serving the People.* Moscow: Progress Publishers, 1971.

Mörz, Kurt. "Mannerheim und Maginotlinie." *Österreichische Militärische Zeitschrift,* 21:2 (Mar./Apr. 1983).

Munch-Petersen, Thomas. *The Strategy of Phoney War: Britain, Sweden, and the Iron Ore Question, 1939–1940.* Stockholm: Militärhistoriska Förlaget, 1981.

Nevakivi, Jukka. *The Appeal That Was Never Made: The Allies, Scandinavia, and the Finnish Winter War, 1939–1940.* London: Hurst, 1976.

Niitemaa, V. *Finnland und der zweite Weltkrieg in der historischen Literatur.* Bibliothek für Zeitgeschichte, 1:4, Stuttgart 1957.

Nyman, Kristina, ed. *Finland's War Years.* Helsinki: Publications of the Society of Military History, No. 4, 1973.

Palm, Thede. *The Finnish-Soviet Armistice Negotiations of 1944.* Stockholm: Almqvist and Wiksell, 1971.

Reddaway, W. F. *Problems of the Baltic.* Cambridge, Eng.: Cambridge University Press, 1940.

Rhodes, Benjamin. "The Origins of Finnish-American Friendship, 1919–1941." *Mid-America,* 54 (Jan. 1972), 3–19.

Rodzyanko, Paul. *Mannerheim: An Intimate Picture of a Great Soldier and Statesman,* recorded by Anita Leslie. London: Jarrolds, 1940.

Schwartz, Andrew J. *America and the Russo-Finnish War.* Washington, DC: Public Affairs Press, 1960.

Spring, D. W. "The Soviet Decision for War Against Finland, 30 Nov. 1939." *Soviet Studies,* 38:2 (Apr. 1986), 207–226.

———. "Stalin and the Winter War." *Yearbook of Finnish Foreign Policy* (1990), 37–42.

Stein, G. H., and Krosby, H. Peter. "Das finnische Freiwilligen-Bataillon der Waffen-SS." *Vierteljahrshefte für Zeitgeschichte,* 4 (1966).

Tanner, Väinö. *The Winter War.* Stanford, CA: University of Stanford Press, 1957.

Turtola, Martti. "Guilty or Innocent? Approaches to the Winter War in Research and Memoirs." *Yearbook of Finnish Foreign Policy* (1990), 43–46.

Ueberschär, G. R. *Hitler und Finnland 1939–1941. Die deutschfinnischen Beziehungen während des Hitler-Stalin Paktes.* Wiesbaden: Steiner, 1978.

Upton, Anthony F. *Finland, 1939–1940.* London: Davis-Poynter, 1974.

———. *Finland in Crisis, 1940–1941: A Study in Small-Power Politics.* London: Faber and Faber, 1964.

———. "TheWinter War: Finland October 5, 1939–March 13, 1940"; "Barbarossa, the Finnish Front: Finland/USSR, June/December 1941"; and "End of the Arctic War: Finland, June/October 1944."

In *History of the Second World War,* vols. 1, 2, 5. London: Purnell, 1966–1968.

Warner, Oliver. *Marshal Mannerheim and the Finns.* London: Weidenfeld and Nicolson, 1967.

Wuorinen, John H., ed. *Finland and World War II, 1939–1944.* New York: Ronald Press, 1948.

Ziemke, Earl F. *The German Northern Theater of Operations, 1940–1945.* Washington, DC: Government Printing Office, 1960.

INTERNAL POLITICS IN FINLAND SINCE WORLD WAR II

Alestalo, Matti, and Kuhnle, Stein. "The Scandinavian Route: Economic, Social, and Political Developments in Denmark, Finland, Norway and Scandinavia." In *The Scandinavian Model: Welfare States and Welfare Research,* ed. Robert Erikson et al. Armonk, NY: Sharpe, 1987.

Allardt, Erik. "Facteurs économiques et sociaux du vote à gauche en Finlande." *Cahiers de sociologie économique,* 6 (1962), 258–266.

————. *Institutionalized Versus Diffuse Support of Radical Political Movements.* Helsinki: University of Helsinki, Publications of the Institute of Sociology, No. 27, 1962.

————. "Patterns of Class Conflict and Working Class Consciousness in Finnish Politics." In *Cleavages, Ideologies and Part Systems: Contributions to Comparative Political Sociology,* Ed. Erik Allardt and Yrjö Littunen. Turku: Westermarck Society, No. 10, 1964.

————. "Social Sources of Finnish Communism." *International Journal of Comparative Sociology,* 5:1 (Mar. 1964), 49–72.

Allardt, Erik, and Bruun, Kettil. *Characteristics of the Finnish Non-Voter.* Turku: Westermarck Society, No. 3, 1956.

Allardt, Erik, and Pesonen, Pertti. "Cleavages in Finnish Politics." In *Party System and Voter Alignments,* ed. Seymour Lipset and Stein Rokkan. New York, 1967.

Allardt, Erik, and Weslowski, Wlodzimierz, eds. *Social Structure and Change—Finland and Poland: Comparative Perspectives.* Warsaw: Polish Scientific Publications, 1978.

Anckar, Dag. *Liberalism, Democracy and Political Culture in Finland.* Turku: Åbo akademis bibliotek, Acta Academiae Aboensis Ser. A62:5, 1983.

————. *Parties and Law-Making in Finland: A Policy Framework.* Turku: Abo akademis bibliotek, Acta Academiae Aboensis Ser. A56:2, 1979.

————. *A Proposal for Reforming the Presidential Elections in Finland.* Turku: Åbo akademis Statsvetenskapliga institutionen, Communications Ser. A.150, 1980.

Anckar, Dag, and Helander, Voitto. *Remise Participation and Associations: A Survey of Some Finnish Data.* Turku: Statsvetenskapliga institutionen, 1980.

Archer, Clive, and Maxwell, Stephen. *The Nordic Model: Studies in Public Policy Innovation.* Farnborough, Eng.: Gower, 1980.

Arter, David. "All-Party Government for Finland?" *Parliamentary Affairs,* 31:1 (1978), 67–85.

————. *Bumpkin Against Bigwig: The Emergence of the Green Movement in Finnish Politics.* Tampere: University of Tampere, Publications of the Institute of Political Science, No. 47, 1978.

————. "Communists in Scandinavian Local Government." In *Marxist Local Governments in West Europe and Japan.* London: Pinter, 1986.

————. "The Finnish Election of 1979: The Empty-Handed Winner?" *Parliamentary Affairs,* 32:4 (1979), 422–436.

————. "The 1983 Finnish Election: Protest or Consensus?" *West European Politics,* 6:4 (1983), 252–255.

————. "The Finnish Christian League: Party or Anti-Party?" *Scandinavian Political Studies,* 3:2 (1980), 143–162.

————. "Die finnische sozialdemokratische Partei." In *Sozialdemokratische Parteien in Europa,* ed. W. E. Paterson and K. T. Schmitz. Bonn: Verlag Neue Gesellschaft, 1979.

―――. "Kekkonen's Finland: Enlightened Despotism or Consensual Democracy?" *West European Politics,* 4:3 (1981), 219–234.

―――. *The Nordic Parliaments: A Comparative Analysis.* London: Hurst, 1984.

―――. *Politics and Policy-Making in Finland.* New York: St. Martin's Press; London: Wheatsheaf, 1987.

―――. "Social Democracy in a West European Outpost: The Case of the Finnish SDP." *Polity,* 12:3 (1980), 373–375.

Bellquist, Eric C. "Finland: Democracy in Travail." *Western Political Quarterly,* 2 (June 1949), 217–227.

―――. "Government and Politics in Northern Europe: An Account of Recent Developments." *Journal of Politics,* 8:3 (Aug. 1946), 369–377, 390–391.

―――. "Political and Economic Conditions in the Scandinavian Countries: Finland." *Foreign Policy Reports,* 24 (May 1948), 52–56.

Berglund, Sten, and Lindström, Ulf. *The Scandinavian Party Systems.* Lund: Student-litteratur, 1978.

Berglund, Sten, and Sundberg, Jan, eds. *Finnish Democracy.* Helsinki: Finnish Political Science Association, No. 9, 1990.

Beyer-Thoma, Hermann. *Kommunisten und Sozialdemokraten in Finnland.* Wiesbaden: Otto Harrassowitz, 1990.

Billington, James H. "Finland." In *Communism and Revolution: The Strategic Uses of Political Violence,* ed. Cyril E. Black and Thomas P. Thornton. Princeton, NJ: Princeton University Press, 1964.

Birnbaum, I. "The Communist Course in Finland." *Problems of Communism* (Sept.–Oct. 1959), 42–47; (Jan.–Feb. 1960), 63–64.

Borg, Olavi, and Paastela, Jukka. *Communist Participation in Governmental Coalitions: The Case of Finland.* Tampere: University of Tampere, Institute of Political Science, No. 80, 1985.

Constitution Act and Parliament Act of Finland. Helsinki: Government Printing Office, 1967.

Democracy in Finland: Studies in Politics and Government. Helsinki: Finnish Political Science Association, 1960.

Eklin, Mikko. *The Role of a Planning Organisation in Collective Decision-Making: The Anatomy of a Finnish Government Commission.* Helsinki: University of Helsinki, Yleisen valtio-opin laitoksen tutkimuksia, C Deta 11, 1975.

Elder, Neil, et al. *The Consensual Democracies? The Government and Politics of the Scandinavian States.* Oxford, Eng.: Martin Roberts, 1982.

Form of Government Act and Diet Act of Finland. Helsinki: Ministry of Foreign Affairs, 1947.

Forster, Kent. "The Silent Soviet Vote in Finnish Politics." *International Journal,* 3 (1963), 341–352.

Haranne, Markku. *Community Power Structure Studies: An Appraisal of an Ever-Green Research Tradition with a Finnish Example.* Helsinki: University of Helsinki, Research Group for Comparative Sociology, Research Reports No. 23, 1979.

Helander, Voitto. *A Liberal Corporatist Sub-System in Action: the Incomes-Policy System in Finland.* Turku: University of Turku, Politiikan tutkimuksen ja sosiologian laitos, Yleinen valtio-oppi, tutkimustiedotteita no. 1, 1979.

Helander, Voitto, and Anckar, Dag. *Consultation and Political Culture: Essays on the Case of Finland.* Helsinki: University of Helsinki, Commentationes Scientiarum Socialium 19, 1983.

Hodgson, John H. *Communism in Finland: A History and Interpretation.* Princeton, NJ: Princeton University Press, 1967.

———. "Finnish Communism and Electoral Politics." *Problems of Communism,* 23:1 (1974), 34–45.

Husu, Erkki. "The Economic Stabilisation Programmes and Their Political Consequences in Finland, 1967–1970." *Scandinavian Political Studies,* 7 (1972), 260–265.

Iivonen, Jyrki. "State or Party: The Dilemma of Relations Between the Soviet and Finnish Communist Parties." *Journal of Communist Studies,* 2:1 (1986), 1–30.

Jansson, Jan-Magnus. "Post-War Elections in Finland." *Bank of Finland Monthly Bulletin*, 36:4 (Apr. 1962), 22–27.

Junttila, Lars. "Prospects of Overcoming the Split in the Trade Unions of Finland." *World Marxist Review*, 8 (1965), 49–55.

Kastari, P. "Grundrechte und Freiheiten in der finnischen Verfassung und Politik." *Zeitschrift für ausländisches öffentliches Recht und Völkerrecht*, 19:4 (1958), 693–707.

————. "The Position of the President in the Finnish Political System." *Scandinavian Political Studies*, 4 (1969), 151–159.

Krosby, H. Peter. "The Communist Power Bid in Finland in 1948." *Political Science Quarterly*, 75:2 (1960), 229–243.

Krusius-Ahrenberg, Lolo. "The Political Power of Economic and Labour Market Organizations: A Dilemma of Finnish Democracy." In *Interest Groups on Four Continents*, ed. Henry W. Ehrmann. Pittsburgh, PA: University of Pittsburgh Press, 1960.

Kuusisto, Allan. "Parliamentary Crises and Presidial Governments in Finland." *Parliamentary Affairs*, 11:3, (Summer 1958), 341–349.

Leskinen, V. "Socialist View on the Political Situation in Finland." *Socialist International Information*, 9 (1963), 131–136.

Lindblom, O. "The Finnish Social Democratic Party and Foreign Policy." *Socialist International Information*, 12 (1961), 190–192.

Littunen, Yrjö. "The Attitude Adopted by the Press During a Labour Strike at Kemi." *Transactions of the Westermarck Society* (1953), 206–220.

Marshall, F. R. "Communism in Finland." *Journal of Central European Affairs*, 19:4 (1960), 375–388.

————. "Labor, Politics and Economics in Finland." *Southwestern Social Science Quarterly* (June 1959) 5–15.

Matheson, David. *Ideology, Political Action and the Finnish Working Class: A Survey of Political Behavior*. Helsinki: Societas Scientiarum Fennica, Commentationes Scientiarum Socialium 10, 1979.

Matti, Bengt. "Finland." In *Communism in Europe: Continuity, Change and the Sino-Soviet Dispute.* Vol. 2, Ed. W. E. Griffith. Cambridge, MA: MIT Press, 1966.

Mylly, Juhani. *Tradition and Change in Finnish Political Culture, 1944–1948.* Turku: University of Turku, Political History Publications, No. C:36, 1991.

Mylly, Juhani, and Berry, Michael, eds. *Political Parties in Finland: Essays in History and Politics.* 2nd ed. Turku: University of Turku, Political History Publications, No. C:21, 1987.

Nopsanen, A. "Communism in Finland." *Norseman,* 16 (1958), 20–23.

———. "Finland's Non-Communist Parties." *Norseman,* 16 (1958), 289–295.

Nousiainen, Jaakko. *The Finnish Political System.* Cambridge, MA: Harvard University Press, 1971.

———. "Political Research in Scandinavia, 1960–1965: Finland." *Scandinavian Political Studies,* 1 (1966), 28–43.

———. *Research on the Finnish Communism.* Turku: University of Turku, Institute of Political Science, Report Series, No. B5, 1969.

Nyholm, Pekka. *Parliament, Government and Multi-Dimensional Party Relations in Finland.* Helsinki: Societas Scientiarum Fennica, Commentationes Scientiarum Socialium 2, 1972.

Oittinen, R. H. "The Ideological Development or Democratic Socialism in Finland." *Socialist International Information,* 1 (1957), 1–18.

Paasio, R. "The Aims of the Finnish Social Democratic Party." *Socialist International Information,* 33 (1963), 475.

———. "Finland in 1963." *Socialist International Information,* 3 (1964), 33–34.

Paavonen, Tapani. *Welfare State and Political Forces in Finland in the Twentieth-Century.* Turku: University of Turku, Political History Publications, No. C:34, 1991.

Pakarinen, Erik. "News Communication in Crisis: A Study of the News Coverage of Scandinavian Newspapers During Russian-Finnish Note Crisis in the Autumn of 1961." *Cooperation and Conflict,* 3–4 (1967), 224–228.

Pesonen, Pertti. "Finland: Party Support in a Fragmented System." In *Electoral Behavior: A Comparative Handbook,* ed. Richard Rose. New York: Free Press, 1974.

———. *The Political Science Profession in Finland.* Helsinki: University of Helsinki, Acta politica 10, 1978.

———. "Studies on Finnish Political Behavior." In *Essays on the Behavioral Study of Politics,* ed. A. Ranney. Urbana: University of Illinois Press, 1962.

Pesonen, Pertti, and Rantala, Onni. "Outlines of the Finnish Party System." In *Small States in Comparative Perspective,* ed. Risto Alapuro et al. Oslo: Norwegian University Press, 1985.

Porevuo, Mervi. "Presidential Election Campaign, 1987–1988." *Yearbook of Finnish Foreign Policy* (1987), 34 et seq.

Puntila, L. A. *The Evolution of the Political Parties in Finland.* Helsinki: Työväen kirjapaino, 1953.

Rantala, Onni. "The Political Regions of Finland." *Scandinavian Political Studies,* 2 (1967), 117–140.

Rintala, Marvin. "The Problem of Generations in Finnish Communism." *American Slavic and East European Review,* 17:2 (Apr. 1958), 190–202.

Sakslin, Maija, ed. *The Finnish Constitution in Transition.* Helsinki: Finnish Society of Constitutional Law, 1991.

Sipponen, Kauko, et al. "Constitutional Reform and Foreign Policy." *Yearbrook of Finnish Foreign Policy* (1974), 55–63.

Suhonen, Pertit. "Finland." In *Western European Party Systems,* ed. Peter Merkl. New York: Free Press, 1984.

Tarkiainen, Tuttu. "The Stability of Democratic Institutions in Postwar Finland." *Parliamentary Affairs* (1966) 241–250.

Timonen, Pertti. "The Finnish Presidential Election." *Yearbook of Finnish Foreign Policy* (1981), 19–24.

Törnudd, Klaus. *The Electoral System of Finland.* London: Hugh Evelyn, 1968.

Tuominen, Arvo. "The Northern Countries and Communism." *Norseman,* 12:4 (July–Aug. 1954), 217–229.

Upton, Anthony F. *The Communist Parties of Scandinavia and Finland.* London: Weidenfeld and Nicolson, 1973.

————. "Finland". In *Communist Power in Europe, 1944–1949,* ed. Martin McCauley. London: Macmillan in association with the School of Slavonic and East European Studies, University of London, 1977.

Vartola, Juha. *Administrative Change, Strategies of Development and Current Problems in the Central Administration of the State of Finland.* Tampere: University of Tampere, Department of Administrative Sciences, Division of Public Administration, Recent Reports, No. 3, 1978.

Wagner, Ulrich. *Finnlands Kommunismen: Volksfront Experiment und Parteispaltung 1966–1970.* Stuttgart: Verlag W. Kohlhammer, 1971.

Wiberg, Matti, ed. *The Political Life of Institutions: Scripta in honorem professoris Jaakko Nousiainen sexagesimum annum complentis.* Helsinki: Finnish Political Science Association, No. 14, 1991.

————, ed. *The Public Purse and Political Parties: Public Financing of Political Parties in Nordic Countries.* Helsinki: Finnish Political Science Association, No. 13, 1991.

Wihtol, Robert. "The 1978 Finnish Presidential Elections." *Yearbook of Finnish Foreign Policy* (1977), 59–64.

Wikstroem, O. "Disintegration in the Finnish Communist Camp." *Socialist International Information,* 41 (1953), 735–736.

Wuorinen, John. "Democracy Gains in Finland." *Current History,* 21:122 (1951), 327–330.

Zilliacus, K. "Parliamentary Democracy in Finland." *Parliamentary Affairs,* 9:4 (Autumn 1956), 427–43

FOREIGN POLICY SINCE WORLD WAR II

Albrecht, Ulrich, et al. *Neutrality: The Need for Conceptual Revision.* Tampere: Tampere Peace Research Institute, Tutkimustiedotteita no. 35, 1988.

Allison, Roy. *Finland's Relations with the Soviet Union, 1944–84.* London: Macmillan in association with St. Antony's College, 1985.

Anderson, Stanley V. *The Nordic Council: A Study of Scandinavian Regionalism.* Stockholm: Svenska Bokförlaget/Norstedts, Scandinavian University Books, 1967.

Antola, Esko. "Security and Cooperation in the CSCE." *Yearbook of Finnish Foreign Policy* (1985), 5–12.

Apunen, Osmo. *Détente: A Framework for Action and Analysis.* Tampere: University of Tampere, Politiikan tutkimuksenlaitos, no. 61, 1981.

——."The FCA Treaty in Finland's System of Treaties." *Yearbook of Finnish Foreign Policy* (1977), 41–42.

——."Geographical and Political Factors in Finland's Relations with the Soviet Union." *Yearbook of Finnish Foreign Policy* (1977), 20–31.

——."The Treaty of Friendship, Cooperation and Mutual Assistance and Finland's Security Policy." *Yearbook of Finnish Foreign Policy* (1983), 27–32.

Berner, Örjan. *Soviet Policies Toward the Nordic Countries.* Lanham, MD: University Press of America for the Center of International Affairs, Harvard University, 1986.

Bjøl, E. *Nordic Security.* London: IISS, Adelphi Papers, No. 181, 1983.

Blomberg, Jaakko. "Finland's Policy of Neutrality in Times of Détente and Tension." *Yearbook of Finnish Foreign Policy* (1984), 2–4.

Brodin, Katarina, et al. "The Policy of Neutrality: Official Doctrines of Finland and Sweden." *Cooperation and Conflict,* 4:1 (1968), 18–51.

Brundtland, A. O. "The Nordic Balance." *Cooperation and Conflict,* 2:2 (1966).

———. *The Nordic Balance.* Oslo: Norwegian Institute of International Affairs, NUPI notat no. 229 (Dec. 1981).

Dancy, Eric. "Finland Takes Stock." *Foreign Affairs,* 24:3 (Apr. 1946), 513–525.

Denisov, Y. "USSR-Finland: Model of Cooperation." *International Affairs* (Moscow), 22:5 (1977), 50–58.

Essays on Finnish Foreign Policy. Vammala: Finnish Political Science Association, 1969.

Etzioni, Amitai. *Political Unification.* New York: Holt, Rinehart and Winston, 1965.

Finnish Foreign Policy: Studies in Foreign Politics. Helsinki: Finnish Political Science Association, 1963.

Gillessen, Günther. "Finnlands behinderte Neutralität." *Europa Archiv,* 30:11 (1975), 361–368.

Gräsbeck, K. "Les fondements de la neutralité finlandaise." *Revue des Deux Mondes* (Dec. 1, 1969).

Häikiö, Martti. "Finland and the German Question." *Yearbook of Finnish Foreign Policy* (1974), 40–42.

Hakovirta, Harto. *East-West Conflict and European Neutrality.* Oxford, Eng.: Clarendon Press, 1988.

———. "The International System and Neutrality in Europe, 1946–1980–1990." *Yearbook of Finnish Foreign Policy* (1980), 39–48.

Hodgson, John H. "The Paasikivi Line." *American Slavic and East European Review,* 18:2 (Apr. 1959), 145–173.

——. "Postwar Finnish Foreign Policy: Institutions and Personalities." *Western Political Quarterly,* 15:1 (Mar. 1962), 80–92.

Holsti, K. J. "Strategy and Techniques of Influence in Soviet-Finnish Relations." *Western Political Quarterly,* 17:1 (1964), 63–82.

Höpker, Wolfgang. "Moskaus Schlinge um Finnlands Hals." *Aussenpolitik,* 13:2 (1962), 99–105.

Jakobson, Max. *Finnish Neutrality: A Study of Finnish Foreign Policy Since the Second World War.* London: Hugh Evelyn, 1968.

——. "Finnish Neutrality Is Still Expedient." *Yearbook of Finnish Foreign Policy* (1974), 28–30.

——. "Substance and Appearance." *Foreign Affairs,* 58:5 (Summer 1980), 1034–1044.

Julkunen, Martti. "A Documentation of Information and Emotions: Paasikivi Set Himself Up as the Guarantor of Finland's Preservation." *Yearbook of Finnish Foreign Policy* (1985), 36–40.

Karsh, Efraim. *Neutrality and Small States.* London: Routledge, 1988.

Kekkonen, Urho. "CSCE and Finland." *Yearbook of Finnish Foreign Policy* (1973), 7–8.

——. *Neutrality: The Finnish Position.* London: Heinemann, 1970.

——. *A President's View.* London: Heinemann, 1982.

——. "The Treaty of Friendship, Cooperation and Mutual Assistance: Historical Background and Present Significance." *Yearbook of Finnish Foreign Policy* (1973), 32–36.

Kenney, Rowland. *The Northern Tangle.* London: Dent, 1946.

Kivimäki, Erkki. "The Finnish Policy in the U.N. Human Rights Commission." *Yearbook of Finnish Foreign Policy* (1986), 19–21.

Kolehmainen, John I. "Finland Is Not Afraid." *Christian Century* (Mar. 9, 1949), 300–303.

Korhonen, Keijo. "The Foreign Policy of President Urho Kekkonen." *Contemporary Review,* 227:1317 (Oct. 1975), 194–197.

——, ed. *Urho Kekkonen: A Statesman for Peace.* Helsinki: Otava, 1975.

Krymov, P., and Golovanov, K. "Finland's Foreign Policy." *International Affairs* (Moscow) (Oct. 1969).

Krymov, P., and Lavrov, L. "The Paasikivi Policy." *International Affairs* (Moscow), 9 (1957), 160–164.

Larsen, Knud. "Scandinavian Grass Roots: From Peace Movement to Nordic Council." *Scandinavian Journal of History,* 9:3 (1984), 183–200.

Lehtinen, Risto. "Development Characteristics of the Finnish Foreign Policy Elite." *Yearbook of Finnish Foreign Policy* (1982), 59–65.

——. "Foreign Policy in the Presidential Election Campaign." *Yearbook of Finnish Foreign Policy* (1981), 24–32.

Leppänen, Markku. "Finland's Change of President and Foreign Policy Status in the Eyes of the Foreign Press." *Yearbook of Finnish Foreign Policy* (1982), 34–38.

Linderg, Steve. "Are We Counting Our Chickens . . ." *Yearbook of Finnish Foreign Policy* (1984), 4–11.

——. "Finnish Neutrality in a Changing Environment." In *European Neutrals and the Soviet Union.* Stockholm: Swedish Institute of International Affairs, Conference Paper No. 6, 1986.

Lipponen, Paavo. "Policy of Neutrality and the FCA-Treaty." *Yearbook of Finnish Foreign Policy* (1974), 31–33.

Littunen, Yrjö. "The Development of Public Opinion on Foreign Policy Since World War II." *Yearbook of Finnish Foreign Policy* (1977), 32–42.

Lübbe, Peter. *Kulturelle Auslandsbeziehungen der DDR. Das Beispiel Finnland.* Bonn: Friedrich-Ebert Stiftung, 1981.

Lundestad, Geir. *America, Scandinavia, and the Cold War, 1945–1949.* Oslo: Universitetsforlaget, 1980.

Lyon, Peter. *Neutralism.* Leicester, Eng.: Leicester University Press, 1963.

Maude, George. *The Finnish Dilemma: Neutrality in the Shadow of Power.* London: Oxford University Press for the RIIA, 1976.

——. *The Finnish-Norwegian Tangle.* Turku: University of Turku, Department of Sociology and Political Science, Studies on Political Science, No. 9, 1987.

——. "Foreign Policy and the Change of Power." *Politiikka,* no. 1 (1984), 74–82.

——. "Problems of Finnish Statecraft: The Aftermath of Legitimation." *Diplomacy and Statecraft,* 1:1 (Mar. 1990), 19–39.

Mazour, Anatole G. *Finland Between East and West.* Princeton, NJ: Van Nostrand, 1956.

Metcalf, Michael, and Väyrynen, Raimo. *The End of the Cold War and Four Small European Democracies.* Boulder, CO: Westview, 1993.

Möttölä, Kari. "Finnish Foreign Policy in the Koivisto Era: The First Two years." *Yearbook of Finnish Foreign Policy* (1983), 2–11.

——. "Kekkonen's Major Achievement Gave New Opportunities." *Yearbook of Finnish Foreign Policy* (1985), 2–4.

——. "Managing the Finnish-Soviet Relationship: Lessons and Experiences." In *European Neutrality and the Soviet Union.* Stockholm: Swedish Institute of International Affairs, Conference Paper No. 6, 1986.

——. *Ten Years After Helsinki: The Making of the European Security Regime.* Boulder, CO: Westview, 1986.

Neutrality and the EC, ed. Kari Joutsamo. Turku: University of Turku, Oik. tiedekunnan julkaisuja C9, 1990.

Nevakivi, Jukka. "Communists as a Foreign Policy Problem: Aspects of the Postwar Finnish-Soviet Relations." *Yearbook of Finnish Foreign Policy* (1987), 26–34.

The Nordic Region: Changing Perspectives in International Relations, ed. Martin Heisler. Newbury Park: Sage, 1990.

Øberg, Jan. "Towards Understanding Common Nordic Security Alternatives." *Current Research on Peace and Violence,* 1–2, (1986).

Ochsner, Alois. "Länderbericht Finnland." In *Neutralität im Internationalen Vergleich,* Leitung Prof. Dr. Alois Riklin. St. Gallen: Hochschule St. Gallen für Wirtschafts und Sozialwissenschaften, 1979.

Ørvik, Karen Erickson. *The Foreign Policy of Finland: A Study of the Sources, Development and Direction of Finnish Foreign Policy.* Washington, DC: Department of State, Office of External Research, 1967.

Ørvik, Nils. "Scandinavia, NATO, and Northern Security." *International Organization,* 20:3 (1966), 380–396.

———. *Sicherheit auf finnisch: Finnland und die Sowjet-Union.* Stuttgart: Seewald Verlag, 1972.

Owen, John E. "Ten Year Tightrope!" *World Affairs Quarterly,* 29:3 (1958), 278–290.

Polvinen, Tuomo. *Between East and West: Finland in International Politics, 1944–1947.* Porvoo: Söderström, 1986.

Porevuo, Mervi. "Finnish Neutrality and European Integration." *Yearbook of Finnish Foreign Policy* (1988–1989), 18–22.

Rantanen, Paavo. "Global Changes and Finland: Is a New Approach Needed?" *Yearbook of Finnish Foreign Policy* (1988–1989), 5–6.

Record of Recommendations by the Conference on the Draft Peace Treaty with Finland. Paris: Imprimerie Nationale, Paris Conference to Consider the Draft Treaties of Peace with Italy, Rumania, Bulgaria, Hungary and Finland, 1946.

322 / Historical Dictionary of Finland

Reimaa, Markku. "The Significance of the CSCE Yesterday and Now."
Yearbook of Finnish Foreign Policy (1990), 20–25.

Rinehart, Robert, ed. *Finland and the United States, 1919–1989: A Review of Seventy Years of Diplomatic Relations.* Washington, DC: Georgetown University Institute for the Study of Diplomacy, 1992.

Rinne, Irene. "Finnish Policy on Refugees Suffering from a Lack of Planning." *Yearbook of Finnish Foreign Policy* (1990), 26–29.

Rosas, Allan. "Finnish Human Rights Policies." *Yearbook of Finnish Foreign Policy* (1986), 9–19.

Saarinen, Hannes. "Finland in the West German Press in 1979." *Yearbook of Finnish Foreign Policy* (1979), 40–47.

Sandén, Christer. "Foreign Policy Debates in Finland in the Seventies." *Yearbook of Finnish Foreign Policy* (1980), 49–58.

The Scandinavian States and Finland: A Political and Economic Survey. London: RIIA, 1951.

Scheinin, Martin. "The Importance to Finland of the European Convention on Human Rights." *Yearbook of Finnish Foreign Policy* (1988–1989), 7–9.

Schiller, Bernt. "At Gun Point: A Critical Perspective on the Attempts of the Nordic Governments to Achieve Unity After the Second World War." *Scandinavian Journal of History,* 9 (1984), 221–238.

Siika, Marita. "China und die beiden nordischen Neutralen: Finnland und Schweden." *China und die europäischen Neutralen.* Shanghai: Shanghaier Institut für China-und Südostasienforschung, 1987.

———. "China and the Nordic Countries, 1950–1970." *Cooperation and Conflict,* 18 (1983), 101–113.

———. "The People's Republic of China and the Nordic Countries in the 1970s." *China Report* (New Delhi), 19:6 (Nov.–Dec. 1983), 19–42.

Söderling, Ismo. "Finnish Refugee Policy in Search of a Shape." *Yearbook of Finnish Foreign Policy* (1987), 8–13.

Spencer, Arthur. "Finland Maintains Democracy." *Foreign Affairs,* 31:2 (1953), 301–309.

———. "Soviet Pressure on Scandinavia." *Foreign Affairs,* 30 (1952).

Ståhlberg, Krister. "Finnish Neutrality and Public Opinion." In *Between the Blocs: Problems and Prospects for Europe's Neutral and Non-aligned States,* ed. Joseph Kruzel and Michael H. Haltzel. New York: Woodrow Wilson International Center for Scholars and Cambridge University Press, 1989.

———. "Foreign Policy Initiatives in the Finnish Parliament, 1950–1983." *Yearbook of Finnish Foreign Policy* (1986), 21–27.

———. "Public Opinion in Finnish Foreign Policy." *Yearbook of Finnish Foreign Policy* (1987), 17–26.

Stenström, Bo. "From Liturgy to Lemmings: Discussion on Foreign Policy in Finland." *Yearbook of Finnish Foreign Policy* (1983), 11–16.

Sundelius, Bengt, ed. *Foreign Policies of Northern Europe.* Boulder, CO: Westview, 1982.

———, ed. *The Neutral Democracies and the New Cold War.* Boulder, CO: Westview, 1987.

Törngren, Ralf. "The Neutrality of Finland." *Foreign Affairs* (1961), 601–609.

Törnudd, Klaus. "East-West Relations and Finland's Scope for Action." *Yearbook of Finnish Foreign Policy* (1983), 38–42.

———. *Soviet Attitudes Towards Non-Military Regional Cooperation.* Helsinki: Societas Scientiarum Fennica, Commentationes Humanarum Litterarum 28:1, 1963.

Treaty of Peace with Finland, Paris, 10th February, 1947. London: H. M. Stationery Office, Cmd. 7484, Treaty Series, No. 53, 1948.

Tuomisto, Tero. "The Birth of the Paasikivi Society." *Yearbook of Finnish Foreign Policy* (1978), 53–56.

Vanhanen, Vesa. "Foreign Policy Debate, 1983." *Yearbook of Finnish Foreign Policy* (1983), 22–25.

Väyrynen, Raimo. "A Case Study of Sanctions: Finland and the Soviet Union in 1958–59." *Cooperation and Conflict*, No. 3 (1969), 205–233.

———. "Challenges to Neutral Countries." *Yearbook of Finnish Foreign Policy* (1985), 27–35.

———. *Conflicts in Finnish-Soviet Relations: Three Comparative Case Studies.* Tampere: University of Tampere, Acta Universitatis Tamperensis, A47, 1972.

———. "Finland's Role in Western Policy Since the Second World War." *Cooperation and Conflict*, 12:2 (1977), 87–108.

Verosta, Stephan. *Die dauernde Neutralität.* Vienna: Manzsche Verlags - und Universitätsbuchhandlung, 1967.

Vesa, Unto. " 'The Crisis of the UN' and Finland." *Yearbook of Finnish Foreign Policy* (1982), 17–23.

———. "Determining Finland's Position in International Crises." *Yearbook of Finnish Foreign Policy* (1979), 2–19.

Vesala, Heimo. "A Survey of Foreign Language Literature on Finnish Foreign Policy." *Yearbook of Finnish Foreign Policy* (1974), 63–65.

Vital, David. *The Survival of Small States: Studies in Small Power/Great Power Conflict.* London: Oxford University Press, 1971.

Vloyantes, John. "Finland." In *Europe's Neutral and Nonaligned States: Between NATO and the Warsaw Pact,* ed. Victor Papacosma and Mark R. Rubin. Wilmington, DE: Scholarly Resources Reprint for the Lemnitzer Center for NATO Studies, Kent State University, 1989.

———. *Silk Glove Hegemony: Finnish-Soviet Relations, 1944–1971 — A Case Study of the Theory of the Soft Sphere of Influence.* Kent, OH: Kent State University Press, 1975.

Wagner, Ulrich. *Finnlands Neutralität. Eine Neutralitätspolitik mit Defensivallianz.* Hamburg: Verlag Christoph von der Ropp, 1974.

Wahlbäck, Krister. "Finnish Foreign Policy: Some Comparative Perspectives." *Cooperation and Conflict*, 5:4 (1969), 282–298.

Wendt, Frantz. *The Nordic Council and Cooperation in Scandinavia.* Copenhagen: Munksgaard, 1959.

Wiberg, Håkon. "The Nordic Countries: A Special Kind of System?" *Current Research on Peace and Violence,* 1–2 (1986), 7 et seq.

Wiklund, Claes, and Sundelius, Bengt. "Nordic Cooperation in the Seventies: Trends and Patterns." *Scandinavian Political Studies,* 2.2 (1979), 99–120.

Wuorinen, John. "Continuing Finnish Neutrality," *Current History,* 36:212 (1959), 224–228.

———. "Finland and the USSR, 1945–61." *Journal of International Affairs,* 16:1 (1962), 38–46.

———. "Finland in Today's Cold War World." *World Affairs,* 125:3 (1962), 161–166.

———. "The Finnish Treaty." *Annals of the American Academy of Political and Social Science,* 257 (1948), 87–96.

Zartmann, W. "Neutralism and Neutrality in Scandinavia." *Western Political Quarterly,* 7 (1954).

DEFENSE, DISARMAMENT, AND SECURITY POLICY SINCE WORLD WAR II.

Antola, Esko. "Arms and Stability in the Finnish Disarmament Policy." *Yearbook of Finnish Foreign Policy* (1982), 4–9.

Apunen, Osmo. "A Nordic Nuclear-Free Zone: The Old Proposal or a New One?" *Yearbook of Finnish Foreign Policy* (1974), 42–50.

———. "Nuclear-Weapon-Free Areas: Zones of Peace and Nordic Security." *Yearbook of Finnish Foreign Policy* (1978), 2–19.

———. "The Three Waves of the Kekkonen Plan and Nordic Security in the 1980's." *Bulletin of Peace Proposals* (1980), 1.

Archer, Clive, ed. *The Soviet Union and Northern Waters.* London: Routledge for RIIA, 1988.

Archer, Clive, and Scrivener, David. *Northern Waters*. London: Croom Helm for RIIA, 1986.

Blomberg, Jaakko. "The Shaping of Finland's Disarmament Policy." *Yearbook of Finnish Foreign Policy* (1982), 2–4.

——. "The Security Policy of the Northern Sea-Areas from the Finnish Point of View." *Yearbook of Finnish Foreign Policy* (1976), 4–6.

The Defence Forces of Finland. Special supplement to the *Army Quarterly and Defence Journal* Tavistock, Eng., 1974.

Finnish Disarmament Policy, by Unto Vesa. Helsinki: Ministry of Foreign Affairs, 1984.

Finnish National Defence. Helsinki: General Headquarters Information Section, 1983.

"Finnish Security Policy Views in 1982." *Yearbook of Finnish Foreign Policy* (1982), 11–13.

The Frontier Guard in Finland. Helsinki: Headquarters of the Frontier Guard, 1985.

Hägglund, Gustav. "Defence Policy: The Tasks and Tools." *Yearbook of Finnish Foreign Policy* (1983), 16–22.

Halonen, Ilkka. "Aufgaben und Gliederung der Finnischen Verteidigungskräfte." *Allgemeine Schweizerische Militärische Zeitschrift,* 151:10 (Oct. 1985).

Härkönen, Seppo. "Eurostrategic Weapons, Northern Europe and Finland: New Weapons Technology as a Finnish Security Problem." *Yearbook of Finnish Foreign Policy* (1979), 20–26.

Holm, Heli. "The Nordic Nuclear-Weapon-Free Zone: Prospects After the Meeting of Nordic Parliamentarians." *Yearbook of Finnish Foreign Policy* (1985), 18–22.

Hyvärinen, Risto. *The Finnish Defence Forces in the Service of Neutrality*. Helsinki: Söderström, 1963.

Kalela, Jaakko. "The Dimensions of Finland's Peace Policy." *Yearbook of Finnish Foreign Policy* (1975), 23–25.

Karjalainen, Ahti. "Finland and Military Security in Europe." *Yearbook of Finnish Foreign Policy* (1973), 9–11.

Klenberg, Jan. "The Military Situation in the Baltic." *Yearbook of Finnish Foreign Policy* (1984), 11–14.

Komissarov, Yuri. "The Future of a Nuclear-Weapon-Free Zone in Northern Europe." *Yearbook of Finnish Foreign Policy* (1978), 26–31.

Korhonen, Keijo. "Finland and the Disarmament Negotiations." *Yearbook of Finnish Foreign Policy* (1973), 15–19.

Lång, K. J., and Rosas, Allan. *Scandinavian Seminar on a Nordic Nuclear-Weapon-Free Zone: Legal Aspects—Papers Presented at the Second Scandinavian Seminar on a Nordic NWFZ in Espoo, Finland, Aug. 30–Sept. 1, 1984.* Mänttä: Finnish Lawyers' Publishing Co., 1987.

Lellenberg, Jon L. *The North Flank Military Balance.* McLean, VA: BDM Corporation, 1979.

Lindberg, Steve. "Towards a Nordic Nuclear-Weapons-Free Zone." *Yearbook of Finnish Foreign Policy* (1980), 28–38.

Mällinen, Teuvo. "The Nordic Nuclear-Weapon-Free Zone: Like a Salmon." *Yearbook of Finnish Foreign Policy* (1986), 5–7.

Maude, George. "Conflict and Cooperation: The Nordic Nuclear-Free Zone Today." *Cooperation and Conflict,* 18 (1983), 233–243.

———. "Finland, Norway, and the Prospective Nordic Nuclear-Free Zone." *Journal of Baltic Studies,* 16:1 (Spring 1985), 18–32.

———. "Finland's Security Policy," *World Today,* 31:10 (1975), 404–414.

———. "The Finnish Dilemma Today: The Defence of Lapland." *Yearbook of Finnish Foreign Policy* (1983), 32–38.

———. "Neutrality and Finnish Security Policy." *ELSA Law Review,* 1:1 (Winter 1989), 51–59.

Möttölä, Kari, ed. *Nuclear Weapons and Northern Europe: Problems and Aspects of Arms Control*. Helsinki: Finnish Institute of International Affairs, 1983.

———, ed. *The Arctic Challenge: Nordic and Canadian Approaches to Security and Cooperation in an Emerging International Region.* Boulder, Co: Westview, 1988.

"Nordic Nuclear-Weapon-Free Zone: Concluding Remarks of the Working Group Appointed by the Ministry for Foreign Affairs." *Yearbook of Finnish Foreign Policy* (1986), 3–5.

A Nuclear Free Zone and Nordic Security. Helsinki: Finnish Institute of International Affairs, 1975.

Nyberg, René. "The Finnish Defense Posture." *Security Dilemmas in Scandinavia*. Ithaca, NY: Cornell University, Peace Studies Program, Occasional Paper No. 217, 1983.

Pajunen, Aimo. "Finland's Security Policy in the 1970's: Background and Perspectives." In *Five Roads to Nordic Security,* ed. J. J. Holst. Oslo: Universitetsforlaget, 1973.

Penttilä, Risto E. J. *Finland's Search for Security Through Defence, 1944–1989*. London: Macmillan, 1991.

Rajakoski, Esko. "A Finnish View on the Situation in European Disarmament Negotiations." *Yearbook of Finnish Foreign Policy* (1980), 25–27.

Reports of the Finnish Parliamentary Defence Committees. Helsinki: Government Printing Centre, 1976 (Second Committee Report); and 1981 (Third Committee Report).

Ries, Tomas. *Cold Will: The Defence of Finland*. London: Brassey's Defence Publishers, 1988.

———. *Consequences of START for the Nordic Region*. Oslo: Institutt for forsvarsstudier, no. 7, 1991.

———. "Finland's Defense Forces: Isolated but Unbowed." *International Defense Review,* 17:3 (1984).

———. "Reorganization of the Finnish Defense Forces." *International Defense Review,* 19:4 (Apr. 1986).

———. "Swedish and Finnish Defense Policies: A Comparative Study," with comments by Kari Möttölä. In *Between the Blocs: Problems and Prospects for Europe's Neutral and Nonaligned States,* ed. Joseph Kruzel and Michael H. Haltzel. New York: Woodrow Wilson International Center for Scholars and Cambridge University Press, 1989.

Rosas, Allan. "Comments on a Draft Resolution." In *Nuclear Disengagement in Europe,* ed. S. Lodgaard and Marek Thee. London: Taylor and Francis for SIPRI, 1983.

Ruhala, Kalevi, and Järvenpää, Pauli. "A Nordic Nuclear-Free Zone: Prospects for Arms Control in Northern Europe." *Yearbook of Finnish Foreign Policy* (1978), 20–25.

Rutila, Asko. "Finnish Defence Appropriations." *Yearbook of Finnish Foreign Policy* (1982), 13–17.

Sixma, H. J., and Laukkanen, J. "Far Northern Fighter Force: The Finnish Air Arm Today." *Air International,* 31:1 (July 1986), 7–13.

Tillotson, H. M. *Finland at Peace and War 1918–1993.* Norwich: Michael Russell, 1993.

Väyrynen, Raimo. "The Nordic Region and the World Military Order." In *Dynamics of European Nuclear Disarmament,* ed. Alva Myrdal. Nottingham, Eng.: Spokesman, 1981.

Vesa, Unto. "Small State Contribution to Disarmament: The Case of Finland." In *TAPRI Yearbook, 1986: Challenges and Responses to European Security,* ed. Vilho Harle. Aldershot, Eng.: Croom Helm, 1986.

Viitasalo, Mikko. "Challenges of New Arms Technology to Nordic Security." *Yearbook of Finnish Foreign Policy* (1985).

Visuri, Pekka. "Die Entwicklung der finnischen Verteidigungsdoktrin nach dem Zweiten Weltkrieg." *Österreichische Militärische Zeitschrift,* 23:1 (Jan.–Feb. 1985), 9–16.

Voronkov, Lev. *Non-Nuclear Status to Northern Europe.* Moscow: Nauka, 1984.

Zakheim, Dov S. "Nato's Northern Front: Developments and Prospects." *Cooperation and Conflict,* 18:4 (1983).

ECONOMIC ISSUES SINCE WORLD WAR II, INCLUDING THE ECONOMICS OF INTEGRATION

Addison, John. *Finnish Incomes Policy.* Aberdeen, Scot.: University of Aberdeen, Department of Political Economy, Discussion Paper No. 14, 1980.

Agricultural Policy in Finland. Paris: OECD, 1975.

Alasoini, Tuomo, and Pekkala, Juhani. *New Model for Rationalization and Labour Relations in the Finnish Paper Industry.* Helsinki: Ministry of Labour, Working Environment Division, Research Branch, 1989.

Alho, Kari. *Analysis of Financial Markets and Central Bank Policy in the Flow-of-Funds Framework: An Application to the Case of Finland.* Helsinki: ETLA, 1988.

——. *Deregulation of Financial Markets in Finland: A General Equilibrium Analysis of Finland.* Helsinki: Research Institute of the Finnish Economy, 1989.

Anatolyev, Andrei, and Nadezhdin, Yevgeni. "Northern Europe: An Invitation to a Dialogue." *International Affairs* (Moscow), no. 12 (1987), 82–86.

Antola, Esko. "Developing Countries in Finnish Economic Relations." *Yearbook of Finnish Foreign Policy* (1979), 27–31.

——. "Finland and the Prospects for Western European Integration in the 1980's." *Yearbook of Finnish Foreign Policy* (1981), 37–49.

Berry, Michael. *Deep Waters Run Slowly: Elements of Contrast in European Integration.* Part 3. *The Case of Finland.* Helsinki: ETLA, Research Institute of the Finnish Economy, Discussion Paper No. 345, 1991.

Breitenstein, Wilhelm. "On Volume Targets in International Development Cooperation: A Small Donor Country's View." *Yearbook of Finnish Foreign Policy* (1982), 23–35.

"Finnish Consumer Goods Industries: An Overview." *Bank of Finland Monthly Bulletin,* 51:9 (Sept. 1977), 20–25.

Finland's Development Assistance: Annual Report to the OECD. Helsinki: Foreign Ministry, 1991.

Finnish Energy Economy up to 2025: Some Development Paths. Helsinki: Ministry of Trade and Industry, Energy Department, Government Printing Centre, 1990.

The Finnish Energy Policy Programme: Approved by the Government on 24th February 1983. Helsinki: Prepared by the Parliamentary Energy Committee, Government Printing Centre, 1983.

Finnish-Soviet Economic Relations, ed. Kari Möttölä, O. N. Bykov, and I. S. Korolev. London: Macmillan in association with the Finnish Institute of International Affairs, 1983.

Hakovirta, Harto. *Effects of "External Factors" and International Negotiations in the Light of Nordic Integration Negotiations.* Tampere: University of Tampere, Politiikan tutkimus laitos 1, 1977.

Harle, Vilho. "Finland's Economic Relations with Developing Countries in the Light of Development Cooperation and Trade policy." *Yearbook of Finnish Foreign Policy* (1978), 45–52.

Heiskanen, Ilkka, and Martikainen, Tuomo. *The Finnish Public Sector: Its Growth and Changing Role in 1960–1984.* Helsinki: University of Helsinki, Department of Political Science, Acta Politica no. 11, 1989.

Hellsten, Erkki. "The Effects of the New International Economic Order (NIEO) on Finnish Industry." *Yearbook of Finnish Foreign Policy* (1979), 35–40.

Hjerppe, Reino. *Fiscal Policy Reactions in Finland.* Helsinki: University of Helsinki, Department of Economics, Discussion Paper No. 91, 1978.

———. "Measurement of the Role of the Public Sector in the Finnish Economy." *Review of Income and Wealth* (1980).

Johansson, B. O. "Finnish Industry and Development Cooperation." *Yearbook of Finnish Foreign Policy* (1979), 32–34.

Karvonen, Lauri. "Economic Relations in the Nordic Area: Failures and Achievements." *Yearbook of Finnish Foreign Policy* (1977), 52–58.

Kekkonen, Taneli. "Finland's CMEA Policy." *Yearbook of Finnish Foreign Policy* (1973), 29–31.

Kiljunen, Kimmo. "Changing Premises of Finnish Development Cooperation Policy." *Yearbook of Finnish Foreign Policy* (1982), 25–34.

Kirves, Lauri. "Finland and EFTA." *Economic Review* (KOP), 2 (1961).

Kivikari, Urpo. "Finnish-Soviet Economic Relations: A Special Case of East-West Trade." *Yearbook of Finnish Foreign Policy* (1985), 23–26.

———. *Finnish-Soviet Trade in the Light Industries: Impact on the Finnish Textile, Clothing, Leather and Footwear Industries.* Turku: University of Turku, Taloustieteen julkaisuja C18, 1985.

———. *Wealth Holding of Households.* Turku: University of Turku, Institute of Economics, Series B3, 1972.

Korhonen, Gunnar. "Finland's Foreign Trade and the Integration Plans." *Bank of Finland Monthly Bulletin,* 33:9 (1959), 18–22.

Korpinen, Pekka. "Finland and the Enlarging EEC." *Yearbook of Finnish Foreign Policy* (1973), 25–28.

Krosby, H. Peter. "Finland: The Politics of Economic Emergency." *Current History,* 71:415 (1976), 173–184.

Kukkonen, Pertti. *Analysis of Seasonal and Other Short-Term Variations with Applications to Finnish Economic Time Series.* Helsinki: Bank of Finland Institute for Economic Research Publications, Series B28, 1968.

Kuusela, Kullervo. "Forest Resources, Forest Ownership and Their Development in Finland." *Bank of Finland Monthly Bulletin,* 53:1 (Jan. 1979), 20–28.

Laato, Erkki. "Finnish Regional Development Policies." *Bank of Finland Monthly Bulletin,* 49:10 (Oct. 1975), 20–23.

———. "New Aims and Means for Finnish Regional Policy." *Bank of Finland Monthly Bulletin,* 50:12 (Dec. 1976), 20–24.

Laine, Jermu. "The Finnish Model for Foreign Trade Policy." *Yearbook of Finnish Foreign Policy* (1973), 20–22.

————. "The Trade Implications of Finland's Energy Import Requirements." *Yearbook of Finnish Foreign Policy* (1974), 4–9.

Larmola, Heikki. "Official Development Assistance in the Light of Economic Statistics." *Yearbook of Finnish Foreign Policy* (1988–1989), 15–17.

Larno, Kaarlo. "Diversification of Finnish Exports." *Bank of Finland Monthly Bulletin,* 41:6 (1967), 18–25.

Lehtinen, Artturi. "The U.S. as a Source of Finland's Imports and Receiver of Her Exports Since World War II." *Economic Review* (KOP), 2 (1951).

Linnainmaa, Hannu T. "Joint Finnish-Soviet Construction Projects: Their Prospects and Effect on Trade." *Yearbook of Finnish Foreign Policy* (1974), 14–18.

Linnamo, Jussi. *Finland: A Growing Economy.* Helsinki: Ministry of Foreign Affairs, Reference Publications No. 1, 1967.

Lounasmeri, Olavi. "Finnish War Reparations." *Bank of Finland Monthly Bulletin,* 26:11–12 (1952), 20–24.

Mäentakanen, Erkki. "Western and Eastern Europe in Finnish Trade Policy, 1957–1974: Towards a Comprehensive Solution." *Cooperation and Conflict,* 13 (1978), 21–41.

Mead, W. R. "Reconstruction in Finland." *Norseman* (Nov.–Dec. 1947), 397–406.

Miljan, Toivo. *The Reluctant Europeans: The Attitudes of the Nordic Countries Towards European Integration.* Montreal: McGill-Queen's University Press, 1977.

Montgomery, Arthur. "From a Northern Customs Union to EFTA." *Scandinavian Economic History Review,* 8:1 (1960), 45–70.

Möttöla, Kari. "The Finnish-Soviet Long-Term Programme: A Chart for Cooperation." *Yearbook of Finnish Foreign Policy* (1977), 43–48.

Mouritzen, Hans. *The Two Musterknaben and the Naughty Boy: Sweden, Finland and Denmark in the Process of European Integration.* Copenhagen: Centre for Peace and Conflict Research, Working Paper No. 8, 1993.

"Neste Turns in an Excellent Year." *Neste News,* 2 (May 1991).

Nielsson, Gunnar P. "The Nordic and the Continental European Dimensions in Scandinavian Integration: NORDEK as a Course Study." *Cooperation and Conflict,* 6:3–4 (1971), 173–181.

Niitamo, O. E. "National Accounts and National Statistical Service on the Threshold of the 1980's." *Liiketaloudellinen aikakauskirja,* 1 (1980).

Nuortila, Raili. "Finnish Economic Relations with the Scandinavian Countries." *Bank of Finland Monthly Bulletin,* 48:10 (1974), 20–25.

Paavonen, Tapani. *The Finn-EFTA Agreement (1961) as a Turning-Point in the Finnish Economic Policy.* Turku: University of Turku, Political History Publications, No. C:37, 1991.

———. *Finland's Road to Europe: Changes in Institutional Frameworks and Economic Policies.* Turku: University of Turku, Political History Publications, No. C:33, 1991.

———. *Finnish Foreign Trade Policy Between the East and the West in the Post–World War II Era.* Turku: University of Turku, Political History Publications, No. C:38, 1991.

———. "Neutrality, Protectionism and the International Community: Finnish Foreign Economic Policy in the Period of Reconstruction of the International Economy, 1945–50." *Scandinavian Economic History Review,* 37:1 (1984), 23–40.

Parkkinen, Pekka. "The Outlook for the Supply of Labour in Finland up to 2000." *Bank of Finland Monthly Bulletin,* 49:1 (Jan. 1975), 20–24.

Paunio, J. J., and Halttunen, Hannu. *The "Nordic Approach to Inflation": Interpretation and Comments.* Helsinki: University of Helsinki, Department of Economics, Discussion Paper, No. 5, 1974.

Pekkarinen, Jukka. "International Economic Disturbances and Economic Policy in a Small Country." *Yearbook of Finnish Foreign Policy* (1981), 32–37.

Porevuo, Mervi. "The European Economic Space and Parliament." *Yearbook of Finnish Foreign Policy* (1990), 32–36.

Puntila, L. A. *Finnische Aussenpolitik und Finnische Handelspolitik.* Hamburg: Schriften aus dem Finnland-Institut in Köln 3, 1963.

Räikkönen, Keijo. "Milestones in Finland's Trade with Western Europe." *Yearbook of Finnish Foreign Policy* (1974), 19–24.

Rossi, Reino. "Finland and the Economic Integration of Europe." *Bank of Finland Monthly Bulletin,* 35:5 (1961), 18–21.

Runeberg, L. *Trade in Forest Products Between Finland and the United States of America.* Helsinki, 1946.

Rytkönen, Arvo. "Finland's Talks on the Reciprocal Removal of Obstacles to Trade with European Socialist Countries." *Yearbook of Finnish Foreign Policy* (1974), 10–13.

Salminen, Ari. *Institutional Relations of East-West Economic Cooperation: The Finnish Experience.* Tampere: Finnpublications, 1981.

Salonen, Hannu. *Strikes and Commitments in a Wage-Bargaining Model.* Turku: University of Turku, Taloustieteen julkaisuja C29, 1988.

Singleton, F. "Finland, Comecon and the EEC." *World Today,* 30:2 (Feb. 1974), 64–72.

Solem, Erik. *The Nordic Council and Scandinavian Integration.* New York: Praeger, 1977.

State-Owned Companies in Finland. Helsinki: State-Owned Companies' Advisory Board, 1974.

Sukselainen, Tuomas. *Finnish Export Performance in 1961–1972: A Constant Market-Shares Approach.* Helsinki: Bank of Finland Publications Series, No. A36, 1974.

Sundelius, Bengt. *Nordic Cooperation: A Dynamic Integration Process.* Ann Arbor, MI: University Microfilms, 1985.

Sundelius, Bengt, and Wiklund, Claes. "The Nordic Community: The Ugly Duckling of Regional Cooperation." *Journal of Common Market Studies,* 18:1 (1979).

Suomela, Samuli. "Developments in the Structure of Finnish Agriculture in 1960–1975." *Bank of Finland Monthly Bulletin,* 49:12 (Dec. 1975), 20–23.

——. "The Outlook for Finnish Agriculture in the 1980s." *Bank of Finland Monthly Bulletin,* 54:8 (Aug. 1980), 24–28.

Tapiola, Ilkka. "Cooperation Between Finland and the CMEA 1973–1977." *Yearbook of Finnish Foreign Policy* (1977), 49–51.

Törnudd, Klaus. "Finland and Economic Integration in Europe." *Cooperation and Conflict,* 4:1 (1969), 63–72.

Turner, Barry, and Nordqvist, Gunilla. *The Other European Community: Integration and Cooperation in Nordic Europe.* London: Weidenfeld and Nicolson, 1982.

Uusivirta, Pentti. "The Free Trade Agreement Between Finland and the European Economic Community." *Bank of Finland Monthly Bulletin,* 47:12 (1973), 20–22.

Wihtol, Åke. "Some Views on the Present and Future Economic Relations Between Finland and the Soviet Union." *Yearbook of Finnish Foreign Policy* (1984), 31–35.

ECONOMIC HISTORY

Ahvenainen, Jorma. "The Competitive Position of the Finnish Paper Industry in the Inter-War Years." *Scandinavian Economic History Review,* 22:1 (1974), 1–22.

——. "The Competitive Position of the Finnish Sawmill Industry in the 1920s and 1930s." *Scandinavian Economic History Review,* 33:3 (1985), 173–192.

——. "The Paper Industry in Finland and Russia, 1885–1913." *Scandinavian Economic History Review,* 27:1 (1979), 47–65.

Alanen, Aulis J. *Der Aussenhandel und die Schiffahrt Finnlands in 18.*

Jahrhundert. Helsinki: Annales Academiae Scientarum Fennicae 103, 1957.

Anttila, Veikko. "The Modernisation of Finnish Peasant Farming in the Late Nineteenth and Early Twentieth Centuries." *Scandinavian Economic History Review,* 24:1 (1976), 33–44.

Åström, S.-E. "Northeast Europe's Timber Trade Between the Napoleonic and Crimean War: A Preliminary Survey." *Scandinavian Economic History Review,* 35:2 (1987), 170–177.

———. "Technology and Timber Exports from the Gulf of Finland, 1661–1740." *Scandinavian Economic History Review,* 23 (1975), 1–14.

Aunola, T. "The Indebtedness of North-Ostrobothnian Framers to Merchants, 1765–1809." *Scandinavian Economic History Review,* 13:2 (1965), 163–185.

Dencker, Rolf. *Finnlands Städte und Hansisches Bürgertum bis 1471.* Cologne: Böhlau Verlag (Herausgegeben vom Hansischen Geschichtsverein 77. Jahrgang), 1959.

Harmaja, Leo. *Effects of the War on Economic and Social Life in Finland.* New Haven, CT: Yale University Press, 1933.

Heikkilä, Hannu. "Credits of the Export-Import Bank to Finland, 1945–48." *Scandinavian Economic History Review,* 30:3 (1982), 207–225.

Heikkinen, Sakari. "On Private Consumption and the Standard of Living in Finland, 1860–1912." *Scandinavian Economic History Review,* 34:2 (1986), 122–134.

Heikkonen, Esko. "The Coming of Foreign Agricultural Technology to Finland." In *The Impact of American Culture.* Turku: University of Turku, Institute of General History Publications, No.10, 1983.

Herranen, Timo, and Myllyntaus, Timo. "Effects of the First World War on the Engineering Industries of Estonia and Finland." *Scandinavian Economic History Review,* 32 (1984).

Hildebrand, K. G. "Labour and Capital in the Scandinavian Countries in the Nineteenth and Twentieth Centuries." In *The Cambridge Eco-*

nomic History of Europe, vol. 7. Cambridge, Eng.: Cambridge University Press, 1978.

Hjerppe, Riita. "Finland in the European Economy, 1860–1980." In *Festskrift til Kristof Glamann.* Odense: Odense University Press, 1984.

———. *The Finnish Economy, 1860–1985: Growth and Structural Change.* Helsinki: Bank of Finland and Government Printing Centre, 1989.

Hjerppe, Riitta, and Ahvenainen, Jorma. "Foreign Enterprises and Nationalistic Control: The Case of Finland Since the End of the Nineteenth Century." In *Multinational Enterprise in Historical Perspective,* ed. Alice Teichova et al. Cambridge, Eng.: Cambridge University Press, 1986.

Hjerppe, Riitta; Peltonen, Matti; and Pihkala, Erkki. "Investment in Finland, 1860–1939." *Scandinavian Economic History Review,* 32 (1984).

Hjerppe, Riitta, and Pihkala, Erkki. "The Gross Domestic Product of Finland in 1860–1913." *Economy and History,* 20:2 (1977).

Jörberg, Lennart. *The Industrial Revolution in the Nordic Countries.* London: Fontana/Collins, the Fontana Economic History of Europe, No. 4, 1973.

Jutikkala, Eino. *An Atlas of Settlement in Finland in the Late 1560's.* Helsinki, 1973.

———. "Can the Population of Finland in the Late Seventeenth Century be Calculated?" *Scandinavian Economic History Review,* 5:2 (1957), 155–172.

———. "The Distribution of Wealth in Finland in 1800." *Scandinavian Economic History Review,* 1:1 (1953), 81–103.

———. *The Economic Development of Finland Shown in Maps.* Helsinki: Proceedings of the Finnish Academy of Sciences and Letters, 1948.

———. "Finnish Agricultural Labour in the Eighteenth and Nineteenth Centuries." *Scandinavian Economic History Review,* 10:2 (1962), 203–219.

———. "The Great Finnish Famine in 1696–7." *Scandinavian Economic History Review*, 1:3 (1953), 48–63.

———. "Large-Scale Farming in Scandinavia in the Seventeenth Century." *Scandinavian Economic History Review*, 23:2 (1975), 159–166.

———. "Origin and Rise of the Crofter Problem in Finland." *Scandinavian Economic History Review*, 10:1 (1962), 78–83.

———. "Population Structure in Finnish Towns During the Early Industrialisation." In *Det moderna Skandinaviens framväxt*. Uppsala: Uppsala universitets humanistiska fakulteten, 1978.

———. *The Scandinavian Atlas of Historic Towns*, No. 1. *Finland: Turku Åbo;* No. 2. *Finland: Porvoo Borgå*. Odense: Odense University Press, 1977.

———. "Town Planning in Sweden and Finland Until the Middle of the Nineteenth Century." *Scandinavian Economic History Review*, 16:1 (1968), 19–46.

Kallenautio, Jorma. "Finnish Prohibition as an Economic Policy Issue." *Scandinavian Economic History Review*, 24:2 (1981), 203–228.

Kaukiainen, Yrjö. "Finnish Peasant Seafarers and Stockholm." *Scandinavian Economic History Review*, 19:2 (1971) 118–132.

———. "The Transition from Sail to Steam in Finnish Shipping, 1850–1914." *Scandinavian Economic History Review*, 28:2 (1980), 161–184.

Kero, Reino. "American Technology in Finland Before World War I." In *Studia Historica in Honorem Vilho Niitemaa*, ed. Eero Kuparinen. Turku: Turun Historiallinen Yhdistys, Turun Historiallinen Arkisto 42, 1987.

Kiiskinen, A. "A Regional Economic Growth in Finland, 1880–1952." *Scandinavian Economic History Review*, 9 (1961), 83–104.

Kirby, D. G. "The Royal Navy's Quest for Pitch and Tar During the Reign of Queen Anne." *Scandinavian Economic History Review*, 22 (1974).

Korpelainen, L. "Trends and Cyclical Movements in Industrial Employment in Finland, 1885–1952." *Scandinavian Economic History Review,* 5:1 (1957), 26–48.

Luukka, A. "The 'Annual Budget' of North Finnish Farmers at the End of the Seventeenth Century." *Scandinavian Economic History Review,* 6:2 (1958), 132–143.

Mäkelä, Anneli. "Deserted Lands and Tenements in Hattula and Porvoo to 1607." *Scandinavian Economic History Review,* 25:1 (1977), 62–87.

Markkanen, Erkki. "Wealth and Credit in the Finnish Countryside, 1850–1910." *Scandinavian Economic History Review,* 21:1 (1973), 28–42.

Mauranen, Tapani, ed. *Economic Development in Hungary and Finland, 1860–1939.* Helsinki: University of Helsinki, Communications of the Institute of Economic and Social History, No. 18, 1985.

Myllyntaus, Timo. *Finnish Industry in Transition, 1885–1920: Responding to Technical Challenges.* Tammisaari: Tekniikan museon julkaisuja, 1989.

——. *The Gatecrashing Apprentice: Industrialising Finland as an Adopter of New Technology.* Helsinki: University of Helsinki, Communications of the Institute of Economic and Social History, No. 24, 1990.

——. *The Growth and Structure of Finnish Print Production, 1840–1900.* Helsinki: University of Helsinki, Communications of the Institute of Economic and Social History, No. 16, 1984.

——. "Initial Electrification in Three Main Branches of Finnish Industry, 1882–1920." *Scandinavian Economic History Review,* 33:2 (1985), 122–143.

Nummela, Ilkka, and Laitinen, Erkki. "Distribution of Income in Kuopio, 1890–1910." *Scandinavian Economic History Review,* 35:3 (1987), 237–253.

Oakley, Stewart P. "The Geography of Peasant Ecotypes in Pre-Industrial Scandinavia." *Scandia,* 47:2 (1981), 199–223.

Oksanen, Heikki, and Pihkala, Erkki. *Finland's Foreign Trade, 1917–1949*. Helsinki: Bank of Finland, Studies in Finland's Economic Growth, No. 6, 1973.

Orrman, Eljas. "The Progress of Settlement in Finland in the Late Middle Ages." *Scandinavian Economic History Review*, 29:2 (1981), 129–143.

Paavonen, Tapani. "Reformist Programmes in the Planning for Post-War Economic Policy During World War II." *Scandinavian Economic History Review*, 31: (1983), 178–200.

Peltonen, Matti. "The Agrarian World Market and Finnish Farm Economy: The Agrarian Transition in Finland in the Late Nineteenth and Early Twentieth Centuries." *Scandinavian Economic History Review*, 36:1 (1988), 26–45.

Pihkala, Erkki. "Finnish Iron and the Russian Market, 1880–1913." *Scandinavian Economic History Review*, 12:2 (1964), 121–144.

Pipping, Hugo E. "Centenary of the Finnish Mark." *Bank of Finland Monthly Bulletin*, 34:3 (Mar. 1960), 18–22.

———. "Swedish Paper Currency in Finland After 1809." *Scandinavian Economic History Review*, 9:1 (1961), 68–82.

Rosenberg, A. "Mobility of Population in the Finnish County of Uusimaa (Nyland), 1821–1890." *Scandinavian Economic History Review*, 14:1 (1966), 39–59.

Schybergson, P. "Joint-Stock Companies in Finland in the Nineteenth Century." *Scandinavian Economic History Review*, 12:1 (1964), 61–78.

Singleton, F. *The Economy of Finland in the Twentieth Century*. Bradford, Eng.: University of Bradford, 1987.

Sjögren, Bror. *Water Power Development in Finland*. Helsinki: Finnish Water Power Association, 1936.

Soikkanen, H. "Finnish Research of Changes in the Standard of Living." *Scandinavian Economic History Review*, 34:2 (1986), 167–170.

Soininen, A. M. "Burn Beating as the Technical Basis of Colonisation in

Finland in the Sixteenth and Seventeenth Centuries." *Scandinavian Economic History Review,* 7:2 (1964), 150–166.

Soltow, Lee. "Wealth Distribution in Finland in 1800." *Scandinavian Economic History Review,* 29:1 (1981), 21–32.

Suviranta, B. *Finland in the World Depression.* Supplement to the *Bank of Finland Monthly Bulletin,* No. 4 (1931). Helsinki: Valtioneuvoston kirjapaino, 1931.

Tudeer, H. *The Bank of Finland, 1912–1936.* Helsinki, 1940.

Virrankoski, Pentti. "Anders Chydenius and the Government of Gustavus III of Sweden in the 1770's." *Scandinavian Journal of History,* 13 (1988), 107–119.

———. "Replacement of Flax by Cotton in the Domestic Textile Industry of South-West Finland." *Scandinavian Economic History Review,* 11:3 (1963), 27–42.

Virtanen, Pekka, and Halme, Pekka. *Land Reforms in Finland.* Helsinki: Ministry of the Environment, Government Printing Centre, 1984.

SOCIAL, CULTURAL, AND LEGAL QUESTIONS

Alapuro, Risto. *Finland: An Interface Periphery.* Helsinki: University of Helsinki, Reports of the Research Group for Comparative Sociology, 1980.

———. "Regional Variations in Political Mobilization: On the Incorporation of the Agrarian Population into the State of Finland, 1907–1930." *Scandinavian Journal of History,* 1:3–4 (1976), 215–242.

Alestalo, Matti, et al. "Structure and Politics in the Making of the Welfare State: Finland in Comparative Perspective." In *Small States in Comparative Perspective,* ed. R. Alapuro et al. Oslo: Norwegian University Press, 1985.

Allardt, Erik. *Changes in the Conception of the Quality of Life: Scandinavian Experiences.* Helsinki: University of Helsinki, Department of Sociology, Working Papers, No. 24, 1982.

———. *Dimensions of Welfare in a Comparative Scandinavian Study.* Helsinki: University of Helsinki, Reports of the Research Group for Comparative Sociology, No. 9, 1977.

———. *Finland's Swedish-Speaking Minority.* Helsinki: University of Helsinki, Reports of the Research Group for Comparative Sociology, No. 17, 1977.

———. *Finnnish Society: A Relationship Between Geopolitical Situation and the Development of Society.* Helsinki: University of Helsinki, Reports of the Research Group for Comparative Sociology, No. 32, 1985.

———. *Institutional Welfare and State Interventionism in the Scandinavian Countries.* Mannheim: University of Mannheim, Sonderforschungsbereich 3, Microanalytische Grundlagen der Gesellschaftspolitik, Arbeitspapier no. 185, 1985.

———. *Welfare Production, Welfare Consumption and State Interventionism in the Nordic Countries.* Helsinki: University of Helsinki, Department of Sociology, Working Papers, No. 32, 1984.

Allardt, Erik, and Husu, Liisa. *Sociology in Finland.* Helsinki: University of Helsinki, Department of Sociology, Working Papers, No. 21, 1981.

Allardt, Erik; Miemois, K. J.; and Starck, C. *Multiple and Varying Criteria for Membership in a Linguistic Minority: The Case of the Swedish-Speaking Minority in Metropolitan Helsinki.* Helsinki: University of Helsinki, Reports of the Research Group for Comparative Sociology, No. 21, 1979.

Allardt, Erik, and Miemois, K. J. *Roots Both in the Centre and the Periphery: The Swedish-Speaking Population in Finland.* Helsinki: University of Helsinki, Reports of the Research Group for Comparative Sociology, No.24, 1979.

Alvesalo, Anne, and Laitinen, Ahti. *Perspectives on Economic Crime.* Turku: Publications of the Faculty of Law of the University of Turku, Criminal Law and Judicial Procedure, Series A20, 1994.

Anckar, Dag. *Political Science in the Nordic Countries: An Overview.* Turku: Meddelanden från Ekonomiskstatsvetenskapliga fakulteten vid Åbo Akademi A210, 1985.

Anna, Luigi de. *Nord e sud. Immagine e conoscenza della Finlandia e del Settentrione nella cultura classicomedievale.* Turku: University of Turku, Annales Universitatis Turkuensis B 180, 1988.

Aromaa, Kauko; Cantell, Ilkka; and Jaakkola, Risto. *Cohabitation in Finland in the 1970s.* Helsinki: Research Institute of Legal Policy, Government Printing Centre, 1983.

Asp, Erkki. "Les Lapons finlandais d'aujourd'hui et leur différenciation." *Inter-Nord,* 10 (Mar. 1968), 279–284.

Asp, Erkki, et al. *The Aged and the Society: Some Factors Influencing the Status of the Aged in Finland.* Turku: University of Turku, Sociological Studies, No. A15, 1989.

———. *The Lapps and the Lappish Culture.* Turku: University of Turku, Sociological Studies, No. A4, 1980.

———. *The Skolt Lapps: On Their Way of Life and Present-Day Living Conditions.* Turku: University of Turku, Sociological Studies, No. A6, 1982.

Brusiin, Otto. "Legal Philosophy in Seventeenth Century Finland: Some Reflections." *Scandinavian Studies in Law,* 18 (1974), 11–25.

Collinder, Björn. *The Lapps.* Princeton, NJ: Princeton University Press for the American Scandinavian Foundation, 1949.

Crottet, Robert. *Am Rande der Tundra. Tagebuch aus Lappland.* Hamburg: Christian Wegner Verlag, 1966.

Dahlerup, Drude. "From a Small to a Large Minority: Women in Scandinavian Politics." *Scandinavian Political Studies,* 2:4 (1988), 275–298.

Finnish-American Academic and Professional Exchanges: Analyses and Reminiscences. Espoo: Weilin and Göös for the Foundation for Research in Higher Education and the U.S. Educational Foundation in Finland, 1983.

Finnish Criminal Policy in Transition. Helsinki: University of Helsinki, Publications of the Department of Criminal Law, No. 4, 1979.

Finnish Drinking Habits: Results from Interview Surveys Held in 1968,

1976, and 1984, ed. Jussi Simpura. Jyväskylä: Gummerus for the Finnish Foundation for Alcohol Studies, 1987.

The Finnish Legal System. 2nd ed. rev., ed. Jaakko Uotila. Helsinki: Finnish Lawyers' Publishing Co., 1985.

Fried, Anne. *Literatur und Politik in Finnland. Wechselwirkung zwischen Nachkriegsliteratur und Politik.* Hamburg: Buske, Schriften aus dem Finnland-Institut in Köln, 1982.

Gebhard, H. *Cooperation in Finland.* London: Williams and Norgate, 1916.

———. *Population agricole, ses rapports avec les groupes professionels et sa composition sociale dans les communes rurales de Finlande en 1901.* Helsinki: Keisarillisen Senaatin Kirjapaino, 1907.

Gosse, Edmund. *Northern Studies.* London, 1890.

———. *Studies in the Literature of Northern Europe.* London, 1879.

Grönvik, Axel. *The Character of the Finnish Press.* Helsinki: Työväen kirjapaino, 1953.

Haapanen, Pirkko, et al. *Women and Politics.* Tampere: University of Tampere, Politiikan tutkimuksen laitoksen tutkimus 33a, 1974.

Haavio-Mannila, Elina. "History of Women's Paid Work in Finland: A Brief Introduction." In *Toward Equality: Proceedings of the American and Finnish Workshop on Minna Canth,* ed. Sirkka Sinkkonen and Anneli Milen. Kuopio: University of Kuopio, 1986.

———. *Women in the Economic, Political and Cultural Elites in Finland.* Helsinki: University of Helsinki, Sosiologian laitoksen tutkimuksia no. 209, 1977.

Haavio-Mannila, E., and Stenius, K. *The Social Construction of Psychiatric Diagnoses and the Rates of Mental Illness in Finland and Sweden.* Helsinki: University of Helsinki, Research Reports of the Institute of Sociology, No. 201, 1974.

Haranne, Markku. *Elements of Life Styles: Leisure Time, Work and Cultural Activities in Present Finnish Daily Routine.* Helsinki: University of Helsinki, Research Reports of the Institute of Sociology, No. 212, 1977.

Heikkilä, M. *Poverty and Deprivation in a Welfare State*. Helsinki: Sosialihallituksen julkaisuja, no. 8, 1990.

Helistö, Paavo. *Music in Finland*. Huhmari: Finnish-American Cultural Institute, 1980.

Hidén, Mikael. *The Ombudsman in Finland: The First Fifty Years*. Berkeley: University of California Press, Institute of Governmental Studies, No. 16, 1973.

Immonen, Kari. "Changes in the Finnish Image of the Soviet Union: Is It Now Time for Shame?" *Yearbook of Finnish Foreign Policy* (1988–1989), 23–28.

Jaakkola, Magdalena, and Karisto, Antti. *Friendship Networks in the Scandinavian Countries*. Helsinki: University of Helsinki, Reports of the Research Group for Comparative Sociology, No. 11, 1976.

Jallinoja, Riitta. "Independence or Integration: The Women's Movement and Political Parties in Finland." In *The New Women's Movement: Feminism and Political Power in Europe and the USA*, ed. Drude Dahlerup. London: Sage, 1986.

Jutikkala, Eino. "Bauernehrung in Finnland." *Odal, Monatschrift für Blut und Boden*, 10:10 (1941).

Kallio, Veikko. *Finland: Cultural Perspectives*. Porvoo: Söderström, 1989.

Keränen, Marja, ed. *Finnish "Undemocracy": Essays on Gender and Politics*. Helsinki: Finnish Political Science Association, No. 12, 1990.

Klami, Hannu Tapani. *A History of Finnish Legal Science: An Outline*. Vammala, 1986.

Knoellinger, Carl Erik. *Labor in Finland*. Cambridge, MA: Harvard University Press, 1960.

Koskimies, Jaakko. "Finland." In *International Handbook of Industrial Relations*. Westport, CT: Greenwood, 1981.

Kujala, Matti. *The Cooperative Movement in Finland*. Tampere: University of Helsinki, Department of Cooperative Research, 1975.

Laitinen, Ahti. "Finnish Drug Control Policy: Change and Accommodation." In *Drugs, Law, and the State*, ed. Mark S. Gaylord and Harold Traver. Hong Kong: Hong Kong University Press, 1992.

———. "The Police of Finland." In *Police Practices: An International Overview*, ed. Dilip K. Das. Metuchen, NJ: Scarecrow Press, 1993.

———. "The Use of Social Power and Organizational Crime." In *Rapport från 31. Nordiska forskerseminariet i Larkollen, Norge 1989*, ed. Torbjörn Thedeen. Stockholm: Nordiska samarbetsrådet för kriminologi, 1989.

The Lapps Today in Finland, Norway and Sweden: Conference Proceedings, vol. 1, La Haye: Mouton, 1960; vol. 2, Oslo: Universitetsforlaget, 1969.

Layton, Robert. *Sibelius*. London: Dent, 1965.

———. *Sibelius and His World*. New York: Viking Press, 1970.

Lehto, Juhani. *Deprivation, Social Welfare and Expertise*. Helsinki: National Agency for Welfare and Health, Research Reports, No. 7, 1991.

Levas, Santeri. *Jean Sibelius: A Personal Portrait*. Helsinki: Söderström; London: Dent, 1972.

Lilius, Carl-Gustaf. "Self-Censorship in Finland." *Index on Censorship*, 4:1 (1975), 19–25.

Manninen, Merja, and Setälä, Päivi, eds. *The Lady with the Bow: The Story of Finnish Women*. Helsinki: Otava, 1990.

Mead, W. R. "Anglo-Finnish Cultural Relations." *Norseman*, 6:6 (Nov.–Dec. 1948), 376–387.

———. "Figures of Fun: Further Reflections on Finns in English Fiction." *Neuphilologische Mitteilungen*, 14 (1976).

———. "The Finn in Fact and Fiction." *Norseman*, 16:3 (1958).

———. "The Finnish Outlook, East and West." *Geographical Journal,* 113 (Jan.–June 1949).

———. "The Image of the Finn in English and American Literature." *Neuphilologische Mitteilungen,* 16 (1963).

Mikkola, J. J. "The Social Culture of Finland." *Baltic Countries,* 1:1 (Aug. 1935), 1–5.

Nelson, George R., ed. *Freedom and Welfare: Social Patterns in the Northern Countries of Europe.* Copenhagen: Munksgaard, 1953.

Niemi, Päivi. *Adolescents and the Family: Images and Experiences of Family Life in Finland.* Turku: University of Turku, Annales Universitatis Turluensis B181, 1988.

Numelin, Ragnar. "Edward Westermarck and the Finnish Sociological School." *Le Nord,* 4:4 (1941), 268–282.

The Parliamentary Ombudsman in Finland: Position and Functions. Helsinki: Government Printing Office, 1976.

Pitkänen, Kari. "The Reliability of the Registration of Births and Deaths in Finland in the Eighteenth and Nineteenth Centuries: Some Examples." *Scandinavian Economic History Review,* 25:2 (1977), 138–160.

Rapportti culturali tra Italia e Finlandia: atti di convegno. Turku/Åbo, 26–27 settembre 1986, ed. Lauri Lindgren. Turku: Henrik Gabriel Porthanin Instituutti, 1986.

Ringbom, Nils-Eric. *Jean Sibelius: A Master and His Work.* Norman: University of Oklahoma Press, 1954.

Ritakallio, Veli-Matti. "Poverty Comes Not Alone: A Study of Accumulated Welfare Deprivation Among Social Assistance Recipients." In *Köyhyys ei tule yksin* (Ritakallio). Helsinki: Sosiaali-ja Terveyshallitus, Tutkimuksia 11, 1991.

Rosas, Allan, ed. *International Domestic Rights Norms in Domestic Law: Finnish and Polish Perspectives.* Helsinki: Finnish Lawyers' Publishing Co., 1990.

Salokangas, R., and Tommila, P. "Press History Studies in Finland: Past and Present." *Scandinavian Journal of History,* 7 (1982), 49–73.

Science Studies and Science Policy: Proceedings of the Finnish-Bulgarian Symposium at the University of Tampere, May 14–15, 1984, ed. Erkki Kaukonen and Veronica Stolte-Heiskanen. Helsinki: Suomen Akatemian julkaisuja 3, 1984.

Seppänen, Paavo. "Social Change in Finland: An Empirical Perspective." In *Small States in Comparative Perspective,* ed. Risto Alapuro et al. Oslo: Norwegian University Press, 1985.

Siika, Marita. "Development of Equality in Finland." *Hypatia* (Athens) (1984), 19–28.

Sinkkonen, Sirkka, and Haavio-Mannila, Elina. "The Impact of the Women's Movement and Legislative Activity of Women M.P.'s on Social Development." In *Women, Power, and Political Systems,* ed. Margherita Rendel. New York: St. Martin's Press, 1981.

Siuruainen, Eino. *The Population of the Sámi Area of Finnish Lapland: A Regional Study with Special Emphasis on Rates and Sources of Income.* Oulu: University of Oulu, Acta Universitatis Ouluensis A40/2, 1976.

Siuruainen, E., and Aikio, P. *The Lapps in Finland: The Population, Their Livelihood, Their Culture.* Helsinki: Society for the Promotion of Lapp Culture, Publication No. 39, 1977.

Social Legislation and Work in Finland. Helsinki: Valtioneuvoston kirjapaino, 1953.

Steinby, Torsten. *In Quest of Freedom: Finland's Press, 1721–1971.* Helsinki: Government Printing Centre, 1971.

Stolte-Heiskanen, Veronica. *Social Studies of Science in Finland.* Tampere: University of Tampere, Department of Sociology and Social Psychology, Working Report No. 4, 1983.

Tawaststjerna, Erik. *Sibelius.* Vols. 1–2. London: Faber and Faber, 1976, 1986.

Törne, Bengt de. *Sibelius: A Close-Up.* Boston: Houghton Mifflin, 1937.

Verkko, Veli. *Homicides and Suicides in Finland, with Their Dependence on National Character.* Copenhagen: G.E.C. Gads Forlag, 1951.

Vuoristo, Kai Veikko. "On the Language Structure of the Finnish Countryside with a Swedish-Speaking Majority." *Acta Geographica,* 20:25 (1968), 365–388.

Waris, Heikki. *Die soziale Struktur Finnlands.* Cologne: Schriften aus dem Finnland-Institut in Köln, 1966.

Wilhelmsson, Thomas, and Svestka, Jiri. *Consumer Protection in Czechoslovakia and Finland.* Helsinki: University of Helsinki, Publications of the Institute of Private Law, No. 32, 1989.

Ylikangas, Heikki. "Major Fluctuations of Crimes of Violence in Finland: A Historical Analysis." *Scandinavian Journal of History,* 1:1 (1976), 83–103.

EMIGRATION AND FINNISH AMERICA

Bogdanoff, O., and Söderling, I. *Minulla on niin ikävä—jar har så ledsamt—I feel such a longing: Finnish American Postcards Exhibition Catalog.* Turku: Institute for Migration, 1988.

Delaware 350: 350 Years of Finnish-American Friendship, 1638–1988. Turku: Institute for Migration, 1988.

Engman, Max. "Migration from Finland to Russia During the Nineteenth Century." *Scandinavian Journal of History,* 3:2 (1978), 155–177.

Haavio-Mannila, Elina. "Social Adjustment of Finns in Sweden." *Siirtolaisuus-Migration,* 3 (1984), 26–53.

Haavio-Mannila, Elina, and Suolinna, Kirsti. "Adjustment Problems and Willingness to Migrate of the Population in the Tornio Valley." In *Ecological Problems of the Circum-Polar Area,* ed. Erik Bylund et al. Luleå: Norbottens Museum, 1974.

Halttunen, David ed. *Sixtieth Anniversary Year Book of the Brooklyn Evangelical Lutheran Church.* New York: Finnish Evangelical Lutheran Church, 1951.

Hammar, Tomas, and Peura, Markku. "Swedish-Speaking and Finnish-speaking Finns in Stockholm in 1975." *Siirtolaisuus-Migration,* 3 (1984), 54–67.

Hoglund, A. William. *Finnish Immigrants in America, 1880–1920.* Madison: University of Wisconsin Press, 1960.

Jaakkola, Magdalena. *Finnish Immigrants in Sweden: Networks and Life-Styles.* Helsinki: University of Helsinki, Research Group for Comparative Sociology, Research Reports, No. 30, 1983.

Jordan, Terry; Kaups, Matti; and Lieffert, Richard M. "New Evidence on the European Origin of Pennsylvania V-Notching." *Pennsylvania Folklife,* 36:1 (Autumn 1986).

Karni, M. G., ed. *Finnish Diaspora 1: Canada, South America, Africa, Australia, and Sweden. Finnish Diaspora 2: the United States.* Toronto: Multicultural History Society of Ontario, Report of the Finn Forum Conference, Toronto (1979), 1981.

———. "Finnish Immigrant Leftists in America: The Golden Years, 1900–1918." In *Struggle a Hard Battle: Essays on Working Class Immigrants,* ed. Dirk Hoerder. De Kalb, IL, 1986.

Karni, M. G.; Koivukangas, Olavi: and Laine, Edward W., eds. *Finns in North America.* Turku: Institute for Migration, Migration Studies C9, Proceedings of Finn Forum III (5–8 Sept. 1984), Turku, 1985.

Karni, M. G.; Kaups, Matti; and Ollila, Douglas, eds. *The Finnish Experience in the Western Great Lakes Region: New Perspectives.* Turku: Institute for Migration in cooperation with the Immigrant Research Center, University of Minnesota, Migration Studies C3, 1975.

Karni, M. G. and Ollila, Douglas, eds. *For the Common Good: Finnish Immigrants and the Radical Response to Industrial America.* Superior, WI, 1977.

Kero, Reino. *Migration from Finland to North America in the Years Between the U.S. Civil War and the Finnish Winter War.* Turku: University of Turku, Annales Universitatis Turkuensis Ser. B 130, 1974.

———. *The Roots of Finnish-American Left-Wing Radicalism.* Turku: University of Turku, Publications of the Institute of General History, No. 5:2, 1973.

———. *The Social Origins of the Left-Wing Radicals and "Church Finns" Among Finnish Immigrants in North America.* Turku: University of Turku, Publications of the Institute of General History, No. 7:3, 1975.

Koivukangas, Olavi, ed. *Scandinavian Emigration to Australia and New Zealand Project: Proceedings of a Symposium Feb. 17–19 1982, Turku*. Turku: Institute for Migration, Migration Studies, No. C7, 1982.

———. *Scandinavian Immigration and Settlement in Australia Before World War II*. Turku: Institute for Migration, Migration Studies, No. C2, 1974.

———. *Sea, Gold and Sugarcane—Attraction Versus Distance: Finns in Australia, 1851–1947*. Turku: Institute for Migration, Migration Studies, No. C8, 1986.

Kolehmainen, John. "Finland's Agrarian Structure and Overseas Migration." *Agricultural History,* 15 (1941), 44–48.

———. "Finnish Overseas Migration from Arctic Norway and Russia." *Agricultural History* (1945), 224–232.

———. "Hanko–Liverpool–New York." *Turun Historiallinen Arkisto,* 28 (1973), 345–360.

———. "Harmony Island: A Finnish Utopian Venture in British Columbia." *British Columbia Historical Quarterly,* 5 (Apr. 1941), 11–123.

———. *A History of the Finns: In Ohio, West Pennsylvania, and West Virginia—From Lake Erie's Shores to the Mahoning and Monongahela Valleys*. Fairport Harbor, OH: Finnish-American Historical Society, 1977.

———. "The Last Days of Matti Kurikka's Utopia: A Historical Vignette." *Turun Historiallinen Arkisto,* 31 (1976), 388–396.

Kostiainen, Auvo. "A Dissenting Voice of Finnish Radicals in America." *American Studies in Scandinavia,* 23:2 (1991), 83–95.

———. *Features of Finnish-American Publishing*. Turku: University of Turku, Publications of the Institute of General History, No. 9:3, 1977.

———, ed. *Finnish Identity in America*. Turku: Turku Historical Archives, No. 46, 1990.

———. "For or Against Assimilation? The Case of the Finnish Immigrant Radicals." In *American Labor and Immigration History, 1877–1920s: Recent European Research,* ed. Dirk Hoerder. Urbana: University of Illinois Press, 1983.

———. *The Forging of Finnish-American Communism, 1917–1924: A Study in Ethnic Radicalism.* Turku: Annales Universitatis Turkuensis, Ser. B147, 1978.

———. "Radical Ideology Versus Ethnic Social Activism: The Finnish Americans and the Communist Party of the United States, 1927–1932." *American Studies in Scandinavia,* 21:1 (1989), 3039.

Kultalahti, Olli. "Migration and Periods of Rapid Industrial Development in Finland." *Siirtolaisuus-Migration,* 3 (1984), 95–116.

Louhi, E. A. *The Delaware Finns; or, The First Permanent Settlements in Pennsylvania, Delaware, West New Jersey and the Eastern Part of Maryland.* New York: Humanity Press, 1925.

Majava, A. *Migration Between Finland and Sweden from 1946 to 1974.* Göteborg: University of Göteborg, Demographic Institute, 1975.

Mead, W. R. "The Adoption of Other Lands: Experiences in a Finnish Context." *Geography,* 48 (1963).

———. "A Finnish Settlement in Central Minnesota." *Acta Geographica,* 13:3 (1954).

Migration Research in Scandinavia: Proceedings of the Nordic Seminar on Migration Research Held at Siikaranta, Finland, on Jan. 3–5, 1973. Helsinki: Ministry of Labour Places Division, Migration Reports, No. 4, Dec. 1973.

Niitemaa, Vilho, ed., et al. *Old Friends: Strong Ties.* Turku: Institute for Migration in cooperation with the Ministry of Education and the U.S.A. Bicentennial—Finnish Committee, 1976.

Ollila, Douglas J. "Defects in the Melting Pot: Finnish-American Response to the Loyalty Issue, 1917–1920." *Turun Historiallinen Arkisto,* 31 (1976), 397–413.

———. *The Emergence of Radical Industrial Unionism in the Finnish*

Socialist Movement. Turku: University of Turku, Publications of the Institute of General History, No. 7:2, 1975.

———. "Ethnic Radicalism and the 1916 Mesabi Strike." *Range History* (Dec. 1978), 1–10.

———. *A Time of Glory: Finnish-American Radical Industrial Unionism, 1914–1917*. Turku: University of Turku, Publications of the Institute of General History, No. 9:2, 1977.

Pietilä, Päivi. *The English of Finnish-Americans: With Reference to Social and Psychological Background and with Special Reference to Age*. Turku: University of Turku, Annales Universitatis Turkuensis B188, 1989.

———. "American Finns as Language Learners: The Age Issue." *Siirtolaisuus-Migration*, 3 (1990), 4–8.

Pilli, Arja. *The Finnish-Language Press in Canada, 1901–1939: A Study in the History of Ethnic Journalism*. Turku: Institute for Migration, Migration Studies, No. C6 1982.

Puotinen, Arthur E. *Finnish Radicals and Religion in Midwestern Mining Towns*. New York Mills, MN, 1977.

Ross, Carl. *The Finn Factor in American Labor, Culture and Society*. New York Mills, MN, 1977.

Siikala, K. "The Turning-Point in Finnish Emigration Policy in the 1970s." *Siirtolaisuus-Migration*, 3 (tenth anniversary number, 1974), 12–14.

Turner, Arthur W. *Rebels on the Range: The Michigan Copper Miners' Strike of 1913–1914*. Hancock, MI, 1984.

Virtanen, Keijo. *The Finns in the United States: The Project on Finnish Immigration of the Michigan Historical Collections*. Ann Arbor: Michigan Historical Collections Bulletin No. 26, 1976.

———. "The Migration of Finnish-Americans to Florida After World War II." *Turun Historiallinen Arkisto*, 31 (1976), 432–445.

———. *Problems of Research in Finnish Re-Emigration*. Turku: Institute for Migration, Migration Studies, No. C3, 1975.

———. *Settlement or Return: Finnish Emigrants (1860–1930) in the International Overseas Return Migration Movement.* Helsinki: Finnish Historical Society 1979.

Ward, C. L. "Delaware Tercentenary." *American Swedish Monthly,* 32 (June 1938).

Wargelin, Raymond W. "Salomon Ilmonen: Early Finnish-American Historian." *Siirtolaisuus-Migration,* 3 (1987), 3–11.

Women Who Cared: The History of Finnish-American Women, ed. Carl Rose and K. Marianne Wargelin Brown. St. Paul, MN, 1986.

Wuorinen, John. *The Finns on the Delaware, 1636–1655: An Essay in American Colonial History.* New York: Columbia University Press, 1938.

FINLANDIZATION

Anna, Luigi de. "Finlandizzazione. Un termino del linguaggio politico recente." *Settentrione. Rivista di studi italo-finlandesi,* no. 3 (1991), 30–35.

Berry, Michael. "Finlandization." In *Dictionary of Scandinavian History,* ed. Byron J. Nordstrom. London: Greenwood, 1986.

Garfinkle, A. M. *"Finlandization": A Map to a Metaphor.* Philadelphia: Foreign Policy Research Institute, Monograph No. 24, 1978.

Giniewski, Paul. "La Finlande face aux 'reconstructions' européennes." *Rivista di studi politici internationali* (Oct.–Dec. 1989).

Gruber, K. *Zwischen Befreiung und Freiheit.* Vienna: Ullstein, 1953.

Halsti, Wolf. "Finlandization." In *Détente,* ed. G. R. Urban. London: Temple Smith, 1976.

Kennan, George. "Europe's Problems, Europe's Choices." *Foreign Policy,* 14 (1974), 3–16.

Krosby, H. Peter. "Finland and Detente: Self-Interest Politics and Western Reactions." *Yearbook of Finnish Foreign Policy* (1980).

———. "Scandinavia and Finlandization." *Scandinavian Review,* 63:2 (1975), 11–19.

Lafond, J.-M. *Finlandisation.* Dijon: Université de Dijon, Faculté de droit, 1974.

Laqueur, Walter. "Europe: The Specter of Finlandization." *Commentary,* 64:6 (Dec. 1977), 37–41.

Mäentakanen, Erkki. "The Myth of Finlandization." *Yearbook of Finnish Foreign Policy* (1974), 34–39.

Maude, George. "Has Finland Been Finlandized?" In *Soviet Foreign Policy Toward Western Europe,* ed. George Ginsburgs and Alvin Z. Rubinstein. New York: Praeger, 1978.

——. "The Further Shores of Finlandization." *Cooperation and Conflict,* 17:1,3 et seq.

Minc, Alain. *Le syndrome finlandais.* Paris: Editions du Seuil, 1986.

Mouritzen, Hans. *Finlandization: Towards a General Theory of Adaptive Politics.* Aldershot, Eng.: Avebury, 1988.

Punasalo, V. I. *The Reality of "Finlandisation": Living Under the Soviet Shadow.* London: Institute for the Study of Conflict, Conflict Studies, No. 93, 1978.

Rusi, Alpo. "Finlandization Without Finland?" *Yearbook of Finnish Foreign Policy* (1987), 13–17.

Sariola, S. "Finland and Finlandization." *History Today,* 32 (Mar. 1982).

Singleton, F. "The Myth of 'Finlandisation'." *International Affairs,* 57:2 (Spring 1981).

Wagner, Ulrich. "Finnland und die USSR. Das sogennante Finnlandisierungs Problem." *Osteuropa,* 25:6 and 25:7 (1975), 423–433, 463–476.

NB: Readers seeking the wider application of the Finlandization concept to relations between the Soviet Union and other European states should consult *Soviet Foreign Policy Toward Western Europe,* edited by Ginsburgs and Rubinstein.

ABOUT THE AUTHOR

GEORGE MAUDE (B.A., Ph.D., University of London) studied history at the London School of Economics and was Bryce Memorial Scholar of the University of London. He is currently Docent in International Relations at the Law Department of the University of Turku. In 1984 Dr. Maude was Fulbright Fellow in Peace Studies at the College of Wooster, Ohio. He is the author of *The Finnish Dilemma* (1976), *The Finnish-Norwegian Tangle* (1987), and co-author (with Michael Berry and Jerry Schuchalter) of *Frontiers of American Political Experience* (1990). Maude is also a member of the Porthan Society and a knight of the Order of the Lion of Finland. He is married to a Finnish wife and has a daughter and a son.